BOUNDEN DUTY

**The Memoirs of a
German Officer 1932-45**

Frontispiece. Adjutant to Field Marshal von Manstein 1944.

BOUNDEN DUTY

The Memoirs of a German Officer 1932-45

Alexander Stahlberg

Translated by
PATRICIA CRAMPTON

BRASSEY'S (UK)

(Member of the Maxwell Pergamon Publishing Corporation)

LONDON · OXFORD · WASHINGTON · NEW YORK · BEIJING
FRANKFURT · SÃO PAULO · SYDNEY · TOKYO · TORONTO

English language edition copyright © 1990 Patricia Crampton

First published in German under the title *Die Verdammte Pflicht: Erinnerungen 1932 bis 1945*.
© 1987 Verlag Ullstein GmbH Berlin–Frankfurt/Main

First English edition 1990

UK editorial offices: Brassey's, 24 Gray's Inn Road, London WC1X 8HR
Orders: Brassey's, Headington Hill Hall, Oxford OX3 0BW

USA editorial offices: Brassey's, 8000 Westpark Drive, Fourth Floor, McLean, Virginia 22102
Orders: Brassey's/Macmillan, Front and Brown Streets, Riverside, NJ 08075.

Distributed in North America to booksellers and wholesalers by the Macmillan Publishing Company, N.Y., N.Y.

Library of Congress Cataloging in Publication Data
Stahlberg, Alexander, 1912–
[Verdammte Pflicht. English]
Bounden duty: the memoirs of a German officer, 1932–1945/Alexander Stahlberg; translated by Patricia Crampton. — 1st English language ed.
p. cm.
Translation of: Die verdammte Pflicht.
1. Stahlberg, Alexander, 1912– . 2. Anti-Nazi movement—Germany. 3. World War, 1939–1945—Personal narratives, German. 4. Soldiers—Germany—Biography. 5. Germany. Heer—Biography. I. Title.
DD256.3.S7213   1990   S40.54′8243—dc20   [B] 89-23908

British Library Cataloguing in Publication Data
Stahlberg, Alexander
Bounden duty: the memoirs of a German officer 1932–1945.
1. World War. 2. Army operations by Germany. Heer. Biographies
I. Title   II. Die Verdammte Pflicht. *English*
940.54′82′43

ISBN 0-08-036714-3

Printed in Great Britain by B.P.C.C. Wheatons Ltd, Exeter

In memory of those whose paths crossed mine

DIETRICH BONHOEFFER

ERICH FELLGIEBEL

EBERHARD FINCKH

EWALD VON KLEIST-SCHMENZIN

HANS OSTER

GEORG SCHULZE-BÜTTGER

CLAUS GRAF SCHENK VON STAUFFENBERG

HENNING VON TRESCKOW

Contents

LIST OF PLATES   x

LIST OF MAPS   xii

FOREWORD TO THE ENGLISH EDITION   xiii

ACKNOWLEDGEMENTS   xiv

PROLOGUE   xv

Part I The Thirties, 12 April 1932–15 July 1939

The Thirties	3
Friedrich-Wilhelms University Berlin	3
A Day's Shooting	8
74 Wilhelmstrasse on 30 January 1933	11
The Reichstag Burns	23
On the Brandenburg Gate	26
Potsdam, 21 March 1933	29
Göring's Secretary of State	33
From Berlin to Hamburg	36
30 June 1934	42
London	47
To Join the Nazi Party?	58
In the 6th (Prussian) Cavalry Regiment	63
'You Share the Responsibility'	68
Years of Peace?	77
Dietrich Bonhoeffer	81
Private Concerts	84
Crisis Years 1938 and 1939	87
Goodbye to Peace	100

Part II The Start of World War II, July 1939–July 1940

The Start of World War II	113
To Poland	113
Campaign in France	129
Amiens Cathedral	135

A French Lady 142
To Brest and Bordeaux 145
Pomerania Again 146

Part III Attack on the Soviet Union, August 1940–November 1942

Attack on the Soviet Union 153
The Eve of the Attack 153
To Moscow 160
Not Moscow: Leningrad 172
Not Leningrad: Tikhvin 174
My Diary for 1942 183
Home Leave 189
To Leningrad Again? 193
Tresckow and Schlabrendorff 199

Part IV Field Marshal von Manstein, November 1942–March 1944

Field Marshal Von Manstein 207
My New Job 207
Stalingrad 217
Hitler on the Telephone 223
The Fate of the Sixth Army 227
Captain Behr's Mission 233
Stauffenberg and Manstein 239
At the Führer's Headquarters 248
Colonel Schulze-Büttger 256
Three Days of Hitler 258
Conferences at Saporoshie 270
'And you didn't shoot him?' 279
Correspondence with Colonel General Beck 283
Meetings 287
Hitler in Saporoshie Again 290
Hitler's Berghof at Berchtesgaden 295
Danger! 299
A Show for the Turks 301
Operation Citadel 303
Rommel and Kluge 306
Vinnitsa 310
Albert Speer, Armaments Minister 316
'Total War' 317
An Interjection 323
The 'Oath of Allegiance' 328
Reichsführer SS Heinrich Himmler 332
The Dismissal 337

Part V The Last Year of the War, 3 April 1944–6 May 1945

The Last Year of the War	343
Liegnitz–Dresden	343
Major General Henning von Tresckow	348
Ambassador Herbert von Dirksen	351
Offensives from the West, South and East	353
Berchtesgaden, 11 July 1944	355
On the Autobahn between Liegnitz and Breslau	358
20 July 1944	361
At the Tannenberg Memorial	367
Towards the End	373
Another Wedding	377
A Sinister Journey	385
The Agony Begins	388
April 1945	394
Hitler is Dead!	398
Field Marshal Montgomery	400

NAME INDEX   407

List of Plates

Frontispiece   Adjutant to Field Marshal von Manstein 1944.

1. The Author 1927.

2. The Author's father 1948.

3. The Author's mother in Red Cross uniform 1942.

4. The house at Klein–Krössin bei Kieckow (Pomerania) – home of the Author's grandmother.

5. Bible study in the park at Kieckow with Dietrich Bonhoeffer.

6. The Author's godfather, Herbert von Bismarck.

7. Confirmation Day at Kieckow.

8. The Brandenburg Gate 1933.

9. Potsdam Day 21 March 1933.

10. Berlin 20 April 1939. Hitler's 50th Birthday Parade.

11. No. 3 Squadron, 6th (Prussian) Cavalry Regiment.

12. Furtwängler conducting in the Philharmonic Hall 27 February 1933.

13. Antoinette, Countess Esher, the Author's cousin.

14. Inge Schweitzer.

15. July 1939. Wedding in Paetzig/Neumark.

16. Claus Graf Schenk von Stauffenberg.

17. Heinrich Graf Yorck von Wartenburg.

18. Henning von Tresckow.

19. Fabrian von Schlabrendorff.

20. Amiens Cathedral (aerial photograph).

21. Amiens Cathedral – the great West Front.

22. On the Field Marshal's telephone – November 1942.

23. South of Belgorod May 1943. Field Marshal von Manstein visiting forward positions.

24. Colonel Georg Schulze–Büttger with Lieutenant Otto Feil.

25. On the airfield at Saporoshje 19 February 1943. Hitler says 'Goodbye' to the Field Marshal.

26. Planning Operation 'Citadel', July 1943.

27. General Guderian visits during 'Citadel'.

28. General Hans Oster.

29. Aerial photograph of the ruins of the Stahlberg factory in Stettin. November 1943.

30 Hitler's former headquarters at Vinnitsa (Ukraine).
& (Inset) The print in Hitler's bedroom.
31.

32. At Vinnitsa. The Field Marshal with his dog 'Knirps'.

33. Field Marshal von Manstein at Hitler's desk in Vinnitsa.

34. At the armoured demonstration for the Turkish Commander-in-Chief. Ukraine June 1943.

35. The Great Hall in the 'Berghof' at Berchtesgaden.

36. A typical planning conference with Hitler.

37. The surrender at Luneburg 4 May 1945. General Kinzel, watched by Field Marshal Montgomery, signs for the Army.

38. Safe conduct issued to the Author after his visit to Field Marshal Montgomery 6 May 1945.

List of Maps

1. The Polish Campaign 1939   115
2. Blitzkrieg 1940   134
3. Operation Barbarossa 1941 – The Plan   158
4. Stalingrad November 1942   221
5. Von Manstein's Counterstroke – Kharkov March 1943   291
6. Operation Citadel – Kursk July 1943   305

Map Symbols

The following formation symbols have been used on all maps, where appropriate:

Army Group	South	Panzer Group*	Pz Gp Guderian
Soviet Front	Voronezh	Panzer Corps	48
Panzer Army	1	Corps	56
Army	3	Panzer Division	7
Army Detachment	Det Kempf	Army Boundaries	—xxxx—

* Note: On Map 3, for simplicity, the Panzer Groups are numbered thus **1**

Foreword to the English Edition

I owe my survival in World War II to friends who gave their lives to redeem the honour of my Fatherland. To some of them, who crossed my path in those years, I dedicate this book. In their name, I am grateful that my records have now been translated into English. My book is intended to tell the world that in the darkest years of our country's recent history, there were also upright, courageous men and women who sacrificed themselves, out of grief for the shameful acts committed by Germans in the name of Germany.

Berlin, ALEXANDER STAHLBERG
December 1989

Acknowledgements

I owe my thanks to those who have advised me over the writing of my reminiscences and have helped me to check several of the episodes I have recorded and to search my own memory.

Dr. Uta Freifrau von Aretin née von Tresckow
Professor Dr. Eberhard Bethge
Dipl.-Ing. Gottfried von Bismarck
Ludwig Freiherr von Hammerstein-Equord
Dorothee Freifrau von Hammerstein-Equord née Claessen
Institut für Zeitgeschichte Munich
Dr. Manfred Kehrig
Bundesarchiv-Militärarchiv Freiburg
Professor Dr. Helmut Krausnick
Professor Dr. William G. Moulton, Princeton University
Luitgarde von Schlabrendorff née von Bismarck
Nina Gräfin Schenk von Stauffenberg née Freiin von Lerchenfeld

Erich Fellgiebel and Fabian von Schlabrendorff did not divulge my name, even under torture.

I owe the fact that I can still write to Professor Dr. Josef Wollensak, who saved my eyesight with four eye operations.

Photographs are from my private collection except where stated in the plate section.

Prologue

THE PUPILS at the Grunewald-Gymnasium in Berlin had gathered for the school-leaving ceremony of the class of 1932, to which I belonged. The party was to have a musical framework. The principal, Dr. Wilhelm Vilmar, had asked me to play a classical piece on the violin, 'for the last time', since, for over two years, it had been my responsibility each Monday to provide the musical setting for the interdenominational morning prayers.

I had been reckless, suggesting the first two movements of Bach's Solo Sonata in G minor, by heart of course. I was to pay for that, because at the very beginning of the second movement, I was overcome by an icy dread that I might get stuck in the fugue and go on playing round and round in circles, always arriving at the same place without making the next 'switch'. It was going to be a nightmare.

I extricated myself with a not very creditable and frivolous trick. When the theme of the fugue came round for the second time, I passed from *forte* to *piano* and then to *pianissimo*, finally allowing the music to die away in mid-movement, as if barely audible in the distance.

My audience were apparently delighted and applauded enthusiastically, either because this sound effect of a musical farewell amused them, or because the difficult piece was over so promptly, because as soon as the ceremony was over, school would be out.

Following my musical farewell, it was the turn of our leading scholar, our *primus omnium*. He discharged his duty with a speech in Latin, if I remember rightly, on the tag so familiar to every schoolboy: *non scholae, sed vitae discimus*. I for my part was no longer listening, happy to have Latin and Greek behind me.

Then the principal rose to his feet in the front row and advanced to the platform with measured stride. As always, Dr. Vilmar's speech was perfectly constructed. He praised his progressive school. He quoted the special statute of the Prussian Ministry of Culture of 1920, which had bestowed on upper school pupils their freedom to concentrate on this or that classical or modern discipline. He did not forget to mention the co-education system. Every head turned towards the two girls sitting in front, who were in fact among the best scholars of their year, living proof of the principal's words of praise. After all, one of them was his very own daughter!

Then he read out the names of the school-leavers one by one, jamming his monocle on its thin black ribbon into his eye, only to take it out again each time he handed over the school-leaving certificate.

Dr. Vilmar was a born headmaster. Nor did he make the slightest attempt to disown his erstwhile membership of a student duelling society. His insistence on the automatic observance of punctuality and order in his school did not conflict in the smallest degree with liberal thought and genuine tolerance.

The unusual thing about our class was that more than half its members came from Jewish families. At a time when political passions and racist ideologies were producing the most freakish off-shoots, even we students realised that we were by no means living in an ivory tower. On the contrary, there were lively discussions of current events in the breaks between lessons, and our various political views often clashed vigorously. Each defended his own as if he alone knew all the answers, but I do not remember any harsh words, and it would have been unthinkable for one of my classmates to express anti-Semitic ideas. To have done so would have been to cut himself off from the rest of the class.

At the end of the celebration, the school choir rose. We knew what they were going to sing, because the school-leavers were dismissed with the same song year after year. We loved it, especially as every pupil was living for the day when it would apply to him. That year it would be sung for the last time. Of course it had been written by Heinrich Hoffmann von Fallersleben, author of our National Anthem, but the composer of this beautiful choral song was Felix Mendelssohn-Bartholdy.

Now that we must part,
keep with cheerful heart
this beside you on your way.
Brave your journey face,
and in every place
health and fortune with you stay.
We must wander on the earth,
joys and sorrows know from birth:
whether up or down,
still the road leads on.
This must be our lot on earth.

Fifty years later we were to meet again in Berlin. Almost everyone who was still alive came. Some came from South and others from North America, a few from England, very few from Germany. The only one who was still living in Berlin – or rather, living in Berlin again – was myself. We walked together through the 'Grunewald Colony', founded by the first Chancellor of the German Reich*, and we glanced into the classroom of our Grunewald-Gymnasium, which now bears the name of Walther Rathenau†, who was murdered not far from there. As we were waiting at Grunewald Station for the train to Wannsee, one of us pointed to an outlying, unused platform from which, in the darkest years of German history, human beings were loaded into goods wagons at night, never to return.

From Wannsee we took the steamer, passing idyllic 'Peacock Island', once the refuge of Prussian kings, to land at Glienicke Castle. As we toured the rehabilitated Lenné Park, a lofty argument took place on art and humanism in Prussian history. And lo and behold, the 'Englishmen' and 'Americans' still had just as much to say about it as if they had passed their school-leaving exam at Grunewald-Gymnasium only yesterday! We were still debating when the sun set behind the silhouette of Potsdam across the Havel.

Then came the final evening of our reunion. In an intimate circle, almost as if nothing had happened in the past fifty years, one after another began to talk. It was a long night, during which we also spoke of those who had not survived.

I had asked to be the last to speak, but when my turn finally came, both strength and time had run out. I promised to write

* *Reich Chancellor* von Bismarck.
† German Minister for Foreign Affairs (died 1922).

down my experiences, because although I had been one of the many drawn into the midst of political and military events in the years between 1932 and 1945, today I am one of the few left who can make a free and frank report.

Hence this book, which is addressed above all to the young people who find it difficult to understand the time of their fathers. 'Why didn't you stop it?' 'Why did you follow that psychopath?' And every time I struggle to find answers.

My book is not intended to replace the history books, which are now so numerous. I shall report my own experiences, and in so doing I do not propose to avoid writing about the unpleasant aspects. Because word has got around that I am working on my notes, there has been no lack of attempts to influence me: 'Must you stir that up again? Can't you keep quiet about it?' My answer has always been, simply: 'I shall not keep quiet about anything that seems to me important in terms of the historical facts.'

'Why are you publishing your memoirs after all this time? Having survived the war, it would have been better if you had got to work at once!' I had no time for writing then. Our family having lost its livelihood, there was work to be done.

In contrast, my friends gave me no peace: 'You lived through too much that should not be lost. You met people who should not be forgotten. It's your duty to write it all down.' So my resolution grew, and when at last I had the time, I began.

PART I

THE THIRTIES

12 April 1932 – 15 July 1939

The Thirties

Friedrich-Wilhelms University Berlin

I was now a 'mulus'. In student jargon, students who had not yet started at university were called 'mulus': no longer donkey and not yet horse, but a hybrid, a mule.

My father asked me what I wanted to be. Preferably a musician, best of all a conductor, was my answer. I had been so greatly impressed by the innumerable concerts given by Wilhelm Furtwängler with the Berlin Philharmonic. For years I had listened to them from the platform steps rather than the stalls, often with the pocket score on my lap.

My father seemed prepared for my answer. For the first time he told me that he wanted me, sooner rather than later, to enter into the management of his Stettin firm, which would one day belong to my brother and me. He said he hoped I would not shirk this task that had fallen to my lot.

I had suspected this, although I had never dared to question my father on the subject, but now I asked him to agree to my spending a few terms on 'general studies' before my commercial training. To my delight he agreed at once.

The year 1932 was one of hectic drama in Germany's home affairs. After seven years, Reich President von Hindenburg's term of office was over and in accordance with the Weimar Constitution a new president was to be elected by the direct vote of the German people on 13 March. The array of candidates available for election was as scintillating as the political landscape at the close of the Weimar Republic: Hindenburg, still in office, now no longer supported by the parties which had elected him seven years earlier but by his former opponents, the SPD, the Centre (Catholics) the *Deutsche Volkspartei* (DVP), the liberal *Deutsche Staatspartei* and the Bavarian *Volkspartei*; Adolf Hitler, candidate for the National Socialists (NSDAP) and Hindenburg's most serious opponent;

3

then the Communist Ernst Thälmann (KPD) and the *Stahlhelm* leader Theodor Duesterberg, the candidate of the conservative *Deutschnationale Volkspartei* (DNVP).

After a savage smear campaign that cost the office of Head of State more than it did the candidates (blood actually flowed!), the election produced no result. Hindenburg had the most votes, 18 million, but the old gentleman achieved only 49.6 per cent, thus failing to gain the necessary absolute majority. Hitler received 30.1 per cent and Thälmann 13.2 per cent.

So there had to be a second ballot. On 10 April, Hindenburg was elected with 53 per cent – but Hitler's percentage had risen to 36.8!

Although, at 19, I was not yet of voting age, I was deeply concerned with political events. I did not belong to a party or other grouping, but I would certainly have voted for Hindenburg in the second ballot.

Since March 1930, Heinrich Brüning, a man of the Catholic Centre, had been Chancellor of the Reich, but since his government did not have a majority in the Reichstag, he governed by means of emergency decrees issued by the Reich President in accordance with Article 48 of the Constitution.

Immediately after Hindenburg's re-election on 13 April, the Reich Government banned, by emergency decree, the paramilitary organisations of the National Socialists, the SA 'Storm Troopers' and the *Schutzstaffel* (SS). There was hope now of internal peace.

So there sat the 'mule' in his dark blue 'confirmation suit' on the morning of 12 April 1932, awaiting the ceremony of matriculation for the following term in the great hall of Friedrich-Wilhelm University on Unter den Linden in Berlin, to receive the certificate composed in Latin from the hand of His Magnificence the Rector Heinrich Lüders. '*Pomeranus Studiosus phil.*' was my new estate.

I could elect my own subjects for study. At the Grunewald-Gymnasium I had by no means been a zealous pupil, except in music, but now, when I was free to make my own untrammelled choice, I was seized by a thirst for knowledge. I went to Martin Wolf for Civil Law. His lectures could be followed only with the utmost concentration, because he spoke in a low voice, though without notes and with crystal-clear emphasis. His lecture hall was always packed and to sit in front you had to reserve a seat in good time.

With Eduard Kohlrausch I read the principles of Criminal Law and was fascinated at the very first lecture by his realistic description of the worth and worthlessness of eyewitness accounts.

I went to Emil Dovifat for Journalism, because I was fascinated by newspapers and the intricate process of their production. I realised now what a high degree of responsibility was borne by any serious newspaper.

Finally, I listened to Romano Guardini, the Catholic religious philosopher, not because I was attracted by Catholicism, but because I wanted to break out of the pietistic Protestantism of my Pomeranian relations. I understood little of Guardini's philosophical thought, but I was impressed by the beauty of his language and the precision of his thinking. I had never before heard a theologian of such quality – what a high intellectual level Berlin University offered us!

But what a contrast was revealed in that summer of 1932 outside the lecture halls, when in the breaks we went to the great entrance hall or, if the weather was good, the front garden on Unter den Linden, for the 'standing convention'. Members of student societies met by their own 'blackboards' and political groups took up positions which seemed to them 'tactically', or even 'strategically' favourable.

The political circles would scarcely have gathered before they began to harass one another, especially the Communists and the National Socialists, generally on completely trivial grounds, but often quite obviously without the slightest cause. Again and again, in a few seconds, the hall would become the scene of savage and generally bloody battles. Suddenly, behind the 'fighters' at the front, their 'auxiliaries' would appear, usually women students who produced from their briefcases everything a nursing orderly could need.

The Communists seemed to have this organised even better than the National Socialists. There was also a German National, or conservative group, and not far from that the members of the *Stahlhelm* met, an equally right-wing, almost paramilitary association, at that time quantitatively significant throughout Germany. I left my name with the German Nationalists and the *Stahlhelm*, initially only to keep in touch with them, since at that time it seemed almost inconceivable not to declare one's allegiance to one student organisation or another. But in my two terms at Berlin I never actually became a member of either. When a year later, on Hitler's instructions, the *Stahlhelm* was transformed into the *Sturm Abteilung* (SA), I sat down on the very day I heard the news and wrote a letter announcing my resignation – 'in case I was already listed as a member of the *Stahlhelm* without my knowledge'. I never received any answer or confirmation.

But to return to the summer term of 1932. Since I was interested in anything to do with politics, I also enjoyed attending mass meetings in the sports palace on the Potsdamer Strasse, a meeting place for others besides the major indoor sports organisations of Berlin.

Now the emphasis was on party events, those of the German Nationalists dreadfully laboured and *petit bourgeois*, those of the *Deutsche Staatspartei*, as the Liberals called themselves, before a yawningly empty auditorium, the *Stahlhelm* in their grey wind-jackets in the midst of a forest of standards from the Kaiser period, and finally the National Socialists in a sea of brown shirts and red swastika banners, which seemed completely alien to me. But there was one thing in which the Nazis excelled over all the others: their mass proclamations were brilliantly organised and as entertaining as a review. The climax was the appearance of 'the Doctor', which meant Joseph Goebbels. If Hitler himself was announced, he would enter the hall to the strains of the 'Badenweiler March', which was reserved for him alone.

I had already heard Goebbels with Hitler while I was at school, at the Neue Welt conference hall in the Hasenheide. At that time I had interrupted Goebbels from the floor with an interjection consisting of two phrases. I have forgotten what I shouted, but it was certainly not a greeting. What I do remember is that he let me finish, and then went on with the sentence I had interrupted. Only later, towards the end of his speech, did he turn to me, the young man who had thought it proper to interrupt him – he now wanted to address a further comment to him: that youth down there should first consider how unseemly it was to interrupt the leader of the largest party in Berlin. Pointing his finger at me, he read me a lecture on good behaviour and discipline in public and although I had certainly not mentioned that subject in my interjection, the entire hall enthusiastically applauded their 'Doctor'.

Then, in a loud, ringing voice, Goebbels announced the principal speaker of the evening: Adolf Hitler.

I remember that Hitler spoke without notes, not behind, but in front of the lectern. I also remember that he began very quietly, though so distinctly that not a word was lost. Whereas the tone of the previous speaker had scarcely changed, Hitler varied his constantly: pitch, volume, colour, tempo. This showed that the speech had been carefully planned, and even at the beginning of a sentence the audience generally knew whether the speaker was expecting applause at the end. It was impressive to see how firmly he held his listeners in his hand, less with the content than the methods of his rhetoric.

In May 1932, my godfather, Herbert von Bismarck, invited me to attend a plenary session of the Reichstag. He was a deputy of the *Deutschnationale Volkspartei* (DNVP). I accepted at once and met him on 11 May 1932 at the south door, which was reserved for Members of Parliament. There was still some time to spare before the beginning of the session, so my godfather was able to show me the inside of the great building.

Naturally I was impressed by the stately interior, the panelled walls and dark red curtains and carpets. Of course one might have objected to so much pomp, but there was no denying that what it radiated could be described in a single word: dignity.

Deputies swarmed in the foyers and corridors, arguing with one another, and my godfather said he was glad to see how many of them could still talk to each other like reasonable people outside the bounds of their own party when they were not in the chamber. He told me to watch how suddenly that would come to an end when the bell rang for them to reassemble.

Then he showed me the way to the visitors' gallery and told me to find myself a seat there as quickly as possible, as it had been annouced that Reich Chancellor Dr. Brüning would be speaking that day.

So, quite unexpectedly, I saw Brüning at an historic moment: it was to be his last speech in the Reichstag. He urged Parliament to give him time, they were 'close to their goal'. The nature of the goal was obvious: to control both the Communist and the National Socialist menace.

Brüning impressed me, and in the nature of things I could only have agreed with him, but he struck me as ascetic. His pale, scholarly countenance betrayed the extent to which the burden of day-to-day politics had weighed on him, but he had nothing to offer that might have enthralled a nation stirred by passions, or 'the man in the street', not even us young students.

Only a few weeks were to pass before Hindenburg dropped Reich Chancellor Brüning, on 30 May 1932. Brüning's party friend in the Prussian *Landtag*, Franz von Papen, became Reich

Chancellor; as the most important man next to him, General Kurt von Schleicher took over the Reich Ministry of Defence.

Papen had been a General Staff Officer in the war and soon grew friendly with the old Marshal. He withdrew from the Centre before he could be excluded from it for his 'betrayal' of Brüning. Papen and Schleicher offered the Reich President a cabinet that seemed trustworthy. Only three Ministers had party (DNVP) ties, the others were non-party specialists. It was hoped that the National Socialists could be appeased and induced to collaborate by offering Hitler the removal of the ban on the SA and new elections to the Reichstag as the price for tolerance of the new government.

The economic hardships of the population and some skilfully veiled propaganda earned the radical parties – the NSDAP and KPD in particular – great popularity and in the 1932 elections to the Prussian Landtag (24 April) and to the Reichstag (31 July and 8 November), the democratic forces were finally on the defensive. Reich Chancellor Papen governed through emergency decrees and the Social Democratic Prussian government was in office only in an administrative sense, until its illegal dissolution by Papen on 20 July ('the Prussian coup'). Still none of these steps contributed to peace in internal affairs.

A Day's Shooting

On one of the last days of September 1932 an unexpected invitation reached me by telephone. My uncle Hans von Wedemeyer from Paetzig in the Neumark invited me to a big shoot on 18 October. To be invited to Paetzig to shoot red deer and wild boar was an honour for a young man, but the fly in the ointment followed: 'No gun'. I asked if I was to go with the beaters, but my uncle said: 'Not with the beaters, with my friend the Reich Chancellor, Franz von Papen.' There were no second thoughts after that; I accepted at once. When I asked him how he had come to pick me, Uncle Hans said that in the first place it was a good job for a young man interested in politics, and in the second one could not let a Reich Chancellor run around in the woods alone, and finally he had thought of me because I knew the Paetzig shoot so well.

When I arrived in Paetzig in my mother's small Opel early on the morning of the shoot, the company was already seated at the long breakfast table, enjoying the local delicacies that my aunt had

had brought up from the cellars for the occasion. I greeted my uncle and aunt, and then came the first surprise of the day: Uncle Hans introduced me to his friend 'Fränzchen', the Reich Chancellor. I had not expected that degree of familiarity. 'My nephew will accompany you today and be at your disposal.' Papen got up and offered me his hand – how unconventional, how friendly, how appealing – that was my first impression.

I went the rounds of the long table. A remarkable company was assembled here. On my aunt's right sat Prince William, the eldest son of the former German Crown Prince, beside him my godfather Herbert von Bismarck, who had so kindly taken me round the Reichstag, then my cousins Henning and Gerd von Tresckow, and finally Klaus von Bismarck from Kniephof, who would later become a Wedemeyer son-in-law. It promised to be an interesting day.

And interesting it certainly was, though not from the point of view of the shoot, which turned out to be what experienced guns call a 'talking shoot', more talk than shooting. Papen, whose side I was not to leave all day, started the ball rolling on the way to the forest, describing the Reichstag sitting of 12 September in lively detail. For the first time the merger of the National Socialists and the Communists had become obvious, so that the Reich Chancellor, with an order from Reich President von Hindenburg provided for this emergency, dissolved parliament. All those in the shooting brake listened enthralled. Papen had been personally rather than politically struck by the blatantly tactical behaviour of Reichstag President Hermann Göring.

In the marshy area of the middle lake, I led Papen along a stalking track to the 'Alicen platform'. Soon we were both sitting high up on the narrow bench-seat, awaiting events. The drive had not even been signalled when the distinguished gentleman on my right began to speak. It was certainly not my job to impress the silence proper to the hunt on the Chancellor of the Reich, so I replied in a toneless whisper to some far too loudly spoken words about the natural beauty of the area. But my efforts were quite without effect, because he immediately pounced on me with a highly political question: he would be interested to know what a young student like myself thought of his action against the Prussian state government. In particular, he would like to know what I would think if the Reich government were to 'prevent' the expected legal proceedings by Prussia against the Reich.

I still remember vividly how much the Reich Chancellor's question shocked me. No special knowledge was needed to assess the monstrous nature of such a question to a young student. I begged him awkwardly – still in a whisper – to understand that I could not possibly answer his question off the cuff. Then, at last, I was released by the horn signalling the start of the drive and there was peace at last on the Alicen platform.

It was now that the dramatic part of the hunt should have begun all round us, since the Alicen platform in the middle lake was the best that Uncle Hans could offer such a prominent guest from his game-filled shoot. Nevertheless, on that day absolutely nothing came. There were a few shots at a great distance, but even on the second drive of the day the bag was worse than paltry. However, since in accordance with time-honoured custom a hunt must have its King, one of the guests was simply declared King. The honour fell to my cousin Henning von Tresckow, so it was the Adjutant of the Potsdam 9th (Prussian) Infantry Regiment (IR9) who would give the Hunt King's speech at dinner, which was excellent, for Henning was a brilliant speaker.

In general, politics were discussed at every available opportunity on that day. I can see them before me now: the Reich Chancellor, generally surrounded by a circle of respectful admirers and undeniably wearing the finest hunting costume of them all, made to measure by a first-class tailor. In stark contrast to him were the local Brandenburgers and Pomeranians in their shabby Loden coats (the older and shabbier the coat, the more credible the sportsman). There were also my godfather Herbert von Bismarck, the ex-District Administrator of Regenwalde, now, as a Reichstag Deputy, behaving with Prussian correctness, mostly in conversation with Prince William of Prussia, the very essence of a bright and breezy old warhorse; or Franz-Just von Wedemeyer from Schönrade, Uncle Hans's elder brother, always ready to make jokes about those who superfluously 'took politics much too seriously to be successful'; or cousin Henning, generally seeking in his relaxed, candid way to maintain contacts with old acquaintances or initiate new ones; equipped with some of the finest qualities that nature can bestow on a man: wit and charm.

The dinner was to be a formal occasion; older gentlemen had not failed to wear their 'miniature' medals. Now came the ladies: Henning's wife Erika – Eta, as she was always called – was the jewel in the assembly. I have never met another married couple who radiated as much harmony and beauty as Henning and Eta Tresckow. The first speech was to be the challenge to the King of the Hunt by the Lord of the Hunt. Uncle Hans performed this diplomatically and in rhyme, blaming the rainy weather for the wretched bag; it was all the fault of Peter the Fisherman, the Lord's disciple, for pouring too much water down from heaven.

I do not remember Henning Tresckow's response, but I do remember some of the Reich Chancellor's ideas. He began with the usual eulogies: he had enjoyed the day, even with no bag, he felt at ease among Prussian conservatives and, turning to the German royal Pretender sitting opposite him, he concluded with a spirited declaration of his belief in the monarchy.

But despite all the fine words, the evening ended on a bitterly discordant note. There had, of course, been plenty to drink and a row blazed up over a trifle. One of the guests had fastened his *Stahlhelm* insignia above instead of below the chain with the Hohenzollern battle and family orders. The host had to intervene to pacify the disputants over the rank of the *Stahlhelm* insignia and restore calm. This embarrassing incident disturbed me: a piece of my Prussian conservative world had received a blow.

74 Wilhelmstrasse on 30 January 1933

On 6 November 1932, for the fourth time in that year and the fifth in Prussia itself, the German electors went to the polls (two ballots for the election of the Reich President, one for the Prussian Landtag and two Reichstag elections).

When the results were announced next day the sensation was complete. Hitler and his NSDAP had lost no less than two million votes since 31 July. Had National Socialism passed its peak? About half the seceders had apparently voted Communist, others had simply grown sick of the constant voting and stayed at home, while others had returned to the Conservatives. Yet the KPD and NSDAP together still commanded an absolute majority in the Reichstag, so that parliament was still inoperative.

Reich Chancellor von Papen was unable to push through his ideas of an authoritarian government by-passing the Reichstag, either in Cabinet or with the President of the Reich, and had to resign on 17 November. Two weeks later, on 3 December, Hindenburg appointed former Reich Minister of Defence General Kurt von Schleicher to the Chancellorship. He informed Papen that the Schleicher Cabinet was to be merely an interim solution and he would like him to remain available. The Reich President was sick of the constant haggling for the parties' favour. Papen was to bring together a supra-party Cabinet of 'national concentration', which was to include Hitler.

So the ex-Chancellor went on living for the time being in his official residence on the upper floor of the rear apartments at 74 Wilhelmstrasse. (Schleicher did not move into an official residence). From Papen's flat one could use the garden stairs at the back of the house to reach the walled garden and from this the gardens of all the ministries, through side doors, from garden to garden. In this way the ex-Chancellor could visit Hindenburg unseen by passers-by in the street. In other words: the acting Chancellor, von Schleicher, had direct access to the Head of State like his predecessor – provided that one had the keys to the connecting doors. Papen had them.

In those weeks there was a great deal of conjecture on the internal state of the NSDAP. This was fuelled not only by the loss of votes on 6 November but by the information that trickled through that the Party was financially in jeopardy. Some of its powerful patrons in industry and the economy were in the process of withdrawing. There was criticism of Hitler himself, even in the ranks of his followers. Not Hitler, but his deputy Gregor Strasser, who was reputed to belong to a 'leftist', that is more moderate, wing of the party, was the coming man. In any case, it was widely known in Berlin that the new Reich Chancellor, Schleicher, was making contact with Strasser, which pointed to an attempt by Schleicher to split the NSDAP.

This was the general political situation when, a few days before Christmas, the telephone rang in our house in Bismarckstrasse and my uncle Hans von Wedemeyer asked to speak to me. He was with his friend Papen now, to advise and help him, Papen was politically active even after his dismissal, but was at present in need of a small planning staff. Another young man was needed in the Secretariat and with Papen's agreement he had called to ask if I would be prepared to help for a time.

I did not have to think it over for long, and Uncle Hans asked me to come to him at 74 Wilhelmstrasse – rear apartments – first floor. I took a bus to the Brandenburg Gate at once and a few minutes later I was entering the house for the first time. I crossed a small courtyard to the 'rear apartments', which turned out to be an extraordinary misnomer.

I reached the first floor by a wide marble staircase; as I learned later, this had for many years been the official residence of the Reich Minister of the Interior.

I pressed the bell beside a large glass door with spendid art nouveau decoration, through the coils of which one had a shadowy view of the inside of the flat. No hint of security measures; in those days a senior politician could live with his family as 'openly' as that.

A charming girl opened the door to me and said she was one of the daughters of the house. Then Uncle Hans appeared and we proceeded, with me on his left, into an extremely dark office. The room gave onto the courtyard and needed artificial light even by day.

A cousin of Uncle Hans, Maria Countess Bredow, was sitting at the desk. I was amazed to see her here: 'Aunt Manni', as her family called her, was running a house and an agricultural business in Pomerania close to Stargard, for her father, a retired General. Aunt Manni was well known and respected in Eastern Pomerania, where she had not earned her nickname 'the Dragon' for nothing. So now we three would represent 'the Secretariat of ex-Reich Chancellor von Papen'.

Uncle Hans made it clear that there would be a great deal for the three of us to do in the coming weeks, as Papen had been given a political commission by Reich President von Hindenburg. We were to be bound to extreme secrecy – I learned no more than that at first, but I thought a good deal. It was quite obvious that Papen's return to power was being planned here.

When I asked him what my own job was to be, Uncle Hans said that they had taken me on as 'maid of all work'. That was fine with me.

Then we crossed the hall to a large, elegantly furnished drawing room where Papen greeted me like an old acquaintance and introduced me to his wife, a lady of great presence and natural distinction. Tea was served and I felt I had been accepted into their circle.

Soon I was given my first job. Since he had left office, Papen no longer had a press attaché and I suggested that I should look through all the important newspapers across the political spectrum in the reading-room of the University Library and then buy those he should read from a stand on Unter den Linden and prepare them for his attention. He agreed. 'Do use lots of red pencil and scissors, to save me time,' he added.

Then I had to look after the official diary which lay open in the office, answer the telephone and receive visitors with an appointment (or get rid of others). Finally there was the incoming post – mountains of it every day – to be sorted.

In so far as I read letters addressed to Papen at that time, I cannot remember a single writer suggesting that Papen might ally himself politically with Hitler. On the contrary, I well remember the opposite. If a trend could be read from these letters, it was the desire to have done with the party state and to establish a constitutional monarchy.

After the Christmas break, Papen's residence came to life. On 4 January, he had a secret meeting with Hitler at the house of the banker Freiherr Kurt von Schröder in Cologne. Both Hitler and Papen wanted to keep their disussion secret, but on 5 January the *Tägliche Rundschau* reported as its lead story the meeting in Cologne: 'in the house of a friend of the NSDAP'. I believe people are right in assuming now that this Cologne meeting set the stage for the Third Reich. In any case, events moved fast in the days that followed up to 30 January, because the political public was now wide awake.

There was constant coming and going in Papen's flat. Meanwhile, on 15 January 1933, a new Land parliament had to be elected in the small Land of Lippe where Hitler's entire party leadership descended for 10 days on a mere 100,000 voters, because the NSDAP wanted to force a result which would show the whole German public that the defeat of 6 November 1932 in the Reichstag election had been reversed. Nevertheless, Hitler did not suceed in achieving the intended absolute majority in Lippe. The NSDAP did become the strongest party, but gained only $3\frac{1}{2}$ per cent over the previous Reichstag election result. Immediately after this election, which the National Socialists exploited for propaganda in their newspapers as best they could, politicians seemed to arrive at our door in an endless stream. I recognised many of them from the newspapers and illustrated journals.

Alfred Hugenberg, party chairman of the German Nationalists (DNVP), did not look at all as one would have expected of a politician of his rank. From his appearance he could have been the senior accountant of an industrial concern. His adviser and usual companion, Otto Schmidt-Hannover, seemed to me of far better calibre. I had known him for years, having often been a guest in his house, so I was well aware that this man had a much clearer picture of Hitler than his chief.

As is so often the case, the second man at the head of the million-member *Stahlhelm* also seemed to me better than the first. From what I gathered on the fringe of these conferences the number one, in the person of Franz Seldte, looked completely insignificant, while Theodor Duesterberg seemed to have a far more sensible grasp of the political power relationships. Papen offered him ministerial office as well, but Duesterberg suddenly announced that he had Jewish blood in his veins and for that reason alone he could not be considered for government. This episode clearly demonstrates that in these discussions the ideological and racist implications of a chancellorship in Hitler's hands were clearly understood. His own reason for refusal actually seemed to please Duesterberg, who later argued all the more freely against Hitler. The fact that Papen was so intent on *Stahlhelm* participation in government, although it did not have the status of a party, proved that a plan was being devised here which should not be offered to a democratically and freely elected parliament, at least not for the time being.

It became more and more apparent that Papen was working towards a change in the form of government. We did not in fact mourn the Weimar Republic, either, since it had proved to be so weak. I, at least, did not then suspect that a democracy can very well be strong.

One day the big glass door to the hall opened and I found myself face to face with Hitler. Behind him were two or three other people. My first impression was one of astonishment – astonishment that he was at least half a head shorter than I was. His photographers and poster painters must always have portrayed him from below so that he seemed taller than he really was. Before he entered he stopped for a moment and fixed me with his startlingly blue eyes.

I had known for a long time that Hitler's gaze was said to be 'incredibly fascinating', so I was not unprepared; but I felt at once, at this first personal meeting with him, that his gaze was not genuine, it was a pose, nothing but a pose, rehearsed in front of the mirror.

He gave me his hand, dismissed some of his entourage and followed me to the cloakroom, willingly allowing me to help him out of his trench-coat. When it was in my hands I thought for a moment that it felt unusually heavy.

Then I took him to Papen in the large drawing-room. There were other men present, but I was so preoccupied by the leading figure and the significance of the visit that I can no longer remember who else was there.

When I closed the drawing-room door behind me and passed the cloakroom on my way to the office, I was met by one of Papen's daughters. She had been inspecting their famous visitor's trench-coat and now, under my eyes, she plunged a hand into each coat pocket and simultaneously drew out two pistols: special model Walther pistols, high gloss nickel-plated, with loaded magazines.

Late on the afternoon of that day, when the visitors had left, Hans von Wedemeyer and I were invited to tea. Understandably there was only one subject of conversation: we must risk the experiment with Hitler, Papen repeated over and over again — with no more than three National Socialists in the government 'practically nothing could go wrong', they could easily be out-voted and controlled and the chairman of the strongest party must be given a democratic chance. He, Papen, was convinced that as soon as he was bearing the weight of governmental responsibility Hitler would 'reduce himself *ad absurdum* in a few weeks'. 'Unfortu-nately there are no politics without risk,' he added.

On another day – probably 25 January 1933 – I opened the big glass door of Papen's flat again, and there stood my uncle Ewald von Kleist from Schmenzin in Pomerania. Without so much as a greeting he asked me, in a tone which was by no means friendly: 'What are you doing here?' I felt like a schoolboy caught copying by his teacher and stammered out something about 'helping in the office'. His retort was prompt 'So, as I see it, you're helping to make Hitler Chancellor of the Reich?' Not another word, as I helped him out of his coat, then, cold as only Uncle Ewald could be: 'So announce me to your Reich Chancellor.' (It had got about that even now Papen liked to be addressed as 'Reich Chancellor', though he no longer was.)

The 'Schmenziner' – that was what they called Uncle Ewald in Pomerania, as there were so many Kleists there – now came to see Papen daily, sometimes even twice a day. He was in and out, so to speak, until 29 January. This had been initiated by Wedemeyer because 'the Schmenziner' was certainly the man of highest calibre among those conservatives diametrically opposed to Hitler who could then be thrown into the fray.

This arch-conservative belonged to no party, not even the German Nationals, whose chairman, Hugenberg, I had once heard him describe as no more than 'a manikin'.

The Schmenziner was, moreover, one of the very few people who had taken the trouble to read Hitler's *Mein Kampf*, and had done it so thoroughly and critically that he had one day decided to seek out the author of the book in order to 'clear up' a series of rather vaguely expressed passages in personal conversation. Kleist's conversation with Hitler produced distinct results and the Schmenziner never tired of interpreting these to anyone who would listen. Our 'nation without space' – from the title of a book by Hans Grimm – would not survive unless it could expand eastward to the Urals and the Black Sea ports . . . so Hitler has told him. After that meeting with Hitler in 1932, Kleist published a brochure entitled 'National Socialism – a Danger', which aroused interest. He had yet another arrow to his bow – his kinship with the old Hindenburg. At the time of which I am writing, he had recently obtained a private audience with the President to warn him against Hitler. So the Schmenziner's political weight was of considerable importance *vis-à-vis* Papen, for Hindenburg had assured his nephew that he had not the remotest intention of making Hitler Reich Chancellor.

So it was undoubtedly more than a mere matter of tactics when he wrested from Papen a concrete alternative to the planned Hitler–Papen government, consisting of a cabinet with Papen as Reich Chancellor and Kleist-Schmenzin as Reich Minister of the Interior. It was intended as an interim government until a revision of the Weimar Constitution could be worked out and agreed.

When the three of us, Wedemeyer, Countess Bredow and I, were in the Secretariat together, the prospects of this alternative were frequently and intensively discussed. We were agreed that the interim government proposed by Kleist would be possible only with the support of Hindenburg and the Reichswehr and could not survive without the use of force against Hitler's SA.

We also told each other repeatedly that Hindenburg still felt some sense of guilt about the events of November 1918, when he had given the Kaiser the final impetus to abdicate and so to end the monarchic form of government. Perhaps the old gentleman now sensed an opportunity to make some reparation.

I remember a telephone call at that time from Reich Chancellor Schleicher. Such a personal, direct call was quite unusual.

'Schleicher here, connect me with Herr von Papen!' I heard him say, but for some reason I could not connect him immediately. I told him so, and offered to call back as quickly as possible. To my astonishment Schleicher immediately started to shout and even became abusive. I had no choice but to listen in silence. To put it quite simply: the Acting Reich Chancellor flew into a rage at the other end of the line, and then hung up abruptly.

I went in search of Papen in the big flat, soon found him and reported the call, but when I asked if I should connect him with the Reich Chancellor he said 'No.'

I never discovered the reason for Schleicher's unusual behaviour, but the episode, trivial in itself, was a sign of the tension in the political situation.

On 27 or perhaps 28 January, Papen told us in the Secretariat to make certain that Kleist-Schmenzin never left the flat without giving one of us his current address and telephone number. These were to be noted on a pad of paper and left open on the first desk in the Secretariat. We were responsible for ensuring that he could be reached at any time. I remember the Schmenziner often left the address of a club in Bendlerstrasse.

A new name – new to us – came up at that time: General Werner von Blomberg, who was with the German delegation at the League of Nations in Geneva, was to be Reich Minister of Defence. A 'non-political' General, so they said, in complete contrast to General von Schleicher.

Suddenly rumours were circulating in the flat, first coming to my knowledge through one of Papen's daughters. Reich Chancellor von Schleicher and General Kurt von Hammerstein-Equord, the Chief of the Army Command, were said to be planning a *coup d'état* with the Potsdam garrison. It would not have been the first time in history that such rumours had been deliberately leaked to the outside world. Then, on 28 January, came the news of Schleicher's resignation, and now it seemed that events were once more moving very fast.

I should explain that the bulk of the telephone calls made to and from Papen's residence were conversations with Hindenburg's Secretary of State Meissner or Hindenburg's son and adjutant, Colonel Oskar von Hindenburg.

On 30 January, when I arrived from the university with the daily papers, I found the door to the big drawing-room left open. Standing at the glass door to the garden stairs was Frau von

Papen, who turned to me, calling: 'Come out, Herr Stahlberg, come out quickly and look! There they go!' I looked down into the garden, still thinly covered with snow, where the last four or five men, dressed in ceremonial black, were disappearing through the door to the left-hand neighbouring garden. Genuinely 'through the back door', as was so often claimed later on. 'They are going to take the oath before old Hindenburg,' said Frau von Papen, her voice shaking. After a long pause – still gazing at the garden gate – she said softly to herself: 'Oh my God, oh my God, I'm afraid.'

At that moment there was a ring at the flat door. A telegraph boy handed me an 'urgent' telegram to Papen 'in person'. It was clearly an unusually long one, in view of the plumpness of the envelope. I gave it to Frau von Papen, who opened it, read it through and passed it to me. I can no longer remember the sender's name, which was unknown to me, but I do remember that it came from Munich and I remember what it said: the sender, evidently a personal friend of Papen, begged him to prevent Hitler's nomination as Reich Chancellor, or at the very least to postpone it. Absolutely reliable information was available in Munich that the NSDAP faced financial collapse, the banks collaborating with the Party had refused further credits and it would only be a matter of days before they closed the Party's accounts.

I looked at Frau von Papen and asked her if I should run after her husband with the telegram. 'No, it's too late. It would do no good. My husband has made up his mind,' she replied. Then she turned away and I saw that she was crying.

I sat down in the empty office and began to deal with incoming mail and newspapers. The paper with Ewald von Kleist's address and telephone number was still in front of me. A little later Frau von Papen came to the office to tell me that the new government had just taken the oath. Her husband had telephoned the news to her.

So I no longer had to be ready to alert the Schmenziner, in case the President of the Reich changed his mind at the last minute. I picked up my hat and coat to go to the university and dine in the hall, the tension of the last few days over and the die cast.

On my way downstairs I conceived the rather curious plan of speaking to the first three people I met in Wilhelmstrasse and asking them whether they knew that Hitler had become Chancellor and what they thought of it.

On reaching the street, I saw that to the south a huge crowd of people had gathered by the Reich Chancellery, in front of Hindenburg's offices (the Presidential Palace was in the process of renovation). I walked off in a northerly direction and spoke to three passers-by one after another in the almost empty street, the first in front of Number 74 itself, the second in front of the British Embassy and the third in front of Braun's fashionable dress shop on the corner of the Adlon. None of them had heard the news and none was prepared to give me his views one way or the other. However much the formation of the government had moved me, all three of my respondents were indifferent – or perhaps simply uncertain.

Dissatisfied with my meagre opinion poll, I asked a fourth passer-by, in Unter den Linden, somewhere in front of the Prussian Ministry of Culture: 'Did you know that Hitler...' This time I was unable even to move on to the second question, because without stopping the man retorted: 'So what?' I abandoned my research.

After lunch I went straight back to Wilhelmstrasse. I was just in time. Papen was standing in the middle of the drawing-room, surrounded by his family. He would have to revise his opinion of Hitler quite fundamentally, he said: the new Cabinet had already met and Herr Hitler had conducted it quite excellently. He, Papen, would not have believed it of him.

The new Reich Chancellor, he continued, had summoned his Party organisations to a great torchlight procession that evening through the Brandenburg Gate and along Wilhelmstrasse. Herr Seldte had immediately announced that the *Stahlhelm* would join in, and Berlin radio had already been asked to summon the entire population to the march in the city centre that evening. Similar torchlight processions would take place in every German city, and in Berlin it would be a tremendous event. It was impressive, Papen said, how purposefully and authoritatively Hitler had organised and announced it all.

Then Papen asked me to go to the Adlon Hotel and book a room with a balcony on the first floor in his name for that evening and accompany his daughters there, so that they could watch the torchlight procession. He and his wife would watch from the Chancellery.

I did as I was told, only to find that the first floor of the Adlon was already fully booked, but I obtained a room on the second floor.

When we arrived at the hotel and went out onto the balcony, the head of the procession, with bands playing, was just appearing, in the central arch of the Brandenburg Gate. Since its erection at the end of the 18th century, this central arch had been used exclusively by the Head of State and his guests of equal rank, which made it painful for me to watch the brown-uniformed columns marching through it.

Every German today has seen the photographs of the SA marching through the Brandenburg Gate on the evening of 30 January 1933. They seem to provide impressive evidence of the exemplary order and the huge numbers in which the SA streamed through the three central arches.

However, I have to disappoint the readers of these historical reports, victims even now of the propaganda of Dr. Goebbels, Hitler's propaganda chief. The familiar pictures were not taken that evening but set up years later on Goebbels' orders for filming purposes, as the perfect lighting of the squares on either side of the gate reveal.

In fact, the Brandenburg Gate was almost in darkness, the streets practically free from snow; the feeble street lamps, with the brown uniforms and red swastika banners, created a grim, sinister atmosphere. Nor was there any question of cheering crowds of onlookers at the Brandenburg Gate. There was no 'cheering' there that evening, only round the Chancellery in Wilhelmstrasse, where Hindenburg appeared at one window and Hitler at another.

Beneath our balcony at the Adlon, the pavement was occupied to about a quarter of its width and the popular mood was controlled.

The scene changed suddenly, for on the balcony below ours appeared a merry company, led by the famous film star, Hans Albers. His loud, uninhibited 'Hallo, here I am!' resounded from the balcony, his well-wined, more or less décolleté companions joined in casually, waving their champagne glasses and toasting the people on the pavement. Hans Albers' success was overwhelming, for the people below us now turned their backs on the brown columns and cheered their popular 'blond Hans'. He showed his appreciation: one of his beauties suddenly had a silver tray in her hands, covered with cigarette packets of all kinds. The great film star helped himself, tearing open packet after packet with broad gestures: their contents rained down on the people. It was no longer the SA but blond Hans who held the stage, until the silver tray was empty. Then, as swiftly as they had appeared on the balcony, they all vanished again into the room below us, for the evening was very cold.

After the brown columns with their sea of banners had marched past us, the *Stahlhelm* appeared. The glum grey of their wind-cheaters and the far smaller number of torches were visible proof that they had now become the tag-end.

After I had returned the young ladies in my care to their flat, I decided to take a look at the southern end of Wilhelmstrasse, where the Chancellery was. I did not get far, because here the street really was jammed by crowds and although the last of the marching columns had already dispersed, people were still shouting and waving at the window where Hitler continued to appear at intervals. Hindenburg had apparently withdrawn by this time.

Once I was on my way home, the tension of the day slackened and I began to wonder what would happen now. Probably the sheet of paper with Ewald Kleist-Schmenzin's telephone number on it was still on my desk at 74 Wilhelmstrasse. Apart from Hans Wedemeyer, he was the only man who had tried, up to the very last moment, to hold Papen back.

In Papen's memoirs '*Der Wahrheit eine Gasse*' (1952) you will seek Kleist-Schmenzin's name in vain. Ewald von Kleist-Schmenzin died under the guillotine on 9 April 1945 in Berlin-Plötzensee, only a few days before the end of the war he had so often predicted.

From 30 January 1933 onwards, Papen's official title was 'Deputy to the Reich Chancellor and Reich Commissar in Prussia'. His offices as Reich Commissar were in the Prussian Ministry of State, the official rooms of President Otto Braun until 20 July 1932. There he had a press office at his disposal again, under Herbert von Bose, a senior civil servant. This put an end to my activities as 'press consultant', but Papen asked me if I would continue to be available. At the very least my task would be to accompany him on public occasions and be prepared to carry out special orders.

After all, the arrival of a politician carries more weight if there is at least one consultant or aide, call him what you will, accompanying him, not to speak of the notebook in the said person's pocket, since it is often necessary to catch snippets of conversation or dates. In my case there was never any question of payment, either before or after 30 January.

As deputy to the Chancellor, that is as Vice-Chancellor, Papen at first had no offices for his use, until my successor, Fritz Günther von Tschirschky, procured some for him. It was to him that Papen owed the planning, staffing and budgeting for his post, and finally, towards the end of May, his move into the new offices in the Borsig Palace on the corner of Vossstrasse and Wilhelmplatz, immediately beside the Chancellery.

Meanwhile, Hans von Wedemeyer and I continued to go in and out at the flat at 74 Wilhelmstrasse.

The Reichstag Burns

The evening of 27 February 1933 began with some irritation for me at home: my radio receiver once again refused to function. I had put the thing together myself from a construction kit. It sometimes went on strike and the business of finding the fault would then present me with a major problem. On this occasion, as I searched and tested, I suddenly heard a newsflash, through all the crackling and piping, reporting that the Reichstag was in flames.

I rushed down the stairs and reached the Brandenburg Gate by bus in fifteen to twenty minutes.

The great building was burning from end to end and flames were even flickering from the dome.

The blaze was cordoned off by police over a wide area, so that, in spite of my curiosity, I could not get close to it. I went to Siegesallee to see if I could find a gap in the cordon, and passing the white marble memorials to Brandenburg and Prussian rulers, came to the victory column, which still stood in front of the parliament building at that time, but here too I met a dense cordon of police. On the other hand, the full width of the main façade of the Reischstag was now before me. A truly phantasmagoric sight it made, and one did not need much imagination to assess the political significance of this fire – six days before the coming Reichstag elections on 5 March. Innumerable fire engines were still trying to extinguish the flames.

I sought out an elderly, grey-haired police official and asked him who could have started the fire. His answer came as freely as my question: 'Someone has already been arrested.' 'Only one?' I asked. 'Yes,' said the policeman, 'only one.' I went on probing – it was easier to talk like this in the darkness: 'How long would he have taken to set this huge buiding on fire?' 'About ten to fifteen minutes, they say,' was his reply, but he and his colleagues had only arrived at the same time as the fire engines and by then flames were already shooting from the dome.

Encouraged by the frankness of our conversation, I asked him if he could not let me through the cordon, as I was secretary to Vice-Chancellor von Papen. 'Have you got an official pass?' he asked. 'No, I have no pass,' I had to tell him. He was sorry, but I could go to the Brandenburg Gate, where there was admission for 'authorised persons'.

Unfortunately I did not follow up his suggestion: what point would there have been? There was no lack of curious onlookers already.

Had I known or discovered that Papen was at the site of the fire at that very time with Hitler, Goebbels, Göring and their followers, I might have been able to witness something remarkable at close range.

On the next day, 28 February, I dropped in at 74 Wilhelm-strasse before my morning lecture but Papen was not there. He was at the Reich Chancellery, his wife told me. So I came back that afternoon to see if there was any work for me, and this time I found him there. As so often, he invited me to take tea with him.

Papen was excited by the events of the last few hours and immediately referred to the 'Communist' arson. He has been one of the first to reach the burning Reichstag, having seen the fire very quickly from his club in Vossstrasse. One of the first people he had met at the Reichstag was Herr Göring. Both Hitler and Goebbels had appeared later. Göring had – these were Papen's words – 'burst into shouts of joy' again and again, joy that the Communists had given the government the satisfaction of being able finally and ruthlessly to proceed against their party. Göring had slapped his thigh.

I took a moment to compose myself and said: 'I saw the fire last night, Sir, and I simply cannot believe that one man could have set that great building alight in a few minutes.' Papen responded at once: 'Have you or anyone else got proof that there were other arsonists?' I said: 'No. Just a suspicion.' Papen replied that only evidence would do – an arsonist had been caught in the act and arrested. 'That is proof, and it fits with the Communist plan.' The man had actually admitted to starting the fire and to being a Communist. Still unwilling to give in, I said that I was not completely convinced that the fire was part of the KPD's design.

Then I asked him: 'Will the Reichstag be rebuilt, Sir? I think that, in spite of all the upsets of past years, the Reichstag is a symbol for the whole German Reich. We shouldn't forget that it was built under Bismarck's government.' Papen looked at me in some surprise, was silent for a moment and then said that there had been no mention of rebuilding, either last night or this morning at the Cabinet meeting. On the contrary, Hitler had expressed his satisfaction that the 'talking-shop' no longer existed.

I felt there was something wrong in the Vice-Chancellor's quoting the Reich Chancellor so blandly, but what was a young student to say? Hitler and Papen knew, without my help, that the Reichstag fire was a highly political issue, but at the time of this conversation I was unaware that on that very day old Hindenburg's signature had been obtained for the latest emergency decree in accordance with Article 48 of the Constitution. Not only had the KPD been banned – that on its own would not have disturbed me personally at all – but the basic rights of the free constitution had been removed, as I was to learn from my radio receiver that evening.

At home my mother showed me the latest edition of *Die Woche*, with photographs from the first German concentration camps. I had already seen the paper in the University reading room and on the next morning I took it to Wilhelmstrasse and laid it on the Vice-Chancellor's desk, open at the page covering Oranienburg.

Even now, half a century later, the origin of the Reichstag fire is still controversial. The Dutchman Marinus van der Lubbe, who had been caught in the act on that evening of 27 February, must certainly have been the arsonist. He was condemned to death by the Reich Court in Leipzig and executed. But the rumours that Göring, President of the Reichstag and Prussian Minister of the Interior, had been involved, together with a group of SA men, via the underground passage between his official residence and the parliament building, have never subsided.

And there were other suspicions, for instance in connection with the brilliant figure of the 'clairvoyant' Jan Hanussen, well known in the city, who was said to have pulled the strings behind van der Lubbe. A few weeks after the fire, Hanussen was found murdered not far from Berlin. Finally, there was talk in Berlin of Gempp, Head of the Fire Service, who had directed its activities that night. Gempp was said to have had inflammable materials collected and stored in a room in the burning building, in such quantities as to arouse the suspicion that there had been several arsonists. Gempp was said to be in prison and later we heard that he had been found dead in his cell.

For me, suspicion of Göring and the National Socialists has not been dispelled, for they alone deliberately and methodically reaped benefit from the situation.

On the Brandenburg Gate

The Reichstag elections took place on 5 March 1933. An unprecedented fusillade of propaganda and promises had descended on the Germans. The NSDAP, which had been faced with bankruptcy only in January, now, as the 'governing party', could apparently lay its hands on as much money as it wanted. Despite massive street terrorism and pressure on the voters, the National Socialists were unable to achieve their goal of an absolute majority, and historians agree that at this time the election results were still correctly counted, which makes the results of 5 March 1933 extremely instructive:

	Seats	Percentage of Votes
National Socialists (NSDAP)	288	43.9
German Nationalists (DNVP)	52	8.3
Centre (Catholics)	73	11.2
Social Democrats (SPD)	120	18.3
Communists (KPD)	81	12.3
Other parties	33	6.3
	647	100.0

So the NSDAP and DNVP had 340 seats between them, in other words (with 51.9 per cent) an absolute majority. According to democratic rules, the Conservatives, now also supported by the former Centre Party member and present Vice-Chancellor, Papen, were in an extremely strong position, holding the balance of power as they did. But the National Socialist government had used a dirty trick: it had presented the German electorate with a voting paper on which the KPD, which owing to the Reichstag fire had been prohibited on 28 February, five days earlier, was apparently still offering itself for election. Now, however, after the election, the

Government declared the Communist votes 'invalid'. Without the 81 KPD members, the newly elected parliament therefore consisted of only 566 instead of 647 members. Hence the NSDAP now had a parliamentary majority without a coalition partner. This converted the indisputable election success of the Nazis by 'legal means' into a *coup d'état*.

When the results became known on the morning after the election, I was at the university. As usual, we met in the lunch break for our 'standing convention' in the front garden on Unter den Linden, when suddenly, as if controlled by an unseen hand, swastika flags were hoisted on the flagpoles of the public buildings around us. On the instant, there was tremendous excitement among the hundreds of students, the Nazis breaking into shouts of 'Heil!', organised democratic and conservative students producing a shrill concert of whistles. Once again, the university had turned into a seething witches' cauldron. Trying to get my bearings, I hurried through the building to Dorotheenstrasse and saw that, there too, flags were flying on roofs and from windows. However in contrast to the house on the main road, there were far more black, white and red flags than swastikas, since that street had less official premises than flats and private businesses. As I ran back to the front garden, I was wondering what could be done. The idea that the swastika could become the flag of the German Reich through what had undoubtedly been a well-organised *coup de main*, was intolerable to me.

In the front courtyard I bumped into Ernst Wolf Mommsen, a fellow-student whom I knew well, who turned out to be a hair's-breadth ahead of me. He already knew that the Nazis had ordered their SA to hoist the swastika banners simultaneously on all public buildings at a pre-arranged time, not only in Berlin but throughout Germany. The election victory was to be celebrated and the swastika flag elevated from Party to national symbol.

Mommsen already had a rolled-up black, white and red flag under his arm and, in ringing tones, he summoned the students about him to run with him to the Brandenburg Gate and hoist the flag on the victory pole of the quadriga on the Gate. The symbolic significance of the Brandenburg Gate could decide which was to be Germany's new national flag. 'The first flag to fly on the Gate is the winner!' he cried.

We young men, and many older ones too, felt no inward response to the colours black, red and gold at the time of the

Weimar Republic. They could say what they liked: black, red and gold were the colours of defeat in the war, of the recognition of the 'Versailles diktat', of poverty through inflation, unemployment and reparations. Black, red and gold represented the feeble Weimar Republic and the failure of the 1848 attempt to create a united German Reich.

But black, white and red belonged to Bismarck's Reich and its advance since 1871. The change in the German national flag in 1919 had been a mistake, despite the fact that black, red and gold had been the colours of the Holy Roman Empire of the German Nation. But we found it unthinkable that a party flag should now become our national flag: 'Black white and red to the Brandenburg Gate!' cried Mommsen once again. 'Who's coming with me?'

I was, naturally, and Mommsen received general support – we were off! There seemed to be fifty or a hundred of us altogether, but after we had passed the iron gate to Unter den Linden, there were no more than twenty starters for the thousand-metre dash. At the monument to Frederick the Great we swung across to the central promenade so as to see the Brandenburg Gate as soon as possible between the bare trees. When the Friedrichstrasse crossing was behind us the Gate appeared ahead of us: no flag on the quadriga! Now I was running in front beside Mommsen, asking him as we ran how we were to get up there. He shouted that we should cross the Pariser Platz diagonally left to the colonnaded extension to the south. The police guardroom inside had a staircase to the top. As we ran I objected that there should really be no flag at all on top of that classical building – a flag there would be stylistically incongruous. 'You're right,' said Mommsen, 'but that's not the point today.'

Panting, we crossed the Pariser Platz – still nothing to be seen on the Gate. Mommsen was the first to reach the door of the police station. We recoiled. A wall of brown uniforms barred our way! Too late! Probably by only a few minutes.

To the front, by the barrier, people were shouting at each other. Once again my six feet three inches paid off and I could see that the police and SA were in confrontation, the police refusing to hand over the keys. Who would be the first to use force? But then two or three SA men leaped the barrier, having spotted to the right of the stairs the key cupboard with 'Stairs to the Gate' written on it. All the keys landed in an SA cap and the police gave in, quite probably having already received orders to do nothing. One key after another was flung away when it failed to fit, then, suddenly, the door was open, the SA men vanished one after another up the stairs and when the last brown shirt had gone, the way was open for us, the 'civilians'.

When Mommsen and I stuck our heads out of the open trapdoor at the top one of the brownshirts had already secured his swastika flag to the top of the victory symbol.

We waited until the 'victors' had passed us, going down again, and then crawled, most of us on all fours, (since I, for one, was liable to vertigo), over to the quadriga. There we secured the black, white and red flag to the two copper carriage wheels so that it hung over the frieze of the Gate on the city side. Mommsen had even remembered to bring plenty of curtain cord.

Meanwhile, a large number of people had gathered down below, filling the corners of the Pariser Platz and the beginning of the central promenade of Unter den Linden. We stopped to look down on Unter den Linden once again – what a majestic street, especially from up here!

Then we went down the dark, narrow stairs again. The key to the 'Stairs to the Gate' was still in the door. We locked up carefully and returned the key to the police, just as we should.

Potsdam, 21 March 1933

Barely six weeks had passed since, on his appointment as Reich Chancellor, Hitler had promised the President that he would not change the composition of the new government. But now he succeeded in persuading Hindenburg that a 'Reich Minister for Popular Information and Propaganda' was needed, and so, on 13 March, the Berlin Gauleiter of the NSDAP, Joseph Goebbels, joined the Cabinet.

A few days later, I learned through the Vice-Chancellor that the opening of the new Reichstag was to be celebrated in a formal ceremony in Potsdam. I had the distinct feeling that Hitler's dynamism had made a lasting impression on Papen. The plan to inaugurate the new parliament in Postdam in early Spring, by the tombs of the Prussian kings, seemed to be extremely welcome to Papen and the other non-party ministers. They were surprised that Hitler should turn so overtly to Prussianism.

Papen gave me one of the sought-after participants' tickets for a seat right beside the Potsdam Garrison Church and asked me to maintain eye contact with him there so that I could join him at a sign.

He was clearly thrilled with the whole idea of this occasion, which, he said, had originated with Goebbels. This made it all the more astonishing that a Chancellor from Austria and his Rhineland Propaganda Minister should want to declare themselves so convincingly for Prussia. There was not a word of suspicion that the whole thing might be nothing but a propaganda move to impress conservative Prussia.

I learned over the next few days that the 'question of dress' for Potsdam had been thoroughly discussed in Cabinet. Hitler had at first decided that dress uniform should be worn, with full-sized medals; the 9th (Prussian) Infantry Regiment (IR9) should march past; Prussian banners and old standards should also be displayed: in short, the official ceremony must look as 'Prussian' as was humanly possible. Papen said he had pointed out that, in that case, protocol called for a black morning coat and top hat to be worn by civilians, but Hitler had accepted this only after some hesitation. Papen concluded: 'We shall therefore see Herr Hitler in public for the first time in quite *bourgeois* dress. I count that as something of a success.'

On 21 March I took the train to Potsdam very early. I did not attend either of the two services for new members of parliament, at the Nicolai church and the Catholic municipal church. On the way from the station, I could see from the Lange Brücke the IR 9 marching on the parade ground by the Town Hall, together with units of SA and the *Stahlhelm*. I passed the 'Petition Lime', which had impressed me from early childhood. A centuries-old, stunted tree with an unusually thick trunk, the lime took its name from the time of Frederick the Great, when the citizens of Potsdam used to pin their requests and petitions to the tree so that 'Old Fritz' could read them without having to dismount from his horse.

That morning, passing the Town Hall, I had to make a detour through the inner city in order to reach the garrison church on Breite Strasse. Potsdam was smothered in a sea of flags, with swastikas in the minority, but there were many old Prussian black and white flags, the white often yellowed by age, and some with the Prussian eagle. From the tower of the garrison church, whose crypt sheltered the coffins of Frederick the Great and his father Frederick William I, the bells rang out at the appointed hour with the tune of '*Üb' immer Treu und Redlichkeit*'. Immediately beside the church, to the East, three stands had been erected, the middle one for the new government and the ones for invited guests to right and left. I found my seat on the left-hand stand, so I had my back to the church. On the first floor of the corner house opposite I saw Eta von Tresckow, Henning's wife, with their children, on the balcony. They had put out the old imperial ensign with the eagle and the Iron Cross. Years after the war, Henning's son Rüdiger told me that there had been a long debate beforehand in the family as to which flag was to be flown, and his father had decided on the old imperial ensign (*1867–1921: black-where-red*).

First, the newly-elected members of the Reichstag appeared on foot, giving rise to whispers that the SPD members were missing. I learned later that they had not even been invited, but only a few people noticed this at the time. Then shouts of 'Heil' were heard from the old *Stadtschloss* in the distance and soon Hitler and Papen appeared, walking at a measured pace, their top hats in their hands, as if *en route* to a funeral. Behind them came the Reich ministers, including Göring and little Goebbels, with their top hats on their heads.

When they were seated in the church, the President's two cars arrived, the big, high Mercedes special models well known to all Berliners, built high enough for Hindenburg to get in and out without difficulty wearing the spiked helmet of the Imperial Army. A genuine living memorial to imperial might and greatness, his marshal's baton in his right hand, he strode to the entrance of the church.

From my seat I was unable to hear Hitler's and Hindenburg's speeches, but the hymns sung inside rang out mightily, the organist having pulled out all possible stops: the 'Netherlands Prayer of Thanksgiving', 'We come to pray before the God of Justice', then 'Lord, make us free' and finally the choral hymn 'Now thank we all our God'.

While all the bells rang out from the church tower, the old President Hindenburg was the first to appear in the doorway of the church and each person took the place allotted to him by the organisers: Hindenburg in the middle, before the three VIP stands, behind him, in military formation, his son and aide Oskar with General Werner von Blomberg, the new Minister of Defence. In the first row of the central stand sat the government, and centrally below it – specially noted by the onlookers – the Papal Nuncio, Monsignor Cesare Orsenigo.

When the church bells fell silent, the salute by the cannons of the
Potsdam Artillery Regiment began in the park before the old
Stadtschloss. Then the band of the 9th (Prussian) Infantry Regiment
struck up in the distance and as the musicians wheeled before the
VIP stands towards the President's standard, the head of IR9
appeared, marching in review order, led by its commander,
Colonel (later Field-Marshal) Ernst Busch and his Aide, my
cousin Henning von Tresckow. One has to have watched the
ceremonial march-past of that regiment to have an idea how a
traditional regiment of the former Prussian Guards could look.
What a sorry bunch of SA and *Stahlhelm* followed behind!

When the march-past was over, the President's huge car arrived
first to pick him up, followed by the open black 7-litre Mercedes of
the Chancellor. While Hindenburg drove away without body-
guards, there was not an inch to spare, as usual, in Hitler's state
limousine when his black-uniformed *SS-Leibstandarte* had been
packed as tightly as possible into the car and on its running-
boards. I estimate that there were ten to fifteen guards.

While the crowds were leaving their seats on the stands, my
cousin Eta von Tresckow called to me: 'Come up and have a dish
of soup with us. Bring Papen with you, if you like.' She had already
vanished again in the crowd to assemble her party according to
inclination or practicality: the daughter of the Great War Chief of
General Staff, Erich von Falkenhayn, did this kind of thing to the
manner born. Finally I managed to reach Papen and passed on the
Tresckows' invitation; their house at 8 Breite Strasse was only a
few steps from the garrison church. Papen begged me to excuse
him, as he still had a number of other engagements, and released
me for the day. I would have liked to take him to the Tresckows,
for I knew of no more interesting house in Potsdam than that of
Henning and Eta.

The front door of the beautiful old town house stood hospitably
wide open, as did the doors on the first floor. The guests were
crowded inside the large sitting-room and I joined a circle by the
hearth, where the debate was loud and lively. A single theme
dominated the conversation: what does today mean? Some thought
Papen's policy of integrating National Socialism into the 'National
Concentration' was bearing its first fruits. Others went further and
said this was the start of a development which would result in a
constitutional monarchy under one of the Hohenzollern princes;
but there were also those who said that the day had been a notable

chess move and a great victory for Hitler in capturing for himself and his party those of our people who adhered to the tradition and spirit of Prussia. No one could escape the fascination of the day, not even our host, but I remember clearly that Henning was one of those who was ultimately sceptical. He declared with a mischievous smile that he was clear about one thing at least: none of those present was likely to have another chance of enjoying the sight of Herr Hitler in morning coat and top hat in public. When Henning had passed him on the way to the garrison church, he had presented a highly comical figure.

Whatever the verdict, the majority of Germans in those days were going over to Hitler 'with all flags flying'. They were captivated by the illusion that a great and brilliant future lay just over the horizon. Only my godfather Herbert von Bismarck, recently appointed Secretary of State at the Prussian Ministry of the Interior, adhered to his silent scepticism, quietly indicating his doubts.

Göring's Secretary of State

A few days later Herbert von Bismarck asked me to come and see him in his office, bringing my camera and a good supply of film. He would tell me the rest in person.

The ministry lay on the north side of Unter den Linden. I was shown up to the first floor and told that the Secretary of State was in the first room on the left.

'I want to ask you to take a few pictures of me here at the desk, because in a few days I shall have left this place.' I must have looked quite astonished, because my godfather had held this post for only a few months. I set up the stand, because my little box camera was not really the right equipment for indoor portrait photography, so it was some time before I used up the film. Then he offered me a chair and said I must be surprised at his asking me rather than a professional photographer. He would explain.

'I have handed in my notice,' he began, 'and now I am going to tell you how it came about. You know that the Minister of the Interior who has been my superior for a short time now is Herr Göring. I cannot take the responsibility of working with him. When he first came to this house he called me in at once for a talk. These were his first words to me: "Bismarck, tell me first of all what I have here". I replied: "I don't understand your question,

Minister." He flared up as if he were dealing with a schoolboy, and shouted: "Don't be like that, Bismarck, I want to know from you what I have under me here".

'I said: "I still don't understand your question, Minister. Would you like to see the civil servants and employees who are working here in the Ministry? I'll get them all to come to a meeting."

'Then he yelled at me: "Bismarck, you seem to take me for a fool. I haven't the time to talk to every single person on the premises, that's what you're here for, as my Secretary of State. I want to know from you about everything I govern from this office!" My answer to that was: "I have to disappoint you, Minister, nothing at all is governed from this office," and I went on to say that the Minister of the Interior for Prussia was to some extent the head of the internal administration. From here he administered the twelve provinces of Prussia, and I listed the provinces for Göring. The head of a provincial administration had the official title of *Oberpräsident*, and I began to give him the names of the Prussian *Oberpräsidenten* and their official quarters in the provincial capitals. After a few names he interrupted me, saying this was too boring for him and he had neither the time nor the inclination to learn the names by heart. He was satisfied that I had obviously memorised them. I then went on to tell him that every province had several administrative districts, each headed by a *Regierungspräsident*. Once again he interrupted me, shouting: "Bismarck, you made a mistake, you got *Oberpräsident* and *Regierungspräsident* mixed up. The *Regierungspräsident* is the head of the province and the *Oberpräsident* heads the administrative district." I said this was not so and I must regretfully correct him. He replied irritably that if this was true – and he would have it checked – then it was quite wrong, because to the simple man '*Regierung*' was higher than '*Ober*'. Then Göring leaned back in his chair and said in a peremptory tone: "Bismarck, take notes, draft a decree at once. I hereby decree that the official titles *Oberpräsident* and *Regierungspräsident* change places with immediate effect!" I explained that this could not simply happen: These official titles had existed for generations and were deeply rooted in the minds of the internal administration as well as of the people of Prussia. To change them over would result in dangerous chaos. I had myself been administrative head of Regenwalde District in Pomerania and could judge from practical experience. He then dismissed me, saying that that was enough for today and he would return to the matter later.'

I listened almost incredulously to my godfather as he spoke, his voice filled with emotion. Then he went on:

'That kind of thing could have been endured, you know. I would gradually have made him aware of the structure of the Prussian administration. But it did not stop at such absurdities: it grew worse from day to day. He very rarely called me in for a talk again. Instead, many of our reliable civil servants have been sacked overnight, and the people who have moved in have not the slightest qualifications, let alone the training for ministerial civil servants. The Minister does not care at all whether there are posts for the new people or not, which has led to an unholy muddle. I am still Secretary of State at present, but I have been virtually reduced to a cipher. However, since a ministerial decree is not legally valid until the minister's signature has been countersigned by the Secretary of State, files I have never seen before arrive almost daily on my desk, already signed by Göring, and therefore only needing my signature. Naturally I read and check them very thoroughly, and what I am now going to tell you *(Uncle Herbert looked straight at me, his eyes wide)* is the honest truth: a constantly increasing number of decrees and decisions concern matters which according to the Reich Penal Code are punishable by imprisonment, penitentiary and even death. Up to now my name has not appeared under any such document, nor will it in the future. I simply return those signature files to the Minister, with a note asking to see him.

'Initially I did succeed once or twice in preventing the worst, but nowadays the Minister appears less and less often at the ministry. I suspect that he has the things I am not supposed to see brought to his palace and completed without me. Recently I did meet him in the corridor here, when he took me – in the best of spirits – to his room, offered me a chair in the most friendly way and said, as if it were the most innocent thing in the world: "Bismarck, I don't think we suit each other."

'I agreed at once, and am now awaiting my discharge. That is why I asked you for a souvenir photograph of my time as Secretary of State.'

I had listened to my godfather in silence, but now I burst out spontaneously: 'Uncle Herbert, wouldn't it be better if you stayed and tried to prevent the worst?' He waved his hand. 'You heard me speak of the penitentiary and the death sentence, so you know what all this is about. I also have the strongest suspicion that the Reichstag building was not set on fire by the Dutchman van der

Lubbe on his own. On the night of the fire, in my official capacity as the superior of Walter Gempp, the Chief Fire Officer, I was in the underground passage leading to the palace of the President of the Reichstag (Hermann Göring). But we have no proof. Only a few days ago, Göring said in a clash with me that he was proud not to know what was right and just. I cannot go on working with this man. I would be sharing his guilt, so it is now my duty to go.'*

Bismarck left Berlin soon afterwards, giving up his flat near the Botanical Garden and retiring to his little estate of Lasbeck in the district of Regenwalde in East Pomerania, where he had once been District Administrator.

From Berlin to Hamburg

I went to see my father at that time in his wonderful flat at 10A Corneliusstrasse in the Tiergarten-quarter, on the Landwehrkanal. We generally sat in the conservatory, with a view of the neighbouring house where the Papal Nuncio lived. I had intended to tell him about my day in Potsdam and my visit to Uncle Herbert but did not have a chance to do so as father had news for me. By now the Reichstag had approved the Enabling Act presented by Hitler on 23 March at the Kroll Opera House. Only the SPD had voted decisively against it (in so far as their members had not already been forced to take flight or been arrested). Hitler could now pass and promulgate in person any law, even an unconstitutional one. My father was in a state of great excitement about it and a personal experience had added to the emotion aroused by the news.

He had made an appointment with his dentist in Uhlandstrasse and had as usual been taken to the waiting-room by the receptionist. But first she had closed the door carefully and told him that a few days earlier her employer had been taken from the surgery by two SA men in brown uniform with the white 'Auxiliary Police' armband, and had not been seen since. When he had failed to arrive at the surgery next day, the receptionist had gone to the police station to report him missing, but her report had been rejected because the dentist had already been taken to Oranienburg concentration camp where he would undoubtedly

---

* Luitgarde von Schlabrendorff, née von Bismarck, confirmed in 1986 that her father strongly suspected that Göring was implicated in causing the fire.

have to stay for some time. When the horrified receptionist asked what charge had been brought against the doctor, she was told that one of his patients had informed against him for criticising the government while he was treating him. The receptionist then tried to find out which patient had done this, but of course she was not told.

My father was now profoundly anxious lest someone should suggest that he was the patient in question, since – so he told me – he had had political discussions with his dentist at almost every treatment, and for many years. The two had become politically close in their admiration for the late Reich Foreign Minister Gustav Stresemann.

I asked if the dentist was a Jew, but my father was not sure. He thought it was possible, he said, but what was important was that this dentist was the best he had ever had. Finally, the receptionist had apologised for not cancelling the appointment by telephone. Since her employer's disappearance she no longer used the telephone, because there was a suspicious crackling on the line as soon as a connection was made and she was certain that the phone was being tapped.

I asked my father to write down the dentist's name and address and promised to report the affair to the Vice-Chancellor next morning and ask for his help.

Now at last, I could tell my father about Potsdam. As a former reserve captain of the Pasewalk Cuirassiers, he was naturally most interested in the military ceremonial. He asked me how many squadrons of the Potsdam cavalry regiment had filed past, and when I told him that there had been no cavalry there at all, he simply uttered a dry: 'Aha'.

Then I told him about my visit to Herbert von Bismarck. He listened quite calmly, without interrupting, then gazed thoughtfully into the distance for some time.

Suddenly he rose and looked out of the window, as if watching for something in particular. I too stood up and followed the direction of his gaze. Over in the neighbouring house the Papal Nuncio Orsenigo had come into sight and my father gave a slight bow, which was returned. 'You are surprised at this odd ceremony,' said my father. 'It started when the Monsignore's predecessor, Eugenio Pacelli, was living there. We often greeted each other through the window when we happened to be sharpening our razors the window at the same time. One day Pacelli surprised me

by lowering his razor to me like a rapier in greeting, and Orsenigo
has inherited the custom. Our friendship goes no further than that,
but it gives both of us some pleasure.'

Then we went for a walk in the Tiergarten, walking in silence
through the big park for some time, until at last my father began to
speak.

Thanks to my frequent reports, he had taken a very lively
interest in my work with Herr von Papen, but from the beginning
the whole affair had not really 'agreed' with him. Of course it was a
unique opportunity for such a young man to find himself suddenly
in the midst of the political events of this period, but my report
about the visit to Herbert Bismarck had pushed the 'Potsdam
performance' to one side. He was surprised that so few people in
our country seemed prepared to recognise the way things were
going. In any case he did not want to see his son being manoeuvred
into a situation from which one day he might no longer be able to
escape. To put it briefly: he advised me to say goodbye to Herr von
Papen and leave Berlin.

Basically I had no objection; on the contrary, I was quite
relieved that he had more or less made the decision for me. Papen
had made such demands on me recently that my general studies, so
enthusiastically embarked on, had inevitably fallen behind.

The next day I asked to see Papen personally. He introduced me
to Fritz Günther von Tschirschky, who had just arrived. He asked
me to join them and told me that in future Tschirschky would also
be working with him. I took the opportunity to tell him that I
intended to leave Berlin in order to begin my business training in
foreign trade, as I had already agreed with my father.

Papen was very sorry that I was going and was kind enough to
assure me that he would be glad to have me with him again later.
Then he went to his desk and took one of the portrait photographs
kept for such occasions from a drawer. 'I would like to show my
gratitude by writing you a dedication on my picture. Is there
anything you would like me to write?' I said that it was entirely up
to him, so he thought for a moment, undid his fountain pen and
wrote:

> One kind of politics is based on faith!
> With thanks . . .
> Your . . .

I was rather startled by his parting gift and have often wondered
why he dedicated those words to me in particular. Perhaps it

sprang from a sentiment from the Catholic to the Protestant – or was there no deeper reason at all?

I stayed with him and Tschirschky for about an hour and was actually very glad that I would not be the third in this group. On first acquaintance I found Tschirschky quite simply 'too loud'. Since my departure was now decided, Papen commented very sweetly that it was only now that he realised what a valuable assistant he had had in me, because Bose, as chief of his press section, had taken over one half of my work, while Tschirschky would now accompany him as his 'aide' and be responsible for the other half.

I still had no notion that, by prompting this decision, my father had been my guardian angel. He had an instinct for approaching danger.

Before I left, I told Papen about the disappearance of the dentist from Uhlandstrasse. Papen listened with consternation, but Tschirschky simply burst out: 'There we have it. Yet another case!' Tschirscky took the paper with the address on it. 'Your first job,' Papen told him.

*   *   *

On my arrival in Hamburg, I ordered the daily paper *Hamburger Fremdenblatt*, to look for a furnished room in the advertisement section. An old lady in an old house on the Esplanade showed me two, one for forty, the other for forty-two marks, because it contained an old piano. Two marks a month for a piano – I took it at once. There was only one condition attached to renting this attractive room: no female visitors! When I left Hamburg eighteen months later, the old lady wept bitter tears.

I now started work with Carlowitz & Co. in the Molenhof, an important import/export firm with branches in many large East Asian towns. My father felt that it was crucial to his edible oil factory in Stettin to make the 'most suitable' purchases of raw materials.

We worked with calculating machines, cabling all over the world in code so that it would not be too easy for the competition to spy on us. In the typists' room were the first electric typewriters, which made a deafening noise.

Then I was put into accounting. The chief clerk clapped his hands to his head when he read my figures, sat me down at a high desk and made me write out the numbers from 1 to 100 by hand! I was piqued, but I could see he was right. Then I moved to the foreign currency department and had to spend two or three weeks accepting cheques in foreign currencies, converting them and making them out in another foreign currency. It really was not easy! One day a cheque arrived from somewhere in South America. The startled chief clerk took the cheque to the bank; the bank that had made out the cheque did not exist! At great trouble and expense it was just possible to forestall the damage.

At lunchtime I met with friends at the vegetarian restaurant in the Alster Arcades, where delicious dishes cost only a few pence.

For me the day began early in the morning. I would run the few hundred metres from the Esplanade to the Hamburg Rowing Club on the outer Alster in my tracksuit. I had been welcomed very kindly as a member because my great-grandfather Heckscher[*] had been one of the club's founders in 1841. In the large picture of the founder members he appeared as stroke in the 'Coxed Six'.

We rowed, generally in sculling fours and sometimes in eights, down to the Uhlenhorst ferry house and back. Then it was under the shower and back to my room on the Esplanade where a tray of hot coffee and fresh rolls was waiting. This too came out of the forty-two marks per month – in all, this was a spendid time for a young man with a monthly allowance of two hundred marks.

My father had given me a letter of recommendation to his regimental friend Burchard-Motz. On the first Saturday I handed in the letter and visiting cards at Klein-Flottbek on the Elbe and was received with open arms. For the first time I could watch from the dining table as the ocean steamers sailed in and out. Hamburg was a fascinating city.

Paul Stahl, a friend of my father's from the pre-war period in Stettin, ran a different, and also very sociable kind of house. In Stettin, Stahl had been director of the Vulcan shipyard. When the warships built there grew larger, the Stettin shipping channel to the Baltic was no longer big enough and the shipyard was moved to Bremen. Now the retired director was living in Hamburg, preferring this city to the smaller Bremen.

Once the Stahls had welcomed one in, one could come and go as one pleased. There were almost always interesting people to be met there, but politics was scarcely ever discussed: anyone whose politics did not suit his host was not invited again.

---

[*] Johann Gustav Wilhelm Moritz Heckscher (1797–1865), 1848 Hamburg delegate at St. Paul's Church in Frankfurt, Reich Minister of Justice and Foreign Minister.

Even at that time, Hamburg's sporting events were already outstanding. In the jumping Derby I was an eager supporter of young Irmgard Georgius, who not only rode wonderfully but was also very beautiful to look at – horse and rider in perfect harmony.

One Sunday I was stretching my legs at the Horner race-track among the thousands who had come to the German Derby. Between races there was a sudden burst of applause, although there was no sporting activity to be seen. Then I saw that Vice-Chancellor Papen had appeared in one of the boxes in the centre of the main stand and the continuous ovation, which he greeted with a beaming smile, was for him.

For the first time I registered with astonishment how popular Papen was – at least here among the public of the first rank.

Then something quite unreal happened: the applause of thousands was abruptly silenced for one or two seconds. Then came a shrill whistle, the first in a concert of whistles such as I had never heard at a race-track before. At whom was this aimed?

At the extreme right of the stand, in the last box, in which previously only brown and black uniforms had appeared, the new Propaganda Minister Goebbels, wearing a light trench-coat, had taken his seat.

The whistling concert did not end until Papen rose to his feet in his box some twenty metres away, not to join his cabinet colleague but to leave the stand and show himself in the ring where the horses were parading.

As it is not easy for me to hide my height in a crowd, he soon spotted me, greeted me kindly, introduced me – somewhat absently – to his aide Tschirschky – he must have forgotten for the moment that we had already met at his house – and now he had two 'aides' on his further passage through the crowd.

So it was from Papen's box that I watched the main race of the day, which was won by the Graditz stallion 'Alchimist', which, if I remember rightly, had led the field from start to finish. Grabsch, the jockey, in the black-and-white striped livery of the Prussian State Stud, provided a certain amount of excitement after the race, caused not by him but by Goebbels, who left his box immediately after the race in order to take his own 'dip in the crowd'. He was led, as we could easily see from above, to the place where, according to racing rules, all the jockeys have to be weighed again after the race. However, on his way to the weigh-in, the minister put up a hand to congratulate the jockey, who was still on his horse, and Grabsch, one of the most experienced German jockeys, who knew the racing rules very well, took the propaganda minister's hand. Many people must have seen them. According to the regulations Alchimist should have been disqualified. There was a good reason for this rule. Any of the lead weights which might have 'gone missing' during the race could have been replaced 'by hand' before the re-weighing. After all, great fame was at stake for the sportsmen and trainers, and a great deal of money as well – but in this case no one dared to follow up the breach.

Papen offered me a seat in his car for the drive back to town and Tschirschky made use of it for a fervent report, but he spoke so loudly that both the driver and I could hear every word. He was speaking of new infringements by the SA and SS and of the disappearance of people whose relations had turned to the Vice-Chancellor for help. Tschirschky spoke of hair-raising matters. The driver beside me kept a poker face.

As before, Papen allowed his aide to call him 'Herr Reich Chancellor'. What must our driver have thought? Or was he in the Vice-Chancellor's confidence?

The drive ended in front of the Atlantic Hotel, where Papen invited me to be his guest at the Derby dinner that evening. The chauffeur was dismissed with a tip and, as the car drove away, I saw a Hamburg registration number, so the driver was, in all probability, a stranger.

I walked home thoughtfully across the Lombard Bridge, glad that I was no longer a member of that staff.

I remember nothing of particular interest from that evening, with its unimaginative seating plan, good food, after-dinner speeches, duty dances – all surrounded by a babble of conversation.

'Life is good, but expensive. One could live more cheaply, but then it's not so good!' So I wrote to my father to ask if he could raise my monthly allowance a little. The answer came by return. From the first of the following month he would have two hundred and twenty marks a month transferred to me, instead of two hundred!

30 June 1934

This is a very significant date in the history of National Socialism, for on that day, a Sunday, the National Socialist leadership removed political opponents from their own ranks and others from outside them, in a murderous operation. We did not discover this until later on, as we gradually learned what had really happened. Nor had I any idea how easily it might have been a fateful day for me.

About a week before, I had received an anonymous letter, a typed copy, not very legible. 'Extract from the Marburg speech of Vice-Chancellor Franz von Papen' was the headline. It was a brilliantly written opposition speech against the government in power, expressing everything that had been worrying me for more than a year now. I read the letter several times and decided to follow the example of the person who had sent me the letter. Next day I stayed on at the office after working hours, the chief clerk having agreed to my staying on to deal with private mail. I typed the letter out twice on one of the new electric typewriters, with as many copies as possible, and addressed the letters anonymously to suitable-seeming recipients. I posted them in Stephansplatz, as far from our office as possible. This speech – I felt – was worth the effort.

It must have been on 2 or 3 July when I was called to the telephone at the office for a private call. My mother was speaking from Berlin and as soon as she heard my voice she cried: 'Thank God, you're alive!' 'What's the matter?' I asked, but she could not tell me on the telephone; I must come to Berlin the following weekend if possible.

By the time I was with her in Berlin, the newspapers and radio had already announced what was alleged to have happened.

The SA had been on the verge of organising a coup in Germany. Ernst Röhm, the leader of the National Socialist party troops, which were said to number more than three million, had tried to turn them into a regular armed force, into which he intended to incorporate the 100,000-strong army of the Weimar Republic as the 'first arm of the Reich'.

Hitler, on the other hand, had taken the contrary route, because for years the Reichswehr had been structured in such a way that it could become the core of an army worthy of the greatness of the German Reich and capable of the defence of its frontiers, overnight. From the controversy between one method and the other, a power struggle had arisen between Hitler and Röhm and so, with the political instinct of the revolutionary, Hitler had undertaken a 'preventive' strike.

In special editions, the compulsorily conformist daily papers had reported that 'the Führer' had stepped in at the last minute and 'saved Germany from a débacle'. Röhm and a number of other SA leaders had been shot on 30 June. The *Putsch* had been 'defeated by the courageous personal intervention of the Reich Chancellor'. General von Blomberg, the Reich Minister of Defence, had expressed 'gratitude and loyalty' to Hitler in the name of the German Army. To me in Hamburg, of course, all this had sounded bizarre, but what had made my mother ring up to ask if I were still alive?

On 4 July, the press had reported on a Reich law, promulgated on the previous day, which had achieved nothing but to add fresh fuel to the countless rumours travelling the country from mouth to mouth. Literally, the law ran: 'The government of the Reich decrees that, as [an act of] national self-defence, the measures taken on 30 June and on 1 and 2 July 1934 to defeat treasonable attacks are legal'.

In Berlin it has been proved time and time again that scarcely anything can be kept secret. The Berliner is simply too intelligent and too inquisitive when it comes to sniffing out the news. When my mother told me what she had heard in the past few days, I could not believe my ears. The SS *'Leibstandarte Adolf Hitler'* had assumed something like executive power. It was still not known who had been in command, but in the Lichterfelde part of town, in the former barracks of the Prussian cadet school, where the SS *Leibstandarte* was now quartered, the salvoes of the firing squads had been crashing out for three days. Nearby residents had listened in horror. My mother had given tea to two ladies from Lichterfelde, who had described what they heard in detail. Then it had trickled through that the SS operation had not been directed against the SA and their alleged coup alone, but that groups of SS had been busy arresting or abducting political opponents of the NSDAP, or simply shooting them on the spot. My mother already knew that Hitler's predecessor as Reich Chancellor, General Kurt von Schleicher, and his wife had both been shot in their house in Babelsberg. Elsewhere, the chief of the ministerial office at the Reich Ministry of Defence, General Ferdinand von Bredow, died in the same way.

Now I also discovered why my mother had telephoned me in Hamburg. She had been called by some acquaintances who asked if I was still working with Papen, and had discovered that Papen's offices, the Vice-Chancellery in Vossstrasse, had been attacked and occupied by the SS and the Gestapo. The press attaché, Herbert von Bose, had been shot at his desk and everyone who worked in the Vice-Chancellery had been arrested and had disappeared. The offices had been sealed and the telephone lines cut. Günther von Tschirschky, my successor as aide, had also disappeared.

At last I could see the danger I would have been in, had I not left Papen and Berlin the previous year. Another of Papen's colleagues, whom I had not met, the lawyer and writer Edgar Jung, had also been shot, 'liquidated' in Oranienburg concentration camp, it was said.

I returned to Hamburg from my weekend in Berlin in a state of shock. My mother had had good reason to telephone me.

But what, I wondered, had got into this government? An internal controversy about the method of increasing the standing army had been seized on by the Reich Chancellor in order to get rid of the opposition within the party by cold-blooded murder. And it had seemed a good opportunity to get a lot of other unpleasant people out of the way – at that time it was impossible to tell how many. And what had become of Papen himself? His office no longer existed, so we heard, and there were rumours in Berlin that he too had been shot by the Gestapo. Others claimed to know that Papen had 'only' been arrested.

A few days later, the public learned through the press that the Reischstag had been convened on 13 July 'to receive a declaration from the Reich Chancellor'. All factories, offices, and so on were ordered to listen to the broadcast. Loudspeakers were installed on stations, streets and squares. It must have been the first time that all Germans listened together to a proclamation from Hitler – there was scarcely any chance of avoiding it.

In a long speech Hitler assumed full responsibility for the events of the days in question, describing the course of events in such a way that the man in the street was bound to see Hitler as the saviour of the nation. Thanks to him and his personal courage, Germany had been preserved from chaos and revolution. He had claimed the right of self-defence and resolutely done what duty and responsibility for the community demanded of him. The members of parliament – which now consisted of a single party, the NSDAP – cheered him, but there was no parliamentary debate. Göring, as Reichstag President, concluded the occasion with plaudits, jubilation and 'professions of loyalty to the great and glorious leader of all the Germans'.

Probably the most politically important question debated among friends at this time was that of the behaviour of the Army. Since the beginning of June, we heard, its supreme commander, the President of the Reich, had not been in Berlin but at his Neudeck estate in West Prussia. At eighty-six, Hindenburg was not in good health, his strength was said to be dwindling.

His son, who had been his aide for many years, and his Secretary of State, Otto Meissner, were with him, keeping the old gentleman informed of everything that happened. Meissner had already held the post of Secretary of State under Friedrich Ebert, the Social Democrat Reich President. How could his son Oskar and Meissner have informed the old gentleman, who wanted only to be left in peace, about the incredible events? It was only possible to conjecture. The fact remains that a telegram from the Reich President in Neudeck arrived in Berlin and was published immediately: Thanks and congratulations to him who had arranged for the murders. General Werner von Blomberg, Reich Defence Minister, and General Walther von Reichenau, chief of the Wehrmacht office, had certainly done nothing to prevent them. Presumably it suited them that Hitler should eliminate the leaders of the SA.

Before the end of July I travelled back to Berlin, having requested a few days' leave from Hamburg. I wanted to hear how 30 June and the days that followed had affected other people, possibly including my relatives and friends.

I soon heard the essential details. The murders of General von Schleicher and his wife, of General von Bredow, of the former Deputy Chairman of the NSDAP Gregor Strasser, of Von Bose, of the writer Edgar Jung, who had composed Papen's 'Marburg speech', and of a number of senior SA leaders were confirmed. Papen, whose two closest colleagues on his staff had been murdered, had suffered 'only' a few days house-arrest at his new flat in Lennéstrasse. As a sign of protest, he had asked Hitler to accept his resignation. Of his aide, Günther von Tschirscky, there was still no sign, but he was presumably in a concentration camp. Uncle Hans, Countess Bredow and I had been left unscathed. We three had made our 'retreat' at the right moment.

On one of the last days of my brief leave, still before the end of July, I had agreed to meet a young lady for tea at the Café Bristol opposite the Kurfürstendamm Theatre. We were talking; I was sitting with my back to the other people there, facing her, when I suddenly felt the friendly pressure of a hand on my shoulder. I looked up into the face of Von Papen! He was perfectly willing to be introduced to my lady, but did not accept my invitation to sit with us, as he had agreed to meet some other people who were already waiting for him on the far side of the room.

So there I was, standing beside Papen at our table. He at once began a conversation with me while the whole restaurant looked on with interest. I had the feeling that Papen was using the scene to demonstrate: Look, everyone! I'm still here!

He said he was pleased to see me again and asked about my work in Hamburg. I found it painful to be having such a trivial conversation with this man in this place, in front of so many people and after the events of the last few weeks. Since he was still standing beside me, I tried to find words, because there was total silence all round us. Everyone knew the former Reich Chancellor and Vice-Chancellor. So I said I had heard such terrible things in my few days in Berlin that words simply failed me. He looked at me, his eyes wide, and said: 'Yes, my dear fellow, isn't it terrible?'

That was all.

Then he said goodbye and wished me well. We left the Bristol as quickly as possible. I never saw Papen again.

London

Before leaving Berlin, I visited my father, who now wanted me to go to England for about six months. He gave several reasons.

Firstly, if he had any influence on political decision-making in Germany, he would make sure that every German student spent at least one term in England or France, and preferably both countries in succession.

Secondly, the political events that had been taking place in our country might be repeated, because he could not see the slightest sign anywhere that conditions in Germany were going to change in the foreseeable future. Then my father surprised me with the news that Papen had declared his willingness to go to Vienna as German Ambassador. This showed such lack of character that he would be thankful if I would break off all communication with Papen.

Thirdly, he, my father, would be grateful if I resumed contact with our English relatives. He mentioned for the first time the name of his cousin, Antoinette Heckscher, who had married Viscount Esher.

Fourthly, he too had been very worried about me after the events of 30 June. It must be assumed that my name was known and suspect to the Gestapo in connection with Herr von Papen's circle, so it would be a good idea for me to spend some time abroad until the grass had grown over that affair.

I could only agree with my father's conclusions, but how was a longish stay abroad to be financed? Extremely strict currency controls prevailed in Germany: not more than 10 marks could be taken out of the Reich, on pain of severe penalties. My father evaded the question. He would discuss it with his chief clerk in Stettin and in any case I could refer to our English relations – why should they not have invited their nephew to England? The family connection with the Eshers in England was new to me. My parents had been separated before the Great War and our mother had not talked to us children about our father's family. We had grown up in Pomerania almost as if our name were not Stahlberg but Kleist.

The news that Papen was going to Austria as Hitler's ambassador was a blow to me. Did he really need to re-enter the service of those who had had two of his closest colleagues murdered – or at least declared the murders 'legal' before the Reichstag? He could have withdrawn to his wife's estate at Wallerfangen in Saarland.

On 2 August 1934 – I was back in Hamburg by then – Hindenburg died on his Neudeck estate. It had not been difficult for Hitler to prepare in advance for all the consequences which he planned to profit by after the Reich President's death, because the eighty-six year-old's state of health had made the end predictable for a long time.

Franz von Papen, who only a year ago might have been a danger to the National Socialists, was politically played out. General von Blomberg, the Reich Minister of Defence, who had convincingly proved himself on Hitler's behalf on 30 June, had become dependent on Hitler through the events of the summer. Hence, on Hindenburg's death, everything was going 'according to plan', and at breakneck speed. On the very same day, Hitler took over the office of President of the Reich as 'Führer and Reich Chancellor'. This also made him Supreme Commander of the Wehrmacht. Blomberg immediately ordered all soldiers to take the oath of loyalty to Hitler in person, not, as formerly, to the constitution. All this happened by decree, with no regard for whether the Enabling

Act was valid for such a major change in the constitution. In any case scarcely anyone would have shed a tear for the weak Weimar constitution.

A 'referendum' was ordered for 19 August. All those entitled to vote were summoned to declare whether they were in agreement with the regulations of 2 August. I was by now twenty-one years old, and as the law then stood, of age and entitled to vote. I voted 'No'.

Soon after that, my time in Hamburg came to an end.

*   *   *

Until my departure for England, I stayed with my mother, who was then running an unusual three-woman household: in addition to a friend, Klara Ninow, her other resident was the Grand Duchess Anastasia, now known as Anna Anderson, youngest daughter of Czar Nicholas II, murdered in 1918. The 'Anastasia case' had been publicly debated for years and was highly controversial.

Lively political discussion went on at the table. In all innocence, I asked my mother and Klara Ninow whether they had voted Yes or No in the Referendum, but the only answer was silence. I had never known this before at home, because we had always discussed other elections quite openly, so I said as lightly as possible that I had voted No.

I had scarcely finished speaking when Klara Ninow sprang up and left the dining-room without a word. My mother commented that I should not have said that, as her friend had become a member of the NSDAP and an enthusiastic admirer of Hitler. I asked my mother if Frau Ninow would now go to her local group leader to denounce me. 'No', said my mother, 'she would never do that, but you touched her at a very vulnerable point.'

Mrs. Anderson had followed our conversation attentively. Being stateless she was not entitled to vote, but now she spoke up. This Herr Hitler did not appeal to her, either, but politics were not about that. She was content to have him because he was against the Bolsheviks, but she was not convinced that in his opposition to the Bolsheviks he would be a man of deeds as well as words.

Interested, I asked what she meant. She replied at once that as soon as the German Army was strong enough, it should march on Russia and despatch the murderous Bolshevik hordes to the devil.

My mother and I looked at each other without speaking. Then she brought the meal to an end.

When we were alone, I asked why my friend had reacted so emotionally. My mother's answer turned into a plea.

First of all, one must remember that Klara Ninow came from Kolberg, a Pomeranian coastal town whose citizens were imbued with an extraordinary degree of pride and self-awareness. The causes probably lay in the time of Napoleon I, when the French had defeated practically every town in Prussia; only Kolberg continued to resist the enemy troops in 1806/07. Since then the Kolbergers felt they were something special, though they were laughed at for it elsewhere. But it was not as simple as that. One simply had to accept this pride, which was associated with great sensitivity.

Klara Ninow had now become a member of the NSDAP from pure idealism and would allow no one to criticise her party. Above all, she believed blindly in Hitler's great love of peace and regarded any criticism of his questionable methods as malicious slander. Recently she had gone to the Anhalter station to pick someone up from the Munich night train early one morning, when Hitler and a large entourage had stepped out of one of the special carriages attached to the rear. Hitler had walked straight towards her as if he recognised her, and when he was quite close their eyes had met. For a long moment she had looked deep into his eyes and even when he had passed, her heart was still beating wildly. It had been an unimaginable experience for her, and she was more convinced than ever that Hitler was at heart a 'good person'.

In the days that followed she had described this meeting with Hitler many times to the class she taught at what would now be called a vocational training school, and had finally actually given a talk on it at her Party's cell meeting.

Then she had been honoured by being appointed a teller on the voting committee for the referendum of 19 August. Some time before the polls opened she had arrived at her polling station on the corner of Brandenburgische and Xantener Strasse. The chairman had gathered all the tellers together behind closed doors and read out a document binding election officials to the strictest secrecy. The document had been passed round and everyone had to sign it.

When the polling booth closed that evening the chairman had once again assembled the tellers behind closed doors, opened a sealed envelope and read out a further document in which their station was directed to announce a voting figure of 98.5 per cent in favour. The voting papers were not counted or checked at all.

Klara Ninow returned home that night in floods of tears. Naturally, she told my mother everything at once: her faith in the NSDAP was wavering and now she was wrestling with the idea of writing a personal letter to Hitler, since she was convinced that he knew nothing of these election frauds. Only inferior party officers could have wanted to boast of such figures in order to make good in the party.

My mother's opinion of this story was very much more down-to-earth, since it was not only in Berlin that similar reports were covertly going the rounds. Her cousin Henning von Tresckow had told her that in Wartenberg, the Tresckow village in Neumark, the polling figures had been published in the local paper as 100 per cent. Following this, the Evangelical village priest had announced from the pulpit the next Sunday that he himself had voted No. In Berlin, at all events, it was 'all over town' that the voting figures, announced as 84 per cent for Hitler, must have been faked.

Then came the day of my departure for London. Surrounded by four suitcases, my accordion and my violin, I stood at the Zoological Gardens station waiting for my train to the Hook of Holland. My ticket carried me via Harwich to Liverpool Street, London. My travelling money amounted to exactly 10 marks, but in my pocket I had an address that inspired confidence: Barclays Bank, Piccadilly. My father and mother had both come, so that for the first time in my life I saw them together. They waved to me until the train disappeared round the bend.

The night passage – as I had been warned – was stormy, but when the ship finally tied up at the quay I had only a few steps to walk to one of the restaurant cars on the train for London. I still had five marks, which would have to cover a taxi to Piccadilly, and I hesitated, but a friendly railway official seemed to have a clairvoyant understanding of the reason for my doubts. Breakfast was included, he said. My luggage disappeared into the luggage van without the least effort on my part and the train was on its way. A pleasant Englishman sitting opposite me obviously realised that I was German. His German was better than my English and he was familiar with the financial dilemma of Germans arriving in England. The train had barely started when breakfast was served, one course following another without a word to the waiters: I felt that I was in the land of milk and honey. The meal did not end until we reached London.

But my most difficult linguistic hurdle was still before me: now I paid the price for having taken no more than two periods of 'optional English' weekly in my last two years at school, for after my luggage had at last been stowed in one of those original and incomparably practical taxis, I revealed to the driver that although I could tell him the name of my destination in Hampstead, I had no money and must therefore go first to the bank, the name and address of which I showed him on my note. But if I had expected to meet with doubt, or even angry words, I had been mistaken. Of his reply I understood only a single word, because he spoke pure Cockney, but that word recurred more than once: 'German'. By his tone he did not mean it at all unkindly, it was simply his way of making a statement.

Everything that then followed went so simply and rapidly that I could scarcely recover my wits. One could still park in Piccadilly at that time and, after a few minutes, I was back in my taxi. Having presented my passport, I had been handed some documents prepared in advance, signed my name once or twice and was now in possession of an amount calculated by my father to see me through six months. He had been generous.

However, the boarding-house in Hampstead recommended to me at home seemed too dull; I did not want to spend six months in London having to converse with nothing but old ladies, even at breakfast. But I stayed for a few weeks to begin with. Old ladies might be better for my wretched English than young ones.

The next morning I reported to my new firm, the United Baltic Corporation, a branch of the East Asiatic Company from which we had been buying soya beans for the oil factory in Stettin for many years. For legal reasons, I would not be allowed to 'work' here, only to volunteer, I was told. I could look at everything, hear everything, read everything and assist where I liked. This proved far less easy than I had imagined, because more than half the employees turned out to be Danes, who spoke terrible English. Soon, however, I could understand even these.

What impressed me most was a gigantic old copying press. All the correspondence was typed with purple copy ribbon, carbon paper was not yet in use here. If the letter was signed, the original was damped and laid in the big copy book. The trick then was to press the entire day's correspondence in the copy book in just one process. My Hamburg Rowing Club-trained muscles were invaluable to me there.

My boarding-house in Hampstead was soon not only too 'old'

for me, but also too far from the City. I had not come to London to spend my time on the Underground, so for a few days I strolled through the town in the evenings and soon ended up at Hyde Park Corner, where hundreds of people gathered, to argue and to sing. To be an onlooker here was an extraordinary experience for me, as a young German from the land of linguistic prescriptions, censorship, controls, prohibitions and fear of denunciation. Here everyone could not only voice his opinion but shout it out to the crowds from a stepladder. Free speech really did still exist here. I would find myself a furnished room close to Marble Arch and listen and sing with the rest whenever I liked. That was how Speakers' Corner became a kind of language school for me.

The room was soon found: my address was now 4, Hyde Park Place.

My father had given me a letter of introduction to his cousin, Viscountess Esher, née Heckscher, whom I was to visit as soon as possible. Number 21, Hill Street, W.1. was only a step away from Hyde Park – an unassuming three-storey house barely fifty feet across. I rang the doorbell, a butler opened the door and asked in a hushed voice what he could do for me. I gave him my father's letter and my visiting card.

In a very few minutes my new aunt appeared, paused in front of me for a moment's scrutiny and then greeted me with spontaneous warmth like a dear old acquaintance. And so we continued, until the war brought about an enforced separation. But the two of them, Antoinette and Oliver, her husband, were the first to reach out a hand to us again in 1945, as if the years of violence between our countries had never been. What I would continue to owe to the two Eshers was immeasurable.

I had another letter of introduction with me, pressed into my hand by Grandmother Kleist when I paid her my farewell visit. It was to her nephew, Wolfgang zu Putlitz, whom I had not yet met. He was a diplomat in charge of the consular division of the German Embassy. The grand old building was easily found by walking from Piccadilly Circus down Lower Regent Street, passing Waterloo Place, and there were the representatives of the German Reich on the right.

I had myself announced to Putlitz and found him to be an immensely kind man of the world. As it was just lunchtime, he invited me to lunch in one of the wonderful restaurants in that area. He listened with great interest when I told him about my time with Papen in Berlin. Once or twice he stemmed the flow of my words and surprised me with the warning that even here in England I should speak of political conditions inside Germany only with the greatest caution and reserve. Even here in London there might be a National Socialist agent listening attentively at the next table. Scarcely able to believe him, I asked since when one could no longer express one's views in the 'freest country in the world'. 'That's not the point,' he said, 'I share your opinion of the Nazis completely and utterly and you can speak without reservation when you are alone with our present ambassador here, Herr von Hoesch, but in public you must avoid any criticism of Hitler and his policies. The Embassy itself has already been infiltrated with diplomats unworthy of the name, who work directly for the Gestapo. Even the so-called foreign organisation of the NSDAP has its spies here, whose special job is to watch Germans living in England. You must assume that you yourself are also being watched. Of course, they won't touch a hair of your head in this country, but you risk being seized at the frontier when you go back to Germany and vanishing into some concentration camp. And please believe me: as head of the consular branch I know what I'm talking about.'

In the months to come, Wolfgang Putlitz looked after me in the kindest way. He put my name on the Embassy address list so that I met him at a number of Ambassador Hoesch's receptions, but our ways soon parted when his thoughts began increasingly to turn towards the Left. We simply did not see eye to eye. When Leopold von Hoesch died in 1936 and Ribbentrop succeeded him, Putlitz had himself transferred to The Netherlands. On the outbreak of war, he stayed in the West and moved over at the end of the war to the Communist régime of East Germany, where those in power were all too willing, even then, to flaunt a sprig of the ancient landed gentry of Brandenburg.

But to return to London. How much at home I felt when I was invited to Hill Street! Antoinette had asked me to drop the 'aunt' when I spoke to her: in England it was not regarded as very kind to be constantly reminding older relatives of their age by using the prefix. If you were related, you were cousins. At first I did not find it at all easy to remember this. 21 Hill Street was a very sociable house, its reception rooms seeming larger on the inside than the narrow façade led one to suppose. After only a few days, the parents gave a dinner for my 'real' cousins, extremely attractive

and charming young ladies, with their friends of both sexes. And I
made a discovery: the English, notorious in Germany for being
'stiff', were the absolute opposite. I have seldom enjoyed in
Germany such cheerful, relaxed parties as I did in London.

A few days later, Antoinette invited me to tea, but with my
violin. 'Let's begin with Mozart,' she said, while I unpacked it. I
had not practised for a few weeks and discovered that her fingers
were more agile than mine. Oh, shame! Then I suggested
Beethoven's Spring Sonata and did much better. How often we
played sonatas together that winter! I wrote to my mother that I
had already found an 'accompanist' in London, so she now
discovered that there was music in her former husband's family as
well as her own!

Antoinette looked after me like a deputy mother. She gave me a
box radio of splendid quality 'so that I should not be bored in the
evenings in my furnished room'. The radio served me faithfully
until 1945, enabling me to hear half the world at night. But, above
all, she saw to it that I learned about all the things a young man
from Nazi Germany ought to know. I watched the investiture of
new peers from the gallery of the House of Lords and observed the
democratic rules of the game at an important debate in the
Commons. She was conscientious about my visiting the major
museums.

Oliver Esher took obvious pleasure in his wife's preoccupation
with the new German cousin. He held a large number of honorary
offices, as the peerage is expected to in England. I profited from
them, whether at the Royal Opera House or with the Royal
Philharmonic Society.

Meanwhile my 'little cousins' took care that I was invited to the
houses of their friends and to many large balls at the hotels along
Park Lane. 'Oh, you are German, do tell me: are you a Nazi?' How
often I had to answer that question in those days!

One day I heard Jack Hilton's dance and show band at one of
London's big variety theatres. I had bought myself a ticket in the
front row and it was rewarding from the start, but the high point of
the programme was the last number: 'News of the World'. It began
with Hitler's favourite march, the *'Badenweiler'*, which was then
transposed to jazz tempo, each musician showing off his virtuoso
skills, until suddenly the lights went out. When they came on again
after a few seconds all the musicians were wearing brown or black
Nazi uniforms. Some wore masks, of Hitler with a hugely gaping

'trap', of Göring, incomparably corpulent (hung with decorations front and back), of Goebbels as the devil incarnate, Himmler as a middle-aged Grand Inquisitor, and so forth. The public cried with laughter, I no less than the others.

Darkness again, and then the wild, continuous firing of warning pistols whose muzzle flashes illuminated a chaotic inferno. The firing ended – another single shot – of light! An indescribable sight appeared: all the uniformed men had killed each other! Germany on 30 June 1934, the English view, from a variety stage. And the house with its several thousand seats was sold out twice daily, so the papers told us.

Almost as a farewell occasion, Oliver and Antoinette took me to a charity ball in London's West End. While I was being enchanted by the beautiful, witty young lady with whom I was dancing, someone twitched at my sleeve. It was Antoinette: would I come to her straight after this dance.

'I want to present you to one of the most charming ladies in our country,' she began, and taking my arm she crossed the empty dance floor with me. Who was it, I asked. 'The Duchess of York,' she replied. We were already standing before the Duke, later King George VI, and his wife Elizabeth, who was sitting on a sofa. 'My German cousin,' said Antoinette, and both greeted me very kindly. I was asked to sit down and talk to them about Germany. The Duchess spoke excellent German, on which I duly complimented her. She said it was a pleasure for her to speak German again, as she had had a German governess for a time when she was a girl, had visited Berlin with her and greatly admired that beautiful city. Then she asked me if it was true that the lime trees had been removed from Unter den Linden. Yes, the trees had in fact been felled because a new underground was to be built, but fresh lime trees would be planted as soon as it was completed.

Feeling that it was now my turn, I followed the advice of my grandmother, who was well versed in court etiquette: never forget to speak to a mother about her children.

So I told her that I had recently attended an afternoon symphony concert at the Queen's Hall, where I had seen her two daughters, Elizabeth and Margaret, sitting not far away from me with their lady-in-waiting. Although the programme had been very demanding and not particularly popular, the two children had been a truly model audience, listening quietly and attentively. I doubted if I could have behaved so well at their age. 'I'm so pleased,' she said, with her radiant smile. 'Thank you for telling me. I'll tell the girls what you said.'

While she was talking to me the orchestra had struck up a Viennese waltz. Suddenly she asked me if I could waltz, but – 'Look there!' – not like those people, but like good dancers on the Continent? I said I thought I could – not only spinning right-about, but left-about now and then as well. 'Do give me the pleasure of dancing a Viennese waltz with me!' She got up and I soon found that she could waltz perfectly. The other dancers made way respectfully. After circling the room once, I led her back to her seat and she gave me her hand to kiss. I had no idea that I had been dancing with the future Queen of England.

My time in England was now drawing to an end. In my memory it verges on the fairy tale – what a good thing that fairy tales always have an ending. One day I went to 21 Hill Street for the last time, in order to thank them many times over. I could not know that I was never to enter that extraordinarily beautiful and endearing house again. Oliver and Antoinette were giving a reception and their friend Ambassador Hoesch was also present. When their guests had left they asked me to stay on for a little while.

'When you are back in Germany will you become a soldier?' asked Antoinette. I told her that was not my intention, at least I did not want to become a career officer. 'Oh, but you Germans are such passionate soldiers,' she said, 'you will scarcely be able to avoid it. My son Lionel is such a convinced pacifist that he would never put on a uniform.' Unfortunately Lionel was not there that evening, or there might have been a debate between the two cousins on the ancient Roman saying: '*Si vis pacem, para bellum*' ('If you want peace, prepare for war'). I would have been only too glad to talk it over with the Old Etonian.

However, Oliver and Antoinette – who regarded themselves as Liberals – were unusually well-informed on political developments in Germany. How often I had observed them, as on that evening, in earnest conversation with the German Ambassador. Now I once again put forward my view that our country needed an army that could do justice to the defence of its long and open frontiers. They were naturally familiar with that argument and even very sympathetic to it. Their counter-argument related to Hitler himself. They found him sinister, an opinion I unreservedly shared. But what was new to both of them was the idea that we Germans needed a strong army in order to field a genuine force against our

current Head of State. They thought it sounded risky. I had to tell
them about 30 June 1934, but I sometimes had the feeling that they
knew more than I did about the background to those macabre
events in Germany.

When we met again for the first time after the war Oliver
reminded me of my remarks in 1935. In the past ten years he had
often remembered my words and discussed them with other
people.

And how much had changed in those dreadful years of violence!
Number 21 Hill Street was no more. A German bomb had
destroyed the house. And the two cousins – Lionel, the convinced
pacifist and I – had fought as officers on opposite sides. Each felt he
had a duty to his own country: the English pacifist as much as the
German who was not a National Socialist.

When peace came, the two Eshers visited us in Germany.
Antoinette became a godmother to our family, two of my daughters
went to Cranborne Chase thanks to Oliver's recommendation, and
one of our granddaughters bears the name Antoinette.

To Join the Nazi Party?

On the journey home via Hamburg I met one of my friends from
the Hamburg days in the corridor of the Berlin express. We had
scarcely ever discussed politics before; he had simply been a
cheerful and entertaining companion, nothing more. Now I
learned that he had given up his profession in commerce and was
on his way to Berlin because his application to join the 'SS-
Leibstandarte Adolf Hitler' had been accepted. He even wanted to
become an 'officer' in it. After telling me this with shining eyes, he
would not let me out of his sight while he tried to persuade me to go
with him. I told him that when it came to my turn, I would become
a soldier because I felt more drawn to the Army, but he would not
give up. The SS was more 'modern', and 'someone like me' would
be better suited to the SS than to the 'old-fashioned Army'.
Promotion was quicker in the SS than in the Army, too, and it
would only be a matter of time before the SS was given equal status
with the Army. In the foreseeable future, the SS would also have
the social rank previously reserved for the Prussian Guards
regiments. Now one must 'think modern' and move with the times.
I had some difficulty in getting rid of my jolly companion of former
days.

On 1 May 1935 I joined my father's firm in Stettin, but my first duties were not in the office or the works but in front of the main entrance to the firm, because Hitler had elevated labour day to a national holiday. The employees were now called the 'followers' and on every May 1st they had to form up in marching columns and march staight through the city to the mass rally. The leaders of the National Socialist works cell organisations ran busily up and down the lines, ticking them off on their alphabetical lists to be sure that none were missing.

In front of our senior chief clerk and me, the youngest apprentice bore on a pole a sign with the three-line inscription: 'Paul-Julius Stahlberg, oil factory, founded 1841'. Ahead of the firm's sign there was even a marching band of Pommerensdorf-South voluntary fire brigade, which my father had approved 'so that we can at least march in time to the music'. But scarcely more than a third of our column could still hear the big drums; further back people were moving informally, as if on the way to the grave of a dear departed.

So we crossed Stettin to the Krekow parade ground, where a lot of swastika flags were flying, and on a temporary stand sat the 'office-holders of Party and state', almost all in brown uniforms; in Germany they were called the 'golden pheasants'. When we had taken up our appointed position snow and hail began to fall. I was not even wearing a coat. I was soon drenched to the skin and felt morally entitled to begin the retreat. By that time, as I then noticed, more than half of our works column had already 'evaporated'.

I had only been in the firm a few weeks when the local group leader of the NSDAP for Pommerensdorf-South was announced. A short, very stout man in a brown shirt with the red swastika armband greeted me with a brusque '*Heil Hitler*', clicking his heels. I offered him a seat and asked him what brought him here. 'We have heard,' he began, 'that the son of the firm of Stahlberg is now in Stettin, and I have come to see you.' I thanked him for his consideration and asked what I could do for him. I was quite unprepared for his answer: 'I have been ordered to see if you are a Jew. But I can see that you are not a Jew, although you have a Jewish name. Right?' I asked him if he would please explain more precisely what gave him this idea, whereupon he said: 'You know, Herr Stahlberg, someone in our local group told me any name that connected "metal and *berg*" was Jewish. Like Goldberg or Silberberg. All of them are going to be checked now, including

Eisenberg, Kupferberg, and so on. But anyone could see at once that you're no Jew.'

The corpulent little functionary was obviously not happy carrying out his orders, but they came from higher up, so I made an effort to take this incredible call calmly. But I was not rid of the man yet, so I stood up to signal the end of our conversation. Now standing in front of me, the wretched man looked up and stammered something to the effect that he must apologise for his mistake. Then he took two forms from a briefcase and gave them to me: if I would please fill them out in detail, he would come back and pick them up next week.

When my visitor had gone I looked at the papers. The first covered the declaration of the legally stipulated membership of the German Workers' Front and the establishment of my 'work book'. Every working German had to own a work book in which every change of job had to be entered. I had no need to fill in this form as the firm had done it for me as a matter of routine. But the other was an application for membership of the NSDAP. I read it with interest and dropped it in my drawer.

One week later, as announced, the 'golden pheasant' assigned to our firm returned to pick up the completed forms. I explained that my work book was already being dealt with and told him, as nicely as possible, that I did not intend to become a member of his party.

He seemed not to have expected this and was silent for a moment. Then he began: 'Please take more time to consider, because as the future managing director it is your duty to your country to be a member of the Party. It is my duty to warn you.' The Party would not tolerate it if the management of a firm as important to Stettin and the German food industry as this one was not associated with the Party. A firm must be headed by a reliable man and the NSDAP in Stettin would see to it that the same principle was maintained here.

I vividly remember replying, deliberately and unequivocally: 'I would ask you to consider that this firm was founded by my great-grandfather in 1841. What gives you the right to assume that a member of the fourth generation of the founding family is not sufficiently reliable to carry on the work?'

Perhaps my words were not quite without effect, because he said that he had not meant it personally. 'Oh yes, you did,' I cried. 'You were the one who talked about reliability.' If I had taken it that way he was sorry, he said, but we made no progress. He had been asked by the local group 'to make sure that I joined the Party', and that was that. He would come back to me in a week's time.

When he had gone I telephoned to my father to expect me in Berlin the next day.

My father was horrified when he heard my report. 'Let's think it over calmly,' he said. As if forced into making a difficult decision, he began: 'The time has come to tell you that we have an ancestor of the Jewish faith.' I told him that was no news to me, I had known for years. 'How?' he asked. Not from my mother, I said, but often enough from other people. In fact there had even been one person who had called me 'half-breed' in an argument. 'What appallingly bad taste!' cried my father. Now I had to tell him exactly what I knew about our Jewish ancestors.

So I told him what I had found out at the Prussian State Library about my great-grandfather Heckscher from Hamburg, during my first term in Berlin: 'The son of a Jewish banker in Hamburg, baptised as a Protestant (this used to be called 'standing Baptism') at the age of eleven, 1848 Hamburg delegate to the Preliminary Parliament at the Paulskirche in Frankfurt, spokesman for the delegation offering the dignity of Vice-Regent to Archduke John of Austria, Reich Minister of Justice, Reich Minister for Foreign Affairs.'

'And what are we to do now, in Stettin, and with you?' he asked. Neither of us uttered the words that were probably hanging in the air: join the NSDAP after all, for the sake of appearances? Over the last twenty-four hours I had made my plans, and now I revealed them.

Some day I would find my call-up papers in the post, and I would not be found 'unfit', indeed I would have seen that as a stigma: I was positively bursting with health. So I had decided to jump the gun. I would volunteer for the Army, knowing that, as a soldier, I would be automatically deleted from the list of applicants for the Nazi party. As we saw political developments in Hitler's Germany, it was highly probable that there would be a war, so I wanted to make sure that I was on the reserve of officers as soon as possible, before that day came. Moreover, as a volunteer I would be able to apply for the regiment of my choice.

My father agreed with my plan and asked me if I already had a regiment in mind. I told him I intended to join the cavalry at Schwedt an der Oder, but this was not at all to his taste, because, as he said, there were dragoons in Schwedt; I should go to Pasewalk, where his regiment, the 'Queen's Cuirassiers' had been stationed. At late-night parties in the officers' casino there they used to slander the dragoons with ready arrogance. 'They're all half-man, half-beast, of course – infantry sitting on a horse!'

When I told him that nowadays 'only' the Signals Corps was in Pasewalk, whereas the 6th (Prussian) Cavalry Regiment (RR6) was stationed in Schwedt, and one of its squadrons actually carried on the tradition of the former Pasewalk cuirassiers, he was satisfied. But then it occurred to him that he had heard somewhere that for want of horses there would soon be bicycle squadrons in the cavalry regiments, so I promised to do my best not to end up with the bicyclists. The former cavalry captain of the Reserve was now pleased with his offspring and we parted on the best of terms.

The very next week the Pommerensdorf 'golden pheasant' appeared again in my office, this time with an ominous expression, which was no doubt his perquisite as a party official. I was going to disappoint him yet again, so I greeted him at once with the news that I had volunteered for the Wehrmacht. He took out his notebook, and I thought he deleted a name.

In fact I never had any more to do with National Socialist party officials: they had 'written me off'.

I felt free. Oh yes, I felt free, free from the burden of having to belong to those hated brown hordes!

It was, in any case, natural for me to be a soldier. '*Si vis pacem, para bellum*' we had learned at the very liberal Grunewald Gymnasium. All my ancestors, whether aristocratic or middle-class, had been soldiers in order to serve their country, their fatherland. Now the grey uniform had become my refuge.

I spent that summer in Stettin living in a furnished room again, with an elderly couple called Wolf. A few weeks before my period of service in Schwedt began, they invited me to join them in their sitting-room one evening. They were in great trouble and wanted to ask my advice. To my utter astonishment I discovered that for months I had unknowingly been the sub-tenant of a Jewish couple. I told them I had no anti-Semitic feelings and would not dream of giving up the room because I now knew that they were Jews.

The two old people said they were thinking of something quite different. Since I had been living with them they had felt safer, but now that I was to leave Stettin their fear of the Nazi blockleader would become unbearable, he would start harassing them again as he had before I moved in.

What advice could I give them: I asked if they had relatives outside Germany. No, they were quite alone. Friends, perhaps? No. They had no more ideas than I had, and lived in fear for their future. I asked them if they could pay to move abroad. Yes, they could, because they had been gradually withdrawing their savings from the bank and hiding the cash in the house. They were also receiving a monthly pension, but what could they live on abroad? They did not dare to take the money across the frontier, and the pension would certainly not be transferred to them abroad. I advised them to risk going abroad, but what was my advice worth? These were old people, who could not possibly start again from the beginning. I was ashamed, as a German. That was a terrible evening, which I can never forget.

After more than a year, when my period of service in Schwedt was over, I went to call on them, to see how they were. There was a strange name on the door of the flat. I rang the bell and a strange face appeared. The Wolfs' display cabinet stood behind him in the semi-darkness. I asked if I could have the new address of Herr and Frau Wolf, and a rough voice answered: 'Oh, the Jews who used to live here? No idea!' Without another word he shut the door and left me standing there.

In the 6th (Prussian) Cavalry Regiment

It was the summer of 1935 and in the newly-built barracks area of the 6th (Prussian) Cavalry Regiment (RR6) in Schwedt, the first recruits were arriving in long lines at their squadron quarters after the re-introduction of general conscription (March 1935). Sixty to seventy young men had been allocated to each of the six squadrons, all still in civilian clothes and each with a box beside him in which to send them home.

The commander of the 3rd Squadron, Captain von Lewinski, and his three lieutenants looked over the new faces. For the modern cavalry, the military district headquarters was looking for short young men, but an outsider had obviously wandered into the 3rd Squadron by mistake: over six feet three inches tall.

The captain spoke a few words of welcome and explained that from now on we were no longer Mr. So-and-So, but 'Troopers'. Then he started with the tall man on the right and asked him to give his name loudly and clearly. So Trooper Stahlberg began and the sergeant-major entered the name in his thick book, which was kept ready to hand between his second and fifth uniform buttons. No one else was allowed to leave a button undone.

'Hands up anyone who has completed their school education. Elementary school first, then secondary school, and university entrance last.' Result: one – he wore abnormally thick glasses – had not finished his elementary schooling, no secondary school pupils, one university entrant.

Then came the ages: all the recruits were under twenty, only the tall one at the end was almost twenty-three. He was asked how he had arrived in this squadron. 'I don't know, Sir!' 'Ah, are you the volunteer?' 'Yes, Sir.' The Sergeant-Major made a note. Then the captain asked: 'Shouldn't Stahlberg have been in the 1st Squadron with the other volunteers?' Sergeant-Major's answer: 'It's probably because he's not noble, Sir.' Pause.

Next order: 'Hands up who can ride!' Six hands flew up. 'One step forward, those six. Enter them.'

Of course I could ride, otherwise I would not have enlisted in the cavalry. I had sat horses from childhood, in Kieckow, in Paetzig, I had ridden across the fields with my uncle, had gone on horseback to bathe and to visit the Tresckows in Wartenberg, and with Uncle Ewald von Kleist in Schmenzin, and even in Berlin, when one of my many uncles came visiting and paid for me to ride from Tattersall Beermann by the Zoo Station across the Tiergarten to the Brandenburg Gate.

Then we were divided up, six to a room. The man with thick glasses was in my room. On the top floor was the Quartermaster's store, where we collected the first items of our uniform: underwear, footcloths (instead of socks), breeches and boots, overalls, our coarsely-woven working uniform. Then the young soldier learned to stuff his pallet with fresh straw. Even the things that one's mother did at home had now to be learned by every recruit 'according to regulations', including sewing on a button!

The three hundred metres from our quarters to the stables were not walked but marched, generally singing. The tall fellow had to give the note, he seemed to know something about music.

Then we were assigned to groups, or 'patrols', and acquired our 'instructors', a sergeant and a lance-corporal, known as 'twelvers' because they had signed on for twelve years in the old Reichswehr.

There were over a hundred horses in each squadron. I was given a chestnut gelding called 'Heldensang', because he was the biggest horse in the squadron, an eleven year-old crib-biter, hard-mouthed and still harder-jowled, as would soon appear, but hardest of all in the trot. But he 'covered' me, so that in silhouette my heels were scarcely visible, a veritable 'monument of a horse'!

We learned grooming and everything else connected with our horses' well-being. Even as a country child, I had never dreamed how much pampering is meted out to the horses of the Prussian cavalry. 'Horse first, weapons next, man last!'

The first riding lesson came on the third day. The shining horse, without blanket and saddle, was led out of his stall on the snaffle. More than sixty recruits stood with their horses at the end of the barrack square, ranged in one line down the middle of the jumping ground. The oldest of the lieutenants, who was in command of riding training, ordered: 'The six who can already ride, three paces forward.' Then came the next order: 'Trooper Stahlberg, three more paces forward. Mount!' I had learned that in Kieckow as a child. I leaped and sat on the horse's back. The lieutenant's next order was: 'Scissors about face!' A sergeant stepped up to my horse, to hold him if necessary, but Heldensang knew it all and stood as if rooted to the spot. So now I was sitting backwards on the gelding's shining back, facing his tail, awaiting the lieutenant's next order. When it came it was not what I expected: 'One round of the jumping ground, gallop!' I looked down at my lieutenant in astonishment. 'Didn't you understand the order?'

I heard the sergeant whisper: 'Not possible, let yourself fall on the jump and keep relaxed'. So I gave Heldensang my knees and slapped him on the buttock. The sergeant, with his hand on the snaffle, ran a few paces in the direction of the first obstacle, Heldensang jumped, and I was rolling in the sand. Heldensang, the old trooper, stopped immediately after the jump and waited until I was up again.

The remaining five who, like me, 'could ride already' went through the same manoeuvre. None of us was seriously injured, and yet I found the exercise a macabre joke. Probably it was meant to be like crossing the equator for the cavalry.

Of course a cavalryman's training calls for hardness: in order to have his horse under his control later on in every conceivable situation, the rider must first sit deep in the saddle. But the military saddle in those days was hard and the recruits had to take the saddle they were given, including some that were poorly suited to the shape and size of their own bodies. After a few weeks, the young soldiers were sitting their horses so well that the squadron could go to the parade ground in closed ranks and the instructors could begin with the first simple dressage exercises.

Inevitably, we had to take the oath, to the person of Adolf Hitler, as the regulation stood since the death of Reich President Hindenburg on 2 August of the previous year. The officers had to prepare the recruits over a good many hours of instruction, of which the one before the oath was taken was conducted by the squadron commander himself. I looked forward to it in some suspense.

Today, Lewinski began, he would talk through the words of our oath with us. He said that the oath had been changed the year before, the former Reichswehr had sworn a different oath from the one we would be taking tomorrow. I put up my hand to ask a question: would he recite the former oath to us for purposes of comparison, so that we could hear the difference? The captain looked at me in some astonishment. 'Well, why not,' he said eventually. He still knew it by heart, and we could certainly hear it:

'I swear by God this sacred oath, that I will always serve my people and Fatherland faithfully and honestly and be prepared as a brave soldier to risk my life for this oath at any time.'

The new oath that we were to swear tomorrow ran otherwise:

'I swear by God this sacred oath, that I shall be unreservedly obedient to the leader of the German Reich and people, Adolf Hitler, Supreme Commander of the Wehrmacht, and prepared as a brave soldier to risk my life for this oath at any time.'

The chief then said we need not learn the oath by heart; at the ceremony next day he would recite passages aloud and we had only to repeat them. That was the end of our lesson.

Each evening, as darkness fell, we heard the duty trumpeter at the barrack gates sounding the Last Post. Then the duty sergeant went through the rooms to make sure all the recruits were in bed and to put out the lights. That night I started a conversation in the darkness with my five room-mates – all of them came from Silesia. 'What do you think of the oath we're going to take tomorrow?' I asked. A long silence. 'Are you all asleep?' I asked. All five said 'No' almost simultaneously. But what were we meant to think, said one, orders were orders. Then I heard our little fellow, the one with the thick glasses: 'At home we do something that makes the oath invalid.'

I had never heard of this and asked him to tell us about it. 'Right then, listen,' he began. 'You raise your right hand to swear and at the same time you make a fist with your left. That way you can swear what you like but the oath is no good. Only afterwards – or that's the way we do it – you have to confess it to your minister.'

I thought this was priceless, but all my other room-mates confirmed it. At all events it would be a good idea to put your left hand in your pocket during the procedure. 'All the same,' I began again, 'I wouldn't advise this left fist tomorrow. When we're standing in ranks anyone behind you might see you and denounce you later which would mean you'd be in a lot of trouble.' 'You're right,' he said, 'then I shall clench my fist in my mind and I'll still confess it, my minister will go along with that.' I said: 'So you don't want to swear?' Oh yes, he wanted to swear, but not for Adolf. He liked the old oath the chief had told us about today much better. 'So do I,' I said, 'all the same I'll be swearing for Adolf tomorrow.' Then the questions came from all sides: 'Aha, then you're a Nazi?' 'I'll tell you something,' I said angrily, 'I'm no Nazi, and I don't care for Adolf, but I'll do it for my Fatherland.' Another long pause. Then I heard the little man with the thick glasses again: 'I like that, you know. But it means a lot of care tomorrow.' 'No,' I said, 'you have only to say "Adolf Hitler" and think "Fatherland". That's not difficult, and in any case it will be much easier for you tomorrow than for me because you were conscripted by the army district command and I am a volunteer.'

The next morning the whole cavalry regiment was drawn up in the great barrack square on foot, in square formation. For the first time I heard our excellent body of trumpeters. For the first time I saw and heard our regimental commander, Lieutenant Colonel Arno von Lenski. As he walked along the lines, I found myself briefly eye to eye with him. He was wearing a monocle; I did not care for him. Then he made a rousing speech, speaking not of the 'Führer, Adolf Hitler', but of 'our beloved Führer Adolf Hitler'. No wonder that, with all these protestations of affection, he later became a member of the notorious National Socialist People's Court. However, it was not until the war was over that he attained his highest military honours, ending his career as a General in the National People's Army in the German Democratic Republic.

Officer tuition generally appeared on the duty roster once a week. One day the subject was 'Orders and Obedience'. Question: 'What orders must the soldier carry out?' Answer: 'Every order must be carried out.' Question: 'What orders should the soldier not carry out?' Pause. Laborious thought by the recruits. Lieutenant's answer: 'An order should not be carried out if the soldier realises that by carrying it out he would be committing a crime.' Question: 'What does the soldier do when he realises this?' Answer: 'He refuses to carry out the order.' Next question: 'Give examples.' Answer: 'Murder, manslaughter, looting, rape, killing prisoners.'

In another lesson we were taught about The Hague Convention on Land Warfare of 1899 and its regulations on the distinction between civilian personnel and soldiers, the treatment of the wounded and prisoners, peace emissaries, respect for the person, honour and property of inhabitants of foreign countries in the event of war. These matters were treated with great conscientiousness in our regiment.

On another occasion we discussed the law of self-defence, because we young soldiers were now bearing arms. The relevant paragraph of the German Reich Penal Code had to be learned by heart and we were questioned on it a week later. I remember it now:

'No punishable action has been committed if the action was necessitated by self-defence. Self-defence means the defence which is necessary in order to prevent an immediate, illegal attack on oneself or another person.'

After a number of recruits had repeated the paragraph correctly and in full, the rest of the period was spent explaining each individual word, with examples. The greatest value was attached to the words 'illegal attack . . . on another person'.

The case of self-defence became complicated if, for instance, one happened to witness a crime. Was it then better simply to look away, to avoid the disagreeable consequences one might incur by intervening, or should one act to prevent the obvious crime in time? After all, the wording actually was: '. . . defence which is necessary . . .'

'You Share the Responsibility'

Infantry training with machine-gun practice was also on the duty rota. This part of the basic training demanded extreme physical effort from the young soldier. We were young and healthy and did not mind being pushed to the limit of our capacities. I myself thought of it as intensive training in a sport.

But we had the little fellow with the thick glasses in our group. Though he sometimes astonished me with extremely intelligent remarks, I often noticed that immediately afterwards he would be dreaming away absentmindedly. In any case he was physically not up to the riding training and drill. His gait was hunched and he could not straighten himself up. When we had to march singly across the barrack square with our backs straight, he always relapsed into a kind of amble. His left hand swung forward with his left leg, the right did the same. I could not understand why he had been sent to the Army at all when he was called up. He looked to me like a case for the doctor, and probably for the psychiatrist.

Unfortuntely, our sergeant and lance-corporal saw things differently and took pleasure in teasing and tormenting him from the very first day. If he was given an order in arms drill he had to think before carrying it out after a fashion. So the two instructors took pleasure in making an unwilling clown of this unfortunate at every opportunity.

Today it was time for machine-gun practice. In groups, close to a toolshed, with the MG 13 Dreise in our hands, we obeyed the orders: 'Up, at the double' – 'Down, up, at the double – down' · three, four, five, six times and more. Suddenly our problem child was on the ground, face down. One more pitiful effort, then – so it seemed – he passed out. Our two instructors were already standing beside him, shouting at the prostrate man, but to no effect: there he lay still, face down.

Then something extraordinary happened. The sergeant and the lance-corporal grabbed the man and set him on his feet. At first his legs would not carry him, but finally he was standing up. Then our sergeant shouted, so loudly that we could all hear him: 'We'll make a soldier out of you, like it or not!' They took him between them by the arms and disappeared round the other side of the toolshed.

We stayed where we were, bewildered. After only a few moments loud screams came from behind the shed. I froze, but then I heard quite clearly: 'Help – help!' I ran round the shed.

There he lay, on his back now, our room-mate. Beside him stood the sergeant and lance-corporal, kicking the prostrate man in the stomach again and again. I shouted as loudly as I could: '*Herr Unteroffizier!*' The two spun round, stared at me, and came towards me as if nothing had happened. The three of us rejoined the rest of our group, the sergeant ordered two others to bring him to our room because he was not feeling well. They did not pass us on the way to the barracks but went round the far side of the shed, supporting our fellow soldier like a wounded man.

At lunchtime we found him lying on his bed in our room. He said he was better already and did not need to report sick, he would come out and join in the afternoon duty.

My account of that day is not over. In the afternoon I was called to the telephone in the orderly room: an officer wanted to speak to me. Who could it be? This was my first telephone call as a soldier. 'Trooper Stahlberg speaking,' I announced. 'Henning here,' was the reply. It really was Henning Tresckow, who had just concluded a General Staff tour in Schwedt and told me to get two hours off and meet him at the Café Wieck on the Schlossfreiheit.

The sergeant-major, evidently impressed that one of his recruits should have a General Staff* officer for a cousin, agreed but insisted that I should report to him correctly dressed. When I reappeared in his office, having changed my clothes, he stood me to attention and walked round inspecting me. So off I went to town at top speed, my heavy sword at my side.

A number of military vehicles were parked in front of the Café Wieck and I went in to the building in some excitement. Frau Wieck, well known in Schwedt as a 'soldiers' mother', stopped me this time at the entrance. I could not go in, because she had reserved the house for a single party. She was all the more astonished when I said that I had been invited to that very party. 'But then you could at least have put on a decent uniform jacket instead of those fatigues!' she exclaimed. 'We haven't collected them from the stores yet,' I excused myself – but the sergeant-major had approved my dress.

When I opened the door to the restaurant, all I could make out was that the room was filled with officers under a cloud of tobacco smoke, and that they all had a red stripe on their trousers. I closed the door behind me and, as instructed under 'conduct in public', stood to attention to await events.

---

* Translator's note: The term 'General Staff' was used twofold in the German Army. First as a general term for what in most Western Armies is merely called 'the Staff' and secondly as a much coveted designation for a highly selected and trained body of staff officers who represented the acme of German military professionalism and were members of the General Staff Corps. As such they were held in deep respect and their professional advice to the commanders carried very great weight. To become a General Staff Officer, an officer must have shown himself to be an outstanding field soldier. Virtually all major military command posts were held by members of the Corps. To distinguish a General Staff officer in uniform, he wore a broad red stripe down his trousers. Even at the peak of World War II, the General Staff Corps never exceeded about 2,000 members.

After a brief moment Henning was before me, shaking me by the hand. The room had fallen silent and I felt all eyes on me. Henning called in a loud voice: 'Gentlemen! May I present my nephew Stahlberg. He is serving here as a volunteer and I have asked him to come because I want to hear from him how he likes military service.'

I hung my sword, belt and cap on the clothes-stand and found myself sitting at one of the little café tables, hemmed in by General Staff officers. I was relieved that no one started questioning me immediately, so that I could devote myself exclusively to the apple pie and whipped cream that Henning had ordered for me. Only once Henning commented drily: 'Well, how do you feel in the midst of the top brass of the German General Staff?' I have no idea whether and how I answered and I no longer remember which of the Army's later celebrities were sitting round me. What I do remember is that I was astonished how casually and openly they talked.

As soon as my plate was empty, Henning got up to take a short walk with me on the Schlossfreiheit. I could never have guessed how many, many 'short walks' he would take with me in the future.

Outside the door I was no longer nephew, but 'cousin' and now he positively showered me with questions. He wanted to hear my impressions, my views and my criticisms of the training for the first year of general conscription. I was to talk to him quite freely and without regard to the difference in our military rank.

My judgement was predominantly positive, but finally I also told him the nasty story of that morning, including the fact that my shout to the sergeant had put a stop to the sadistic abuse. Henning stood still. 'You undoubtedly did the right thing,' he said, 'but that's not enough. You now share the responsibility of ensuring that nothing like this ever happens again in your squadron!'

'How can I do that, as a recruit?' I asked helplessly. Henning's face was grave. 'Who's your squadron commander?' he asked. I gave him Lewinski's name. 'You will go to him today and report the incident. In all probability you will have to repeat the story, the way you told it to me, before a court martial, under oath. Can you do that? In other words, will you stick to what you said?' I drew a breath and said: 'Yes'.

Then he gave me a friendly clap on the shoulder, said goodbye and told me to give his greetings to Captain von Lewinski.

The rest is quickly told. When I told our sergeant-major after the evening roll-call that I wished to speak to the commander on a personal matter, he wanted to know my reasons. I said that it was personal and I would only tell the Captain himself. 'Very well,' he said, 'you are entitled to insist, every soldier has the right to speak to his chief personally.'

Next morning I was standing before the Captain. 'I have a report to make, Sir,' I began, 'but before I begin there are two things I have to say. Firstly, I had two hours' leave yesterday to meet my cousin, Major von Tresckow of the General Staff, in the town. He has been a kind of godfather to me for many years, though he is not officially my godfather. He told me yesterday to make the report that I am now making to you, Sir. He also asked me to give you his greetings.

'Secondly, I wish to say that I am very glad to be a member of the 3rd Squadron and would like to remain so.'

Then I described the events of the day before in detail.

Lewinski was chalk-white when I finished. 'That happened in my squadron?' he stammered. Then he asked if none of his officers had been present at machine-gun drill. I said no, and he dismissed me with the words: 'Thank you for your report.' But I felt that he was struggling for self-control.

Some two weeks later I was a witness at a court martial called at regimental headquarters. My examination was brief and I did not have to take the oath because the accused had confessed. When the verdict was pronounced I was already back on stable duty, but the word soon went all round the Regiment that the two accused men had been condemned to a suspended prison sentence and demotion. They had also been transferred to another regiment. Our room-mate with the pebble glasses was released from the Army a few days later as unfit.

Never again was I to witness such an assault in the Army. The service remained hard, but correct. I was certainly 'cut' by some sergeants for months and treated with icy reserve, but I believe there are many advantages in a certain solidarity among NCOs. There were some sergeants in the squadron who 'out of comradeship with the victim of recruit Stahlberg', 'revenged themselves' on me. I took it in good part, and am glad to have spent a year as a cavalry recruit. You have to have ridden with a squadron to understand the fascination exerted by horses *en masse*, for the horse is a herd animal by nature.

Captain von Lewinski told us one day that squadron drill in

closed ranks was unfortunately no longer part of cavalry training, although this was a touchstone for ability and discipline as a rider. If the cavalry had a future now, it lay exclusively in military reconnaissance and scouting in small groups, and yet one day he drew his sword and explained the old command signals with the weapon to the squadron. We tore off across the parade ground, the horses' hooves thundering on the earth. It was like some mighty natural cataclysm. What must it have been like in the days when not only a squadron, but a whole regiment or even several brigades appeared on the horizon?

Even our regimental trumpeters practised on horseback. If a squadron had performed particularly well it might be rewarded by the mounted band waiting outside the town to station itself in front of the squadron, the drummer, with his Kaiser Wilhelm beard and white gauntlets, on his magnificent, large-framed grey, the kettle-drums decorated with yellow saddle-cloths on either side. He guided his horse with his feet, the snaffle-reins ending at his stirrups.

The music started up at the first house on the edge of town and it was like the old nursery rhyme: 'When the soldiers come marching through the town, every maiden puts on her favourite gown . . .' Then the captain, riding at the head of his squadron, drew his sword, and at the command: 'Draw swords!' a hundred gleaming side-arms hissed into the air, to be propped for the parade on the right thigh, so that the blade lay on the shoulder, glittering in the sun.

And so we crossed the town, to the 'Cavalry March of the Great Elector' or even our regimental march, the 'Hohenfriedberger', which had been my father's regimental march as well.

My year's service as a soldier in Schwedt ended quite unexpectedly and not without drama. At the end of an afternoon duty I had agreed to meet my friend Peter Haniel from the neighbouring 2nd Squadron for a 'real' coffee at the Café Wieck instead of the foul-tasting barracks coffee. But Peter was not in his barracks, he was ill, they told me, in the town sickbay. So instead of going to Mother Wieck, I went to the sickbay to look him up.

To my horror, I found him lying unconscious in bed. I searched the building for a doctor, but found only a medical orderly. On enquiry I found that the doctor was on leave, and an elderly colleague from the town was deputising for him, but he had been there an hour before and seen my friend without giving a diagnosis.

He thought it best to wait for the following day and then see what sort of disease it might be. When I asked the orderly what disease he suspected, he shrugged his shoulders and said he had never seen anything like it before. About half an hour earlier the patient had asked for a glass of water, but when he had tried to lift the sick man's head his neck had been rigid and immovable.

Now we were both at a loss. I asked for the doctor's private address or the address of another doctor in the town, but the orderly said there was no doctor in Schwedt at present because the deputy who had looked at Peter that afternoon was now in his car visiting out-patients in the surrounding villages. Speechless at this state of medical provision for a town of about ten thousand inhabitants, I considered what to do next. In the building I came across a young lieutenant from another squadron who was also visiting. Well, what were we to do with Peter Haniel, who was seriously ill and without medical attention? I decided to take the sick man to the Municipal hospital at Stettin straight away. The lieutenant said he was not entitled to give me permission but he too thought this was the right thing to do.

The medical NCO, on the other hand, was delighted with my plan; it was certainly the right thing to do and in any case he had a girl-friend in Stettin whom he could visit, but where could we get hold of a car at short notice? I could set his mind at rest about that, because I kept a car in Schwedt, hidden away on the edge of town with a tobacco farmer on the Tenne because regimental orders forbade recruits to keep a car where they were stationed. So I ran off to fetch my car, hoping that as it was already dusk I would not be recognised.

We laid Peter Haniel on a stretcher – his body was completely rigid – and carried him out of the building. Fortunately my car had a hood which we opened to get the sick man in and we were soon on the road to Stettin. The assistant registrar on duty at the municipal hospital had scarcely begun to examine the patient when he lifted his head and stared at me, wide-eyed. Soon no less than three more doctors had gathered round, while I was shown to a seat in the corridor and forbidden to leave the building. My medical orderly had by now disappeared towards the town centre by tram.

An elderly doctor came out to tell me that the patient we had brought in unfortunately had an advanced case of infantile paralysis. He would inform the regiment in Schwedt by telephone.

I drove in to town and sat in the Café Ponath on the Paradeplatz, where I had arranged to meet my NCO at midnight. I waited till the café was closed, but it was several hours before he knocked on the window of my car. He was sorry, he had overslept at his girl-friend's house. All right for him, I thought, because there was no guard at the entrance to the Schwedt sickbay, but I would have to report at the barrack gates!

So the sun was already in the sky when I got back to barracks, and I heard my companions in the 3rd Squadron singing as they marched to their morning stable duty.

I reported to the sergeant-major and was soon standing before my squadron commander. 'Now what have you been up to, Stahlberg!' was his greeting. I told the whole story. 'So, to sum up,' said Lewinski:

'1. Contrary to regimental orders, you keep a car hidden in Schwedt.

2. You removed a critically ill patient from the sickbay without a doctor's authority.

3. You left your garrison, that is, the Army, without permission.

4. Without orders from your regiment, and without his consent, you delivered the patient to a civilian hospital of your choice instead of taking him, if anywhere, to a military hospital.

5. You persuaded a medical orderly to abandon the sickbay in his care, leaving the patients on their own, and leaving the station.

6. You failed to return to barracks before Last Post. In other words, you "kicked over the traces".'

I confirmed all six offences with a 'Yes, Sir'. He was sorry, he concluded, but I must expect a court martial. 'Yes, Sir,' I replied, because the degree of my transgressions was outside the competence of a squadron commander.

Then – after a pause – he said he must tell me that everything I had done and caused to be done had been criminal. Nevertheless, it had been right – except for keeping a private car in the garrison town. In fact, he would have done exactly the same in my place. But now the whole regiment was in quarantine and I myself was ordered to leave the barracks and the garrison immediately, without even shaking hands with anyone. 'Good luck, Stahlberg,' he finished.

I was dismissed, leaving my mother's Berlin address in the Orderly Room and vanishing from Schwedt without even taking my personal effects out of my barrack-room cupboard.

At about lunchtime, my mother opened the door of her flat at 28, Brandenburgische Strasse in Berlin, and I could not prevent her from throwing her arms round me. She had already received the bad tidings about me by telephone from Schwedt and had been discussing what should be done with me now with my sister, who happened to be there, and who was married to the medical director of Schreiberhau Hospital (district of Hirschberg in Silesia). He had told her (again by telephone) that Behring had developed a serum from horses, not yet generally released, with which I should be treated immediately. Then the two ladies had telephoned several doctors and chemists without success, until at last they discovered that there was a small stock of the serum in Berlin. They could enquire at the Reich Ministry of the Interior. They did, but unsuccessfully, of course; in fact, a civil servant told my mother quite simply: 'Listen, dear lady, as you describe the case, your son should go to hospital at once.' But he had missed his mark there, because my mother had a lifelong, deep-rooted mistrust of hospitals. A sick man, she used to say, should only be in hospital for an operation: hospitals were more likely to spread diseases than to cure them. And after all, as far as I was concerned, I was not even ill, but only – and then only possibly – infected with the poliomyelitis virus. At that the civil servant had hung up quite abruptly.

In these circumstances my mother turned for help to her friend Frau von Weizsäcker, wife of the later Secretary of State at the Foreign Office, Ernst von Weizsäcker. We had been friendly with the Weizsäcker family for many years, had often been to their house to play chamber music and have dancing lessons with the three eldest children, Carl–Friedrich, Adelheid and Heinrich. Frau von Weizsäcker, known for helping wherever help could be given, took the matter up energetically. While we sat discussing what else could be done, the call came, giving the address where the Behring serum could be found. My sister swooped into her car, returned swiftly with the lifesaving package and injected a yellowish fluid into my thigh. She was a doctor's wife, after all, and knew what she was doing.

Then it was a question of what to do next. I suggested going to the cinema and we soon found ourselves at the evening showing in the Ufa Palace at the Zoo.

Then what had to happen, happened. Some time in the middle of the film I lost consciousness. As if from a distance I could hear helpful people suggesting this and that. I was aware that I had been carried into the street and put in a taxi and I heard my mother's loud voice declaring that this was her son and he was not going to hospital but back to her home. I still cannot understand how the two ladies managed to get me, in a state of complete paralysis, from the taxi into the house and by lift to the fourth floor. I kept to my bed for only a few days as the paralysis gradually faded, and then I was on my feet again. But I could not yet return to my regiment. The quarantine in Schwedt actually meant that all the recruits there had to extend their year of service by a few days.

I learned later that by using the still restricted Behring serum I had become an extremely welcome human guinea-pig. One day a letter arrived from the regiment announcing that I had been promoted to lance-corporal and was a candidate for the reserve of officers. There was no mention of a court martial. Peter Haniel, though severely damaged, had survived the disease.

Years of Peace?

In Germany the years 1936 and 1937 were outstanding for a chain of extraordinary successes, skilfully publicised by the Ministry of Propaganda using the technique of 'linguistic prescription' on press and radio. Any news that was not welcome to the National Socialist authorities was suppressed, or simply forbidden, so that the public received an impression of constant successes. By far the greater part of the German population was convinced that this government could achieve absolutely anything.

Naturally, this could only continue to go well when undeniable facts were demonstrated, of which the most important was the decreasing numbers of unemployed. Of course, no one could check the published figures, but the man in the street saw no more unemployed people. Before 1933 they had been standing around on street corners, but now building sites sprouted from the ground, with thousands of 'labour service' men, working on the reclamation of swampland here, and the construction of new autobahns there. In those days they worked with spade and shovel, there was no massive building machinery. Similarly, after March 1935, general conscription ensured that the mass of unemployed disappeared. The young soldiers enjoyed showing themselves among the population in their new uniforms, and on holidays the regiments marched with bands playing through the garrison towns to parade.

Begging was now forbidden, under pain of arrest. In short, the physical constitution of our country had undergone a complete transformation, and other countries began to admire the 'new' Germany.

Industry and agriculture were encouraged as never before – what entrepreneur is not keen to invest, if he can profit from his investments for two years completely free of tax. We in Stettin, for example, attacked our major item of expenditure, electricity consumption from the town power supply, and built our own electric power station. Never before had the edible oil and soap factories risked an investment of anything like this volume. The building industry began to blossom, not only through the building of new barracks and airfields but also through state-subsidised home-building. In Hamburg, for instance, everyone could see that on the lower Elbe the 'ships' cemetery', a vast quantity of abandoned, rusting ocean liners, had disappeared. Whether they had been taken into service or gone for scrap interested no one; it was enough that we could no longer see them. The shipyards were happy to be working to capacity because the German government had concluded a ship-building agreement with Great Britain: the German Navy was now allowed up to 35 per cent of the British tonnage. In England this was known as the appeasement policy.

Few people realised that the price for this breathtaking economic success would be paid in evil and irresponsibility. Hitler had announced that Germany was big and strong enough to finance it all, and that the 'best and most reliable' of all economic systems was autarchy, national self-sufficiency.

Now our Stettin factory, with its end products of vegetable oils, foodstuffs, soaps, and so forth was dependent chiefly on raw materials from overseas. Then the Reich Ministry of Economics undertook the purchase of our raw materials, especially soya beans, and distributed them to producers. Our quota was $10\frac{1}{2}$ per cent of the total volume. We were relieved of the risk of buying in the world market and, on paper, our earnings were good. However, in the background there was the menacing question of the real value of the money. This was the perfect planned economy, the kind we see in the Socialist countries today. If Father State was short of money, he simply ordered the money presses to run a little faster. As my father said drily: it may be all right for a while, but one day the German Reich will have to get its raw materials from beyond our frontiers without paying for them.

We had not yet reached that pass in 1936, which was to be a 'year of peace', by order of Hitler. True, he had marched troops across the Rhine in March and revoked the demilitarisation of the German territories on the left bank of the Rhine. The world protested, but that was all. We were faced with a *fait accompli* and we were all glad that the teeth of one article of the infamous 'Versailles Diktat of 1919' had been drawn.

In March, too, the Germans had been summoned to the polling booths yet again to declare whether they agreed with this policy. The result was overwhelming: 99 per cent voted 'Yes'. Once again, my mother's friend Frau Ninow, as a faithful party member, was on the election committee at the polling station. Once again the lists were ticked off with minute care, but the votes were not counted this time, either.

The peak of the peace euphoria was reached with the Olympic Games of 1936. It does not take much imagination to transform the Olympic ideal into the visible documentation of a desire for peace. With thousands of white doves, with the première of a hymn by Richard Strauss, and with the idea of having an Olympic flame carried, for the first time in the history of the Games, by relay runners from the Peloponnesus in Greece to Berlin – with all this came an unbelievable atmosphere of celebration of peace. Even the big French delegation succumbed to it, filing past the head of state of the German Reich with right arms raised. Had I not seen it for myself I would scarcely have believed it, because in German families at that time the use or non-use of the 'German greeting' amounted to a confession of faith.

I had got myself a ticket to the stadium not only for the opening ceremony but also for the athletics play-offs and the equestrian finals, as well as for the victory ride by the dressage winner.

I saw Jesse Owens when he won four gold medals in succession for the USA, but I also witnessed the unparalleled treatment of this unique athelete when the token of his victories, especially for the world record in the 100 metre sprint (10.2 seconds) was hung round his neck by one of the members of the International Olympic Committee. As an honorary award from Germany each winner received with his medal a terracotta pot containing a small oak seedling which he could plant in his own country. In addition every winner of a gold medal was led to the VIP rostrum to receive in full view of the crowd the personal congratulations of the highest German official present. If the Head of State was there, the victor could return home with a handshake from Hitler.

When Jesse Owens ran his sensational world record, Hitler was present. So now the Führer and Chancellor of the German Reich, known to be a fanatical racist, would have to shake hands with a dark-skinned athlete.

My seat was diagonally across from the VIP rostrum and I watched the episode tensely through my binoculars. In the usual way, Jesse Owens was escorted up the steps to the right of the VIP rostrum by two young ladies dressed in white. But when the trio reached the platform immediately below the rostrum, about a hundred black-uniformed SS men suddenly stepped out of the darkness and blocked the last section of the steps. Jesse Owens was close enough to touch them. Would they give way? By no means. Quite obviously they had not appeared there for security reasons but to bar the black athlete's way.

Up on the rostrum, only another five to ten metres away, there was a disturbance among the guests of honour of the International Olympic Committee and some of the officials could be seen running to and fro. Seconds later Hitler had vanished. Had he gone home? Even now the barrier of SS men did not open. Finally Jesse Owens turned round and walked down the steps again, dignified as a king, accompanied by the two white-clad girls: an unforgettable image. Only then was the tension in the stadium released, and it seemed to me that the explosion of applause exceeded all previous dimensions. It was as if the people had spoken.

I remember one day I went to see my mother, who had invited a number of ladies to tea. I greeted the company, all of whom were known to me, and begged them to continue their interrupted conversation. Frau G. had been reciting a deeply committed hymn of praise to 'our Führer', which she took up again. To hold one's tongue was almost unbearable, as the old clichés came out: 'our Saviour', to whom every one of us owed 'such inexpressible gratitude'. At that 'my paper collar burst' as the Berliners say, and I threw in: 'Only he's sometimes a bit short on the truth'.

The company fell into a startled silence. My mother looked at me reproachfully, but Frau G. rose without a word and left the room and the flat.

A few days later my mother received a letter from Frau G. My remark had faced her with a grave moral conflict: as a Party member it was her duty to denounce me to the Gestapo. Only her friendship of many years with my mother kept her from her duty this time, but she hoped my mother would understand that she could never cross her threshold again.

Decades have passed since then. I sometimes come across Frau G., still very sprightly, at a theatre or concert in Berlin and we say a friendly hallo. After all, I still owe her my thanks for failing to denounce me back in 1933.

In October 1933 Hitler announced Germany's withdrawal from the League of Nations. The many grievous years spent by our former Foreign Minister and Reich Chancellor Gustav Stresemann restoring international confidence in our country were lost at a stroke. 'No longer to wish to enter the forum of nations' – what hubris that decision revealed!

In July 1934 the Austrian National Socialists had also attempted to seize power in their country, not 'by legal means' like Hitler, but with a *putsch*. They murdered the Austrian Federal Chancellor, Engelbert Dollfuss. Who gave the order? I never found out, but many people had their own ideas. The *putsch* failed, but on the day after Dollfuss's assassination it occurred to Hitler to send, of all people, Herr von Papen, his former Vice-Chancellor, 'unemployed' since 30 June 1934, to Vienna as his special envoy to clear the poisoned atmosphere there. And as we have already seen, Papen agreed! What weakness of character, we thought. Papen negotiated an Austro-German treaty of friendship; now the Austrians too were yielding to his eloquence and charm. 'No indirect or direct interference with Austria's internal affairs,' Papen promised in Hitler's name, and signed the Treaty in July 1936.

Not two years were to pass before Hitler gave the order to invade Austria, in March 1938. He was no doubt fulfilling the old dream of a great German Empire, but at what a price: suspicion of murder, treaty-breaking and blackmail.

The glory and rejoicing of the Berlin Olympic Games was still fresh in our memories when Germany and Italy became allies in a 'Berlin-Rome Axis' in October 1936.

In November of the same year an anti-comintern pact was concluded between Germany and Japan, with a great deal of propaganda. It could only be directed against the Soviet Union. The hectic activity in which our country was now indulging no longer bore any relation to the size and importance of the German Reich. Hitler never tired of declaring again and again in every one

of his speeches that all this was in the cause of peace, but if one
thought about it, or took the trouble to look at an atlas or a globe,
one could begin to feel very uneasy.

Dietrich Bonhoeffer

In 1937 I met the theologian Dietrich Bonhoeffer at the home of
my grandmother Ruth von Kleist-Retzow in Stettin. In
Finkenwalde, not far from the town, he was leading a preachers'
seminar of the Confessional Church, a free association of
Evengelical theologians and parishes who refused to see
Christianity obscured by new political maxims. This institution
had naturally been an irritant to the National Socialists from the
start. The régime was trying to bring the entire Evangelical
Church under its control. It had already enthroned a National
Socialist 'Reich Bishop', so the preachers' seminar at Finkenwalde
had been searched several times by the Gestapo for documents
considered suspicious by the government.

Grandmother had rented a spacious old flat in Pölitzer Strasse in
Stettin, where she kept a 'boarding house' for her grandchildren.
Since their families all lived in the country, they would have had to
go to boarding school to prepare for their school-leaving examin-
ations, but now that most boarding schools in Germany were
already under National Socialist influence their parents wanted to
avoid this.

Having no home of my own yet, I was glad to share
Grandmother's lunchtime table with all the many cousins, male
and female. While we ate, Grandmother wanted to know what the
teachers at the schools had said, and if she discovered so much as a
hint of National Socialist doctrine, she would bring it up for
discussion at once, correcting where she saw the need, with the
authority peculiar to her.

I also remember a family story she often quoted. In 1737 one of
our common ancestors, the French Huguenot Vernezobre de
Laurieux, found himself quite involuntarily responsible for the
building of a great palace in Berlin, at the southern end of
Wilhelmstrasse. The building later belonged to the Prussian Prince
Albrecht and went into the history of Prussia and Germany as
'Prince Albrecht's Palace'. Its origins were involved in a macabre
episode, since it was only when he assumed liability for the
building of this costly palace that the French member of the

Reformed Church Vernezobre had achieved the goal for the sake of which he had emigrated to the freer and more tolerant Brandenburg–Prussia: not only religious freedom but also personal freedom. The building had been the price for allowing his daughters to marry the husbands of their choice instead of obeying their overlord's marital plans. So the story of that palace's origins provided ample material for instructive debate, and Grandmother felt all the more personally affected since Prince Albrecht's Palace had become the centre of terror in Germany: the headquarters of the Gestapo, the Secret State Police, and the scene of torture and murder.

But there was more to Grandmother's table: Dietrich Bonhoeffer was a frequent guest at it, brought there by the closeness of his and my grandmother's ecclesiastical and theological interests. And so he had gladly undertaken to instruct the children of this circle who presented themselves for Confirmation. Then the Confirmation ceremony was performed by him at the village church in Kieckow.

It was in the autumn of 1937 that Dietrich Bonhoeffer unexpectedly looked me up late one afternoon at our oil factory. What could he want of me so suddenly? He came straight to the point 'I would be grateful for your help, I hope you will consent to my hereby presenting you with my Bechstein Grand.' He said it apparently without emotion, and so matter-of-factly that he might have come to the factory office to order a supply of oil. He explained the reason for his request in a few words. Naturally he did not like parting with the instrument, but he had received confidential information that the Gestapo would be coming to Finkenwalde again next day and this time they would probably seal up the house. He simply wanted to make sure that the grand piano escaped the Gestapo's grasp in time.

I picked up the telephone at once and found one of our lorry drivers who was still in the factory, and some workers who were quite willing to do a few hours' overtime. So a lorry was dispatched at once to Finkenwalde with two or three muscular men and a lot of empty soya meal sacks for wrapping, and Dietrich Bonhoeffer phoned through to say that the piano would be picked up.

'And now,' I said, 'we need a bit of paper to confirm this strange "business" between us. Somehow we must certify that the Bechstein really is your property. We will both sign this paper and I will put it in the secret back compartment of our safe.' He replied at once: 'No, please don't do that. It could mean trouble for both of us and do no one any good. And you must please promise me not to put anything about this on paper on your own.'

I wanted to argue, but he cut me off after the first few words: 'If it should happen that you and I survive the time ahead, then I shall be pleased if you give me back the piano one day. Today I am simply grateful to you for accepting my gift without reservation.'

He was in a hurry to leave in order to be there when his Bechstein was prepared for transport. The instrument was in my house that very evening, a very fine, black concert grand which I have played often and which has given me much pleasure.

The old family house in Pommerensdorfer Strasse and everything inside it was looted in 1945, and finally razed to the ground. Although Dietrich Bonhoeffer's connections with my grandmother and the cousins whom he prepared for Confirmation grew closer year by year, I never met him again.

When, for reasons of health, Grandmother had to give up her flat in Stettin and return to Klein-Krössin, he was often a guest there. They enjoyed discussing theological matters, and in order to read the original text from which Martin Luther translated the Bible and understand it better, my grandmother began to learn Greek. When I visited her in Klein-Krössin she often asked me to 'hear' her Greek vocabulary. Through Dietrich Bonhoeffer, Klein-Krössin and Kieckow became a much-frequented refuge for persecuted members of the Confessional Church.

During the war Dietrich Bonhoeffer became engaged to my cousin Maria von Wedemeyer from Paetzig.

The National Socialists arrested him and imprisoned him without trial in Tegel penitentiary, where Maria visited him whenever she could get a visitor's permit. Dietrich Bonhoeffer did not live to see the end of the war. When the Russian armies were closing on Berlin the SS took him to Flossenbürg concentration camp in the Upper Palatinate, where he was murdered on the morning of 9 April 1945 together with Admiral Canaris, General Oster and Judge Sack, the Judge Advocate General.

Private Concerts

With the same intensity that my grandmother dedicated to ecclesiastical affairs all her life, my mother distanced herself from them. As a member of a Pomeranian Pietist family, she was certainly a very convinced Christian, but she had a deep dislike of pastors. I remember that sometimes at the Sunday service she would get up at the end of the liturgy and leave the church with us children in order not to have to hear the sermon. Once out in the open she would give vent to her feelings: 'All that sanctimonious stuff – unbearable!'

My mother's form of worship was music. With her as conductor and organist we three children took part in innumerable concerts, medieval mysteries and passion plays: when in Berlin, mostly at the German Church on the Gendarmenmarkt, and when travelling, in Brandenburg and Magdeburg cathedrals, and famous churches in Goslar, Quedlinburg, Stargard in Pomerania and in Silesia as far as Breslau.

One day – in 1925, I think – she had explained to my brother and me that she was going to give a concert at the Berlin women's prison in Barnimstrasse with her women's choir and us two boys. Welfare work there was the responsibility of our aunt 'Kätzchen' – Katharina von Tresckow. My brother and I, aged eleven and thirteen, protested vigorously: it simply would not do – but no one was asking for our opinion. It was our Christian duty and that was that!

So off we went with cello and violin, and after passing through a good many iron-barred gates we attacked our instruments with the greatest possible abandon and still more vibrato, because, after all, this particular audience had moved us deeply. We had – so to speak – a smash hit such as we children had never experienced before. At all events, over the course of the next few years there was not a single prison in Berlin whose portals we had not entered, cello and violin in hand. These included the penitentiary in Tegel, where our listeners arrived chained together in the great hall, where they were shut up in small cubicles in such a way that from the platform we could see only their heads. All this was part of our mother's 'practical Christianity'.

But now the year was 1937 and times had changed. Our mother had always organised her social life in the form of private concerts. Now she informed her many contacts in Berlin's musical life that a new problem of great importance had arisen. There were musicians who were no longer allowed to give concerts and even some who could no longer give music lessons because the National Socialist authorities had forbidden them on political or racial grounds to practise their profession. And there were still other musicians who now refused to appear on a concert platform, although they were in no way 'affected'. So some artists were now in extremely straitened circumstances.

My mother no longer issued invitations to private concerts, but to 'private charity concerts'.* Artists performed there who were well known in Berlin but could no longer be heard in public. First among these was the violinist Karl Klingler, Professor at the Berlin College of Music. Attempts had been made to force him to dismiss his cellist from his internationally-known string quartet. When one day, on top of this, the bronze bust of the founder of the college, the great violinist Joseph Joachim, disappeared from the foyer, Klingler never set foot in the place again.

Now he was playing Mozart's Symphonia Concertante for violin, viola and orchestra at our house, on the famous Stradivarius which had once belonged to Joseph Joachim, with his assistant Beatrice Bentz, and with the young Hans Chemin-Petit conducting.

The dining-room was big enough to contain a chamber orchestra. Among my mother's guests of honour in the now overcrowded flat were Max Planck and the two Weizsäckers. The younger listeners had to sit on the floor because there were not enough chairs.

In her opening words my mother appealed to her guests' generosity, indicating the charitable purpose of her gathering unmistakably, without naming a single one of those in need of support. Astonishing sums of money were collected in the large, open bowl left standing in the entrance hall.

At another of these concerts, once again with Chemin-Petit conducting, we played Bruckner's String Quintet, with each part filled four times over, and with the addition of a double bass, taken over by Linus Wilhelm, solo double bass of the Berlin Philharmonic. This time the guests included Gertrud Bäumer, Tatiana Gsovsky, Ricarda Huch and the writer Jochen Klepper and his wife, who no longer went to public concerts because, as a Jewess, Frau Klepper was not allowed to enter a concert hall. In December 1942 they and their daughter committed suicide.

On another occasion we accompanied Wilhelm Kempf in a Mozart concerto. The great pianist, accustomed to playing in the biggest concert halls, made an unforgettable impression as he adapted mother's Blüthner grand acoustically to the area of the flat.

* Karla Höcker, *Hauskonzerte in Berlin*, Rembrandt-Verlag, Berlin 1970.

I remember yet another concert, when we played the octet by Felix Mendelssohn-Bartholdy, the greatest of all Berlin composers, whose music was now forbidden in public. But mother's concerts were not 'public'. Guests were just asked to telephone in advance if they could come, so that enough refreshments could be prepared for later on. But of course there were always more visitors than we expected.

There was never any question of fees at my mother's private concerts. The professional musicians received a sealed envelope, handed over 'discreetly' beforehand, but I noticed several of them putting some of the contents, equally discreetly, into Mother's big bowl. Mother distributed the receipts as she thought fit and was able to alleviate much misery.

Crisis Years 1938 and 1939

The year 1938 was remarkable for extraordinary political activity by Hitler. Towards the end of the previous year there had already been news to set the critical reader thinking. In February Hitler undertook a reshuffle of the Cabinet and the Wehrmacht leadership which was intended to strengthen the National Socialist regime: the Supreme Commander of the Wehrmacht and Reich Minister of War, Werner von Blomberg, was deprived of his office, as was the Supreme Commander of the Army, Werner von Fritsch. Hitler formed a Wehrmacht Supreme Command as his own direct instrument of command. Reich Foreign Minister Konstantin von Neurath, a traditional career diplomat, was replaced by the National Socialist party member and former champagne sales representative Joachim von Ribbentrop. Ribbentrop was regarded as utterly 'enslaved' by Hitler. The National Socialist State and its Führer had now taken complete control of the military as well, without meeting any opposition from within the officer corps.

It was only after the war that we learned the extent of the intrigues and unfounded accusations which the National Socialist authorities had used as means to their ends, but everyone could already see the facts, and something else besides: all three branches of the Wehrmacht, the Army, Navy and Air Force, were being strengthened quite openly and at positively hair-raising speed. Could this really be nothing more than a manifestation of the peace policy tirelessly broadcast in all the propaganda?

When, on 12 March 1938, I switched on my first new car radio in Stettin and heard the special announcement that troops had crossed the German frontier to Austria on that day, I pulled in to the side of the road for a minute to catch my breath. 'Hitler in triumphal procession with the soldiers of the Army on the way to Vienna!' – 'The Austrian people in transports of joy on the country roads' – 'Hundreds of thousands on the Heldenplatz in Vienna'.

The centuries-old German dream, the unification of all German-speaking citizens in a single German Reich, the rebirth of the old Holy Roman Empire (of the German Nation) and the 1848 Frankfurt National Assembly's hope of a confederation of German states including Austria, for which my own great-grandfather Heckscher had sacrificed himself in vain, seemed to have come within reach.

And Goebbels, Hitler's propaganda minister, was already drumming out the new slogan: '*Ein Volk, ein Reich, ein Führer!*' – 'One people, one empire, one leader!'

For the great majority of Germans, those days were an intoxicating experience. Who could resist it?

The newspapers carried pictures of the new German frontiers, revealing at a glance that the Czechoslovak Republic, founded in 1919, was held in the jaws of the German Reich. And Bismarck's 'European balance' was a thing of the past. Nevertheless, France and Great Britain accepted the *fait accompli* 'for the sake of peace'. Hitler had played for high stakes, but he had won.

Now we would see how the German Führer's statesmanlike qualities would really turn out. Was he shrewd enough to be satisfied with the consolidation of his incredible success? The organic coalescence of the two now united German countries could be his life's work. In those March days all those who had seen Hitler as a great politician seemed to be justified; more than ever, they saw their Führer as one of the greatest of Germans, one who could triumph over all the small-minded and the sceptics.

I met Ewald von Kleist-Schmenzin at a family party in Kieckow, my mother's family estate. 'Read about it in Hitler's book *Mein Kampf*,' he told me. 'That's the only way to see the aim of his policies.' I had often heard him talk like this, but who wanted to read that huge tome!

Now he added; 'We are on the brink of a second world war. You will live to see it.'

A month or two after the German invasion of Austria a rumour reached me. It concerned Franz von Papen, whose usefulness as German Ambassador to Vienna must have ended with the

Austrian *Anschluss*. When the German troops marched in, the Gestapo also arrived in Vienna and at once seized everyone who was not acceptable to the NSDAP. Once again, as on 30 June 1934 in Berlin, Papen's offices were one of their first targets. Papen's aide, Günther von Tschirschky, was apparently able to escape by taking flight in time, but Papen's legation counsellor, Wilhelm von Ketteler, was kidnapped and murdered. A few days later his body was taken from the Danube below Vienna.

In the days that followed, the rumour was confirmed from mouth to mouth and soon afterwards the papers were reporting that the former German Ambassador to Vienna, Franz von Papen, would now go to Ankara as German Ambassador to Turkey.

The news affected me personally, and once again I asked myself what could be going on in this man's heart. In the pursuit of his soaring political ambitions the murder of his closest colleagues apparently left him cold. Packed deep down in a chest at home I still had his photograph with the dedication of March 1933: 'One kind of politics is based on faith!'

In May and June, German newspapers became remarkably full of items about clashes in the frontier zones of Czechoslovakia inhabited by Germans. Many people rightly suspected a repetition of the tactics preceding the invasion of Austria by German troops: there too the National Socialists had organised assaults, street fights and political murders months before March 1938, until Hitler had intervened with an ultimatum. That had been his policy.

Was the Czechoslovakian Republic now being softened up for the attack?

Some time in July I was called up for my first exercise with the 2nd Anti-tank Battalion grouped with the 2nd Infantry Division in Stettin. On 1 September 1938 I reported, no longer as a cavalry trooper but as 'Sergeant of the reserve and candidate for the Reserve of Officers', to the Battalion Adjutant,* Lieutenant

---

* In relation to the practice in the German Army, the word Adjutant can prove a little confusing. As used here, its first meaning was that generally understood, i.e. the executive staff officer to the commanding officer of a battalion or similar unit. In its second sense, it would be translated in the British Army as Military Asssitant, i.e. personal staff officer to a formation commander or a general on the staff. Thus we shall find Stahlberg later as Adjutant to his battalion before becoming ADC (*Persönlichen Ordonnanzoffizier*) to Field Marshal von Manstein, looking after the Field Marshal's day-to-day personal and military needs but not becoming his Adjutant until after Manstein was dismissed and the scope of Stahlberg's duties expanded. We shall also see that Hitler, as Supreme Commander of the Armed Forces, had a number of Adjutants whose activities were co-ordinated by a Chief Adjutant, who features frequently later in this book.

Heinrich Graf Yorck von Wartenburg.

I had first to undergo a period of additional training. There were a lot of new things to be learned. Soon I had all the driving certificates, from motorcycle to lorry and tracked vehicle, and finally a driving instructor's certificate as well, and I learned how to use the small 37 millimeter anti-tank gun. With this weapon you could even make a hole in the turret of a modern tank, the astonished newcomer was told.

For the second time in four years I was a soldier again and so absorbed in the conversion to my new arm of the Service that I scarcely took in such news of political events as reached the public during those weeks. On the other hand, I gained two new friends, to whom I was to remain attached until their deaths: Heinrich Yorck and Achim Oster. Yorck, the Adjutant, had told me when I reported for duty that in a few weeks' time there were to be 'important manoeuvres', and a day or two later he told me that I was to be assigned to battalion headquarters for these manoeuvres, so I would be directly subordinate to him.

In mid-August came news which concerned us greatly: the Chief of the Army General Staff, General Ludwig Beck, had retired. Yorck knew him personally and together with his friend, Lieutenant Achim Oster (Adjutant of our 2nd Artillery Regiment also from Stettin), had eagerly fostered the connection. As someone with non-commissioned status, I was observing something completely novel: at every opportunity officially available to them, the two young officers drove to Berlin to catch up with the latest news. Achim's father, Hans Oster, was Chief of the Central Division and Chief of Staff at the Foreign Intelligence Office. Above him the line led to General Beck and General Erin von Witzleben, the general commanding the Berlin garrison. Colonel Oster had undoubtedly encouraged the two lieutenants in this connection, well aware that, even for generals at the top, it could only be useful to have such a close association outside official channels with two young and intelligent officers.

Yorck and Oster included me in their friendship. We met off-duty and discussed events. These retirements at the top of the Army could scarcely be routine; there must have been fundamental differences at the highest level.

I bought myself a large radio receiver which was really beyond my financial resources, but it was worth the money because it enabled me to hear the best foreign broadcasts on short wave.

Anyone who was content – or had to be content – with the new 'people's receiver' for 35 marks would hear scarcely anything but 'Reich radio', which broadcast nothing but material filtered by censorship and linguistic prescriptions. But now the three of us, Yorck, Oster and I, had such excellent information sources that at my home we analysed and debated affairs in the evening as if we were authorities with high responsibilities instead of being young men in the Forces – a prerogative of youth, and a good one, in my view.

With the second half of September came our marching orders. 'So it's really happened!' we young men exclaimed, knowing at the same time that for this 'manoeuvre' we would not simply be using blanks but live ammunition.

We left Stettin, travelling west, which meant that we were passing north of the capital – except for part of our 5th Infantry Regiment. Some infantry companies had an extremely unusual and unmilitary task to perform: they drove straight into Berlin and marched past the Reich Chancellery. A few days later they told us that the Führer had actually shown himself at the window for a moment, but the streets had been almost empty. The Berliners had a 'nose' for what this demonstration meant, and they did not like it.

I sat in the battalion commander's car. Major Heinrich Becker, a recalled former participant in the trench warfare of the First World War, listened admiringly as Yorck lectured us like a military historian. What we Germans were apparently embarking on now was a highly risky operation, Yorck commented.

Over the radio we heard about Hitler's negotiations with the British Prime Minister Neville Chamberlain, first at Hitler's mountain refuge in Berchtesgaden, then at the Hotel Dreesen in Bad Godesberg and finally in Munich. Hitler was making the demands: surrender of the German-speaking frontier areas of Czechoslovakia, or else . . . ? Benito Mussolini, Italy's Fascist dictator, had intervened to prevent the worst. Meanwhile the units of the German Army were rolling and marching through the country in full marching order, that is, equipped for war.

We passed Magdeburg and reached Bad Kissingen, wondering whether we would be swinging westwards towards the French frontier or eastwards towards Czechoslovakia. It was not until we were at Kissingen that our destination was revealed: the Republic of Czechoslovakia. The danger that the French would attack Germany if the Germans invaded Czechoslovakia seemed to have passed. We speculated that our division, one of the fastest moving army units with the most modern equipment, would have been thrown westwards if a war on two fronts threatened. The French Army was undoubtedly stronger than that of the Czechs.

As we drove through Kissingen, visitors to the resort were sitting in front of the hotels in their basket-chairs and did not even rise to see the troops at close range, far less to wave to the soldiers. How different it had been when the Schwedt Cavalry Regiment was riding through town! We felt now that the population rejected us.

To the east of Bayreuth we reached the mountain boundary and took up our quarters in the mountain villages.

Although the first rounds of live ammunition had already been issued to the companies, in those late September days, oddly enough, we never thought of a genuine 'shooting war'. We believed that this war of nerves would end as the one against Austria had ended seven months earlier. After all, the people on the other side of the frontier were Germans too.

When, through the intermediary of Mussolini, the Munich Conference did in fact take place on 29 September, we saw Heinrich Yorck's prognosis confirmed: Chamberlain, Daladier and Mussolini had secured peace for their own countries, Great Britain, France and Italy, and, so they thought, for Europe. Was this not yet another incredible 'master stroke' of Hitler's? We would advance into the Sudeten-German frontier zone of Czechoslovakia without having fired a shot, and – as the whole world now learned – Hitler had solemnly declared as part of the Munich Agreement that, with the surrender of Sudetenland, Germany's last territorial claims had been met.

The world breathed again, and Prime Minister Chamberlain announced on his return to London, and afterwards in the House of Commons: 'Peace in our time!'

On 1 October we rolled across the Czech frontier at Eger. Once again I was sitting in the commander's open car, with Heinrich Yorck beside me and Major Becker in front of us, beside the driver. We advanced at walking pace, because the reconnaissance unit marching ahead of us had already been stopped in the first village by an enthusiastically cheering crowd, and pelted with flowers. That was how a despatch rider described it to us. Not without reason, this march into Czechoslovakia became known as the 'War of Flowers'. It seemed to us quite unbelievable that the people lining the streets could have laid their hands on so many flowers.

During the slow advance we had been able to observe the system of fortifications on both sides of the road from our car – a chess-board pattern of bunkers. The field of fire and fire positions had been freshly cleared. Had we been forced to quell the Czechs, we would have suffered severe losses.

Then the first village appeared ahead of us, swastika flags fluttering from the windows of every house. Where had they come from? Many of the banners looked as if they had been run up on the housewife's sewing machine. Still the people thronged the edges of the street, and still the flowers pelted down, now on us.

Towards evening we went into civilian billets. I was billeted on an elderly widow, the rooms of whose house were carpeted with hand-woven, coarse white linen on which I scarcely dared set foot. The old woman spoke fluent German.

After only a few days the return march to Stettin began, and for the first time I saw Karlsbad, once one of the loveliest spa towns, most frequented by the 'great ones' of this world. After crossing the frontier, our tracked vehicles were loaded on to a train, experience having shown that many of our new designs were not capable of long distances – not yet.

The division mustered before Stettin for a ceremonial parade, a victory feast, a popular feast. Once again there were flowers upon flowers, and this time there were not hundreds of people, as there had been in the Egerland villages, but hundreds of thousands coming out to welcome their Stettin soldiers. 'Peace in our time.' The welcome was genuine: the German people did not want war, they wanted peace.

Now I was back at my desk in our edible oil factory, annoyed at the sorry state in which I had recovered my new BMW Cabriolet 'commandeered for the autumn manoeuvres': sprayed with camouflage paint, the bodywork damaged all over. Then I invited my friends Heinrick Yorck and Achim Oster to an evening meal. They had already been back to Berlin and were bursting with horrific-sounding information. In the past two weeks Germany really had been under the gravest threat of war. A hundred or so French divisions had been massed for the attack on the eastern frontier of France, facing not more than five German divisions.

A war on two fronts – against the Czechs in the East and France in the West – would have ended hopelessly for Germany. Accordingly, in the circle around General Beck's successor, the new Chief of General Staff, General Franz Halder, preparations

had been made to eliminate Hitler and his government immediately, by military means, in the event of war. A *coup d'état* had been
planned in the interests of peace. Nothing but the Munich
Agreement and the compliance of the British and French politicians had saved Hitler.

Only as a result of Hitler's unexpected success in Munich had
the move against him been called off. Chamberlain and Daladier
had allowed Hitler to outwit them and the one question still
outstanding was whether the German Führer would keep his
promise, made before the entire world, that this was Germany's
last territorial claim.

After the meal we spread out a newspaper on the table showing
Germany's latest frontiers. We looked at each other, eyebrows
raised. If ever there was an unnatural frontier between two nations
who did not even understand each other's language, then it was the
one with the rest of Czechoslovakia. How long would it be before
Chamberlain and Daladier realised that Hitler had been bluffing,
that he had led them by the nose? Or was he really going to quieten
down at last?

That evening stays in my memory, because only a few months
later the subject of our discussion faced us again in harsh reality.
Memories stay alive when they are fed by subsequent events.

And yet, despite our extraordinarily good information, there was
one event of great significance in those last weeks of which we were
unaware. I heard of it only after the war.

Once again, it was my uncle Ewald von Kleist-Schmenzin who
had involved himself politically, although in fact politics did not
concern him 'by virtue of his office'. He had his estate and his
forest in Schmenzin, which kept him busy, but country life was not
enough for him, because the possession of land gave him a feeling
of personal responsibility to the community. In his cousin
Hans-Jürgen von Kleist-Retzow, my mother's eldest brother, he
had a like-minded companion. It was no great distance from
Schmenzin to Kieckow and neither used the telephone very much,
because it had now been tapped for a long time. But they met as
soon as there was political news to be discussed; it was in the blood
of these two Prussian 'Junkers'.

Kleist-Schmenzin and Kleist-Retzow having agreed in the
summer of 1938 that Hitler was busy steering Germany straight
into war, Ewald Kleist seized the initiative – just as he had in
January 1933, when he tried to stop Papen from making Hitler

Reich Chancellor. He went to Berlin, where he spoke first to the young lawyer Fabian von Schlabrendorff. After the latter had confirmed the two Pomeranian Junkers' judgement of the political situation, the Junker from Schmenzin went to Admiral Wilhelm Canaris and his earliest collaborator, Colonel Oster. There too his fears were shared. Canaris and Oster arranged for Kleist to see General Beck, Chief of the General Staff, and again all doors were open. Then Kleist offered to fly to London in an attempt to stir the British government into taking a decisive stand against Hitler. Beck's words were passed on by Schlabrendorff: 'Bring me certain proof that England will fight if Czechoslovakia is attacked and I will put an end to this regime.'

Kleist-Schmenzin was in London from 18 to 24 August 1938. Canaris and Oster had arranged camouflage for this risky venture. In London Kleist-Schmenzin talked to important political personalities, including the Secretary of State at the Foreign Office, Robert G. Vansittart, David Lloyd George, the chairman of the British Council, and Winston Churchill, then a Conservative Member of Parliament and opponent of government policy. But Kleist's mission of peace missed its target. It was not the people he talked to, but Chamberlain, the Prime Minister, who kept himself informed by word of mouth and in writing on Kleist's mission, who decided the lines of British policy which ultimately led to the Munich Conference.

Superficially it might now look as if, after the nerve-racking events of 1938, a peaceful era had begun at last. Austria and the Sudetenland now belonged to the German Reich – now called 'Greater Germany', presumably in the same context as 'Great Britain'. Great Britain and France had recognised the new German frontiers and declared them 'inviolable'. And in spite of Churchill's warnings an overwhelming majority of the House of Commons had thanked the Prime Minister for his successful peace policy.   ·

But 1938 was not over yet. On the morning of 10 November, I was in Stettin on my way to our factory when I saw crowds of people on the far side of the broad square, the Paradeplatz. What were so many people doing, so early in the morning? When I turned into the Grüne Schanze, leading down to the River Oder on the other side of the square, I could scarcely believe my eyes: the Jewish synagogue down the road on the left had been burned out in the night. I parked my car in a side street and returned to the site of the fire, where a few policemen and uniformed SA men were standing about ordering pedestrians to move on. I crossed the Grüne Schanze so that I was standing opposite the still smoking ruins, where others stood wordlessly staring. I asked someone how the fire had started and the answer came in a single word: 'Arson'. I asked if the arsonist had been caught, but instead of answering the man shrugged his shoulders, turned away and disappeared in the crowd.

Then came a policeman's loud voice behind me: 'Move on please. Please move along!' There were SA men looking busy on the other side of the remains of the synagogue, and gradually I realised whose hand had been behind this.

I walked back further, to the Paradeplatz, where crowds of people stood bunched in front of certain shops, whose windows had been smashed. SA men stood before them like guards though the shattered businesses had obviously already been looted, their furniture destroyed. On the walls of the houses beside the shops one word had been daubed in white with a rough brush: *Jude*, Jew.

Policemen strolled along the road, having no need to keep order. Everything was quiet, so everything was fine. I was ashamed of my home town.

Back in the car, I switched on the radio, and it was then that I discovered what had happened. Throughout the German Reich the German people had that night avenged themselves spontaneously, so the report ran, for the murder of a German diplomat in Paris. A Jew had been the assassin, the people had acted. Apparently not a single synagogue, not a single Jewish-owned shop in Germany had escaped.

Only one person could have been responsible for this act. Whether the German diplomat in Paris had been murdered by a Jew or not, the destruction of all German synagogues and the disruption of the lives of Jewish citizens were unheard-of crimes. One of the grandest achievements of 18th century enlightenment had gone. 'In my country everyone can worship according to his fashion!' Frederick the Great had announced. What had we come to now?

A few days before Christmas, I received an important letter in the post. I opened it, to see my promotion to Lieutenant on the Reserve, 'in the name of the Führer and Supreme Commander of the Wehrmacht'.

On 14 March 1939 I was in my car on the way to Breslau, where

I had arranged to meet our commercial representatives in Silesia. Between Liegnitz and Breslau it had begun to snow. The end of a halted military column suddenly appeared before me. I drove on at walking pace. The soldiers had left their vehicles and seemed to be awaiting orders to march on. The trail of vehicles seemed endless. I found a space where I could stop, got out and spoke to a group of young officers, introduced myself, explained that I was an officer on the reserve of the Stettin Division and began to chat, hoping to find out what kind of extraordinary winter manoeuvre this might be; normally manoeuvres took place in the autumn.

This was no manoeuvre, I was told, they were on standby, ready to cross the Sudeten Mountains. By noon tomorrow they would have occupied Prague. The young officers said this quite innocently, as if it were nothing out of the ordinary. 'My God,' I exclaimed inwardly, 'is Hitler a madman?' Little more than five months ago, in Munich, he had solemnly renounced any further territorial claims for Germany, and now, for no apparent reason, he was breaking a treaty with Great Britain, France and Italy, in order to occupy the rest of Czechoslovakia, a foreign country whose inhabitants were not even German.

I drove on in a trance. Now I began to meet troops travelling in the opposite direction along the autobahn and other military groups crossing it, moving westwards. It was quite clear that an entire army was on the move: would this mean war? There was still the 'Polish corridor', dividing East Prussia from the rest of the Reich, there were still the German minorities in the former Prussian province of Poznan. There was still the strip of land across the Memel, which the Allies had awarded to Lithuania. There were still the Germans in Romanian Transylvania. There were still the former German colonies in West Africa, East Africa, Pacific Oceania. All these could be negotiated, but now we were invading a foreign country. On that day, 14 March, my last doubts were swept aside: we were heading straight for war. My uncle from Schmenzin had been right all along: Hitler meant war.

And once again, only a few days after Hitler's entry into Prague, the newspapers carried an illustration of Greater Germany's very latest frontiers. In the *Völkischer Beobachter*, Hitler's official party newspaper, certain territories were actually hatched-in: the Free State of Danzig, the province of Poznan-West Prussia and the Memel area. At home and abroad, people were to be given a foretaste of what was to follow Prague. Sure enough, scarcely a week had passed after the occupation of the rest of Czechoslovakia when on 22 March the government of the Republic of Lithuania was required by the Reich government to evacuate the Memel area. To give the German demand the necessary emphasis, Hitler embarked on the armoured cruiser *Deutschland* on 23 March and appeared with more than half the German Fleet off the Baltic port of Memel. As quickly as that – and again without a shot being fired – Memel belonged to the German Reich. Neither before the occupation of Prague nor before that of Memel had Germany's Führer and Chancellor deemed it necessary to invite the respective contracting states to a prior conference. The whole world now knew the German Reich to be a treaty-breaker.

*   *   *

There was one particular military spectacle that I was not going to miss: the parade for Hitler's fiftieth birthday on 20 April 1939. The day had long since become an official holiday, as the Kaiser's birthday had once been.

A gigantic audience stand had been erected opposite the Berlin Technical University. The splendid street between the Brandenburg Gate and Charlottenburg Knie had been widened on Hitler's orders. A triumphal way for Hitler had to be broader than the one on which Napoleon I had once marched through Berlin towards Moscow and along which the victorious Prussian troops had returned from Paris in 1871. Not only had many of the trees in the Tiergarten been felled, but Hitler had also ordered that the two great components of the Charlottenburg Gate on the bridge across the Landwehr Canal should be taken down and rebuilt a few metres further apart. Of course this step destroyed the proportions and the organic harmony of the two groups – but, on the other hand, companies could now march past on parade at their full width. In the capital of the Greater German Reich everything was now to be bigger and grander than in the old Prussian royal residence. The birthday parade was to be the biggest in the history of Berlin. Germany and the Germans were being taught to think only in superlatives. I did not want to miss the show. But how could I find myself a place?

I learned that thousands of tickets were being issued solely to party members and prominent personalities, so (quite without authority) I put on my new made-to-measure dress uniform, hung (by special permission) the sword of the Pasewalk Cuirassiers, which my father had given me when I was promoted to lieutenant, at my side and went to the Knie. There I simply followed the signs to the individual groups of seats on the stand. CD – Corps Diplomatique – seemed to me the best chance, and in the twinkling of an eye, there I was amidst all the pomp and circumstance of the foreign military attachés. In the Germany of those days one simply had to wear a uniform to pull off a successful fraud.

Then came the great moment when the birthday boy drove by, standing in his big black 7-litre Mercedes. The good company into which I had so successfully insinuated myself rose, as is proper on the arrival of a Head of State, and saluted in silence (so did I). I did indeed have a wonderful seat, only a few metres away from the great man in the brown uniform with the red swastika armband and the ill-fitting boots. The weather was wonderful, real 'Führer's weather'.

After that, what marched or rolled past us, hour after hour, or roared overhead from the direction of the triumphal column (industriously photographed from our stand) could have had quite an overwhelming effect. The military attachés around me were impressed. What was typical of Germany's policy was of course the immoderate character of this display. It was quantity that was intended to impress, and it became not only wearisome but totally 'un-Prussian', since less would have meant more.

As a whole, the political atmosphere of that spring was like a landscape just before the storm breaks. The German press – to use the military phrase – set its propaganda sights on the next victim: Poland. The technique was familiar from the previous year.

Now, at last, the British Prime Minister Chamberlain had given up the appeasement policy we had thought so foolish the year before. On 31 March in the House of Commons, and in the name of France as well, he guaranteed the sovereignty of Poland and the inviolability of her frontiers. Among close friends, we breathed a sigh of relief when we read that.

A week later Italy, encouraged by Hitler's territorial acquisitions, also satisfied its appetites. Mussolini occupied Albania, on the other side of the Adriatic, by force of arms. Now, in mid-April, the American President Franklin D. Roosevelt spoke, demanding that in future Germany and Italy should renounce all further attacks on other countries. He invited them to a joint conference, but Hitler, now into his stride, refused. Then Great Britain introduced general conscription. Surely all this must have some effect, we thought. But we were wrong.

On 28 April Hitler reacted with a speech to the Reichstag, which in fact consisted only of brown and black-uniformed National Socialist adherents. Throughout Germany factories and industries had to interrupt their work while hours of virulent, rabble-rousing propaganda were transmitted to their assemblies over loud-speakers. I heard them too, in our main factory building. The factory stopped for a full eight-hour shift and as the workers from the previous and following shifts were ordered to be present as well, a full day's production was lost. Hitler concentrated mainly on President Roosevelt, whom he described as 'the puppeteer of an encirclement policy against Germany'. Then came the unmistakable threat: Germany was militarily stronger now than before the outbreak of the Great War in 1915. As if in passing, Hitler declared that he no longer regarded the German–Polish non-aggression pact as valid, because Poland was no longer observing it. Then he turned to France, declaring that the German 'West Wall' (the fortification of Germany's western frontier that had been under construction for some years) 'could no longer be breached by any power in the world'. And with reference to Chamberlain's speech of 31 March he announced 'herewith, to the British government, that Germany no longer regards itself as bound by the Munich Agreement' and 'will take the appropriate steps'. Moreover, he demanded the return by Great Britain of all former German colonies of the pre-1914 period. Even this was not enough for him: he renounced 'herewith' the Naval Treaty entered into by his own government with Great Britain in 1935 and, since appetite comes with eating, he also demanded freedom of action *vis-à-vis* the Free State of Danzig.

This speech was no more and no less than advance notice of a declaration of war, but Hitler had formulated it so skilfully and demagogically that our politically untutored workers were enthusiastic, indeed carried away, to the point that the majority of the audience under the loudspeakers applauded rapturously. 'Adolf's really told them now!' But there was also a significant number who remained silent and thoughtful.

Goodbye to Peace

In those dramatic weeks I received an invitation to the wedding of my cousin Luitgarde von Bismarck to the Berlin lawyer Fabian von Schlabrendorff, arranged for 2 June 1939 in Lasbeck, in Eastern Pomerania.

Luitgarde and I were linked not only by the bond of our close relationship – our mothers were sisters – but also by a genuine friendship 'from the sandpit'.

At first, however, we found it difficult to get used to her choice. Of course we had known Fabian – five years my senior – for quite a long time, but I had never had any special rapport with him.

He had often visited my mother's flat in Brandenburgische Strasse in 1935, to talk to the Russian Grand Duchess Anastasia (Anna Anderson) who was living with us. With Paul Leverkuehn and Erich Vermehren, he was working to achieve legal recognition for the Czar's daughter, declared dead in 1920 in London. But without success, since the severely brain-damaged central figure was not prepared to appear before a judge or even to make the slightest written declaration. 'I have never done anything wrong, consequently I see no reason to go to court and I need no certificate to show who I am. I know that already,' she would say.

Fabian had been in and out of the house of my godfather and uncle Herbert von Bismarck, Luitgarde's father, to advise him while he was politically active in Berlin, and especially when he was Secretary of State at the Prussian Ministry of the Interior. He had also been in close touch with Ewald von Kleist-Schmenzin from 1932 onwards, when the latter was trying to prevent Hitler from forming a Reich government.

So for me, as a younger man, Fabian had previously been little more than a fleeting acquaintance. This changed one day, when the young lawyer was courageous enough to take on voluntarily the defence of the actor and cabaret artist Werner Finck, who had been arrested by the National Socialists. What had happened?

Werner Finck, then very popular for his bold criticism of the regime, had walked on to the stage of the 'Kabaretts der Komiker' on the Kurfürstendamm, when as soon as he appeared the lights went out. With the total darkness the welcoming applause of the audience was also abruptly silenced. They waited for some time in the hushed darkness. No sound came from the stage, either. The audience began to wonder if Werner Finck was there at all.

At last the cabaret artist's voice was heard: 'Ladies and gentlemen, I'm quite sure it's simply a fault in the *Leitung*.'*

---

* Translator's note: *Leitung* in German can mean either 'wiring' or 'leadership'.

A roar of laughter, protracted applause, light – the Berlin audience had understood.

Dictatorships are humourless. They view humour with suspicion: it might show up their weaknesses. Dictators are almost always as weak as they wish to appear strong. Presumably there were other *bons mots* on Werner Finck's record, but the words from the darkness of the 'Kabaretts der Komiker' were decisive, so that the day came when he was in need of a courageous defence lawyer to 'bail him out'. By then there were not many lawyers who would take on such a case, and Fabian did, in fact, save the witty cabaret artist from worse trouble. That impressed me.

One day I asked my future 'cousin' to tell me a little about his family with the remarkable name. It is always a good idea to find out about the 'opposition' in good time before a marriage in the family. I shall never forget his answer: 'From your question I know that you have never seen Frederick the Great's memorial on Unter den Linden.' Slightly embarrassed, I protested, but he went on with a grin: 'The pediment of that splendid memorial is adorned, as you know, by many of the great king's important generals. Only a few civilians were found worthy to be immortalised there. One of them is the Silesian Minister of my name* and I am grateful to the creator of the memorial, Christian Daniel Rauch, for placing the eminent jurist in such a way that the royal horse dung would fall exactly on his head. A committed lawyer must learn to bear such things with dignity.'

Once again I put up some resistance: as a former trooper I was wounded. I made an appeal on behalf of the usefulness of horse dung: 'You seem not to know that freshly-produced, hot horse dung is the tried and tested ideal cleaner for dirty hands.' 'No, I really had no idea!'cried Fabian, 'but I shall make a note of it. It's a good thing to know – and perhaps it will come in really handy one day!' So we found ourselves on much closer terms.

The small, modest manor house in Lasbeck – there were many such unpretentious manor houses in East Pomerania – was not big enough for the many wedding guests on 2 June 1939. In earlier generations it had been the estate manager's house. So for his eldest daughter's wedding Uncle Herbert had a wooden barn built immediately opposite the house on a stretch of turf that was 'kept short' by a flock of sheep. It could be moved later to a different site

---

* Ernst Wilhelm Baron von Schlabrendorff (1719–1766).

for practical purposes. So the wedding banquet would take place in the barn and the former manager's house would have to do for music and dancing after the meal.

For the civil wedding the bridal pair had to seek out the potato distillery, as the chief distiller held the office of Registrar and naturally enough he too was bound to perform the duty of all Registrars in the German Reich, by presenting the bridal pair at the end of the ceremony with Adolf Hitler's literary legacy, *Mein Kampf*. 'My Struggle' – what an apt title for the start of a young married life! Not to mention the fact that the author was paid a royalty by the state for every copy.

One little oddity about Lasbeck should not go unremarked. While, as a rule, the entrances to Prussian manor houses were decorated with the family coat-of-arms or the initials of the builder, Lasbeck had a fanlight window above the entrance door which admitted a little light to the hall. This window was decorated with the figure '1848', carved in wood. It was probably just the year of its construction, and yet no Bismarck and – as far as we know – no Pole has to this day felt impelled to remove the reference to a year of such eminent importance and conflict for Germany, though its removal would have been a matter of minutes.

So it was under that symbolic '1848' that we walked through to the dance after the wedding banquet. Father and daughter opened it with a waltz, all the guests clapping to the rhythm. Then the music for the second dance began and everyone waited for the bridal pair to begin, but Fabian made not the slightest move to ask his wife to dance. I went over to remind him of this 'duty' and he replied quite matter-of-factly that he did not dance. He asked us, her cousins, to take his place in the bridal dance. Luitgarde told us blithely that it had all been arranged with her husband beforehand.

And as so often at weddings, those who were not dancing stood around with others, getting to know the 'new family'.

I asked the young bridegroom where the honeymoon was to be and was astonished when he said 'England'. 'Fabian, you're crazy,' I burst out involuntarily. 'You can't finance a honeymoon with a foreign currency allowance of 10 marks each! Or are you turning out to be some sort of financial genius?' Unmoved, but with a grin, he replied that he did not need more than twenty marks because he had friends in England who had invited him and his wife to stay. They were descendants of friends of Baron von

Stockmar, who had been Queen Victoria's adviser for many years. He himself was related to Stockmar.

So we now had a very unusual cousin in the family, who had had himself invited to stay on his honeymoon by English friends. The sun was still up when we said goodbye to the bridal couple, who wanted to be in Berlin before evening. I had brought my accordion and we sang: '*Muss i denn, muss i denn zum Städtele hinaus*'. If it was to be a sea voyage, if only across the Channel, one could hardly expect that charming farewell song to be played on the ferry from the Hook of Holland, so we sang it ourselves for the two travellers to England.

Only when the war was over did Fabian and Luitgarde tell me that they had used their honeymoon as camouflage for an important political mission. At the Casino-Gesellschaft in Berlin, a liberal-conservative club in Bendlerstrasse, where he also had meetings with Ewald von Kleist-Schmenzin, Fabian had met the English journalist Jan Colvin. The three had got to know each other in the early 30s, and it was Colvin who, with his first-class political contacts in London, had made the preparations for Kleist-Schmenzin's peace mission to London in 1938, in agreement with the British Ambassador to Berlin, Neville Henderson. Kleist's journey had been fruitless, but by now English politicians must have recognised Hitler's true character. The threat of war was now far greater than in 1938 and the success of Munich had actually made Hitler all the more determined to pursue his expansionist policies.

My Stettin friends, Yorck and Oster, and I all suspected that war was coming, but Fabian knew there would be war. He had information on '*Fall Weiss*'*. This was the cover name under which in April, that is soon after the occupation of the rest of Czechoslovakia, Hitler had given the Wehrmacht instructions to prepare for an assault on the Free State of Danzig and on Poland: deadline 1 September 1939.

Once again it was Jan Colvin who took the initiative. This time he suggested to Kleist-Schmenzin that Fabian von Schlabrendorff should be sent to England for this far riskier peace mission. Kleist could not be sent twice, and someone else – perhaps more persuasive? – must now make the attempt. It was a stroke of genius to camouflage the trip with a honeymoon, an event which would

* Translator's note: literally, Case White. All major operational plans were code-named with a colour.

nip any hint of suspicion in the bud. And the young bridgegroom's great-grandfather, who had been so greatly respected in England, could open many doors for his descendants, even then!

On the evening of their wedding day the two newly-weds from Lasbeck took up their reservations in the Hotel Esplanade in Berlin, not far from the Potsdamer Platz. It seems a stroke of destiny now, that only a few hundred metres from the Esplanade, in the cellars of the Gestapo headquarters in Prinz Albrecht Strasse, Fabian was to be tortured almost to death by the vile instruments of the SS. In retrospect it also seems uncanny that, only a few metres to the right of the Esplanade, Fabian would one day be standing before Hitler's bloody judge of the People's Court, Roland Freisler, when an English bomb despatched this personified perversion of a judge into the next world, while the accused survived.

In London the two honeymooners first met the British ex-prime minister and leading Liberal politician Lloyd George. After the war they gave me a vivid description of the meeting.* Lloyd George had made a clear assessment of Hitler and his plans for war, but had spoken disparagingly of the British Prime Minister, Chamberlain. We could expect nothing from him that would impress Hitler.

Nevertheless, the newly-weds succeeded in being invited by Winston Churchill to his country house in Westerham. Churchill was a Conservative member of the House of Commons and a vigorous critic of government policy. Lloyd George had already told them that if it actually came to war with Germany, Churchill would be the man to lead Great Britain.

When the visitors reached Westerham, Churchill was standing in front of his house with his bricklayer's trowel and apron, working on a wall. After he had changed he had tea with them indoors, talking mainly to Luitgarde because he had discovered that she was a Bismarck. He showed them a photograph of the former Chancellor from his father's papers, signed by Bismarck.

Then the two men withdrew and had a long talk, finding at once that they agreed in their judgement of Hitler. When Churchill asked how the German Führer might still be stopped, Fabian told him that the only language that could influence Hitler now would be for the British Fleet to cross the Channel into international

* See also Fabian von Schlabrendorff, *Begegnungen in fünf Jahrzehnten*, Hamburg 1975, pages 138–141.

waters off Heligoland. But Churchill said no: that was not the policy of Chamberlain, the Prime Minister in office, who continued to believe in the power of the desire for peace.

Today – nearly half a century later – I see the fatalism with which we lived through the last weeks of peace in the summer of 1939 as quite unreal. Of course it was not the first crisis we had experienced, and no doubt the majority of Germans did not find the situation particularly unusual, having grown used to the subsequent recoveries. Why should it be different this time? And if it really was to be a 'shooting war' rather than a 'war of flowers', surely Poland would be quickly dealt with. In those days most of our people were so 'unpolitical' that they were quite unaware of the threat of conflict reaching far beyond Poland.

Working on this book, I have been to many archives and historical institutes to check up on my facts. Fortunately, my memory is still fresh enough to enable me to record the events most important to me, but I was still shocked when after almost half a century I found myself one day in the Press Institute of the Free University of Berlin, holding the *Völkischer Beobachter* of 11 June 1939 in my hand. During the Nazi period it had been a torment to me to read this official party paper; I stopped reading it. Now I was seeing that day's edition for the first time. On the front page there is a heading: 'European interim stocktaking'. Europe is divided into groups, with the German Alliance, the 'Axis', put first. Its members are: Germany, Italy, Albania and Libya (both occupied by Italy).

The 'friendly' countries follow: Spain, Yugoslavia, Hungary and Slovakia.

Then the 'neutrals' are listed: Belgium, The Netherlands, Denmark, Norway, Sweden, Finland, Estonia, Latvia, Lithuania, Bulgaria and Switzerland.

Then comes the 'British encirclement front': France, Great Britain and Poland.

This 'European interim stocktaking' of 11 June 1939 clearly reveals Hitler's incredible arrogance and unparalleled cynicism.

In those weeks my brother and I were faced with the question whether, in the event of war, one of us should have himself classified as 'indispensable'. The edible oil factory was among the businesses 'vital to war work' and the continuity of its management was crucial to the food industry. We talked to our father and agreed that neither my brother nor I should put in an application for 'reserved occupation' status. All three of us were of course among those who despised Hitler's warmongering, but we would have regarded it as shameful to evade our duty to serve our country. None of us wanted war, but if it were to come without our doing, that would be our fate. And if our workers and employees had to go to war, then we neither would nor could escape the same fate. That had been taken for granted in our families for generations, and Hitler would have to derive what benefit he could from that outlook. As regards the management of our factory, the decisions on staff were taken promptly. There were enough people who were only too glad to be in a reserved occupation. My brother and I were not National Socialists and had there been any kind of democratic opposition we would both have belonged to it. If we should ever be called upon for other, unforeseeable reasons, then there was not the slightest doubt – for me at least – where my allegiance would lie. For me this too was a cogent reason not to 'dodge' now.

Early in July my friend Heinrich Yorck told me I should expect to be called up on 1 August and that under the mobilisation plan I had been put down as Assistant Adjutant to the 2nd Anti-tank Battalion. I was glad, because I would not be going into the field with the reserve, but with the old, active Stettin Division, where I had friends and acquaintances. If war was coming, that could only be to the good.

Once again the post brought me an invitation to a family wedding: on 15 July Klaus von Bismarck from Kniephof would be marrying our cousin Ruth-Alice von Wedemeyer in Paetzig, in the Neumark. There were a lot of weddings that summer, no doubt because of the uncertainty over our future.

Hans von Wedemeyer and his wife Ruth, my mother's youngest sister, wanted to give their eldest daughter a party which future generations would still be talking about. It was meant to be a 'fairy-tale' wedding, and so it was.

The village church, a medieval quarry-stone building, was far too small for the number of guests expected, since it had to contain not only the guests but also the families of the agricultural labourers. So – just in time – a famous church architect from Hamburg was asked to remove the eastern apex and to build a semi-circular apse in the same material across the whole width of the nave. Without altering the character of the centuries-old fortified church, a considerably more generous and very beautiful internal space was created.

A huge crowd of guests had been invited for three days. The simple, typical Mark Brandenburg manor house was not big enough for such a crowd. It did have electric light, but no running water, and the financing of the church extension had taken precedence with the devout Pietist family. In the dressing-rooms and guestrooms of the manor house there were still china wash-basins and ewers on their marble slabs. In the cloakrooms there were even now closets in which certain seating facilities were emptied once a day, at crack of dawn, down at the sewage pit by the cowsheds. For Paetzig these were all things of minor importance.

More than a hundred and fifty relations and friends from both families arrived, included our two 'English travellers', Fabian and Luitgarde Schlabrendorff. Grandmothers, aunts and uncles stayed in the manor house's few guestrooms, those relations who were 'less close' were put up in inns and houses in the neighbouring villages, while pallets had been prepared on granary floors for the young people.

The engaged couple both came from houses famous for their hospitality in Pomerania and the Neumark.

If this wedding was to be fairy-like, then naturally a fairy-tale drama must be performed. My sister, so well versed in fantasy and poetry, had taken on the job of dramatising the Grimm Brothers' *Frog King*. And of all people I, a philistine in all theatrical matters, had been chosen by the family for the role of Frog Prince: with this miscasting the whole thing could only go wrong. It went wrong at the very first rehearsal, when I got stuck not once but several times, missing my cues, because my sister's version seemed to me too jerky, not to say too 'modern'. Under the shapeless cardboard mask of a toad, hired from Verch, the Berlin theatrical costumiers, I felt as if I were wearing a diving mask and sweated blood and water, so to speak. But there was worse to come.

My partner Maria, the bride's younger sister, was to play the bride. Unlike me, she had learned her part perfectly, but when we reached the high point of the dramatic action, when the princess was supposed to turn the frog back into a prince with a kiss, our dear little cousin rebelled. Instructions from the producer rained down on us, there were offers of compromise, encouragements ('Chin up, chin up!') and someone actually cried: 'Don't put on airs!'; nevertheless our dear Maria stuck to her guns and it ended in tears – but not with a kiss.

So next day our play went on stage without its climax, in other words, without a kiss, not even on the cardboard mask!

But the large audience seemed more amused by the absence of a kiss than if the stage directions had been followed. Involuntary comedy is sometimes even funnier.

In the park at Paetzig there was a fine, broad avenue of chestnuts, the beautiful trees trimmed for generations in such a way that the avenue had become an enclosed, shady space, a magical, living festival hall. In the middle of it carpenters had set up a dance floor surrounded by tables and seats and with a platform beside it for the musicians.

Three evenings we danced away, with events in between, as if we were at a festival of the arts. My mother's Steinway concert grand was in the manor house (it was too big for her Berlin flat) and on it she played Brahms' Piano Trio in B major with her two sons.

Like many other cousins and the two of us, Klaus Bismarck was on the Reserve of Officers. According to Prussian custom, the soldier wore uniform on his wedding day, even officers on the reserve, who actually wore dress uniform. Thus, when we formed up for the procession into the church, Klaus appeared with his bride on his arm, wearing his helmet, sword, dress tunic, aiguillette and riding boots.

There was a festive bridal procession through the park to the church, which was dedicated on that day, with flower girls and pages, bridesmaids and bride's attendants – and at the organ was my mother, who had pulled out all the stops so that we would hear it even from the chestnut avenue.

A beautiful celebration followed – almost too beautiful, it seemed to me. And yet that is no doubt precisely why the image and the ceremony in the new, semi-circular apse are still vivid in my mind after so many years.

The great day was a fairy-tale to the end. We celebrated, we danced to our hearts' content. We were, quite simply, happy, for we had made up our minds to be nothing but happy. This wedding on 15 July 1939 – everyone knew it, but no one said it – was a farewell party, because many of us had already received our call-up orders for August 1st. How else was one to celebrate a wedding, when one knew that war was imminent – when one could not but know that death would take its toll of our happy band? Yes, we were quite consciously celebrating our farewell to peace.

PART II

THE START OF WORLD WAR II

July 1939 – July 1940

The Start of World War II

To Poland

The morning after the Paetzig wedding I made a detour via Berlin on my way to Stettin, to take my mother home. I still had a suit hanging in a cupboard in her flat in case I had to change my clothes in a hurry, arriving from Stettin, but on that day the good suit was missing. My mother was rather embarrassed, saying she had lent it to someone but she thought it would be back very soon. When I asked who the happy man now wearing my best tailor-made suit might be, I learned that far from being a 'happy man', it was her cousin Achim von Rohr from Demmin in West Pomerania, who was escaping from the Gestapo. The Gestapo had entered through the front door of the manor house at Demmin, while he had escaped just in time on the garden side. She did not know how he had travelled from Demmin, but he had said he must assume that the police would guess he was in Berlin. So she had given him my suit, as well as a hat and coat of mine, so that when darkness fell he could leave the house in my clothes, continue his flight and cover his tracks.

I asked what the National Socialists had against Uncle Achim. 'I didn't ask him anything about it,' said my mother. 'He's no Nazi, after all, in fact he hates them and has no intention of carrying out the orders of the party bosses in Demmin. That's enough to make them harass him, or lock him up, as they have done before. So I help him when he asks for help. In any case you must have enough to wear in Stettin and since you'll soon be wearing nothing but uniform you might bring me some more of your wardrobe at the next opportunity. One never knows who else we may have to help.'

Since 1 August I had been a soldier again. Generous short leaves were granted, so I made one or two farewell visits to Berlin as well. I went to Fasanenstrasse and rang the bell to the ground floor at number 68. My visit was less to the esteemed ballet mistress of the State Opera *Unter den Linden*, Tatiana Gsovsky, who ran her ballet school there, than to her assistant in the master class, Inge Schweitzer, with whom I was very friendly. I not only found both ladies at home, but also had the pleasure of listening to the pianist Maria Kalamkarian, who was already at the piano and whom I had previously met as Feodor Chaliapin's accompanist. Tatiana Gsovsky ended the lesson – all too soon for me – and invited us to tea in her flat. The samovar was already steaming and it was a delight to watch the grace with which our hostess prepared the tea.

Scarcely had the cups been filled when she burst out explosively: 'Have you actually gone crazy, making war?' she cried. 'How do you know we are going to make war?' I asked. 'The sparrows are whistling it from the rooftops!' she cried, 'or isn't it true?' I told her it was true, but I had never yet met anyone who wanted war. 'Then why are you wearing uniform?' I tried to explain, using the famous phrase about our 'bounden duty' to our Fatherland. She interrupted me: 'Please stop, it sounds like my childhood in Petersburg. The officers talked of nothing but duty and obedience then, and the Revolution came and we were glad to save our lives. You officers should get together and stop the war by force! That's your duty now!'

'Does that mean 'I asked, 'that you don't think it wrong for me to be an officer?' 'Of course not!' she cried.

How simple, how natural it sounded, from the mouth of that great artist! I was left with an unforgettable picture: this beautiful, passionate young Russian, of the family of the Princes Galitzine.

Then she suddenly struck a different note: 'You will kneel down before me now,' she said, quite calmly and seriously, 'and receive my blessing.' Rather painfully moved, I said: 'My dear Tatiana, that is charming of you, but it is too theatrical for me' As if she had not heard my objection, she repeated: 'Kneel down in front of me now.' I shook myself, not wanting to be a spoilsport, when she was so serious. So I got up and knelt on one knee while she made the sign of the Cross over me three times, kissed me as they had done in Petersburg and told me to stand up. 'You will come home safe and sound from the war. And now we'll have tea.'

On the way back to Stettin I took the road through the Brandenburg Gate. I loved that beautiful edifice, with a kind of personal sentimentality, especially since I had climbed it on 6 March 1933. As I approached it, coming from the Grosser Stern, I

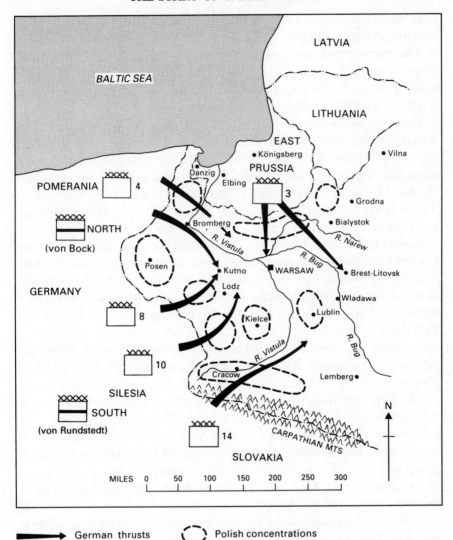

MAP 1 The Polish Campaign 1939

could see a huge, white banner spanning the full width of the Gate, and as I came closer I read the inscription in huge black letters: 'Führer command – we follow'.) What things that gate had witnessed in its mere one hundred and fifty years of existence – and what it would witness in the future!

One evening we rolled across the Oder bridge by the old town of Stettin towards East Pomerania. The population scarcely noticed that 'their regiments' had left the town. None of the brave mood of August 1914, no cheers, no flowers. We stole away in darkness.

The march led straight across my beloved East Pomerania, where the people stood in front of their houses in the villages, waving to us. In the vicinity of Schlochau, not far from the Polish frontier, we found billets and awaited events.

Exciting news came through: on 24 August we learned that Reich Foreign Minister Ribbentrop had signed a non-aggression pact in Moscow with Joseph Stalin, Hitler's deadly enemy. We were playing our evening game of poker in a country house when we heard the news, put our cards aside and argued for hours. There must be more to this news item – Hitler and Stalin must have played for higher stakes than the price of Poland alone.

It was difficult, if not quite impossible for us to form a picture from the confusing information that reached us. One evening when it was already dark, we received orders to march and attack. Then, because we were maintaining radio silence, messengers on motor-bikes suddenly appeared beside the waiting columns. Everyone halt, back to quarters. It got on our nerves. The next evening we were back at our poker table. Our hostess, whose husband commanded a company with a different division, was invited to play with us. She financed her stake with her hen-house earnings. We lowered the stakes, playing with small coins, paper money was taboo. We only wanted to kill time, and a few good wines from the cellar played their part. The paymaster was revealed as our 'court jester', reviving us with macabre humour if there was not enough going on: 'You'll win no fortune if you tarry! You'll get no child unless you marry!' Our hostess doubled her working capital from the hen-coops that evening.

With all this I could only rejoice that our small group of officers was such that we could talk freely among ourselves. There were no fanatical National Socialists among us – one sensed the hand of Heinrich Yorck. Then, one evening in the middle of the jolliest poker game, came the order to attack. It was 31 August 1939.

For the second time within a few days, the companies rolled towards the frontier in total darkness, without lights. Since there were no reports of Polish armour in our reconnaissance sector, we pulled off the road into a thick wood. Our commanding officer, Major Becker, ordered me to go forward with a small radio unit, to report back when radio silence was lifted. I strained my eyes in the darkness, trying to follow the road, until I thought the frontier must be right ahead of us. I called a halt and went on on foot. After a few paces three soldiers appeared before me in the darkness. The frontier was about ten metres ahead, a sergeant of our infantry whispered. The soldiers had removed their helmets in order to hear better. Nothing moved. It was as silent as a graveyard. Only a dog could be heard howling in the distance.

In the East, light slowly began to dawn. Now we could see the German and Polish frontier posts and beyond them a large meadow and – probably a kilometre away – the first trees. Between them we glimpsed the roofs of a village. I searched the area intently, my heart beating so hard that I had difficulty in looking through my binoculars. Nothing indicated that anyone over there was expecting the attack.

The war against Poland was scheduled to begin at 04.45 hours. Our watches had been synchronised yet again.

I stared at my watch. The sun was not yet visible on the horizon. Then at last the large hand reached the given hour.

Abruptly, salvo upon salvo of heavy artillery fire started up to our right at a distance of perhaps ten kilometres. Ahead of us on the meadow and in the village, all was calm, nothing stirred.

Then our infantry began to move up from the rear and pass by me, carrying their rifles under their arms as if they were going hunting. At the frontier posts they swarmed off to left and right. Not a shot was fired. Suddenly one of our battalion commanders from the 5th Infantry Regiment appeared beside me. 'Good morning, Stahlberg,' he cried, 'so what do you say now?' 'Nothing at all, Major,' I called back. What was I supposed to say? We knew each other well. 'You're absolutely right!' he shouted, and turning his head again, gave me a wave. I watched him as he reached the meadow, shaking his head pensively.

Our infantry disappeared into the trees beside the village. Even now no shots had been fired in our area, though we could still hear the rumble of our artillery in the distance. By now the field track by which I was standing had turned into a main road. Column after column rolled by, for well over an hour. I looked at the soldiers' faces, seeing and hearing no excitement, no cheers; they were silent, their faces generally expressionless. '*Ave Caesar, morituri te salutant** came into my mind. After a time the vanguard of my division appeared. No Polish armour was reported, so we still had

---

* In Ancient Rome, when the gladiators marched into the arena, they greeted Caesar with the words: 'We who are about to die salute you, Caesar!'

nothing to do. Later in the morning we heard the broadcast of Hitler's speech from the German Reichstag in the Kroll Opera House: 'Fire has been returned since 4.45 a.m.!' he screamed. Major Becker, Heinrich Yorck and I looked at each other.

We drove from village to village, as if we were on manoeuvres. Here and there people were standing at their doors, but for us the exercise was without incident. Only once an old-fashioned biplane came towards us, clattering loudly. I had last seen such aircraft as a small boy, at air displays in Berlin-Staaken. We could clearly see the red and white Polish national emblem and the silhouettes of two pilots sitting one behind the other. A German fighter was coming up behind the Pole and after a single burst of fire, the old biplane caught alight and plunged to the ground. In the distance we could see the cloud of smoke which continued to rise from the forest for some time.

On the second day, I was on my motorbike on the way to divisional headquarters. A crowd of German soldiers was standing in the middle of a village, gazing silently in one direction. I stopped and asked someone what was going on. 'An execution,' came the answer. When the village was occupied shots had been fired from an attic and there had been losses. The house had been stormed and two marksmen had been found in the attic. They had been wearing civilian clothes without insignia or armbands, their weapons and empty cartridge cases had been found: hunting guns, cases of shotgun cartridges. This was a clear infringement of the international rules of The Hague Convention on Land Warfare. The divisional court martial had met, the two Poles had confessed and the sentence was now being carried out. I looked over the heads of the curious onlookers. At that moment the salvo from the firing squad cracked out: the first deaths I witnessed in that war.

On the third day – it was 3 September – Heinrich Yorck brought the news from the divisional staff that Great Britain and France had declared war on Germany. Great Britain – that meant the Empire, Australia, India, New Zealand. It probably meant Canada and South Africa. It meant World War Two! Would it also mean the United States of America? We stared dumbly at each other.

Heinrich Yorck had other news as well, because he had also talked to Achim Oster, adjutant of our 2nd Artillery Regiment, and Achim had telephoned his father. Hitler had received a severe shock when the bad news came through. No wonder, because he

now had the war which he had described in his book and at
thousands of party gatherings as 'the great crime of German policy
against the German people' in a world war: war on two fronts.

Yorck brought still more news: Heinrich von Weizsäcker, the
second son of the Secretary of State at the Foreign Office, had
fallen in the division next to ours. For Yorck, Oster and me,
Heinrich von Weizsäcker's death held a tragic symbolism, because
his father was one of the few high officials in the German Reich
who had done everything possible within their own sphere of
activity to prevent this war. Naturally only those close to him or his
family knew this. The news of Heinrich von Weizsäcker's death
was also the first to touch my brother and me personally. We had
taken dancing lessons together in a happy, familiar circle of friends
that included Carl Friedrich, Adelheid and Heinrich von
Weizsäcker. Their much younger brother Richard had been given
the job of winding up the gramophone for us. We knew Heinrich as
the brilliant, musically gifted one – he and my brother had been
taught together by the cellist Richard Klemm. The first of our
circle of friends was dead.

In the next few days – we were still advancing, without having
fired a shot – an order came over the radio: 'Turn right off the
road, stop, wait.' We knew that meant that a force urgently needed
further forward was to be let through ahead of us. Sure enough, an
armoured reconnaissance car came up behind us, travelling at high
speed. It was like our own reconnaissance unit's car, but without
our divisional insignia. From the turret protruded the figure of a
general, unrecognisable in his dust-goggles, but round his neck we
spotted the highest Prussian military order, *Pour le Mérite*. As the
dust-cloud moved away we could hear more vehicles approaching
and a large, shapeless open Mercedes appeared, travelling at the
same high speed – a model we had not seen before, a three-axle
cross-country vehicle. In the front passenger seat sat Hitler, in grey
uniform, which was also new to us. A few more vehicles followed
close behind, at breakneck speed, considering the dust-cloud from
the first vehicle. 'That too,' remarked Yorck drily, 'like Lützow's
wild hunt'. I wanted to know who the general in the leading scout
car had been. We would find out at once, Yorck told me, going
over to the radio car behind us. He returned soon afterwards with
the news that it was a general called Rommel, whom the Führer
had selected as commandant of his headquarters. 'Probably
because of his Prussian order,' Yorck added.

Soon afterwards I had a little adventure, something that would have been called a 'baptism of fire' a century before.

We were on the Tucheler Heide, a large wooded area, and our battalion had still had no contact with enemy. For a reason that escapes me, I had to contact one of our companies which was on the march some way off. In our section we were already on the verge of not taking the war seriously, otherwise I would not have travelled without an escort on my favourite means of locomotion, a new two-cylinder BMW motorbike. It fascinated me to have it between my knees and let it go, so I got into my leather coat, put on my steel helmet and drove away. Soon a ruler-straight stretch of road through the woods appeared ahead of me and I 'let her rip'.

Suddenly I heard a strange sound, clear and metallic. My first thought was that my machine had piston trouble. My memory of what happened next is still vague: the front of the machine buckled and I must presumably have somersaulted with it.

When I had collected my wits to some extent, I found myself lying with aching limbs in a roadside ditch. I crawled up the embankment until I could just see the road. There at some distance lay my beautiful machine, its front tyre and rim obviously shot to pieces. What was I to do? I had to assume that somewhere the machine-gun that hit my motorbike so accurately was waiting to fire again. So I decided to wait too, and put my revolver ready beside me. Eventually, one of our own vehicles would appear, because the Tucheler Heide was marked on our situation map as being completely occupied by German troops. But I confess I was not feeling too good: if Germans were still being shot at here, behind the German front, then the courageous marksman might suddenly appear before me in person.

I was lucky. My heart certainly began to pound when I caught the sound of an engine in the distance, but then I saw the bonnet of one of our open cars, travelling in the same direction as I had been. The driver had already slowed down at the sight of the motorbike lying in the road. Now he stopped beside me and with the speed of light my BMW was hoisted on to the back of the truck. The soldiers – part of our division – told me that they too had been fired on by a machine-gun about a kilometre back, but had not been hit. Within a few days I had further evidence that Poles were still fighting, though their situation was hopeless.

One evening we bivouacked in a village where I found an old Polish cobbler, who repaired my leather coat. It had a long tear right across the back. That coat stayed with me as a kind of talisman until the end of the war.

It must have been on about the tenth or twelfth day of war when we received the order to turn and drive in a northerly direction, towards East Prussia. We reached the area of Rastenburg and noticed, with astonishment, that the German population took virtually no notice of us during the march. Despite the military successes of our armies, this war was still not popular. Then we swung southwards, recrossing the Polish frontier, and drove in darkness through the Polish town of Lomza. But what a state it was in! Lomza was a depopulated ruin, with the smell of decay in the air.

At the next bivouac we heard that Lomza had been heroically defended, until the new German dive-bombers, known as Stukas, were brought in. Major Becker commented that in 1917 he had seen places similarly reduced to rubble in France, but they had been fought over for weeks or months, while our new weapons had apparently caused all this in a few hours.

The next afternoon we received our first operation order. The 2nd Anti-tank Battalion had to get to a village a few hours away without delay. There was a prison camp there, organised and guarded by an SS formation. We were to take over that camp today, and as quickly as possible.

Our commanding officer informed the company commanders and drove ahead with Yorck and me, together with the radio car and a few despatch riders. When we reached the village a grisly sight met our eyes. In a marshy meadow lying in a depression beside the village a plough had marked out a square about one hundred metres in length. Into this square had been herded a crowd probably numbering thousands, mostly Polish soldiers, but also civilians, old men, women and children. They sat or lay so closely packed that there was scarcely any grass to be seen. At a distance of about thirty metres a second furrow had been ploughed and at the corners of the outer square were machine-guns mounted on tall tripods which, by the time we arrived, had already reaped a rich harvest. This was obviously the reason why we had been urged to make so much haste.

On the open break surrounding the camp lay at least fifty dead. An SS-man told us that the men at the machine-guns had orders to shoot at once if any of the prisoners crossed the inner line, otherwise it would not be possible to keep the 'upper hand' over the thousands.

A deafening noise met us from the camp, although we were standing about a hundred metres away on higher ground at the edge of the village. It sounded like thousands of people all crying for help at once. SS-men in grey uniforms came up to us – it was the first time I had seen grey-uniformed SS – and asked if we were the expected relief. We agreed to take over the camp as quickly as possible and insisted that the machine-guns were not to fire one more shot. 'On your own responsibility!' one of them told us.

Major Becker went to our radio vehicle to describe the situation to our companies and divisional staff and to arrange for the most essential needs of the thousands of prisoners to be met: food, doctors and nurses.

Yorck and I went down to the outer edge of the camp. First the prisoners had to be told that help was on the way. When we reached the outer furrow the noise swelled and we heard over and over again the German word 'hunger', chanted in spoken choruses. We raised both hands – it must not look like a Nazi salute – and at once there was silence. Yorck began to speak. In his clear, metallic voice, speaking very slowly, syllable by syllable, so that as many as possible should understand him, he told the crowd that we were army officers and would be taking over the camp in a few hours, that food trucks were on the way, that we had also called for doctors and nurses, and would do everything in our power to help them. We also wanted to try to get prisoners of war moved to a proper camp, the next day if possible. We did not yet know where to find clean water and in order to discuss this and all the necessary details with them we therefore asked that within ten minutes, if possible, three German-speaking deputies should be sent out to us. We had the promise of the previous guards that the machine-guns at the corners would not fire another shot, and anyone wishing to relieve himself should go on to the break round the camp. But we must be able to rely on their complying with our request, since we had not yet assumed responsibility.

Then we walked back to the edge of the village, where we found Major Becker surrounded by SS-men, his set face expressing bewilderment and contempt. We rescued him from his entourage and when we got back to our own vehicles, reported on our efforts to enter into a dialogue with the prisoners.

At the end of the agreed ten minutes, Yorck and I returned to the prisoners and stopped again on the outer plough furrow. Opposite us some of the Poles waved, but still did not dare to enter the fatal strip between us. So Yorck and I waved our white handkerchiefs at the SS machine-gun guards to left and right and walked to the middle of the strip. There three elderly men in civilian clothes came to meet us, also waving white handkerchiefs. Together we walked up the slope, taking care to stop in full view of the crowd in the meadow.

Our commander now came up from the edge of the village with some despatch riders. No SS-men had been invited to accompany him: the prisoners must see that we distanced ourselves from them.

We now learned from the Poles that the camp had been in existence for four days, during which no food or drink had been provided. The prisoners had scraped holes in the ground with their hands and slaked their thirst with water from the ground. There were already many sick in the camp and a number of dead as well. There were doctors among them, but they had no medicines and no medical instruments. Most of the dead, who lay on the outer strip, were those who had tried to relieve themselves outside the camp, but some of them had been shot for attempting to escape, mostly by night, when lorries were stationed beside the machine-guns to light the death-strip with their headlamps.

The three Poles could not tell us how many people there were in the camp, but they said there must be several thousand. Since we had not yet been to the village behind us, it was from them that we first learned that the village was empty and most of its inhabitants were in the meadow camp. Only a few had been able to escape in time. The guard squads had apparently used the empty village as their quarters.

We told the three old men that we were bringing help and repeated that we were not with the SS, but when we tried to tell them how to identify the SS we found they already knew: 'Eagle on chest good, eagle on arm bad'.

Major Becker told them that as soon as the first of our companies arrived we would take over guard duties at once, first releasing all the old men, women and children. 'Please SS go first!' the men begged, and we promised.

The old men showed their gratitude and tried to kiss our hands, but they did not dare to return to the camp alone. I accompanied them to the inner line. The story of the rest of that day is quickly told. After we had taken over the camp and the SS had gone, our soldiers worked as if their lives depended on it. Those released moved back to the empty village, water-trucks shuttled incessantly, night and day, between the village and the camp. The entire food reserves of our four companies were unloaded at the edge of the village, the lorries returning at once to fill up again. Our own doctor went straight into the camp with his medical orderlies and helped where he could. Soon he too was back, to replenish his medical supplies. He gave indescribable reports of sick, wounded, dying and dead people. We asked the Poles to form some burial commandos and to bury the bodies in the village cemetery. Temporary hospitals were set up in the village school and church, the division sent us a whole medical unit. We did leave one or two of our tractors and machine-guns near the camp at night, but not a shot was fired: they had decided to trust us. Even before midnight we were able to announce that columns were on the way who would pick up the prisoners-of-war the next morning, so that in about twelve hours the camp would be dispersed.

Bleary-eyed and bemused, we travelled further south, trying to get our thoughts in order. Were the principles of The Hague Convention no longer to apply in this war? Was the treatment of civilians, the sick and wounded, not laid down in internatonal law? After all, the German Reich was one of the powers which had entered into the agreement, as early as 1899.

During the drive, Heinrich Yorck drafted a *Tatbericht* (a military charge on the grounds of a criminal offence) against the SS on his report block. He handed it to me sheet by sheet to read. I had difficulty in deciphering his handwriting and needed his help here and there, which gave us the opportunity to discuss some of the formulations. We were in agreement on the issue, but I tried to damp down the emotion in places. At the next bivouac an NCO typed out the report, which Major Becker signed without alteration. I was told to take the document to Division next morning.

I reported to the First General Staff Officer, the 'Ia', who read the report in my presence. Then he looked up and told me that Division had already heard of this affair and he had been expecting the report. But as the SS group was not a fighting unit it was not answerable to the division. It was probably not answerable to any military authority, never mind the jurisdiction of the Army. He would naturally lay the report before the Divisional Commander, but the procedure was predictable. The document would move 'up' through official channels, in other words to the Corps, Army

Headquarters, Army Group, and the High Command of the Army, (OKH) and finally, for reasons of competence, to the High Command of the Wehrmacht (OKW.)* And then? What court would be prepared to act against an SS unit?

It turned out just as we had expected. None of us was ever called as a witness, and to our knowledge our report of this monstrous crime never came before a court. After the campaign against Poland, I believe Hitler actually proclaimed an amnesty for all infringements.

At that time we were not clear about the status of this SS unit. Perhaps it was one of the first *Einsatzgruppen*, the notorious Task Forces of the Security Service (SD). Not until later were we to learn what lay behind this significant description.

The march continued, now in a south-easterly direction, without meeting the slightest resistance. We were approaching the town of Brest-Litovsk. According to the scant news that reached us, there was fighting round Warsaw far to the west and the pincers of the German forces operating from East Prussia and Upper Silesia would meet at Brest-Litovsk.

On 16 September we rested as if we were not at war but on manoeuvres, on the estate of a Prince Bielski, not far from Brest. We might almost have been on an East Pomeranian estate. According to our ideas, the style was not 'princely' at all, but simple and unassuming. The landowner offered us his guest rooms and invited the officers to eat with his family in the evening, where the conversation was in German and French.

During the meal, Yorck was called to the telephone by an orderly. After a few minutes he came back, grave-faced, and asked the commanding officer to join him in another room. The rest of us remained at table until they returned. Yorck went on with the conversation as if nothing had happened. Prince Bielski told us his memories of the peace negotiations at Brest-Litovsk between Germany and Russia at the end of the First World War. Soon, however, Yorck asked the princess to bring the meal to an end ahead of time, since important news had arrived.

Major Becker took the officers into the adjoining room, where he told them that we would be marching on again next morning, not

---

* Translator's note: OKH Oberkommando des Heeres; OKW Oberkommando der Wehrmacht.
These abbreviations were widely used in Germany and have been used throughout this translation for simplicity

to the East, but to Germany. The 2nd (Motorised) Infantry Division would be taken by train to the Frankfurt area immediately.

So it was war on two fronts! Had the French already attacked?

Then we learned the rest: the next morning the Russian Army would cross its western frontier into Poland. The future frontier between Germany and Russia would run here – the place we were in would become Russian.

This was terrible news. So Hitler and Stalin had decided to divide up Poland between Germany and Russia – the fourth partition of Poland in the history of that sorely afflicted people. The two dictators disposed of other countries as if we were living in the Middle Ages. And what would become of the western half of Poland? Apparently there were no longer to be any 'buffer states' between Germany and Russia. Would Hitler allow the remainder of Poland to disappear from the map? Question after question: our minds revolved round matters of the highest historical importance.

However, on that evening there was no more time for reflection and debate. There was a knock at the door: the landowner, who had heard rumours from the village. Becker dismissed the officers, apart from Yorck and myself, and we sat down. We told the prince that we would be withdrawing the next morning, back to Germany . . . 'I suspected that,' he said, 'I thought as much.' Then came a pause in which no one said a word, though we all knew what the others were thinking. Then the prince began: 'Can you tell me where the frontier between the Germans and the Russians is to run?' We could not tell him exactly. The words had been 'by Brest-Litovsk,' no more. After another long pause Yorck spoke: 'Have you friends or relations in Germany?' Prince Bielski seemed grateful that one of us had broached the subject, rather than he himself. 'Yes,' said the prince, 'a great many, in fact.'

Before 1917 he had had as many relations in Russia, but they had fled to the West during the Revolution. Those who had not wished, or had been unable, to escape had been murdered by the Bolsheviks. Now he too had decided to escape with his family. Cars and horses were available, but he could not decide which road to take, not knowing the military situation. Above all, he did not know whether the German authorities would let him pass.

Yorck, who was conducting the conversation on our side almost on his own, advised him to start packing at once, while we tried to find a solution to the undecided questions. But the prince should assume that no more people and luggage would be travelling than one truck could hold.

When we were alone, our commanding officer began half reluctantly, half anxiously, to tell Yorck that what he was apparently planning seemed to him enormously risky, and besides, this was not a matter for an adjutant but for the commanding officer, and he was to have it approved first by the divisional commander. Yorck overrode him: a divisional commander should not be troubled with 'these little things', an independent battalion commander must take the decision himself. 'Yes, but how do you see this, quite practically, Yorck?' Major Becker was helpless, it was too much for him.

His adjutant, on the other hand, already had a plan in mind: 'We'll release a truck and send it via East Prussia to Stuttgart, to Mercedes. The driver will have orders to pick up urgently-needed spares there, especially tracks for our tractors.' Still the commanding officer would not give in: 'Are you certain our workshop company has no spare tracks in stock, Yorck, and do you know whether Mercedes have the tracks we need?' Yorck parried at once: 'If not, Major, all the better, because then our driver will have to go on looking with the help of Mercedes until he has found the right tracks, and if we now have to march from Frankfurt to the Atlantic – with our Führer one must expect something of the kind – we shall be better off than a lot of other troops, because we shall have no more worries about our tracks.'

'Yorck, you really are a wonder!' cried Becker. But then came further misgivings. 'Just think, Yorck, what trouble we'll be in if the whole story comes out. I think it's simply too dangerous, both for the prince and for us. Think it over: a prince, and a Polish prince at that!' But by now Heinrich Yorck was in his stride: 'Well, Major, prince or no prince, it's all the same to me. He received us hospitably, when none of us knew what to expect. He is an educated, distinguished old gentleman, his daughters are well brought-up girls, his wife is a highly cultivated lady, his only son – he told me "confidentially" – is a Polish officer at the Front and the family has no news of him, they don't even know if he's still alive. If the Russians were to reach this village they would have the whole family "up against the wall". But if, contrary to expectations, the Russians do not get this far, it will be the SS who take over here one day. After our experience of the SS only a few days ago, I don't like to think what they would do with the family of a Polish prince.

Major, I am asking your permission to sign the documents for the drive to Stuttgart as adjutant, on the letterhead of the 2nd Anti-tank Battalion.'

Becker had listened to his adjutant's last words with a light in his eyes, proud of his imaginative, enterprising officer. He agreed to everything, making only one condition: the Commanding Officer, not the Adjutant, would sign.

Meanwhile the manor house came alive, as the family gathered their emergency luggage together at lightning speed. I met the prince returning from the village, where he had told his workers everything, inviting them to take two horses per family from his stables and pick out a wagon each. His people had talked it over among themselves and had decided to stay and try their luck with the Russians.

He himself, said Prince Bielski, and his family, would have only a little luggage, no more than they could carry if need be. Only one problem remained that he could not resolve himself. He asked me to get one of our soldiers to shoot and bury his five dogs at a place he would show me in the park. He could not bear to do it himself.

I put forward a different solution: I could ask if any of my friends was prepared to play guardian to a dog. The prince agreed and in short order I had found temporary owners for four dogs – for they were very beautiful dogs, two rough-haired dachshunds and two German wirehairs. Only the Great Dane, a splendid giant, was left and although I had no feeling for Danes, I took him on. 'Rex' travelled with me to Stettin and my caretaker in Pommerensdorfer Strasse was delighted to have found a good watchdog for the area round the oil factory.

In the darkness of night we waved goodbye to the departing Bielski family. I cannot forget the sight of the flat car, open at the back, with the family crouching inside it. They were the first refugee family I had seen.

A few hours later we too were moving westward. The radio had given us our destination, some villages between Hanau and Fulda. To save the tracks of our tractors, always our biggest technical headache, the division was to be transported by rail, with an advance party driving ahead. Yorck and I took that on, driving first to Stettin and relieving each other at the wheel without interrupting the journey. Even so, neither of us could get any sleep. Our battalion had not had to fire a single shot in Poland, but how much else we had experienced! After a first world war which had been paralysed in trench warfare, where the two sides had bled each other to death, we had returned to the classical style of mobile warfare. Whose could have been the mind behind this campaign? It could not have been Hitler, the eternal corporal of the first war, who had conducted this campaign on the pattern of Clausewitz and Moltke, we were all agreed on that. But this victory over Poland might only have been a foretaste.

And what was to become of Poland? Poland was beaten, but it still existed, and would continue to exist. More than 20 million Poles had a right to stay together, a right to live.

Our dreadful experience with the SS had made us profoundly thoughtful. Had this been simply a botch-up by a single unit, or was it a political weather portent? It left us deeply distrustful.

Travelling along lonely, peaceful roads in East Pomerania, we reached Stettin the next day and, after a few hours' sleep, I handed Rex over to his new master. When we parted, the dog jumped up, his front paws on my shoulders, and tried to lick my face. What depths a dog's instinctive nature holds.

Prince Bielski and his family reached West Germany, but I heard nothing further from them and I do not know if they survived.

Campaign in France

After Brest-Litovsk we had been moved with every evidence of great haste to the West of Germany. Apparently the highest authorities were uncertain whether the military forces astride the Rhine would be sufficient to prevent a French attack. Now we were among the farming villages of Hesse, trying to 'kill' time with the butcher in Hüttengesäss and the chemist in Langendiebach, who often drove to Frankfurt, returning successfully, his savings exchanged for carpets, silver and porcelain, as long as quality goods could still be found in the shops.

In November a rumour went the rounds from village to village: Hitler and his special train had stopped at Hanau, where he had taken the opportunity to stretch his legs. He had spoken to the engine driver, who had plucked up courage to ask the great man: '*Mein Führer*, when will the war be over? When can we go home again?' And Hitler had replied: 'At Christmas time'.

Autumn in Hesse was followed by winter weeks in the Eifel, where Yorck and I drove down to Bad Bertrich and had our backs scrubbed by the women attendants at the thermal baths. There were no visitors to the Spa. In fact, the place was preparing to become a hospital.

In the New Year came another move, back to the far side of the Rhine, to the source of the Selterwasser in the Taunus Mountains. Were these troop movements strategic ruses for the benefit of the Allies?

Then came alarming news: Hitler's treaty partner, Stalin, had had his appetite whetted by the tasty meal of half Poland. Exploiting the fact that, for the foreseeable future, Germany would be tied up in Western Europe, the Red Army attacked peaceful little Finland on the last day of November 1939. Throughout the winter, the Finns maintained a heroic defence against the Russians, while the world held its breath. The Finnish David defied the Russian Goliath, until a compromise, favourable to the Soviet Union, was reached in March 1940.

In April 1940, the daily Wehrmacht report announced that the German Navy had sailed for the North, Denmark had been occupied, offering no resistance, but the Norwegians were defending their country courageously. Our troops had forestalled the British, not for the sake of the northern flank alone, but because of Swedish steel, which was exported via Narvik. No modern war can be conducted without steel. Finally, Norway was in German hands from Oslo to Narvik; the war unleashed by Hitler had now taken on European dimensions.

Then the tension was released for us as well. On the night of 9 May 1940 came the order to attack, not only France, but also Luxembourg, Belgium and The Netherlands, all neutral countries. Was this a repetition of the 'Schlieffen Plan' of August 1914, to encircle Paris, the heart of France, from the North with a strong right wing via neutral Belgium? Or would we also have to make a frontal attack on the French Maginot Line, the most up-to-date line of defence in the world, which ran along the Franco-German frontier – the line that was regarded as impregnable?

None of these. On the contrary, we read – in those extracts which concerned our division – of a bold operational plan. The German armies would invade Luxembourg, Belgium and The Netherlands, foreshadowing the Schlieffen Plan in the first stage of the offensive, thus luring the main Allied forces northwards. Only then would the main thrust of the German forces have to cross the Meuse at Sedan, in order to reach the Channel with massed armour in the area of the mouth of the Somme, cutting off the Allies' main forces which were north of the Somme and advancing to the sea. Our division would be with 'Panzergruppe Kleist' (General Ewald von Kleist), which would lead the breakthrough to the West. We, the 2nd Infantry Division (Motorised), would be on the left wing of this Panzer Group, behind the rapidly advancing Panzer divisions, and would have to protect their left wing, facing south. A truly fascinating plan.

Major Becker, Yorck and I stood in front of the maps – our marching orders had not yet arrived – estimating distances. From the Taunus a good 250 kilometers as the crow flies to Sedan, and 450 to the Channel. Who could have devised this plan – certainly one of the boldest operational plans in the history of war, mobile warfare on the classical model, but now with motorised forces, tanks, radio and aircraft? We belonged to the Army Group which would probably decide this campaign, but we were still in the Taunus, more than 200 kilometres from the French frontier, while the attack was already taking place at this moment.

The plan involved risks. Would the armoured spearhead succeed in negotiating the Meuse below Sedan? Could the supplies for the Panzer Group – especially petrol and ammunition – be brought up quickly enough and in sufficient quantities through the narrow Ardennes? And could the flanks of the attacking spearhead, especially the southern one, be held against relief attacks by the French and British?

While we waited for the arrival of the company commanders for orders, we discussed another topic, one which we had often mentioned in past months, but which had now taken on absolute immediacy. In our area of command we would have to do our utmost to abide by the international rules of fairness and humanity in our campaign against our Western neighbours.

The high cultural standing of our neighbours, their monuments and art treasures must be spared and protected. We did not like the thought of having to fight Frenchmen and Englishmen, Yorck being particularly close to the French and I to the English. Of course, it was they who had declared war on us, but we regarded that less as a declaration of war on us Germans than as a declaration of war on the National Socialist régime.

Towards midday we received our marching orders and palm-sized stencils which were to be issued to the companies. All vehicles without exception were to be marked at once with a white

'K' front and back. K for Panzer Group Kleist. All the vehicles marked K, and there would be many thousands of them, had precedence.

The companies filtered on to the roads with admirable discipline. It was the most efficient military operation I had ever seen, running as if well and often rehearsed.

We crossed the Rhine at Neuwied, part of a gigantic motorised army that was moving westwards. Now and then roads were cleared for us of troops marching on foot or with horses, who stopped or camped in woods or fields until the columns with the white K had passed. We were expecting enemy air attacks against such a massive movement of our troops, but days were to pass before we saw the first French or English aircraft overhead. Up to now, only a few German fighters had roared over us.

We advanced very slowly, often with hour-long pauses, and were still in the Eifel area when we learned that our attacking spearheads had already fought their way across the Meuse at Sedan. We crossed the Luxembourg, Belgian and French frontiers, and as we rolled down into the Meuse valley we saw the first signs of battle. There must have been hard fighting here. We crossed the river on a German pontoon bridge, always moving West, forward, forward. And only now was our advance route lined to left and right with the ruins of a defeated French army: bullet-riddled vehicles, battered and burnt-out tanks, abandoned guns, an unending chain of destruction. Whenever we were held up we jumped down from our cars and subjected the design, dimensions and strength of the French equipment to keen inspection. Our verdict was: out of date, too weak, obviously too slow, hopelessly inferior to ours in technical terms. France must have fallen asleep on military technology.

Even now we had never been in battle. Only above us, in the brilliant blue sky of those days, there were fierce dogfights between German and Allied pilots. We followed them with our binoculars, admiring the courage with which the adversaries, whether Allied or German, hurled themselves at each other. Then, in the distance, we saw our new dive bombers in action for the first time. Engines howling, they plummeted like birds of prey towards their targets on the ground, pulling out at the last moment as they released their bombs. Everything we saw, on the ground and in the air, seemed to add up to great superiority on our side. On we rolled, always to the West.

On one of those days – it must have been about 17 May – we were ordered to make a reconnaissance to the South, something which was basically foreign to an anti-tank battalion. No doubt the High Command had their reasons – after all we were still marching as if on an exercise in peacetime, our flanks unprotected. I suggested to our commanding officer that I should undertake the job myself; my cavalryman's heart was up. I picked out a small reconnaissance troop: two motorbikes with sidecars, each with a crew of three, a small portable radio, machine pistols our only weapons. I impressed on my five companions that their job was to see a lot and defend themselves only in emergency.

It was a remarkable trip, through a depopulated countryside. The French leadership had evacuated the civilian population to the South, the villages were empty. Here and there we saw traces of war, but they were overgrown with grass – we were in one of the First World War battlefields.

I had excellent, reliable German maps in my pocket. Now the Somme-Aisne Canal appeared before us, still empty of people as far as the eye could see. A bridge was marked on my map at no great distance and we soon found it. We hid our two motorbikes in the bushes a few hundred metres back, leaving the two drivers with them. So I now had three men, with whom I intended to cross the canal on foot. We set out with no more than binoculars, pocket map and pistols, and above all without the tiresome steel helmets. Before stepping on to the exposed bridge we searched the area with our glasses. Nothing to be seen.

South of the canal we were still more cautious, because a highway was entered on my map at some distance from the canal and parallel to it. Behaving like hunters stalking their game, we reached a small hill, its top overgrown with bushes, from which we finally had an open view far across the country to the south. I could not believe my eyes: about 500 metres away a military column was marching from right to left – no, not just a column, an army on the march: infantry, light artillery, engineers, heavy horse-drawn artillery – the lot. Was it really conceivable that such troops should be allowed to march in the theatre of operations without any protection on their flanks? Were the French making the same mistake as we had almost made ourselves?

We four Germans lay in our bushes, looking through our glasses, counting the platoons, the companies, the light and heavy guns, the engineer equipment, while I filled page after page of my report

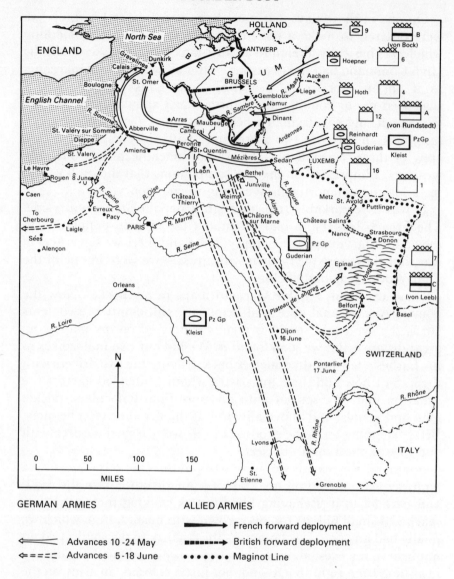

GERMAN ARMIES

ALLIED ARMIES

⟸⟸ Advances 10 -24 May
⟸===⟸ Advances 5 -18 June

■■■■▶ French forward deployment
▬▬▬▶ British forward deployment
●●●●●● Maginot Line

Map 2 Blitzkrieg 1940

pad. Our map revealed the probable goal of the enemy troops: a
further canal bridge, and to the north of it a wood. They might be
planning to form a bridgehead there, north of the Somme-Aisne
Canal. The woods would provide a night-time bivouac.

Now all we had to do was to make our way back again. Would
the bridge we had crossed still be unoccupied? Or would we have

to swim the canal? Would we be able to find our two motorbikes in the darkness?

We set off when it was dark and fortune favoured us. The bridge we had crossed was still open and we found our two companions easily. Then it was a matter of getting back as fast as the darkness would allow, and straight to the divisional command post. There, as expected, they were surprised and pleased with the results of our excursion and were generous with praise and acknowledgement of such accurate reconnaissance material. A battalion of the Stettin Infantry Regiment under the command of Lieutenant-Colonel von der Linde (decorated as a First World War lieutenant in 1914 with the Order *Pour le Mérite* for a successful raid on a fort) was ordered to launch a surprise attack on the French by night in their presumed forest bivouac. From what we heard, there were only small losses on both sides, but many prisoners were taken.

Becker and Yorck were amused when I reported our little adventure to them late at night, but my feeling was one of relief that my five companions and I had not had to fire a shot.

Only years later, after the end of the war, did I read that the French advance we had observed was part of an attempt to strike deep into the flank of Panzer Group Kleist. It had been led by a young general called Charles de Gaulle.

Amiens Cathedral

On 20 May 1940, Kleist's Panzer divisions reached the Channel at Abbeville. The Allies north of the Somme were now in the trap and the Germans had achieved their first operational goal.

On 21 and 22 May we too, still covering the south flank, were now involved in battles. The British tried to attack southward from the Arras area, with the French opposite them, close to us, doing the same to the North, but the operation failed, they did not make contact. On 22 May our Panzer divisions swung northwards along the Channel coast, heading for Boulogne, Calais and Dunkirk. Our division was to take over the defence of the front on the left bank of the Somme, with bridgeheads to the South on the outskirts of Amiens and Abbeville.

The last kilometres before Amiens ran across treeless plains, made unpleasant by the thought that enemy aircraft might suddenly appear and fire on our uncamouflaged marching columns. But our worries were unfounded: apparently the German

Luftwaffe was too much in command.

Then the valley of the Somme opened out before us. We looked down on Amiens as if from a military commander's hilltop and were overwhelmed by the awe-inspiring panorama of its city centre, dominated by the 13th-century Gothic cathedral.

We advanced into the town along the southern boulevard, our side-arms at the ready, but there was no resistance, not a soul moved in the streets. Apart from a few stray dogs and cats, the city seemed swept clean. The atmosphere was eerie: Amiens – so we were told – had more than 80,000 inhabitants, but where were they? We questioned divisional headquarters on the radio and were told that the whole population north of the Somme, including the townspeople, had been evacuated to the South of France. The French were apparently expecting the theatre of war to shift to where it had been from 1914 to 1918.

When our companies had marched off to take up their defensive positions south of Amiens and Abbeville, there was still the question of where we should establish battalion headquarters. Yorck solved the question quite simply: Amiens was the capital of the *département* of the Somme, so there must be a *préfecture* here somewhere. The beautiful old building was quickly found and our radio transmitters moved into the park behind the building. Major Becker, proud of his new dignity as Town Commandant of Amiens, took over the prefect's bedroom, Yorck rejoiced in the unparalleled quality of the bed in another bedroom, but in view of the glorious, high summer weather, I preferred the park and placed my airbed and sleeping-bag under a tree immediately beside an air-raid shelter dug by the French. After all, no one knew what might happen. Now we had everything we needed for our present well-being – with the exception of electricity and water, which were not available.

After everything had been organised and our radio contacts confirmed, Yorck and I made a tour of the town, full of impatience to view the cathedral, in particular.

We left the car in front of the famous west façade and sat down on the steps of a house opposite it. At some time in his school career, each of us had seen pictures of the five most important French cathedrals in lessons on the history of art, but there had to be a war for us to experience the incredible beauty and majesty of this façade.

It was not a quiet night. The sound of aircraft flying in from the

North-West woke me and I listened in suspense, wondering whether it would be advisable to move into the air-raid shelter beside me. Then came the crashes. I counted the explosions, six, eight, ten, perhaps even more. Then the sound of the engines faded, the aircraft had apparently turned and were flying north-westwards. They could only have been British, since there was no reason for our Luftwaffe to attack a town evacuated by the French and occupied by the Germans. I went back to sleep until woken by first light.

The first thing I was aware of in the cool of morning was the smell of fire. I woke my driver, informed the guard and set off for the cathedral, where the smell of burning was considerably stronger. Both of us left the closed car and saw a huge cloud of smoke ahead, travelling from the North-West straight over us and the cathedral. An evil presentiment seized me and we drove in the direction from which the smoke-cloud was coming.

We had not gone far before we were faced by the first burning houses and realised with horror that the north-west wind was driving the fire ahead of it. It had already leaped across several streets and would leap across the Somme, too, since the most of the houses were old and burned like tinder. On the north side of the cathedral stood a number of old half-timbered houses several storeys high. If they caught fire, it would be the end of the cathedral. The wind would send the tongues of flame and showers of sparks under the roof gutters of the building and the roof truss would be bound to catch fire. The thought of the destruction of the biggest Gothic cathedral in France, and one of the most beautiful at that, while we Germans were responsible for Amiens was unbearable. What could I do to prevent it?

I set off at high speed for the *préfecture*, to report what I had seen to our commanding officer, suggesting that the row of houses along the north side of the church would have to be removed. But how? They could not possibly be blown up without severely damaging the cathedral and its windows and sculpture. Or were we to do nothing and pray to God that things turned out for the best?

I suggested that the major send me to divisional headquarters to describe the situation to the general and ask if there were technicians in our regiments, engineers, firemen, explosives experts, demolition experts or fire chiefs who could advise and help. Major Becker agreed to everything and I set off at once. I received every support from the division, one of the companies of our 2nd Pioneer Battalion* would be sent to me immediately, since they were currently unemployed and their ranks included many of the technicians we would need.

On the return journey to Amiens, I wondered what else could be done to make use of the time until the pioneer company arrived. I kept looking across at the cloud of smoke over the town, which seemed to be growing. Should I seek out the fire station in the town? But what use would the engines of the municipal fire brigade be to us, since there was not a drop of water to be had from the hydrants – or should we look for pumps and use the water from the Somme? I abandoned these ideas at once, because something had to be done in a matter of hours. There would not be enough time.

Then I had an idea that sounded absurd: we should find hand-held fire extinguishers, not in order to advance with such insignificant implements on the holocaust approaching the church but, should the Pioneers actually decide to set light to the houses on the north side, to position our soldiers inside the cathedral roof with them as a preventive fire brigade. There might be some in the main department store.

Back in Amiens, I drove first to the fire, which had now leaped a further street and was still moving towards the cathedral. In the *préfecture* I mustered a troop of soldiers to open the department store, by force if necessary. We soon found one, called, if I remember rightly, 'Nouvelles Galeries'. But how were we to get in? At the back of the store we found an entrance for staff and deliveries, barred by an iron expanding gate. This could be opened, with the right tools, and closed again afterwards. A couple of my soldiers set to work, but I did not feel at ease. There was something repugnant about breaking into a strange building.

At last we were inside. A truck from battalion headquarters was already on the spot, the two drivers were left to guard the forcibly opened gate. 'Nothing will be touched,' I ordered. 'We search the staircases and all the floors of the store for fire extinguishers and load them on our truck. Nothing else will be touched!' I repeated, because I had seen a good many things in the windows that were no longer obtainable in Germany.

Inside the building I drew my pistol – there might be guards. I was very excited, though I did not know why. Suddenly I was facing a woman who gazed silently at me with large eyes. I jumped. It was a life-size model in white bridal dress with a white

* Translator's note: Field engineers in the German Army are known as Pioneers.

veil. I looked down at the pistol in my right hand and suddenly feeling ridiculous, replaced the weapon in its leather holster on my belt. My nerves were over-charged. I would have made a most inadequate shop thief!

We found fire extinguishers all over the building, and drove back to the cathedral with our plentiful spoils, which we lined up in rank and file by a small door on the north side of the church, which we would break open in emergency. Neither of the great doors of the west façade were on any account to be damaged. We would also have had to break through the strong iron gates in front of the church that served to protect this great work of art.

At last the Pioneers arrived, a full company, with all their technical gear. At last we had the experts without whom I would not have dared to do anything: qualified engineers, architects, builders, firemen. The divisional staff had also signalled by radio to other units for experts who might be of use. A load fell from my heart – the responsibility would no longer rest on my shoulders alone.

The captain in charge of the company was standing beside me, looking up at the west façade. He was quite silent, his eyes fixed on the great rose window. I almost had to drag him back to the immediate reality. 'It is high time,' he said, when he turned to look at the cloud of smoke blowing over our heads. 'High time,' he repeated.

Everyone agreed that the houses on the north side must be removed. Although they were beautiful medieval half-timbered houses, the cathedral took precedence. There was vehement argument for a few minutes, each of the experts saying his piece. Then the captain asked all round whether anyone had an idea that had not yet been put forward, and when no one else spoke he decided: 'The houses on the north side must go. They will not be blown up. We will prepare to burn the houses very rapidly, but we shall wait. We will need enough petrol to soak all the houses inside, when I give the order, but only then. The houses will be opened at once, and carefully searched, in case anyone is still inside after all. Two canisters (a total of 40 litres) will be prepared for each house. All doors and windows will be opened.'

We were standing in the square before the west façade, watching the soldiers' preparations. The Pioneer captain muttered, so that only I should hear: 'If you want to wage war in a country like France, you ought to take fire brigades with you. We've got the

Somme a few metres away, enough to soak all these houses in water, with good pumps. It's a shame to take the risks we've got to take here.'

His eyes returned to the façade. The banner of smoke was still blowing over our heads, now skimming the upper part of both towers. The fire was still advancing towards us but elsewhere the sky was brilliantly blue. What we needed was pouring rain, a redeeming storm, but nothing of the kind appeared.

Now the Pioneers unloaded a fuel truck and carried the canisters over to the houses. One of the non-commissioned officers came over to us and told us he thought it would be safer and more effective to double the quantity of petrol. The captain agreed – then suddenly, as if he had sprung from the ground, a monk in a dark habit appeared before us.

He stretched his clasped hands towards us and cried, repeating himself over and over again: '*Pas la cathédrale, s'il vous plaît, pas la cathédrale!*'

So there was still someone alive in Amiens! Apparently he had been left to guard the church and he must in fact have been watching us for a long time. Now he had left his hiding-place, assuming that we were bringing up all this petrol to set fire to the cathedral. Since the monk spoke no German it was difficult to convince him that far from setting light to the building, we were about to save it from the flames. Finally, however, I succeeded with my inadequate French in gaining his confidence. '*Nous voulons sauver la cathédrale,*' I repeated two or three times. Then it occurred to me that the monk might be able to bring me the keys to the church doors so that we could reach the roof. '*Il faut que nous avons les clefs de l'église,*' I said. He seemed to believe me, and ran off to the street diagonally opposite, where he disappeared. But he did not return; we never got the keys.

Suddenly Heinrich Yorck drove up at high speed, jumped from his car before it stopped and shouted at us: 'What are you going to do? Time's running out!' I told him we had made all the preparations to burn the houses down, but dared not begin, because of the wind. For answer Yorck turned, raised his right index finger in the air like a hunter before stalking and said quite calmly: 'I think the wind has turned.' Sure enough, a distinct breeze, previously blowing from the North-West, had now backed to the South-West.

Our decision was made; we must act swiftly, before the wind

veered again. The Pioneers had divided their people evenly between the houses and everything was running as if well-rehearsed. Two men, each with two canisters, rushed simultaneously into the houses. All of them reported their presence from the top windows, then came a shrill whistle, previously agreed, and as they ran down, the soldiers emptied the petrol down the stairs. When they were all back in the street again one of the lieutenants gave the loud order 'Fire!', NCOs threw a burning box of matches through every house door at once and literally at a single stroke the entire row of houses was in flames from doors to rooftops.

We watched what followed in extreme suspense. Yorck and I walked down the alleyway between the church and the burning houses, feeling altogether too responsible for what we had done here, and impelled to stay as close to the action as possible. With relief we saw the direction of the flames turn away from the church, though it was almost unbearably hot, and we put our backs to the cathedral wall. After a few minutes drops began to fall from above. At first we thought it was water and wondered where it could be coming from. We sent for our steel helmets to protect us, but then I felt a burning pain on the back of my hand, where a minute drop of lead had landed. It was senseless to stand so close to the fire. The lead must be coming from one of the copings up there and though the buttresses served by the copings would not catch fire, the danger lay behind them, in the guttering. We withdrew to the square in front of the west façade.

The Pioneers had distributed their people in a wide circle round the cathedral to watch the church roof and, as a precaution, had opened one of the small doors to the interior some time before. Our portable fire extinguishers lay ready for use at the first sign of smoke in the roof truss, but they were not needed.

The half-timbered houses had collapsed with astonishing speed, the south-west wind kept faith with us, even the dangerous showers of sparks were moving away from the cathedral. Our daring plan had succeeded. Thank God!

I saw Amiens again, years later. An almost fond relationship binds me to the cathedral. The houses we destroyed have not been rebuilt, and fortunately the iron bars before the west façade have been removed, so that today one can see this incomparable building not only on a straight line but also diagonally from the North-West. So even from the standpoint of an art historian of the town of Amiens I feel that I and my friend Heinrich Yorck, who did not survive the war, were justified in the action we took. May Amiens Cathedral never again be exposed to such a danger as that.

A French Lady

At Dunkirk the fate of the encircled French and British armies was decided. In an admirable operation, the British succeeded in getting hundreds of thousands of their soldiers back across the Channel in ships both large and small, and very small indeed. Their success was originally helped by an event which had got about very quickly among our troops, waiting for the order to attack southward across the Somme. None other than Hitler himself had intervened personally in the operations for the first time in his capacity as Supreme Commander. Believing that the British leaders would be sueing for an armistice after their catastrophic defeat, he had suspended the attack on Dunkirk, which was now surrounded. The German troops had stopped and waited for two days – two days which were a gift from heaven for the encircled troops. Hitler had underestimated the British. In the years that followed we were often to think of the halt before Dunkirk, the mistaken assessment of the enemy which was to decide the war. It became evident here for the first time, and now the British Prime Minister was no longer Chamberlain, but Winston Churchill, who was made of different stuff from his predecessor.

On 4 June 1940 the remainder of the Allied troops capitulated at Dunkirk and on 5 June we were already attacking southwards across the Somme, with two superior German army groups, confident of victory, facing the Allies.

Just as I had on the German–Polish frontier on 1 September 1939, I again took up an observation post before dawn, this time on the Somme, about half-way between Amiens and Abbeville. Our armoured divisions were to advance from the two bridgeheads, aiming to cross the Seine between Paris and Rouen.

The day began with hours of heavy German artillery bombardment. For the first time I was experiencing the uninterrupted howl of shells, flying overhead towards the South. Major Becker suddenly appeared beside us. 'It sounds like Verdun in 1917,' he said, complaining that I had not dug myself in deeper with my radio unit. We must assume, said the old First War warrior, that the French were excellent gunners.

When Becker moved on we began to get bored. Though we

could hear the continuing, distant sound of battle to left and right, nothing was going on in our vicinity. As our radio was netted to a fixed operational frequency, we could not search around to find out what was going on in other sections, so I had my own portable radio brought from the car parked behind us – the excellent instrument that Antoinette Esher had given me in London. We heard the German news bulletin, effusively triumphant, insufferable in its over-bearing arrogance. I turned the knob and suddenly there was music on the loudspeaker: Richard Strauss's 'Don Juan'. Hardly ever had I listened so intently to music, my enjoyment so great that I forgot almost everything else, until the speaker announced: 'You are listening to Wilhelm Furtwängler and the Berlin Philharmonic' – 'my' orchestra!

A few hard days followed, when for the first time our anti-tank battalion faced enemy armour south of Arras; not French armour, which we had previously only seen lying on the roadside, battered and burnt out, but English tanks, fighting bitterly; though they were only a remnant of the British Expeditionary Force, their morale was unbroken. We suffered losses because our guns proved too feeble. I experienced – and survived – that battle against a group of English tanks. I shall never forget their last stand. Our gunners, with their small 37 millimetre guns, fired everything they had, but our ammunition was no match for the English armour and the bullets rebounded off the slanting surfaces. To produce any effect we had to hit the turret ring of the tank or its heavy tracks, which were vulnerable. Hitting a turret ring jammed the turret, destroying a track sent the tank revolving round itself. At that point the upper hatch of the turret usually opened. We obeyed an unwritten law not to fire at soldiers emerging from their useless tanks. However, the crew who came out of the last, crippled tank, which included a young officer, fired off their machine pistols in a circle, throwing them down only when the magazines were empty. I was glad that these three ultimately fell into our hands unhurt.

After a few days resistance on the other side flagged, but caution was still needed: could France be defeated already? This uncertainty probably explains one unfortunate incident that we witnessed. One day we found ourselves approaching a château – I have forgotten its name. We had passed a large and beautiful forest and now a splendid old building lay before us in the middle of an open park. Anyone wishing to reach it would have to leave the woods and cross 100 metres of green turf. We had no idea if the castle was inhabited, or possibly even occupied by defenders, so we waited and the infantry company marching with us waited to see if anything moved behind the windows or up on the battlements.

While we were still inspecting the front of the building through our binoculars, the infantry company, which had halted beside us, sent a troop of soldiers running across and, as they had been trained to do, they crept along the building below the windowsills, when – as we saw through our glasses – a curtain inside suddenly moved. One of the soldiers, his nerves overstretched, reacted without thought and hurled a hand grenade through the window. The crash of the explosion, followed by the desperate screams of women, reached us in the forest. We ran across, to find that the door was not even locked, and soon we found two women, one lying seriously injured on the floor, the other tending her.

Our medical officer arrived at once with some medical orderlies and the wounded woman was carried to an upper floor. It was hours before our doctor reappeared, to report that this was the châtelaine herself, who had been injured by innumerable splinters. He had been able to remove some, but though the patient had borne the inevitable pain admirably, she had to be taken to hospital. She wanted to speak to one of our officers. Yorck and I went up to where the second of the two ladies was waiting to take us into a large bedroom. The wounded lady, lying propped up with pillows on a magnificent bed, received us with a slight gesture. We stayed by the door as Yorck expressed our profound regret at this wretched episode and asked whether we might take her to one of our field hospitals by ambulance. She thanked us quietly and said she intended to wait there until a French doctor could take over further treatment. We asked if there was anything we could do to inform relations or friends of the family, but this too she refused, saying that her husband was himself an officer at the Front and would, as far as she knew, be on the Maginot Line, and hence inaccessible.

Yorck and I were about to leave when she asked us to come a little closer to her bed for a moment. She inspected us from head to foot, dismissing us with a comment which I found so unforgettable that I can quote it now:

'Gentlemen, in my country they say that the cloth from which German officers' uniforms are made is of wretched quality. I see that they are right. Gentlemen, I thank you for your visit.'

To Brest and Bordeaux

To the east of Rouen we advanced towards the Seine. In the distance, a thick black cloud of smoke rose vertically above the town into the bright blue summer sky. Black smoke could come only from burning oil, and we remembered that Rouen too had a Gothic cathedral. But oil stores were not likely to be situated close to churches and art treasures. Yorck and I would have liked to view the cathedral and the market-place in which Joan of Arc had been burned at the stake, but our task now was to cross the Seine as quickly as possible. We crossed the river on 11 June by a pontoon bridge not far from Les Andelys. On the radio we heard fresh news of lunacy: Italy had declared war on France. Mussolini also wanted a slice of the French cake. It sounded to us like body-stripping, for France was already beaten.

We now turned westwards via Rennes towards our new goal, Brest, the naval harbour on the Atlantic. Now towns and villages were inhabited again, with people standing by the roadside, gazing silently at the foreign troops.

On 19 June we stopped before Brest, as if we had only to sit out a traffic jam ahead. Soldiers from the Signals battalion fixed climbing irons to their boots and climbed the telegraph poles. Trusting to luck, they fixed their cables to one wire after another until they made actual contact with the town hall. We were expected, they called down from above, we could come.

To reconnoitre, and from curiosity, I fitted myself and my car in at the head of our armoured reconnaissance vehicles. A barrier opened ahead of us. To left and right the French soldiers had left their concrete pillboxes, rifles under their arms, to take a look at what was rolling in.

I left the vehicles of the reconnaissance section behind, wanting first to see the harbour, the battleships, cruisers and destroyers. Or was it reckless to drive through the town of Brest like this, with only three soldiers and a small radio? We were still at war with France.

Then the bay of the harbour was before us, the sea smooth and lonely. I searched the quays and bays with my binoculars from different positions. Nothing, absolutely nothing. Never before had I seen a large harbour without a single ship in it. I described on the radio what I saw, or rather what I did not see.

Meanwhile the sun was sinking towards the horizon and by its last light I suddenly saw a mounting, dense black cloud. We drove towards it and we soon found the source of the fire: the naval oil depot. The tanks had been opened, the burning oil was flowing down the slopes before our very eyes and spreading out across the water – a prospect of uncanny beauty.

Once again I reported to my division by radio and asked for fresh orders. I was given the numbers of the roads we were now to march along: Nantes – La Rochelle – Bordeaux.

We advanced day and night. The tired slept as the cars moved on, the drivers relieving one another without interruption.

This was a new style of warfare: fighting where the opportunity offered, marching where it seemed possible to wring some advantage from movement, retaining the initiative, waging a mobile war according to the classical models of world history.

On 22 June France capitulated. On 25 June an armistice was signed and immediately afterwards we were rolling back to Germany.

Pomerania Again

In Stettin the caretaker's wife had garlanded the entrance to the house in Pommerensdorfer Strasse. Her first question was whether there would now be peace. Rex, the Polish Prince Bielski's Great Dane, jumped at me, greeting me with howls of joy. There was no news of Rex's Polish master, which was odd, as I had given him my address in Stettin. Rex had become an excellent watchdog and thefts from our neighbouring oil factory had dropped considerably, the caretaker told me.

All major foodstuffs had been rationed since the beginning of the war. We produced edible oil, which the citizen received, gram by gram, for coupons. The oil factory was 'essential to the war effort'.

I made a tour of the sheds, to be greeted everywhere with the same question: would there soon be peace? Our vital raw material, soya beans from Manchuria, previously sent to Stettin by sea, now reached us by rail, via the Soviet Union, with whom Germany had concluded a treaty of friendship in 1939.

In one of the factory yards were the workshops, with the electricians, fitters, plumbers and carpenters that every industrial enterprise needs to carry out its own maintenance and repair work. Here I saw new faces, where officialdom had intervened. Here objects entirely unconnected with oil, foodstuffs or soap were being built. Those familiar with wood were working in a group manufacturing the skeletons for the fuselage and wings of Messerschmitt fighter aircraft; those who could cut and weld metal were producing pontoons of a size I had never seen our Pioneers building. They were intended for the Channel, an engineer whispered to me, but this was top secret and he shouldn't really have told me. I took a closer look at the float. Our little 37 mm anti-tank guns could have made short work of them. I asked the engineer up to what wind speed a fully laden boat would still be able to cross the Channel. He did not know.

Achim Oster, Heinrich Yorck and I were swamped with invitations. We had agreed that whichever one of us received an invitation for the evening should accept for all three – a system that paid off admirably.

One evening the three of us and other friends visited a young married couple. Soon after Achim Oster left the living-room 'in high spirits', the voice of Goebbels suddenly rang out from the dark dining-room 'per people's radio' and 'via all German stations'. After some typical radio crackles and whistles, the Reich Minister of Propaganda came on the air 'personally, for reasons of world historic importance,' in order to 'announce the greatest political speech of all time'. 'We are now going over to London. Our beloved Führer Adolf Hitler will speak to us from London!'

First we froze, then we could not control our mirth. After some more crackling and whistling, the heralded speaker came on the air and in a voice like an organ told the world that after the victorious conquest of the British Isles he had just entered *Boockingham Palast* and was speaking from the balcony to all the nations on earth. Once again German soldiers had sped from victory to victory, for to German soldiers nothing was impossible. The English had capitulated, most of them had come over to us even as our assault boats were landing. *Herr Shurshill*, the old whisky-bibber, had flown to Canada, not on one of the last but on one of the first American flights.

We were no longer laughing, we were howling, doubled up. Achim Oster was proving to be a magnificent actor and cabaret artist. 'Go on, Achim,' we begged, 'go on!'

At that moment the doorbell rang – stunned silence.

Our hostess, a little pale, left the room and we heard voices at the door. It was some time before the brave lady returned. Nothing special, she said, only the couple from upstairs, asking on what wavelength they could hear Hitler's speech – they had been unable to locate the station on their set.

I visited my mother in Berlin. There were no longer any concerts held in her house, someone had reported Mother's 'questionable gatherings' to the district Party office. She had been told that such gatherings were not suitable in time of war. Mother had found another job to do, taking over the management of the Evangelical People's Kitchen in the wooden huts on Eisenzsahnstrasse, where the old and lonely could get a hot midday meal. However, the work soon became too much for her, and Gertrud Oster, Achim's mother, had offered to help, so they were now sharing the load.

In East Pomerania I visited my grandmother, eight of whose grandsons were now army officers. One, Hans Otto von Bismarck from Lasbeck, had fallen in France – the first casualty of our circle, and the merriest. Heinrich von Weizsäcker, Hans Otto – why were the merriest spirits the first to be struck down?

Grandmother read parts of her youngest son Konstantin's last letter. He had been shot down over Verdun in 1917 and he too, she said, had been one of the happy ones. One passage remains in my memory, almost word for word: 'Hermann Göring joined our squadron recently. Since he was awarded the order *Pour le Mérite* he has become quite useless. The commanding officer only lets him fly "tail". He's still the greatest – in the officers' mess.'

Then I had to tell her about France. Suddenly she interrupted me to ask if the Gestapo were already busy in France as well. I told her I did not know, and asked what had made her think of it. She had had Polish refugees here in the Belgarder Kreis once or twice, she said – aristocrats fleeing from the Gestapo, who came at night, stayed for one day and left the next night, moving on from wood to wood. In Poland the SD and the SS were hunting down the intelligentsia, and if that was our war aim, I should know about it, because it seemed to her that the role of the Wehrmacht was a dubious one. Only the German commander in Poland, General Blaskowitz, had protested, the lower-ranking officers apparently no longer had any courage. Blaskowitz had apparently been the only general to stand up to Hitler and now – no doubt for that reason – he had been relieved of his post. That was when I first heard evidence of organised German atrocities in Poland.

Back in Stettin, I talked to Oster and Yorck about what I had heard. Both had meanwhile been in Berlin and had more authoritative information than I. Things were far worse than my grandmother had discovered. We were suddenly reminded of the events of 30 June 1934, the murders of Schleicher, Bredow, Bose, Jung and many others, which had been camouflaged under the title of 'the Röhm *Putsch*'. Did this mean we were in the hands of a criminal state? Were we risking our necks for such a régime?

The deliberately provoked attack on Poland last autumn had certainly been irresponsible, frivolous and in breach of international law. The German–Polish frontier problems could have been discussed without going to war if the will had honestly been there. Our attack on the West was the logical consequence of declaring war on Poland, and so were the occupation of Denmark and of Norway. But now Poland was serving as an example of Hitler's ruthlessness in simply deciding to wipe out those ethnic groups that did not suit him. This no longer had anything to do with warfare.

There were others in our country at that time who, like us, were trying to think things through, but who reached quite different conclusions from ours. All this, they thought, was 'high-level policy', aimed at reorganising and bettering the world, and only the mean-spirited would fail to see it.

Each of us had heard these arguments, as so many Germans had been made uncertain by the many successes – uncertain of themselves, whether they were somehow missing out on the times in which they were living. So they played along. If things went well – they might perhaps go well – then they did not want to have been left out. To be successful, or at least to share in success – was that not a fine thing, for the sake of which one might turn a blind eye?

PART III

ATTACK ON THE SOVIET UNION

August 1940 – November 1942

Attack on the Soviet Union

The Eve of the Attack

When the French campaign was over, we spent almost twelve
months in virtual idleness. Soon after our return to Stettin, we had
been sent off on the march again and now we were spending the
winter of 1940/41 in East Sudetenland, close to Troppau*. In the
spring we were transferred to the former Prussian province of
Poznan. This 'smelt' to us like a strategic move to the East. It was
explained to the troops that our Stettin barracks were needed to
muster new units.

One day we were no longer the 2nd Infantry Division, but the
12th Panzer Division. A completely new Panzer Regiment 29 had
now joined us. Initially we regarded it as a foreign body, because
no one knew a single man, let alone any of the officers in it.

Our 2nd Anti-tank Battalion was also re-christened, to be
known henceforth as '*Panzer–Jäger–Abteilung* 2' (2nd Tank
Destroyer Battalion), but with no change in its structure, with the
exception of a new 50 millimetre gun, which was larger and heavier
than our old 37 millimetre pieces and said to be more effective.

The next change affected me personally. When I returned from a
few days' leave, my friend Heinrich Yorck was missing. He had
been transferred to the War Academy and our commanding officer
told me that I was now Yorck's successor: in other words, his,
Becker's adjutant.

Yorck's promotion to the General Staff was predictable. The
crimson stripes down the trousers had been his 'from the cradle'.

We exchanged a few letters and dreamed of peace, although
neither of us believed we should see peace again as long as Hitler
was at the head of the German Reich. In his last letter Yorck
'nevertheless' invited me to a peace festival at Klein-Öls in Silesia.

* Now Opava.

The best thing about his parental home was the library, he wrote, and I must just come and stay for a long time. Since Yorck had left the battalion I had been missing something important in life. Soldiers we might be and soldiers at war into the bargain, but at least the mental stimulus of our friendship and like-mindedness had offered some compensation. When would I have that again?

We never saw each other again. Heinrich Yorck fell in Russia as a captain on the General Staff. Had he not fallen at the Front, I am certain that, like his eldest brother Peter Yorck, he would not have survived. Hitler's thugs would never have overlooked a man like Yorck.

While we were still quartered in Stettin in August 1940, Stalin polished off a juicy morsel. Not one, but three sovereign states at once, were swallowed up by the Soviet Union: Lithuania, Latvia and Estonia. Hitler and Stalin had, we learned, actually 'negotiated' this in 1939. And Hitler had his eye on a far juicier morsel than the Baltic States: Great Britain. On the French and Belgian Channel coast two German Army Groups with twenty-six divisions stood ready to pounce. Mountain divisions practised climbing the 'White Cliffs of Dover' on suitable sections of the continental coastline, but word had gone round that our Navy shrank from this adventure. To start an offensive is easier than to 'feed' it. At this stage Göring stepped forward with his Luftwaffe: the Luftwaffe alone could bring England to her knees! The results were not long in coming, and the Luftwaffe never recovered from that failure. Where Gaius Julius Caesar and the Emperor Napoleon I had failed, Adolf Hitler was not going to win the prize. But we observed the growing intemperance of the German dictator with anxiety. On his initiative, Germany, Italy and Japan concluded a 'three-power pact' in September 1940 and we wondered what on earth this expansion of the war to the Far East could signify. We still could not conceive that Hitler's crazy fantasies were already leading him to toy with a threat to the United States from both oceans. It was another year before that notion was confirmed.

Further grave news followed in October. The Italians had launched an attack on Greece from Albania, which they had already occupied. Our Allies' noses had been bloodied, however, and their offensive got stuck.

A few days later, on 12 and 13 November, the Soviet Foreign Minister Vyacheslav Molotov visited Hitler at the Reich Chancellery in Berlin. What were these two going to cook up between them, we wondered – certainly no small fry, in the present world situation. Flames seemed to be flickering up all over Europe. So far none of the fires that had been laid since 1939 had been extinguished, leaving the impression that the three powers of the pact were actually busy fanning them and laying fresh ones.

At the beginning of 1941, the British in North Africa had attacked the Italians stationed in Libya from Egypt and apparently driven them westward. Hitler had no alternative but to send his friend Mussolini a German Panzer corps in support, under the command of General Rommel. I remembered how I had seen him tearing past me in his armoured reconnaissance vehicle in Poland, as commandant of the Führer's headquarters. When we were in France, heading towards the Seine from the Somme, Rommel had been commanding a Panzer division to our right and the soldiers of our division who had seen him had exciting things to say about him. He had always stayed in the vanguard of the attack (where a divisional commander really has no business to be, because a Panzer unit cannot be led from its fighting spearhead) and had named his formation the 'Phantom Division', because it should always be popping up where the enemy least expected it. Rommel seemed to be the first real 'warhorse' of our war; at least he made sure that his name was on every tongue.

By April 1941, our Italian friends were in urgent need of help in the Balkans as well. All of a sudden, strong German troop units were stationed in Yugoslavia and Greece and, in May, Hitler had the island of Crete occupied by parachute troops. He was doing his best to conduct not merely a war on two fronts, but a war on many fronts. The Wehrmacht hurled itself on its allotted targets, certain of victory, and with heroic courage. How long could this go on?

In June came an order which clearly showed us what to expect. Every soldier, from simple private to commanding officer, had to learn the Cyrillic alphabet. Everyone had to be capable of reading Russian signposts and Russian maps. That told us something – but had not Hitler and Stalin ceremoniously signed a non-aggression pact less than two years ago? Had not Hitler received Molotov in November of the previous year, to discuss – it had filtered through later – the partition of the British Empire?

Then pocket-sized brochures were distributed to the troops, from which we were to learn – on the lines of a tourist phrasebook – the essential questions and answers between Germans and Russians. For instance, instead of the request to a foreign waiter:

'Please bring me the menu,' the command in Russian was 'Halt! Hands up!' So we were to attack the Soviet Union.

A few days later came the order to march, and the 12th Panzer Division, which, in fact, had never once been on manoeuvres as a Panzer division, rolled towards East Prussia. Our assembly area was in the forests at Suwalki. One look at the map showed where we were heading, because 'Suwalki Point' resembled a prominent nose. The 12th Panzer Division would be in the spearhead of the attack.

The closer we came to the Russian frontier, the more densely the regiments massed. The numbers of troops now mustering exceeded anything we had seen before.

Radio silence was imposed, as usual before an offensive, so that the enemy reconnaissance could not pick us up. But of course there were other types of reconnaissance, such as observation from the air, or espionage. Our approach could not remain hidden from the Russians – unless they were asleep.

I remember a crossroads in open country. For some inexplicable reason the troop concentration plan had arranged for two units to cross one another at this point, so the engineers had built a bridge from freshly-felled timber. The recently-sawn wood gleamed in the sunlight.

On 21 June we drove through a village, where I noticed beside the entrance to a farmyard the insignia of an Army Group headquarters, which could only mean the Headquarters of Army Group Centre, to which we belonged. When we had already left the village, it occurred to me that this might be an opportunity to find out if my cousin Henning von Tresckow was there; after all, Henning was now Ia, First General Staff Officer of Army Group Centre, under the command of Field Marshal Fedor von Bock.

Lieutenant-Colonel Becker, my commander (who, as the reader will see, had now been promoted), agreed and released me, telling me to bring back plenty of news. I took one of our new BMW motorbikes and drove back along the column.

On the first floor of the farmhouse I quickly found the door marked Ia and knocked. Henning received me in his usual extraordinarily affectionate manner, like an old friend: 'Just look at that,' he cried, after I had made my report, 'a reserve officer as adjutant of an active unit! Congratulations! Do you remember when you appeared at the Schlossfreiheit in Schwedt in your overalls?' I told him I would never forget that day. Then he wanted to know how I had become Battalion Adjutant and I told him that I undoubtedly owed it to Heinrich Yorck, my predecessor. 'Yes, I've already had a look at Yorck.' he said, 'you have a good model in him.'

Then he changed the subject: 'And what do you say to what we're doing here?' Well, what was I to say – we were launching another war, without having created political order in a single one of the arenas of war we had already opened up. I asked him if he thought the Russians could possibly have missed our troop concentration. Instead of answering, he led me to the big situation map of the Army Group, with its armies, corps and divisions, which I was seeing for the first time. The enemy units were also plotted, on the far side of the frontier. I was astonished at the huge numbers of Russian units – the Soviets had evidently mustered against us in great strength – but their positions did not reveal whether the Red Army knew of our attack, planned for the next morning. Henning explained it all to me in detail.

I asked about the relative strengths and Henning told me he thought that while the Russians were superior to us in quantity, they certainly were not in quality. We could soon deal with the sort of thing we had encountered up to now.

When I asked what he thought of our chances in this campaign, he said he saw an opportunity for us to bring about the seizure of the whole of the Soviet Union, but only on condition that Army Group Centre had first won the battle for Moscow and occupied the city before the coming of winter. If we succeeded in destroying the centres of Soviet government, the administration, economic control, transport and intelligence, we could expect Russia to collapse. But if we had not succeeded by the onset of winter, he was convinced that our prospects were dismal. Everything therefore depended on the rapid and sweeping success of Army Group Centre.

Then why, I asked him, were we only attacking now, in June? Why not in April or May? 'You'll have to address your question to the great man in Berlin himself,' he retorted. 'We are afraid that this belated attack is an irreparable mistake, but it has been worked out for us at the highest level that this campaign could be over in four months, based on what happened in France.'

Still standing before the big situation map, I asked what the neighbouring Army Groups North and South were to do. Army Group North was to take Leningrad and establish contact with the

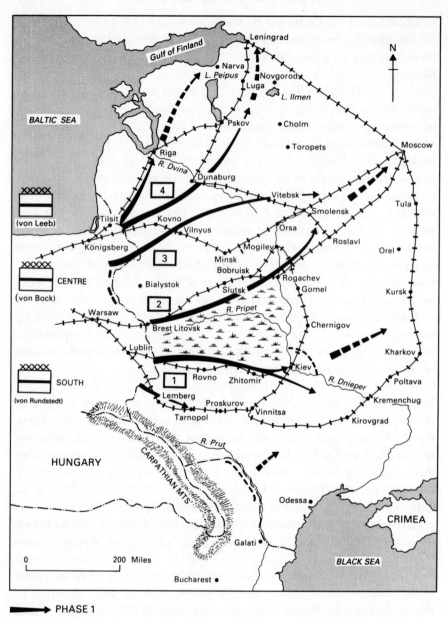

PHASE 1

PHASE 2 (dependant on PHASE 1)

1   Panzer Group 1 von Kleist   3   Panzer Group 3 Hoth

2   Panzer Group 2 Guderian   4   Panzer Group 4 Hoepner

MAP 3 Operation Barbarossa 1941 – The Plan

Finns, he said, while in the South the Ukraine was to be conquered
for its huge agricultural acreage, its mineral wealth and its oil.
Since the three Army Groups were consequently divided geographically, we would in fact have three mutually independent
theatres of war in Russia, which meant that the plan of this
campaign was contrary to all the rules of warfare. Our only chance
of winning was to strike at the 'heart' of the Soviet Union, Moscow,
and here the 12th Panzer Division would be one of the forces with a
decisive role to play.

For me, personally, Henning Tresckow's assessment of the
situation was the first I had heard on this scale, which is why it is
imprinted on my memory. We would often have reason to
remember it later. I asked him other questions, especially what
was known of any Russian reserves deep in the hinterland.
'Largely terra incognita,' he replied; but one must assume that the
Russians had also concentrated considerable forces on their
eastern frontier which could be brought up to the western front.

Then Henning suddenly asked me whether we had yet been
informed about the treatment of Soviet political commissars. I
admitted my ignorance and he went on: 'An order came through
recently that all Red Army commissars, the so-called *Politruks*, are
to be shot on capture.' I was appalled. 'That would be murder!'
'The order is just that,' he replied. 'And for that reason we are not
allowed to give it to the troops in writing, but you will receive it by
word of mouth before the attack begins and will have to pass it on
my word of mouth to the companies.' Still half incredulous at this
atrocity, I asked from whom the order came, and he replied – I
have never forgotten it – 'From the man to whom you gave your
oath. As I did,' he added, with a penetrating look.

Then he was summoned to Field Marshal Bock and had to break
off our conversation.

Still in a turmoil, I drove the BMW back to my unit, where I
found the battalion in a beautiful old forest. The Commanding
Officer had gone to a commanders' briefing at Division, I was told.
Becker did not return before dark and, despite the poor light of his
map-reading lamp, I could see something in his face that I had
never seen before. I knew the reason.

He summoned all the officers and told us to gather closely round
him on the ground.

Then he began: we would attack at 3.15 the next morning, 22
June. Deep in the Russian ranks, our reconnaissance had also

spotted armoured units. It was going to be harder this time than in France. Then he assigned the individual companies to the various battalions of infantry.

After a pause he announced the 'Commissar order'. When he had finished there was deathly silence in our circle, until one of the company commanders asked how one would recognise a Commissar. Lieutenant-Colonel Becker seemed to have been expecting the question and said cuttingly that he had no idea, nor did he wish to know. He and all the other commanders had been ordered by the Divisional Commander to pass this order on to all officers – but only to officers. The order came from the highest level. He, Becker, had now carried out his orders.

After another pause he said: 'Gentlemen, the officers' briefing is not yet over. There is reason to remind you of The Hague Convention on Land Warfare. I am now speaking of the treatment of prisoners and wounded. Anyone who abuses prisoners and wounded I shall have court-martialled. Do you understand me, gentlemen?'

Yes, we understood our commanding officer. We went to our vehicles and tried to get a few hours' sleep.

To Moscow

We were sitting in our vehicles in deepest darkness. Many men had simply lain down on the ground in the forest. Sleep had evaded me, as my conversation with Henning went round and round in my head. In a few hours' time more than three million German soldiers would cross the frontiers of the Soviet Union, from the Baltic to the Carpathians. However this campaign ended, this day, 22 June 1941, belonged to world history. Which of us would survive what lay ahead?

Once again, we Germans would be breaking a treaty, our treaty of friendship and non-aggression with Russia, not yet two years old. Were treaties in the future really to be no more than 'scraps of paper'? 'Pacta sunt servanda' – treaties must be observed – was this time-honoured central element of law no longer valid? Would naked force alone prevail?

The problematic nature of the Treaty of Versailles, which had been imposed on the inferior treaty partner by the victors in 1919 might be open to debate, but the Moscow treaty had been agreed between free partners.

Today we would be attacking whole peoples in order to force them into subjugation. One man had given the order, and we would be his accomplices.

Or would it be quite different? Would the Russians come over to us? Would they welcome us as their liberators from the tyranny of Communism? Had Russian history ever known anything but tyranny, whether under the Tsars or under the Communist dictators? What would happen if they now welcomed us as their liberators? Round and round went my thoughts.

Suddenly the CO was standing beside my vehicle. 'You can't sleep either, Stahlberg. Come over to me, so that we can talk in peace,' he said. When we were sitting on either side of the small map-table in his enclosed command car, he poured out cognac. That was when I reported my conversation with Henning Tresckow. Becker asked me if I knew in what month Napoleon I had invaded Russia in 1812. I had read the memoirs of Caulaincourt, Napoleon's adjutant on his Russian campaign, and remembered that it had been in June; Moscow occupied in September; the burning of Moscow and beginning of the retreat of the Grande Armée in October. We talked on: Panzer and motor-ised divisions were much faster than the infantry of 1812, but we too had to be followed by infantry. Ultimately, even in 1941, the marching troops dictated our speed. Moscow was about 1,000 kilometres away. The talk went to and fro.

I asked Becker if, in his life as a soldier, he had ever wanted war. 'For God's sake, no!' he cried in dismay. He had certainly enjoyed being a soldier, but he had never been war-crazy. He loved peace above everything and that was why he was a soldier. I said it was extraordinary that so many people all over the world regarded war as a matter of course, even a necessity, and I also believed there were people who loved war. I quoted the phrase about 'war as the father of all things', which I had always found incomprehensible. Becker told me that he had met such a person only a few hours before. When, at the commanders' briefing, General Harpe had asked if anyone wished to speak, the commander of our new 29th Panzer Regiment had got up and made an inflammatory speech. He had worked himself up, using such histrionic slogans that one might have thought one was at a Party rally at the Berlin Sports Palace: ranting of Germany's future in the dawn of the East, of the 'chosen people' we now were, of his vision of standing on the heights of the Urals and gazing further eastward to Germany's future. It had been insufferable, and also incomprehensible, that our Panzer regiment should have been entrusted to such a fanatic. There was absolutely no doubt that that regimental commander was war-crazy – but Becker doubted whether he would still be so in a week's time.

The attack on Russia began almost noiselessly. Towards three o'clock, the NCOs went from one vehicle to another, waking up the soldiers. The drivers pressed their starters and slowly the columns rolled out of the forest, like the gradual emptying of a car park after some sporting event. This new 12th Panzer Division made an impressive sight when, crossing open country, one could see the whole body of 14,000 soldiers with their vehicles.

We crossed the frontier of the Soviet Union without opposition. From one side we could hear the sound of fighting in the distance, but where we were the Russians seemed to have been taken by surprise.

Then came the first fighting, though it was becoming clearer all the time that we really had surprised the Russian units which had been mustered against us. Quite small Russian units faced us from time to time, but quickly withdrew. We took our first prisoners and received the first deserters.

We reached the Memel without much difficulty and our pioneers at once began to build a bridge. I drove over to them to look at the lie of the land and watch the work of the bridge-builders. Pontoons and beams were joined together at incredible speed, every movement counted. When the first section of the bridge was finished, I went up to see if there was anything useful to be learned. I was leaning on a railing which had already been completed when a Pioneer sergeant spoke to me: 'You are in our way here, Sir. I would be glad if you would go back to the bank.' Naturally I did as he asked.

At that very moment there was a shattering crash and the half-finished bridge vanished in a chaos of leaping water, splintering wood and men hurled into the air. Our own artillery replied at once, probably firing at random, without any precise target. I pressed myself to the ground – what else could I do? It was a grisly scene. The Russians sent over one or two more salvoes so that, after a few minutes, there was practically nothing left of our bridge – a masterly piece of gunnery which we had not expected of our opponents. After that it was quiet and I helped to recover some of the wounded. We also found the sergeant who had asked me to leave my position by the railing. He had not survived.

Another Pioneer company appeared with its vehicles and set to work. An hour or two later our first tanks were crossing the bridge, and we followed soon after.

The old Polish/Russian frontier was shown on our maps, but since September 1939, when Hitler and Stalin had divided up Poland, it no longer existed. However, there was still the line of pillboxes which the Soviets had once built to defend their country. Now they would have to fulfil their function as defence posts against Western attacks. The 12th Panzer Division was ordered to penetrate this bunker system.

So far our new 50 mm guns had never come up against Russian tanks. Now we would be deployed against concrete bunkers – in other words, we would be making a frontal assault on the chequer-board system of defence, firing at the embrasures. The thick concrete walls would resist the calibre we had available and only accurate hits on the embrasures would be effective.

After our companies had been assigned to their respective sections of the attack, I drove along an avenue as far forward as I had cover. Then, with a radio operator who carried his small instrument on his back like a knapsack, I left the vehicle. Together we crawled metre by metre along the ditch, until we were only about three or four hundred metres from the first bunkers ahead. Our road led almost at right angles into the defence system, but astonishingly the light-grey concrete bunkers were completely 'naked'. The Russians had evidently had no time to camouflage them as they retreated. However, through binoculars one could see that they were manned. The guns stared fixedly from their embrasures.

While I passed my observations back by radio, our guns began to fire. The infantry were also seeking their targets with their light weapons and hostile fire was now returned from the bunkers. Bullets whistled and howled over our heads in both directions.

Pressed deep into the grass, my helmet camouflaged with weeds, I tried to follow the effect of our fire with my binoculars over the edge of the ditch, hoping perhaps to see that one or other of the bunkers was no longer returning fire. But my heart was beating so hard that I could not hold the binoculars steady, so I decided to creep forward another few metres to where I would be able to steady my glasses against a wooden electricity pole on the very edge of the ditch.

It was in fact a tremendous help, but only for a few minutes. There was an ear-splitting explosion above my head, immediately followed by a blow on my helmet which almost knocked me senseless. Instinctively I dropped back into the ditch, where I found myself cheek by jowl with my radio operator. Nothing had happened to him, but what was the matter with me? The radio operator said something but I could not hear him, I could only see that he was speaking. He pointed upwards: a shot had split the wooden pole above us in such a way that its long upper section, separated from the lower, was now swinging merrily to and fro from the cables. It was this that had hit me on the head.

We scrambled back considerably faster than we had crawled forward. I felt I had made a thorough fool of myself. After all, I told myself, there could scarcely be a more satisfying target for a gunner in the enemy bunker than to line up a telegraph pole with his vertical sight. Never again in the field have I spent any longer than was absolutely necessary beside a pole or an isolated tree.

However, even after hours of firing from both sides, the day brought no results. As I could hear virtually nothing, my radio operator took over the task of reporting to the rear and I showed the boy with paper and pencil what to say or ask. Lieutenant-Colonel Becker sent orders for me to rejoin him. He now had a practically deaf adjutant, but our doctor reassured me that it would all be forgotten in a few days' time.

Then a courier reached us with the news that the infantry and pioneers would shortly be storming the line of bunkers, and I saw a side of my Commanding Officer that was new to me. Probably the infantry sergeant of the First World War had awakened within him. How often we had heard him talk with shining eyes of the charges they made during the trench warfare of 1917 in France. No doubt he owed his promotion to lieutenant to his courage then.

He announced that at the start of the infantry attack he too would be driving 'forward'. 'In what?' I asked, seeing something feverish in his eyes, his lips trembling with excitement. 'The *Kübelwagen**,' he cried. We climbed into the unarmoured car bearing the Commanding Officer's standard, Becker in front, beside the driver, I in the back beside Staff-sergeant Knoke, and we were away. 'Full speed ahead!' yelled our Commanding Officer, and there we were, tearing along the open road at high speed, straight toward the enemy bunkers. Wild firing opened up from

* Open cross-country military car (the German equivalent of the 'Jeep').

both sides. Presumably the Russians were shooting at us; our own guns and infantry weapons gave us covering fire. Our windscreen cracked, Becker tried to push the glass fragments away with his elbows. There was no going back for us now. Our driver drove like the devil, constantly flinging the car to left or right in order, as he told me later, to give the impression that we had already been hit. Becker stood upright, holding the frame of the windscreen. Knoke and I, less intrepid, crouched in the back. How would this crazy drive end? The first concrete bunker was no more than 50 metres ahead of us when our driver did something no one had ordered him to do. To our left he had spotted a track that crossed the ditch and, without braking, he wrenched the car to the left across it and landed us with a leap in a sandpit two to three metres deep.

For the time being we were saved, but how we were to get out again? As long as the battle for the bunkers was undecided, it seemed an impossibility. However, for the time being he had intelligently put us out of action.

Our first concern now was for our self-defence. Our arsenal consisted of two machine pistols and two Walther PPs. We had not brought along one of the many radios available in the battalion, so all we could do was to wait, peering with extreme caution over the edge of our pit to see what else was going on around us.

Astonishing things were going on. Even to me, hard of hearing as I was, it was obvious that our division was sending a box barrage of more than impressive proportions over our heads. Soon we could hear German words of command as the Stettin infantry and pioneers made a death-defying rush for the bunkers. It was like the parade ground all over again: down, up at the double, down, up at the double! After a short time they successfully broke through the old Russian line of fortifications, with few losses on our side. Most of the bunker crews had soon given themselves up, faced with the good training and personal courage of our Pomeranian infantry and pioneers and apparently relieved that the war was so quickly over for them.

When Lieutenant-Colonel Becker returned with us to the battalion, a great cheer went up. Word had gone round our section of the fact that the Commanding Officer of the Panzer-Jäger battalion had died, with his adjutant, his staff sergeant and his driver. Some claimed to have seen it happen.

Even in retrospect, I did not like the affair at all. A commanding officer cannot go rushing on towards the enemy lines, far ahead of his gun emplacements, with nothing but a pistol in his hand. Becker was undoubtedly a brave soldier and a decent man, but now and then the soldier inside him cracked up. However, these old warhorses were certainly not peculiar to Prussia.

Daily we told each other: Moscow is our goal, we arrive in the Soviet capital on 31 October at the latest, our intermediate stop is called Minsk, where the encircling ring is to close round the Soviet armies, from Minsk there will a 'runway', something like a dual carriageway, and then we shall move faster still over the remaining 600 kilometres from Minsk to Moscow. So up to now everything had gone according to plan.

Would the tracks of our tractors make it? Yes, it seemed so. They had suffered much less wear and tear in the Soviet Union than in Poland and France, because in the 'workers' and peasants' paradise' we very seldom found a made-up road. As a rule, we moved along deep, sandy tracks. From that point of view, one was almost tempted to think that this country would be a suitable practice ground for the summer manoeuvres of modern troops.

I will describe two episodes from the march towards Minsk, not of any great importance in themselves, but characteristic of the first week of the campaign.

A company of our Panzer regiment was marching in front of us when there was a hold-up further ahead, so that we too had to stop. We were in a country that offered little cover. To our left was a slight elevation, unevenly coverd with young firs. For the moment, we could do nothing but lie down in the grass beside the sandy road and wait.

Then a machine-gun suddenly opened fire to our left and one of the fuel trucks ahead of us burst into flames. The fire certainly provided a unique spectacle, as the twenty-litre canisters blew up like fireworks, exploding in all directions, but nobody knew from where the machine-gun fire had come. In consequence, everyone grabbed a weapon from the mountings on the vehicles and started shooting aimlessly, to the right as well as the left.

For a few minutes the machine-gun was silent, as if it had been moved away, but then came renewed bursts of fire; for a moment I had the feeling that I had seen the muzzle flashes, on the left of the rise, two to three hundred metres away, from a group of young firs. I called to the soldiers nearest to me that I thought I had spotted the machine-gun and asked who wanted to take out the nest 'round the back' with me. One NCO and two young soldiers volunteered at once. Armed with machine pistols for speed and mobility, we worked our way back one or two hundred metres, protected by our column of vehicles, in order to enter the plantation from there. Then we waited quietly to see if the machine-gun would start up again and, sure enough, another short burst of fire soon enabled us to locate its position fairly accurately.

What we did then was more like manoeuvres than war, with the single difference that we were not armed with blanks but with live ammunition. I actually felt I had been transported back to the training ground of my days as a recruit in Schwedt. I told my three companions that we would try to reach the machine-gun by making a wide detour behind it, running forward only when the machine-gun was firing, and trying to take prisoners rather than shoot. We four agreed that there was only a single machine-gun ahead of us, otherwise other guns would have been firing on us as well. But our main conclusion from the shortness of the bursts was that the crew was running short of ammunition and might be only one small group of Russian stragglers.

Events followed quickly and smoothly. The machine-gun fired again once or twice and we exploited the noise to move in closer. Our own people down below on the sandy road were no longer returning fire, which meant that they calculated we were already on the hillock. So for the four of us the moment soon came when according to our estimate we must have the Russians right in front of us. We rushed down the slope for the few metres which probably still separated us from them, raising as much hullabaloo as we could. There, sure enough, were three Russians, lying on their stomachs, their weapons aimed down at our column. They turned in fright, I fired one burst in the air with my machine pistol – just to make sure – they raised their hands and surrendered. My NCO confirmed that the three of them had almost exhausted their ammunition. Then we drove them down the hill ahead of us, literally into the arms of our own people. Our three prisoners seemed happy that we did not shoot them.

That was the casual way we made war in those days.

Another day one of our companies reported that an undamaged Russian T34 tank had fallen into their hands. It had come upon two of our guns on a forest path, the crew had waved a white cloth from the turret on recognising our cannon, and had given them-selves up. They were probably deserters.

As the incident had happened not far from us, I drove over to take a look at the tank, the first we had acquired undamaged.

Together with the company commander, I considered what we should do with our booty: simply leave it there, perhaps to be reoccupied one day by Russian stragglers in the forest? No. Blow it up or set it on fire? No. This might quite possibly be our first intact T34, which would be warmly welcomed at home for purposes of examination and testing. I climbed inside first, sat in the driving seat and pressed the starter. The engine started at once, running roughly and loudly – much too loudly. I found the gear lever and took a test drive. The thing – that was all one could call it – did everything it should, it was so primitive that any idiot could have handled it. Compared with our German tracked vehicles, this was an antediluvian box – but that could also have its advantages as a tool of war.

So, as a preliminary measure, we decided to take it along with us till evening and made the necessary arrangements by radio with battalion headquarters. Above all, the entire division had to be made aware that there was an olive-green T34 in their area, which was not to be fired on.

We received information very soon by radio that all sections of the division had been informed; nevertheless the T34 had to be decorated with a swastika flag front and back. Since the beginning of the Russian campaign all combat troop elements had been supplied with swastika flags which were supposed to identify the forward lines so that our aircraft would recognise them from the air. (What an idiotic order – from whose ivory tower had that been issued?)

So there I was, sitting in a vehicle decorated with the Nazi party flag for the first time in my life (and the last, for that matter). I soon regretted my bright idea. The wooden handles on the levers of the track brakes, which were still used in those days to steer tracked vehicles, proved so recalcitrant and rough that they were too much for the palms of my hands. At the same time the temperature inside the tanks was so fiercely intensified by the sun from above and the heat of the engine from within that I was soon drenched in sweat. In short, I had let myself in for sheer martyrdom. I had no gloves with me – after all, it was summertime – so it was with relief that I consigned the vehicle to our workshop and my bleeding hands to the care of the doctor, who merely commented laconically: 'Wounded by enemy action?' (This would have 'earned' me the decoration for the wounded.) We laughed.

On 22 June we had arrived in East Prussia; on 29 June, a week after our offensive began, the two spearheads of our attack met to the west of Minsk, and on 9 July, the eighteenth day, the last units of the encircled Russian troops gave themselves up. It was reported that more than 300,000 prisoners had fallen into German hands.

Descending from the North, we saw Minsk before us. Since my battalion's reputation from the Polish campaign of being able to deal with the problems of captured enemy soldiers had evidently preceded it, we received the order to set up a camp for prisoners. We chose a large meadow to the north of Minsk, which had the merit of being dry, with a river only a few metres wide running in a semi-circle on its western edge. Thousands of Russian soldiers marched up in columns and understandably started by throwing themselves at and into the water. Supplies ran smoothly from the first day thanks to our prompt, clear organisation.

Our offensive advanced very quickly towards the East, actually taking us from time to time on to one of the roads marked on the maps as a motorway. A motorway had been planned and the route marked out in parts, but it had never got as far as a concrete surface – at least I never saw one.

We were meeting scarcely any resistance now, but the number of villages in which we were welcomed by small reception committees was increasing. Village elders, accompanied by young girls in white dresses, handed us flowers and presented us with bread and salt, the time-honoured symbols of good luck and welcome.

We had a new orderly officer, Baron Helmuth Engelhardt, who came from Estonia and also spoke Russian. Engelhardt told us that the population was awaiting a political signal from us Germans and it would be a simple matter to win over the people of Byelorussia into a community of Western nations.

We moved on eastwards, north of the city of Smolensk, which had capitulated on 5 August. We were counting the kilometres, we were counting the days – when would Moscow lie before us? Then an order reached us which I could not understand. Army Group Centre had received an order from the highest level to halt and go on to the defensive. A line running from North to South was formed to the East of Smolensk. The 12th Panzer Division, one of the units created for fast breakthroughs and envelopments, was demoted overnight to an infantry division. So there we halted, scarcely 300 kilometres from Moscow, while our infantry began to dig in.

Our anti-tank companies took up stand-by positions behind the infantry lines so that they could be put into action anywhere in the event of enemy tank attacks. But there were no Russian tank thrusts, and typical positional warfare developed, with minor advances from both sides.

At last we were also receiving mail from home. I seized the opportunity to distribute the contents of the bulging postbag with the field post number of my staff company, as it gave me the chance of a personal word or two. From time to time I found myself delivering a letter which showed clear signs of having been opened and stuck down again and I drew the recipient's attention to this openly in front of the other soldiers in the hope that this might encourage them to use caution and restraint in their letters home. I regarded the censorship of the private letters of soldiers fighting at the Front as degrading.

My grandmother wrote to me often, anxious that the bonds between her flock of grandchildren should not be broken. Only recently, she wrote, two of my Kieckow cousins, Jürgen–Christoph and Hans–Friedrich von Kleist, had been transferred to my division. She assumed that we might see a lot of each other. In fact I had spotted neither of them so far, which was no wonder considering that the division numbered 14,000 men. If I saw either of them, I was to tell him that their father was in Köslin* again. 'In Köslin' meant in prison; 'again' most probably meant that he had given the prisoners of war allocated to him as farm labourers too much to eat.

One afternoon I received a call by field telephone from the Regimental Adjutant of our 5th Infantry Regiment. My cousin Jürgen–Christoph had not returned from an attack by his company in the forward area. He must be seriously wounded, but it was impossible to reach his last known position by daylight.

My commanding officer agreed that I should go; Sergeant Knoke, who had already shared many an adventure with me, refused to let me go alone. We reached the company while it was still light and when it was completely dark we set off with two NCOs. The four of us crawled slowly forward, metre by metre, over terrain covered with man-high bushes. None of us knew where the Russian line now ran, so we paused frequently, stayed close

---

* Now Koszalin.

together and listened hard. Nothing was moving. Finally, after about an hour, which felt like an eternity, the NCOs indicated with gestures that this was where the lieutenant might be lying. But it was so dark that we had to grope our way across the ground. At last we found him, dead. A bullet had pierced his helmet from the front. We moved him on to the strip of canvas we had brought with us and dragged him back to his company's position.

I asked the company commander if it would be possible to inform his younger brother, Hans-Friedrich, who was a cadet in the same regiment, so that he might attend the burial service for Jürgen–Christoph the next day, but it appeared that his brother was many kilometres away, in a position from which he was 'unavailable'. The 5th Infantry Regiment had been stretched too thinly along too long a defence line and had no reserves. If the Russians discovered that, it would be easy for them to break through here. Every single soldier was needed.

So we laid Jürgen–Christoph in the back of my car and took him away. The next morning Knoke and I buried him at a crossroads near our command post in the canvas on which we had carried him, and placed a little birchwood cross on his grave. I did not succeed in getting either of our two divisional priests, the Evangelical or the Catholic, to the funeral. They too were 'unavailable' that day, because the over-stretched division was suffering mounting losses. So, with my staff sergeant, I repeated the Lord's Prayer over the grave myself.

Then we arranged for Jürgen–Christoph's effects – the usual lieutenant's kit – to be sent to his family. I addressed it to his mother, since I had to assume that his father was still in prison, 'in Köslin'.

A few weeks after Jürgen–Christoph was killed, Hans–Friedrich, also fell in the field, but I did not hear of his death until much later. I also learned later that their father was again in prison when his younger son died, though not this time in Köslin but now, for a different 'offence', in Berlin–Moabit. He was not accused of conspiracy but of quite a different type of activity: the Russian prisoners-of-war allocated to him had sent a delegation to ask his permission, as head of the parish of Kieckow, to bury a dead comrade in the village cemetery. Since the parson from one of the neighbouring villages who was 'responsible' for that village did not dare to give a Russian prisoner a Christian burial, Uncle Hans–Jürgen did it himself. At the Russians' request, he repeated the Lord's Prayer over the grave. The next day, the police returned to Kieckow to arrest him.

Not Moscow: Leningrad

The order to discontinue our advance towards Moscow and go over to a defensive position had been a shock. What strategy was intended? The word had gone round at once that it had come from the highest level, that is from Hitler himself.

After a few days the riddle was solved. The 12th Panzer Division was detached from Army Group Centre, to come under the neighbouring Army Group North. Moscow was no longer the priority, Leningrad was to be taken first.

At a stroke, everything became clear: the supreme command had overturned the whole operational plan almost before it had begun.

The troops who had followed us from home on foot were already appearing, units with high numbers, so they were reserve divisions. The 12th Panzer Division was relieved and rolled northward behind the German defensive front.

During the long days of marching, we wondered what to expect in the Leningrad region. In order to fulfil its purpose, a Panzer division needs room to move, which the vastness of the area of Russia between Smolensk and Moscow seemed to offer. But what awaited us in the narrow passage between the Gulf of Finland, Lake Ladoga and Lake Ilmen?

Our orderly officer, Baron Engelhardt, who was a native of Estonia, knew the area: we would be entering very marshy terrain. A Panzer division, sent into marshland? Who had given that order?

There was another point for us to consider: we had been issued with new maps of Northern Russia, copies of Soviet maps which, in our opinion, did not deserve the name of maps, let alone General Staff maps. They were sloppily penned road maps, not at all accurately plotted. We thought it was irresponsible to issue this kind of thing to a highly modernised Panzer division, and one of our company commanders rightly said they were fit only for use as lavatory paper.

Only Engelhardt was pleased about our transfer to the North, because the 'Baltic Baron' would be seeing his homeland again, the home of his family for many generations. What exile does not rejoice to see his old home again?

For the time being, however, we were not going to Estonia, but west of Lake Ilmen, passing Novgorod, the once-famed capital of trade and industry, with its close connections with the German Hanseatic League.

For us the fighting started up again on the old road from Moscow to Leningrad, the former St. Petersburg. The Russians, using stalling tactics, fell back on Leningrad. Our anti-tank guns accompanied the infantry who were preceding us on foot, but no enemy tanks appeared.

So we reached Chudovo, about a hundred kilometers before Leningrad, a miserable spot to our eyes, but Engelhardt knew that Chudovo had once been famous as a coaching stop.

Now the road to the old capital of the Tsarist Empire lay before us, straight as a ruler. 'Wide as the Champs-Élysées,' commented Engelhardt.

Down the middle of a far too wide break in the old forests ran a lonely causeway, gravelled, yes, but scarred with potholes.

Slowly we advanced, far too slowly it seemed to us, with our marching infantry setting the pace. What could have got into our military leadership? It seemed to us that if only we were allowed, we could be in Leningrad in two or three days. After all, we had the experience. The whole question of the momentum of a well-run Panzer offensive seemed suddenly to have been forgotten.

We were approaching Tosno, shown on the map as the last large town before Leningrad, when we heard the sound of a weapon we had never come across before. From the area to the west of Leningrad rose a deep, ever-growing thunder, roughly comparable to one of the deepest notes of an organ. It passed over our heads and from far to our rear came the sound of a mighty explosion, re-echoing through the surrounding forests.

Later I met an artillery officer who thought it could only have been a shell fired by a Russian warship, presumably lying in Kronstadt harbour. Over the next two days the Russians sent us a few more such 'organ notes', but they had no effect, except on morale: the Russians were poor shots.

On another day we saw a vehicle approaching from a distance at high speed along the straight road. First it was a small point, then it became clearly recognisable as an olive green – in other words Russian – truck, driving flat out towards us and throwing up a great cloud of dust behind it. I had the truck clearly in my binoculars and thought it could only be a deserter, so I shouted as loudly as possible: 'Let it come, don't fire, let it come' As Adjutant I certainly had no right to give such an order, but I was not sure if other officers were present at that moment.

The Russian truck was almost upon us when its driver apparently saw the situation and slammed on the brakes. At the moment when it came to a stop the door opened and a soldier with a pistol in his hand jumped out, pointed the weapon at his temple and shot himself. Immediately after the shot, two more Russians jumped out and raised their hands. We looked at the dead Red Army soldier and were startled to recognise the insignia of a '*Politruk*', a Party Commissar.

This Russian outside Leningrad was the first commissar I had been able to identify as such, now that we had been given small, playing-card size illustrations of the Russian insignia. He was also the last one I saw in the Soviet Union.

Not Leningrad: Tikhvin

We advanced on Leningrad 'with our brakes on' instead of making as much progress as the situation allowed. Nevertheless, parts of our division reached the Neva early in September and on 8 September Schlüsselburg* was taken. Now Leningrad was encircled by the Germans in the South and our Finnish allies in the North. Only on the eastern side could the three million inhabitants maintain a link with the Russian motherland via Lake Ladoga. We were ready to attack the city.

Lieutenant-Colonel Becker took me on a tour of inspection of the investment front. Reaching a height from which we could overlook large parts of Leningrad, we found one of our artillery observation posts, where they let us use the binocular periscope. We saw a factory with a smoking chimney. We saw people in the streets. And then we saw another factory, whose gates suddenly opened and out rolled a tank, straight off the production line. Obviously they had not yet given a thought to camouflage over there.

We released the periscope at once and our artillery fired on the factory. According to schedule, we were ready to attack Leningrad early the next morning.

When we returned to our command post a new divisional order

---

* Now Petrokrepost.

1. At the Grunewald-Gymnasium I was responsible for the music at the non-denominational morning prayers (*see page* xii).

Portrait of the Author circa 1927 by Heinrich Boese, Professor at the Academy of Art, Berlin.

2. My father, Walter Stahlberg (1873–1953). Painted in watercolour circa 1948.

3. My mother, Spes Stahlberg (née von Kleist Retzow) when in the Red Cross 1942.

4. My grandmother's house at Klein–Krössin bei Kieckow (Pomerania). During the war it was a refuge for many persecuted theologians of the Confessional Church.

5. Bible study in the park at Kieckow 1939.
(*Left to right*): my grandmother, Ruth von Kleist Retzow, Dietrich Bonhoeffer and my cousin Konstantin von Kleist Retzow.

6. My godfather Herbert von Bismarck, State Secretary in the Prussian Ministry of the Interior, at his desk in March 1933. A few days later, he resigned because his Minister, Hermann Göring, had tried to make him put his signature to some decrees which were criminal in content (*see page* 35).

7. At Kieckow on the day of a Confirmation service held by Dietrich Bonhoeffer. My grandmother with her son-in-law Hans von Wedermeyer, who was killed in action at Stalingrad. All my four cousins (*left to right*) Jürgen Christoph von Kleist Retzow, Maximillian von Wedermeyer, Hans-Friedrich von Kleist Retzow and Hans-Otto von Bismarck were killed in action. Grandmother was killed by the Russians when they over-ran her estate (*see page* 81).

8. The Brandenburg Gate in Berlin 1933. On 6 March, the day after the Reichstag elections, on which the Nazis raised the Swastika flag on every public building throughout Germany, some student friends and I tried to hoist the black-white-and-red flag of the old Reich on the standard of Victory on the Quadriga before this symbolic building could be besmirched with the flag of Nazism. We arrived a few minutes too late (*see page* 27). (*Photo: Bildarchiv Preussiche Kulturbesitz*).

9. Potsdam Day 21 March 1933. On the crowded VIP stand near the Garrison Church, after the State occasion, one can recognise (*from left to right*): von Neurath, Hugenberg, the Papal Nuncio Monsignor Orsenigo, Frick, von Papen, Hitler, Göring and Meissner (*see page* 29). (*Photo: Bildarchiv Preussiche Kulturbesitz*).

10. I was not going to miss this special military occasion in Berlin – Hitler's 50th Birthday Parade on 20 April 1939. I put on my new parade uniform and managed to get a seat in the crowded VIP stand (*top left*), (*see page* 98). (*Photo: Bildarchiv Preussiche Kulturbesitz*).

11. To avoid having to wear the hated brown uniform of the Nazi Party, I became a soldier in No. 3 Squadron of the 6th (Prussian) Cavalry Regiment in Schwedt/Oder (*see page* 63).

12. When my father asked me what I wanted to become, I answered that, above all things, I wished to become a musician and most of all, a conductor, so deeply had I been impressed by the countless concerts I had attended when Wilhelm Furtwängler was conducting in the Philharmonic Hall. I took this photograph on 27 February 1933 during a concert to celebrate the centenary of the birth of Johannes Brahms (*see page* 3).

13. My cousin Antoinette, Countess Esher née Hecksher (*see page* 53).

14. Inge Schweitzer, assistant at Tatiana Gsovsky's ballet school, who was 'aryanised'. False declarations saved her life, but her sister died in Auschwitz (*see page* 370).

15. July 1939. The wedding of my cousin Ruth-Alice von Wedermeyer to Klaus von Bismarck at Paetzig/Neumark. My cousin Maria, who later married Dietrich Bonhoeffer, is in the first bridal pair. The Author is in the third.

16. Claus Graf Schenk von Stauffenberg. An early picture sent to me by his widow. I last met him at Berchtesgaden when he was returning from Hitler, having achieved nothing with the bomb in his brief case for the second time (*see page* 358).

17. Heinrich Graf Yorck von Wartenburg. By 1938 he had already offered to place himself at the disposal of the General Officer commanding in Berlin, von Witzleben, in the event of a *coup d'état*. He was killed in Russia in 1941 whilst serving on the General Staff. His elder brother Peter was executed in Berlin–Plötensee on 8 August 1944.

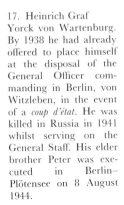

18. Henning von Tresckow (1901–1944) who had so much influence over me when I was adolescent and with whom I was later to become so closely associated. This photograph was taken a few days before he took his own life on 21 July 1944.

19. Fabian von Schlabrendorff, Henning von Tresckow's
ADC. Summer 1944 (*see also the Acknowledgements on page* xi).

20. Amiens Cathedral. This aerial photograph was taken after 1945. At the end of May 1940, Graf Yorck and I were successful in saving it from destruction by fire. We destroyed the neighbouring houses, the remains of which can be seen on the left of the picture (*see page* 135).

21. The great West Front of the Cathedral.

22. On 18 November 1942 I became ADC (in German, literally, Personal Orderly Officer) to General Field Marshal von Manstein. When I asked him to define my duties, he replied 'You will be my constant companion, be present at every conversation I hold, listen in to all my telephone calls, do my writing and look after my files'.

23. May 1943. With Field Marshal von Manstein (*front*) on a visit to the forward positions on the Donetz, south of Belgorod. (*Author at rear of the group*).

24. My best friend on the staff of the Army Group: Colonel (General Staff) Georg Schulze–Büttger who was hanged in Berlin Plötenzee after the 20th July 1944 as an accessory to the plot. With him is Lieutenant Otto Feil, our War Diarist, who was killed in action in Silesia just before the end of the war.

25. On the airfield at Saporoshje 19 February 1943. Hitler says 'Goodbye' to the Field Marshal.

26. A planning conference before the start of the 'Citadel' offensive at the beginning of July 1943, held in the former saloon carriage of the Queen of Yugoslavia which served as a mobile headquarters for the Army Group. (*Left to right*) Georg Schulze–Büttger, the Author, the Field Marshal and Colonel General Heinrici (*see page* 303).

27. Colonel General Heinz Guderian during 'Operation Citadel'. (*Right*) his Adjutant. (*Left*) the Author. As Guderian had no command function in his capacity as Inspector General of Armoured Troops, Manstein found the visit unnecessary, if not downright annoying (*see page* 305).

28. General Hans Oster. Through him I saw documentary evidence at Wehrmacht headquarters in Berlin of the massacre of the Jews. Oster died in Flossenbürg am Galgen Concentration Camp on 9 April 1945 (*see page* 286).

29. British aerial photograph of the destruction caused by a bombing attack on the Paul Julius
'Practically all the buildings are destroyed or seriously damaged and fires are still burning two

edible-oil factory in Stettin, published in a London daily paper in 1943. The caption read:
r the attack'. (*See page* 317).

30 & 31. Vinnitsa (Ukraine) July 1943. A few months earlier, Hitler's headquarters had been here during the attack on Stalingrad. Now the Field Marshal and I took over Hitler's former living quarters (*see page* 311). *Inset.* This print of a portrait in red pastel hung in Hitler's bedroom.

32. Vinnitsa. The Field Marshal with his long-haired Dachshund 'Knirps', who would raise his right paw on the command 'Heil Hitler'. The large BMW, a 1939 prototype, carries the 'Crimean Shield' on its front off-side wing (*see page* 312).

33. The Field Marshal at Hitler's former desk at Vinnitsa.

34. In the Ukraine June 1943. As the result of an initiative on the part of the German Ambassador in Turkey, Franz von Papen, and on Hitler's orders, a perfect demonstration of an armoured attack, employing all the latest weapons, was laid on for a Turkish military mission lead by Colonel General Toydemir, Chief of Staff of the Turkish Army. Field Marshal von Manstein with his guests on the VIP stand. (*Right*) the Author. (*See page* 301).

35. (*Top*). The Great Hall in Hitler's 'Berghof' at Berchtesgaden. I attended a number of meetings with Hitler in this room. Colonel Graf Stauffenburg came there to lecture on 6 and 11 July 1944. On each occasion he had the bomb in his briefcase but could not detonate it because Göring and Himmler were not present. On 15 and 20 July he took the bomb to Hitler's East Prussian headquarters, as the Führer had returned there. On the fourth attempt, he detonated it, causing an explosion (*see page* 363).

36. A briefing conference with Hitler, typical of many I attended with the Field Marshal as his ADC in 1943–44. (*Left to right*): Field Marshal von Manstein, Colonel General Ruoff, Hitler, General Zeitzler (Chief of Staff of the Army) and Field Marshal von Kleist.

37. The surrender of the German Forces in Holland, North West Germany, Denmark and Norway on 4th May 1945 at Luneburg. General Kinzel signs for the Army under the eye of Field Marshal Montgomery.

PASS.

The two occupants of this car:-

Hauptman STAHLBERG, and

Graf PLATEN

have taken a personal message from Field Marshal
MANSTEIN to Field Marshall MONTGOMERY.

They are now returning and will be granted

passage.

BLA

Lt-Col.
GS.
53 (W) Div.

HEADQUARTERS
6 - MAY 1945
53rd DIVISION

38. The safe conduct issued to me after my visit to Field Marshal Montgomery on 6 May at Luneburg. (*See page* 405).

had arrived: Leningrad would not be attacked, the city would remain encircled and come under artillery fire and bombardment by the Luftwaffe until it surrendered.

That evening I was sitting with Becker in his command car, both of us now plagued with doubts. Of course, we had no view of the overall situation, we were only a tiny pebble in a mosaic of many thousands, but we had a sense that the machinery of the military command was grating.

A good twenty kilometres south of Schlüsselburg there was a place with the well-nigh unpronounceable name of Mga. Its strategic importance lay in the fact that two railway lines met here from the South and East of Russia, which supplied Leningrad. At Mga the Russians began to bring in fresh forces from the East to relieve the millions in the beleaguered city. Mga became a battlefield, comparable to Verdun in 1917. There is no doubt that had we attacked the centre of Leningrad a great deal of blood would have been shed, but it was only a few weeks or months before we discovered that Mga had cost us far more than Leningrad would have cost. In this operation we were caught completely on the hop. We had lost the initiative.

In the 2nd Anti-tank Battalion we missed these battles at first, because so far the Russians had not brought out any armour. We were to find out later that they had held back their tanks until the rivers, lakes and marshland were frozen solidly enough to bear them.

Then the 12th Panzer Division received a new order. We were to cross the connecting river from Lake Ilmen to Lake Ladoga further south of the Volkhov, penetrate far to the East and take the town of Tikhvin.

We found Tikhvin on the Russian map, about a hundred kilometres to the East of the Volkhov. A railway line also ran through Tikhvin, leading via Mga to Leningrad. It had, of course, been interrupted by us at Mga, but trains were still running via Tikhvin far enough for goods to be re-loaded on to ships on the south bank of Lake Ladoga and carried to Leningrad. So whoever held Tekhvin controlled the line to Lake Ladoga – or so it seemed from the Russian map.

The Tikhvin order told us something else: at the same time as we were crossing the Volkhov, our Finnish allies would be attacking southward to the east of Lake Ladoga. In Tikhvin we would be shaking hands with the Finns. It sounded wonderful. Of course, we did not know where the Finns were at present, but we felt we had a reasonable and presumably important job to do.

The Tikhvin order contained yet another, apparently extremely weighty reason for our offensive: at Tikhvin, we read, there were considerable stocks of bauxite. The blue bauxite mined on the surface was the raw material of the manufacture of aluminium. Since Germany possessed little or no bauxite, possession of the bauxite mines at Tikhvin was of decisive significance to the war. This also sounded good, though we found it difficult to imagine how the 12th Panzer Division was to quarry the bauxite of Tikhvin in the war zone, or protect the mining operations and arrange for transport of the bauxite to Germany. However, as we used to say in the division, this was an operational order from 'the highest level'. We were glad that the division had finally been given an order to move, at least.

On 19 October 1941 the attack began. A column many kilometres in length crossed the wooden bridges built by our pioneers at Chudovo. Then it began to snow. In the car Becker turned and looked at me, his face grave. Engelhardt, our 'local expert', said that as a rule the first snow arrived 'up here' at the beginning of November. Did this mean an early winter, or even a particularly harsh one? None of our soldiers had any winter clothing.

The first snowflakes turned into a heavy snowfall. Our drivers could see the vehicle in front only from extremely close range. We advanced very slowly, anyone who needed to warm up jumping off and walking beside his vehicle so that at least his feet were warm.

During the column's frequent halts, we strained our ears for any sound in the white landscape, the drivers having been ordered to switch off their engines as soon as they stopped, to save petrol. The noise of battle came from far ahead. We were marching as what we called 'mixed troops'. As long as our troops could not deploy but were compelled to advance along a narrow road, the endless column had to be strong enough not only at its head but throughout its length to defend its flanks immediately.

We now realised that we were no longer driving along a woodland road but – almost exclusively – on a causeway. To the left and right of us the thin covering of snow concealed dangerous marshes. Whenever an ambulance came towards us carrying wounded to the rear, we had to pull over to the right as far as possible and halt. In many places the causeway was so narrow that any flow of oncoming traffic was out of the question.

We had received motorcycles with side-cars, a new product, with a powered side-car wheel. I had myself driven to the front of the column in one of these to size up the situation. The column was headed by a company of our reconnaissance battalion with light armoured scout cars, followed by tanks and infantry combat vehicles. But this group did not dictate the pace of our advance, because the Russians had mined the causeway. The first covering of snow had effectively camouflaged the mines, so our pace was dictated by our Pioneers with their mine-detectors, feeling ahead, step by step. Until now there had been no fighting except up here at the front of the column.

From some way off, I observed the manoeuvring as a couple of our tanks came up from the rear to relieve others at the front. One of the tanks turned, but its driver had apparently over-estimated the width of the causeway as he reversed and, to the horror of all the onlookers, the great machine suddenly pitched backwards down the low embankment and vanished in the swamp before our eyes.

The Pioneers immediately felled a few slender birches and tried to feel out the position of the vanished Panzer. A heavy tractor came up and let go a length of steel cable, but every attempt to hook the sunken monster failed.

It is sometimes possible to help a dying comrade in battle – we had all had that experience – but to stand up here on the causeway, unable to lift a finger, while our comrades below died a slow death was ghastly.

I was about to make my way back when there was a huge detonation from the front, louder than any I had ever heard before. I took my place in the column again, because I wanted to see what calibre of weapon this could have been – presumably an anti-tank mine, whose effects we had to discover.

I soon reached the spot, where the snow seemed to have been swept away with a broom over a wide circumference. Black earth stared back at me. I was told that it must have been a mine of a size previously unknown to us. I asked if there had been any victims and the NCO I had spoken to pointed all round him over a wide circle. 'Everywhere there,' he said. 'A motorbike and side-car with three men.' All I could see were splinters, fragments, remnants, rags. If I had to die here, I wanted it to be like that.

The days were becoming harder, with losses caused by firing on the flanks – we could scarcely ever see the marksmen. Heavy losses, though not a single tank had appeared against us – what could Panzers do here? The swamps were worse obstacles to us than Soviet tanks. The Russians certainly knew where to find the islands in the marshes from which they could fire on us – feeling as we did like targets set up for hunting practice along the causeway from Chudovo to Tikhvin.

We reached Tikhvin at last – on 8 November 1941, as I have now discovered from the archives. There had been little resistance in the town itself – what would have been the point? After all, in Tikhvin we were like rats in a trap. The small town had been evacuated, there was not a soul to be seen. The troops prepared themselves for the defence of this town in complete peace and quiet, an eerie silence filling the market-place, now under deep snow. The infantry dug themselves in, our guns disappeared in defilades, the tanks camouflaged themselves in barns and cowsheds, breaking openings in the walls for their gun muzzles. Tikhvin was now a 'fortress' and the 12th Panzer Division, intended for mobile warfare, was now engaged in positional warfare. Who had given the orders?

We had been ordered to take Tikhvin and we had done it. We had cut the railway line, but after a few days we heard from reconnaissance reports that thousands of Russian soldiers and civilians were building a new road far to the north of the town, out of range of our artillery.

Then the bauxite mines were found, reached by scouts who had actually brought back soil samples. That was all, and there it stopped.

And what of our Finnish allies, who were supposed to be coming from the North to shake hands with us in Tikhvin?

The Finns had not even considered emerging from their 200 kilometre-wide corridor between Lake Ladoga and Lake Onega, where they had reconquered their old frontiers after heavy losses and had the good sense not to be betrayed by Hitler into an adventure in the vastness of Northern Russia.

So the German leadership had not succeeded in closing a second, 'outer ring' round Leningrad. The 12th Panzer Division had crossed the Volkhov in vain, the occupation of Tikhvin had brought nothing but losses. On the contrary, the division was trapped. By now, predictably, the Russians had established a ring around the town. Soon, lively target-shooting developed round this senseless 'fortress', sandwiched between the two fronts.

Far greater dangers attached to the maintenance of our link with the Volkhov. Our supplies and reinforcements could now only be protected or brought through by force of arms, but the transport of our wounded to the rear was the worst problem, because the Russians had no intention of respecting the large Red Crosses on our ambulances.

The Russians facing us had long since seen their chance: firing industriously at our dug-in weapons, but wisely not going in for the attack. Meanwhile, the Germans besieged Leningrad, and the Russians besieged Tikhvin. Daily we expected the order to withdraw beyond the Volkhov, but it was a long time coming. Perhaps our 'Supreme Commander' was still negotiating with Marshal Carl Gustav von Mannerheim, the President of Finland?

Absorbed in such thoughts, we were sitting in a little wooden house, hunting bugs to pass the time, when I saw our Baltic Baron, Engelhardt, struggling towards us through deep snow. His outward appearance had certainly never laid any special claim to adhere to 'Prussian' dress regulations, but at the sight of him words failed us. His head was weighed down by a gigantic fur cap and instead of the prescribed leather boots, his feet and legs were stuck into grey felt boots which did not even have soles.

'Engelhardt, where in the world did you get hold of those impossible garments?' cried Lieutenant-Colonel Becker, and in his rolling Baltic German our ADC replied: 'From the town, Colonel, and I've got lots more of them in my car.' The experienced Baltic officer had taken some soldiers from the staff company to 'weed out' a winter wardrobe from a whole row of houses. This would be a hard, cold winter, Engelhardt predicted, and without furs and felt boots we would be no match for the winter here in Northern Russia.

It was true that all of us, officers and men, were still wearing the clothes and equipment in which we had crossed the Russian frontier on 22 June. At that time not a single article of winter clothing had reached us. The soldiers on guard had to be relieved at shorter and shorter intervals, by day and most particularly by night. The thermometer had already dropped to minus twenty degrees, and Engelhardt said it would soon be much colder. So any winter clothing found in the houses of Tikhvin was requisitioned.

When Engelhardt had emptied out his car, filled to bursting with these items of clothing, he produced yet another 'surprise for our Adjutant', whom he knew to be particularly keen on beautiful antiques. He dragged in a pestle and mortar of finest bronze, of a size and weight I had seldom seen before, and set his trophy proudly on the table.

Becker froze and went for our Baron in a tone which unmistakably revealed his origins as a Prussian NCO: 'Engelhardt, where did you get that mortar?' Addressed in this loud, unfriendly manner our Baron reacted as only a Baltic citizen can react in such a situation, impenitent, friendly and 'in the Baltic way': 'From the chemist's shop on the market-place, Colonel. This was the biggest and best of them.' Becker, still icy, continued to address his orderly officer with biting severity: 'Engelhardt, you will return the mortar at once to where you found it. Otherwise I shall be forced to have you charged with looting.' Engelhardt did not give up. In his appealing Baltic voice he said: 'But it would be a shame to leave such a beautiful mortar behind, because we're surely not going to spend the whole winter in Tikhvin, Colonel, and who knows, Colonel, what kind of people may come into this empty little town after us? So I think we ought to save this unusually beautiful mortar from destruction!'

But in our upright Commanding Officer he had picked the wrong man: 'Engelhardt, you will drive to Division at once, together with the mortar, and show the mortar on my behalf to General Harpe. You will ask him, on my behalf, for his decision.'

Engelhardt came to attention without a word, picked up the *corpus delicti* in both arms, went out to his car and vanished from our sight. Becker muttered something under his breath to the effect that it certainly was an unusually fine mortar, but Engelhardt's ideas on the subject simply would not do.

It must have been at least an hour before Engelhardt returned, advancing through the snow with the radiant smile of the victor, the mortar in his arms. For the second time he set down the 'looted item' before us on the table, and beside it, on a dispatch pad, in his own hand, with the signature of Divisional Commander Harpe, the following note: 'I hereby authorise Lieutenant Stahlberg to take home a mortar from the chemist's shop as a memento of the town of Tikhvin.'

For more than three years the 'memento' stood in our house in Stettin, and I still have General Harpe's 'authorisation' to this day.

That winter grew bitterly cold. The thermometer dropped to below thirty degrees, the snow cover deepened from day to day. We had still received no winter clothing, as our supplies and reinforcements fought their way towards us in Tikhvin.

To camouflage our vehicles we had them dug into the snow. The engines became heaters which their drivers left running night and day. Then petrol supplies grew short, so we had to be economical with our heating arrangements, though if an engine were switched off for too long it was difficult to start again. To spare the batteries, the engines were warmed up before they were started, by putting tin cans filled with diesel oil under the vehicles and setting light to them, but every driver hoarded as much fuel as he would need for the anticipated withdrawal.

Frost-bitten limbs, feet, hands, ears, noses, mounted from day to day, but it was the wounded who were in the greatest danger. If frost penetrated an open wound it was unlikely that the man could be saved. The men preferred death to injury. Doubts were beginning to gnaw at us all, from private soldier to Commanding Officer, but ultimately, we thought, 'them up there' must have recognised the mistakes made by the leadership and would avoid them in the future, so we should have to grit our teeth and not lose hope.

Ammunition was now also in short supply. 'Don't shoot at random!' we told the soldiers. 'Remember we shall probably need more ammunition for the withdrawal than for the defence of Tikhvin.'

Then we had to ration food, having found no cattle we could have slaughtered, not even horses.

It was hard on those whose vehicles or tanks were no longer usable for lack of an important spare part, though sometimes the talent for improvisation, or even invention, which would come to light in ordinary technicians was remarkable. Engine repairs were undertaken in the open, at more than 30 degrees below freezing, often in snowstorms and not infrequently under enemy fire, when lives were in danger and time was short.

We had almost stopped expecting an order to withdraw. So far we had never retreated in this war, so Tikhvin would probably be our end. And then the order came through after all, on 6 or 7 December 1941 – I no longer remember the exact date. Far too late, of course, but at least it came before the Russians attacked.

I remember scarcely anything of that retreat. Only one or two moments are still present in my mind. I had suddenly begun to run a high fever, but neither then nor later did I discover what illness had struck me. I remember only that I was wrapped in blankets and sat or lay for days in a half-track. Sometimes we were on the move, sometimes at a standstill – I lost all sense of time. I remember a good deal of shooting, shouted orders, cries of pain and calls for the medical orderlies. I lay comatose under my blankets, indifferent to it all.

At some point – and this I remember with dreadful clarity – I pushed aside the blanket over my head for a moment, to see all around me bodies upon bodies, sick and wounded, sitting, lying, squatting; and on the back of our tractor lay the dead, or rather, they did not lie but were stacked, bound on with ropes. Our soldiers would not leave a dead comrade lying in the snow, but would load him up whenever possible. The stack behind us rose from day to day, probably contributing decisively to my survival, because when the Russians fired on us from behind, our dead became a bullet-screen, a protective shield.

Some time, probably at the very end of the year, my memory returned. I was lying in a bed that was far too short, with our doctor beside me, telling me I had come through. I wanted to know where we were and he assured me that we had already crossed the Volkhov and were in a village to the south-west of Leningrad, with the vital task of holding the Front against the Russians along the Volkhov.

And what, I asked him, had become of our battalion and our division. Once again the doctor reassured me: it was difficult to see the whole picture as yet. I asked him if I would be sent to hospital, but he said that was no longer necessary.

So Christmas had already passed, and I had some difficulty in sorting out my sense of time. I was left in bed for a few more days and had time to think. Not of what had been: I instinctively resisted thinking about the horrors that lay behind me. What concerned me was what was going to happen now. Brother officers visited me and then I did, after all, allow them to tell me what I had been missing in the days that had passed.

In December 1941 the Commander-in-Chief of the Army, Field Marshal Walther von Brauchitsch, retired – a scapegoat had had to be found. Hitler appointed himself Commander-in-Chief in his stead.

Another, positively incredible piece of news disturbed us more: some of us had heard on the radio that on 11 December, during a meeting of the 'Greater German' Reichstag in the Berlin Kroll Opera, Hitler had announced to enthusiastically cheering 'people's representatives' that he hereby declared war on the United States of America. So we were definitely in the hands of a madman. Nevertheless, even among responsible people in our unit, when the talk turned to Hitler, there were those who quoted the age-old belief in the knife edge between madness and genius and some continued to draw comparisons between Hitler and Napoleon.

At the end of the year, the remnants of the 12th Panzer Division were moved to Estonia. There was a fulsome divisional order about our deeds of glory and the divisional commander was 'decorated by the Führer with the Oakleaves to his Knight's Cross'. I travelled to Estonia by tractor with other convalescents, for the most part on new corduroy roads through trackless marshland. Engelhardt said we should keep our eyes open as there were still bears in this area, but no matter how hard we looked, we never saw a single bear.

My Diary for 1942

A small book, only 12 centimetres long, worn and shabby, lies before me – one of the few documents I still possess from the war. The entries are terse, scarcely more than place names. We had become apathetic.

Towards the end of the little book addresses have been entered, out of alphabetical order, just as they came. Some of the names and addresses have been cut out with scissors, but astonishingly I had overlooked Henning Tresckow – as if he must on no account be forgotten: Potsdam, Burggrafenstrasse 32, telephone number 2689.

Towards the end, the insignia of thirty German Panzer divisions are recorded, clearly and meticulously, for quick recognition of oncoming units.

The last pages show a coloured map of the continent of Europe with the Greater German Reich extending west to Luxembourg and Metz and east to Brest-Litovsk. So the map of 1942 had long been superseded. We were already far beyond Brest-Litovsk to the East. At the beginning of 1942 the remnants of the 12th Panzer Division were in Estonia for 'rehabilitation'. In reality the old Stettin division had been smashed to pieces.

Estonia turned out to be a most beautiful country, its people kindly. Place names such as Dorpat, Fellin and Wesenberg were easy to pronounce or even sounded German. It was not until we went into quarters that we noticed the lack of men: Estonia appeared to be a country of women. 'Where are your men?' we asked, and received a grim reply: 'In 1939, when the Treaty of Friendship was concluded between Hitler and Stalin, the Soviet soldiers arrived. They arrested all the males, including the boys, put them on trains and transported them to the East. We have heard nothing since.'

Our 'rehabilitation' lasted only a few weeks, while fresh battles raged on the Volkhov. The enemy was now deploying Siberian regiments, said to be impervious to the cold. Moreover, they were wearing padded white outer tunics which made them invisible in the snow until they moved.

Then came a new order: return to the Front! With about a hundred soldiers from the remnants of our companies we rolled eastwards again, via Narva into Russia. In Tosno, not far from Leningrad, I had to report to 'Construction Battalion Keppel'. This battalion, under a Pioneer, Major Keppel, consisted almost entirely of older men who had originally been sent to Northern Russia to build roads and corduroy tracks for us. Now the construction battalion had been 'reorganised' in conjunction with our Panzer-Jäger units. In particular, it had been given a new name and was now to be referred to as Combat Battalion Keppel. This 'regrouping' had been the Führer's personal idea!

With a motley mixture of trucks and tractors we moved on towards Chudovo. After more than three months, here we were again, passing through this dismal dump. Then the new combat battalion received its combat orders: to relieve the 3rd battalion of an infantry regiment with the impressively high number of 390 on the Volkhov front. That area had been calm for some days now and only a few units of the soldiers of the 390th Infantry were still about. They had dug trenches and built dugouts, and now the soldiers of the 12th Panzers had turned into infantrymen in a positional war. We had had no previous experience of digging trenches, but our Commanding Officer, who had been stationed before Verdun in 1917, gave us advice.

Combat Battalion Keppel looked like a pack of bandits, because each man saw to it that his garments were, above all, warm. There were dead soldiers, both German and Russian, lying all around us, where hand-to-hand fighting had taken place. The Russians had padded jackets, fur caps and felt boots, with snow tunics over their uniforms, and now we would have to worry about the possibility of confusing German and Soviet soldiers. I had succeeded in finding a seamstress in Estonia who had made me a fur cap from a ragged

German uniform coat and rabbit skin. The cap made me recognisable as a German, but no longer as an officer – who cared!

Early in February I was recalled to Estonia, where we had acquired newly-trained young soldiers from Kolberg* in Pomerania, who were to be distributed according to usefulness among the remnants of our companies. Since there was a shortage of heavy weapons, the companies formed were more like infantry. We agreed to this, since anti-tank weapons were no longer in use. Up to now the Red Army in our area had attacked with infantry alone.

I was not long in Estonia before stand-to orders arrived from the Volkhov front: the entire defence line was in extreme danger, with breakthroughs into our defensive positions, now here, now there. There was hand-to-hand fighting which called for every available soldier to go to the Front at once, regardless of rank or position.

On 8 February 1942 I was back in Chudovo, but this time no battalions or even companies were being deployed: now only small groups were formed, '20 men here, 10 men over there, six to that machine-gun post – You'll find them there, in that direction, but not by day, you wouldn't make it. The people up there will have to hold on until you come!'

When it was dark I found the machine-gun nest we were to relieve. I had five men, including two NCOs who were determined to be in my group because I was regarded as lucky. The three people we found in the machine-gun position fell on our necks as if we were their saviours. 'It's usually quiet here at night, but by moonlight or at first light you have to take hellish care. There are Siberians in the snow a few hundred metres ahead. They suddenly get up and try to advance through the deep snow, with their officers behind the soldiers instead of in front. Make sure you shoot the ones at the back first, and you'll be left in peace!'

Then the three soldiers we had relieved ran back along the communication trench. We organised ourselves as well as we could in the dugout. A raised 'sleeping berth' allowed room for three, cheek by jowl. I took over the first duty on the machine-gun and tried to penetrate the darkness and get to know the sounds of the countryside. A deathly silence lay over the river basin of the Volkhov. I sent two of my soldiers out to collect birch wood, impressing on them that they must be back by midnight, because my calendar showed that the moon would rise after 24.00 hours.

* Now Kołobrzeg.

Birch was the only wood we could use for heating purposes, because it produced little or no smoke.

In the distance, beyond the Russian lines, we heard an aircraft, every single cylinder clattering, obviously an old kite. We knew it, though no one had yet seen it; being a very slow flyer, it came only by night. The entire Volkhov front called it 'Iron Gustav' – after a famous Berlin coach driver – because it arrived so regularly and so slowly. If Iron Gustav was roughly above the German lines our soldiers shot at it with their rifles; after all, a bullet might actually hit it one day! We laughed a lot over Iron Gustav and it did us good.

The two soldiers dragged up as many small birch branches as they could carry and began to saw. Now that there were six of us again, I sent both NCOs off to make contact with our two neighbouring positions. Since the telephone in our hole was dead, they were also to try to use someone else's telephone to request a new line to us. We had no radio.

The NCOs were soon back. The position to our left was about 50 metres away but to our right the neighbouring position was not occupied. The next machine-gun was in the position beyond that. There was no time for further reconnaissance now, because according to my pocket calendar the moon would be rising in a few minutes.

The scene revealed to us when its pale light illuminated the landscape was one of horror: we were in the middle of a graveyard, the dead, German and Russian, lay all round us. Here a helmet was visible through the snow, there only an arm freed by the wind, here an entire body, there only – the unspeakable.

We were staring round, appalled, when suddenly a bullet whistled close over our heads and forced us back into cover.

Together we discussed how we should behave if the Russians were to attack or if they were to lay down artillery fire over our positions. In the dugout we found a pot of white paint, so at least we could whiten our helmets.

This was my first experience of trench warfare. We were there for three weeks. Although we were not attacked, the first days were the worst: living among corpses was inhuman, their possible burial was a daily topic, but we had no chance. Two soldiers arrived every night with food containers, snow provided our drinking water. Any one of us might be hit by an enemy bullet today or tomorrow and have to be thrown over the edge of the trench by his companions. Transport to the rear would not help: better dead than wounded, we told each other. The food-carriers reported that the thermometer had already reached 40 degrees below zero that night. We were simply existing.

My five comrades suffered so badly from lice that hunting them down became their only leisure activity; but no more than three men at a time could devote themselves to the hunt, since it meant removing all one's clothes. The others had to stay on the alert. I myself was spared lice; even when we were sleeping cheek by jowl, the lice were kind enough to avoid me. What I did suffer from were bugs, but they lived only in houses, not in dugouts – lucky again.

We actually did have a latrine, which could be reached only at night. By moonlight I discovered a board on which some joker had painted a verse, lovingly decorated, which I soon knew by heart:

Shit till the bog doors shrivel!
Shit on the sergeant's feet!
Shit in the jaws of the devil!
But – don't shit on the seat!

After three weeks we were relieved at last. Filthy, full of self-disgust, we returned to quarters in Estonia, to clean bathrooms, fresh linen, and an end to the repulsive three-week beard. Since that time I have hated being unshaven. In Narva there was actually a German field dentist, and even if he was no artist, it is only fair to say that he had to drive his drill with his feet like a bicyclist.

As I still have my little diary, I read that after a week we returned to the Front, this time spending four weeks there before we could be relieved. And so it went on, to and fro between Estonia and the fronts to the south of Leningrad, once back on the Volkhov, then on the Neva, then at Mga, which we called 'the bone mill'. We felt like firemen, because we always followed the flames, or like tinkers, mending holes.

Every time there were losses, sometimes 'slight', at other times 'heavy'. Then 'new' young soldiers were brought in from Kolberg, poorly trained, very young lads with no idea what awaited them. One day I realised that my Commanding Officer, Leiutenant-Colonel Becker and I, his Adjutant, who scarcely carried out any of the duties of an Adjutant these days, were the only officers left who had been with the old Stettin 2nd Panzer-Jäger Battalion on 22 June 1941, the day of the attack on the Soviet Union. And let no one imagine that during the months of fighting Lieutenant-Colonel Becker had spent his time sitting somewhere 'to the rear'. He would often grab a hastily assembled platoon in order to intervene at the Front with 20 or 30 men and save the situation.*

Once in April, and then again in May, there was a ray of hope: we received new anti-tank weapons to replace the many lost or worn-out guns. They were actually mounted on self-propelled gun carriages, partly of new German and partly of old Czech origin, which led us to various conclusions. It looked as if the armaments industry at home was in a bad way, and although the gunners on the self-propelled guns could now develop tremendous fire power, woe betide them if, for want of ammunition, they simply became a rolling two-storey house. And woe betide them in the spring, when they were in danger of sinking in the mud because their tracks were too narrow.

More and more we sensed the hand of our new Supreme Commander, as we read operational orders which betrayed the signature of the former lance-corporal. Passivity prevailed along our front, initiatives coming almost exclusively from the other side. Our leadership seemed paralysed.

At this time we came across Spanish soldiers in German uniform between Lakes Ladoga and Ilmen. The Spanish Head of State, General Franco, had sent Hitler a division of volunteers, obviously Spain's payment for the German Condor Legion which Hitler had despatched to Spain in 1936. This Spanish Blue Division, like our own, was unprepared for winter warfare in Russia, the young Spanish volunteers suffering even more from the cold than we did. Why this disregard for the statutory welfare obligations? Was it Hitler's indolence, was it cynicism, or was it even his revenge against Franco for refusing to join in our war? Given only a vestige of fair play, Hitler could easily have used the Blue Division in a more suitable climate – plenty of warmer possibilities existed.

Members of the Blue Division revenged themselves in their own way. Since the Germans had equipped them with the most up-to-date weapons, not infrequently the ones which were in short supply

---

* From the War Diary of the 12th Panzer Division (original in the Federal/Military Archives in Freiburg): Fighting strength of the 12th Panzer Division:

	Officers	Civil servants	NCOs	Men	Total
December 41	295	107	2,268	11.297	13,967
February 42	116	59	1,052	4,802	6,029
July 42	71	48	621	2,550	3,290

in our own units, the word soon went round between Lakes Ladoga and Ilmen: 'Swap weapons for . . . ! No one thought any the worse of our comrades from the Iberian peninsula.

Month after month passed on our northern front without any substantial changes. Since Hitler had taken over the supreme command of the Army himself, we were always on the defensive. But the war grew daily more brutish and many a battle no longer had anything to do with warfare.

At Mga a group of Soviet tanks broke through our thin lines again, as far as one of our assembly points for the wounded. The tanks rolled straight over the big tent in which the doctors were working at primitive operating tables, driving to and fro, across and back, until the last spark of life was extinguished.

Home Leave

On the evening of 12 June 1942 I was ringing at the door of my mother's flat in Brandenburgische Strasse in Berlin. 'My God!' she cried, taking me in her arms, 'my God, what do you look like?'

Only the night before I had been in Estonia, where our 2nd Anti-tank Battalion had been 'rehabilitated' once again for a few days. In the afternoon my Commanding Officer had suddenly said I could take two weeks' home leave. While it was still dark, my driver had taken me to the airfield at Reval, where I just might be able to get myself a free seat in one of the Luftwaffe's transport planes. I avoided the leave train because it would mean wasting several days on the way to Berlin and my entertainment on the journey, sitting on those hard wooden benches, would be confined to bug-hunting. Our Paymaster had supplied me with a stack of ration cards which were worth more than money at home; in the Army they were worthless.

I was in luck. I flew to Riga by Ju 52. It was slow, but we felt extraordinarily safe, having seen machines of this type returning safely, even with rows of bullet holes in them. When I landed in Riga there was a Ju 86 standing there, as if waiting for me. After a flight of seven hours, I was landing at Berlin Tempelhof Airport.

The next morning my mother brought me a princely breakfast in bed, but eating and drinking were not the order of the day: instead, a doctor appeared and diagnosed hepatitis. 'Another one from Volkhov,' he remarked drily. 'Now you'll have to be patient.' It would be three months before the Berlin garrison doctor declared me 'fit for active service' again.

They wanted to move me to a hospital outside Berlin, but my mother protested: she was going to take care of me herself. There was no arguing with my mother, even for a military doctor, especially since she herself had been wearing the uniform of a staff director in the German Red Cross, which gave her additional authority. She telephoned the German Red Cross executive in Berlin, the executive telephoned the German Red Cross in Paris, where my mother was superintendent of the German soldiers' hostels. Her leave was extended.

My mother now spent a great deal of time beside my bed, asking for accounts of the present position in Russia and telling me of her work in the French capital. She loved Paris. She had made up her mind to do all she could to maintain order and decency in the hostels. Truly, the daughter of a Pomeranian Pietist Prussian family was in her element.

I asked what she did for entertainment. 'From time to time I go' – her eyes lit up – 'to Montmartre. I even have a regular haunt there called "*Au Lapin Agil*", a little old house, full of nooks and crannies and a bit grubby, but with an extraordinary atmosphere.' My mother was 54 now and still an attractive woman – she was one of those fortunate people who grow more beautiful with age. I told her I hoped she did not make these risky visits without an escort. 'On the contrary!' she cried, 'I would not feel right at the *Lapin Agil* with an escort.' There was absolutely nothing to eat there, it seemed, but one sat at long tables on rough benches, with only one kind of drink, a bowl of cognac with a cherry in it, and the decoration of the one room consisted of a life-sized crucifix on the wall. But the best thing about this establishment was that anyone who felt like it could turn up there whenever and however he liked. There was one habitué who declaimed poetry, another performed conjuring tricks, every night brought plenty of surprises. On her very first evening she had sat down at the old piano – 'Not a grand piano, unfortunately' – and played Beethoven's *Moonlight Sonata*. 'Surely not the whole sonata?' I asked. 'Only the first part that first evening,' she said, 'but the whole sonata several times later on!'

I wanted to know if she appeared there in uniform and with an undertone of indignation she replied: 'But of course in uniform! Don't you think that's in the spirit of the Red Cross? And it's got nothing to do with "appearing".'

I asked if she had played anything else after Beethoven. 'On the first evening, after the first part of the *Moonlight Sonata*, an old lady came over and thanked me and asked if I could play Ravel or Debussy. I had to say no – as you know, I'm not keen on either of them. Instead I sang two Brahms Lieder.' 'Sang?' I was astonished. 'You haven't got a trained voice.' 'Maybe,' she said, 'but when you're accompanying yourself, you can get away with quite a bit.'

Finally I asked what one could play after Brahms in Paris, because to French ears Brahms was surely not a 'finale'. 'This and that,' she said. 'If possible, I play whatever people ask me to play. But at the end always Bach, one of his chorales, preferably the final chorale from the St. Matthew or St. John Passion. After all, we mustn't forget that we are at war.'

'Have you already joined the Resistance in Paris?' I teased her. She asked how on earth I knew about the Resistance. 'Perhaps from Radio London, after midnight,' I replied. Then she wanted to know if we listened to Radio London in Russia and I said we had neither time nor opportunity in the field, but our radio operators almost certainly listened at night, on their headphones, of course, so that no one else could hear, and with one hand poised on the tuning knob so that the London wavelength could be changed at once if necessary. Naturally we knew that listening to and passing on news from Radio London incurred the death penalty in Germany. Nor did we pass on what we had learned from Radio London, but in conversation with a good friend one was simply 'reliably informed'. My mother said it was just the same in Paris.

Since early childhood I had had no opportunity for such peaceful, intimate talks with my mother. She had always been rather a 'restless soul', always wanting novelty, always making plans, always meeting 'new' people. In the Red Cross it was Frieda Cleve, leader of women's work on the executive, who was genuinely concerned about the 'balance' between the political influences to which the German Red Cross was subject. After all, a prince of the House of Saxe-Coburg Gotha had been elected president, whether because of the high office he held in the party hierarchy or because of his close relationship with the British royal house. In National Socialist Germany the word opportunism was so frequently written larger than large. On the other hand, if it was a question of hiding someone as profoundly loathed by the Nazis as Elisabeth von Thadden,* head of the Wieblingen girls' boarding-school near Heidelberg, from the henchmen of the Gestapo, Frieda

* Elizabeth von Thadden died under the guillotine in 1943.

Cleve was immediately ready to give her a job in a Parisian soldiers' hostel as cover.

From this source I learned something monstrous: Hitler had instructed the German Red Cross to destroy letters from German soldiers who had been taken prisoner by the Russians when they arrived via neutral Sweden. Postbag after postbag was burned.

I was in bed for a month before the doctor allowed me to get up. Lieutentant-Colonel Becker wrote to tell me that the soldiers of the 12th Panzer Division were still being deployed as infantry near Leningrad, still as 'firemen'. Nothing had changed since he had sent me on leave. In the next letter he wrote that I was to become '01' (1st ADC) of the 12th Panzer Division. Since he had said goodbye to me in Estonia I knew that he had put my name forward for training as a General Staff Officer. Had we really reached the stage when the Army had to call on reserve officers to replenish the General Staff?

Towards the end of July, I was ready to think about making plans for my leave, but the doctor insisted on another week or two of convalescence before that. So I drove off to Bansin on the Baltic, to a guesthouse on the promenade, where my brother and I had spent many a delightful weekend, driving out from Stettin in the last years of peace. Frau Karow, the owner of 'Seeschloss', had diet food specially cooked for me and in an astonishingly short time she had made a normal human being of me again.

Then one day I took the train to visit my grandmother in Klein-Krössin, where her son Hans-Jürgen Kleist-Retzow had arranged a comfortable half-timbered house as a 'dower house' for her.

Grandmother was not pleased with me for coming to see her in civilian clothes, so to please her I went back to my room and put on my uniform. When I returned she had another grumble: my uniform was incomplete – after all I was an adjutant. She brushed aside my objection that the adjutant's lanyard was worn only on duty. She was proud that her eldest grandson was an adjutant in the Stettin division and she wanted to see me as an adjutant just once.

So I went back to my room once again, took the silver lanyard out of my case and put it on. Now at last Grandmother seemed satisfied. She poured tea and told me that she had another reason for seeing me in full rig, because she wanted to tell me what she thought of 'our' war. Straightening a little in her armchair, she began gravely: 'I am not opposed to war as a last political resort, but this war is a criminal war and its initiators are criminals. Nothing worse could befall our German Fatherland than to win this war.'

I was stupefied. This was the most uncompromising statement I had heard and I said nothing, because basically we were of one mind. Then she said: 'And now, would you please bring in a good bottle of red wine. You know where my French wines are and as far as I am concerned you can take the best.'

The next day I drove over to Kieckow, little more than three kilometres away.

Uncle Hans-Jürgen Kleist and Aunt Maria walked up the old village street with me to their church. One or two things had changed: the crypt underneath the church had been cleared out, because the coffins were beginning to collapse. In the graveyard my uncle pointed to fresh graves, carefully tended, but without a cross. 'My Russian workers had set up Orthodox crosses, but the local Nazi leader had them taken away and I was sent "to Köslin" for a few weeks as a result.'

In the family graveyard a mass grave had been designed, where Uncle Hans–Jürgen had had all the coffins from the crypt deposited with their contents. All the names, dates, ranks and decorations were to appear together on a granite slab to be put up after the war. It would have to be thought out in peace and quiet, because the stone was intended to record a slice of Prussian and German history. After all, Kieckow had been owned by the family for over 700 years.

Beside the mass grave stood two fresh oak crosses for the cousins who had fallen in our division.

At dinner two or three people I did not know were sitting at the far end of the extended table. Oddly enough, I never learned their names, nor did they take part in the conversation. Aunt Maria whispered to me that they were guests of Dietrich Bonhoeffer from Berlin. Kieckow had become a refuge of the Confessional Church.

To Leningrad Again?

On 24 August 1942, I reported back to the Berlin garrison doctor and at last he signed me 'fit for active service'.

At last! Yes, that was how I saw it. I had received letters not only from my commanding officer but from other friends in the battalion. 'We miss you,' they said. We were at war, that was our

fate, so as soon as one was fit again one should be back at one's
post – as soon as possible – at last.

Early next morning, I was at Tempelhof Airport, looking for any
chance of getting back to Estonia as quickly as possible.

Soon I was sitting in a courier plane flying to Riga via Danzig*
and Königsberg†. The pilot agreed to let me sit in the co-pilot's
seat. I told him I came from Pomerania and asked him to fly as low
as possible, which he did, although it was forbidden. He enjoyed
getting me to tell him the names of so many little towns, villages
and estates, and we liked seeing the farmworkers at their harvest-
ing. Some of them waved to us because we were flying so low,
including men in olive-green shirts – prisoners of war. Eastern
Pomerania in harvest time – what a lovely place it was!

In Riga I had to find another aircraft and in a few hours I was
sitting in a Ju 52, fully loaded with spare parts for tanks and
tractors.

It was much more difficult getting from Reval to Wesenberg
than from Berlin to Reval, although the little country town was
scarcely more than 100 kilometres away. In fact I did not reach it
until the next day, and by train. Since I had announced myself by
telephone from Reval, there was my batman, standing on the
platform. He gave me a military salute, then lost his head a little
and fell – quite unmilitarily – on my neck. 'You've come just in
time, Sir, we're going to the Front tomorrow evening!' I asked
where we were bound. 'Back to the Neva this time.' The front line
was more or less unchanged, only our 2nd Panzer–Jäger Battalion
had changed a great deal and I was to see predominantly new
faces. But the Lieutenant-Colonel was still there, although it was
rumoured he would soon be promoted to colonel and take over a
Panzer regiment in Southern Russia.

Meeting my old battalion again was half joyful, half bewildering.
I now knew only a few officers, and having believed I was at last
returning to 'my' battalion, in fact I felt almost like a stranger.

The next evening, 27 August, we left Wesenberg and rolled
through Narva into Russia. The great news came: Leningrad was
to be attacked and taken.

A year ago, as we saw it then, we could quite simply have driven
into the great city. Now, a year later, it was going to be a tough
battle, because the Russians had had a whole year to make

* Now Gdansk.
† Now Kaliningrad.

thorough preparations for the German attack. A new Army Commander-in-Chief would be in charge. The victor of the Crimea, with its legendary fortress of Sevastopol, was the man to take the two million-strong city of Leningrad: Field Marshal von Manstein had already arrived. To give the necessary impetus to the operation, the Führer had sent the latest tanks, the first Tigers, fresh from the factory, to our front. Four brand new Tiger tanks, which the Soviets could not match. And more were to follow.

This was stirring news. Had the top brass really roused themselves to get the front moving again, after a year of virtual paralysis? The name of Manstein and the hopes associated with it said as much. There was also the allegedly unbeatable new heavy Tiger tank. So into the centre of Leningrad, with four of the monsters! That was something.

Our companies took up their positions on the Neva. We waited.

By now my pocket diary showed 1 September. 'Beginning of the fourth year of war,' I had noted. The First World War had lasted for four years – how much longer would the Second last?

On 2 September the 1st General Staff Officer, Major Bergengruen, a cousin of the writer Werner Bergengruen, sent for me. I was to become his senior *aide-de-camp* (01 to the Ia). I seized the opportunity to ask him whether and where I could see the new Tiger tanks – one should at least know them from the outside, if we were to take Leningrad with them. But he put me off. One of the monsters had a technical fault and was not usable, the other three had proved too heavy for the log roads and bridges of northern Russia, Bergengruen told me, his face expressionless.

Whatever else we owed to the personal strategic initiative of our Supreme Commander as regards the final conquest of Leningrad is quickly told. Before we opened the attack on the city, the Russians attacked us. They crossed the Volkhov again and made deep inroads into our defensive front. Undoubtedly, it was thanks to the leadership of Field Marshal Manstein and the courage of our soldiers that – once again – the Soviets were beaten in bitter fighting near the notorious village of Mga (the battle of encirclement on Lake Ladoga). But there were heavy casualties on both sides, until, at the beginning of October, the two fronts came to a standstill again in the positions they had now occupied for a year. Neither side had achieved anything.

Then came the news of the expected promotion and transfer of my old Commanding Officer, Becker. He still had a bottle of

French red wine in his luggage; together we reviewed once again what the two of us – the last of the 'old' officers – had been through: the 'War of Flowers' in the Sudetenland in 1938, the beginning of the war in 1939, with our gigantic army reserves against a hopelessly inferior Poland, together with our first doubts about the morality of the German conduct of the war, 1940 in France, the feeling of security in being part of a military operation which could be ranked as classical warfare, and now, since June 1941, the insanity of a war wilfully launched on two fronts and the declaration of war on the United States. We soldiers were being used to plunge the whole world into blood and horror. Again and again we asked each other the question we regarded as crucial: Why had Hitler started to attack the Soviet Union on 22 June, instead of in April?

That was to be my last conversation with this simple and personally irreproachable man. Quite soon we received the news of his death on the battlefield, where he had fallen in the first assault at the head of his Panzer regiment. I thought back to our desperate drive together into the Russian pillbox line in June of the previous year. Something similar had happened this time too, we heard.

Now I really was 'the last of the old ones' in the 2nd Panzer–Jäger Battalion, and among the officers I knew no one with whom I could speak freely.

Then a new Commanding Officer arrived from home, a nice, friendly old man, but pursued by ill-luck. Late one evening, an old log cabin we had just occupied burned down when our stove was lit. When we rushed at the last moment from the blazing wooden hut, he broke his leg.

By now what was left of the 12th Panzer Division had been withdrawn from the Front. The companies had been made up with many young soldiers from home and older ones returned from convalescence. Only equipment was in short supply: we had now received horses as draught animals, which saved the Panzer division petrol.

One day the entire unit, now so motley and muddled, rolled southward, mostly by train. Farewell Volkhov, farewell Leningrad, farewell Estonia! We mustered in the Nevel area, where we became part of Army Group Centre again. At last 'them up there' had realised that the marshes between Leningrad and Lakes Ladoga and Ilmen were not suitable terrain for a Panzer division. What an incredible amount of blood that recognition had cost.

We had no new commanding officer and responsibility for the battalion now rested with me. I was stationed with my head-quarters staff in a village surrounded by woods. There were only one or two women still living in the houses with their children, and relations with them were conducted with civility and trust. Matter-of-factly, it seemed, the women took over the laundry and helped in the field kitchen. There were no difficulties. Initially we were unable to discover where the men of the village were, until one day our night guard reported that a few women were visited by their husbands at night. There was more life in the surrounding woods than we had suspected.

By the second week of November, the men in the forest had apparently reached a stage when they could begin to fight us in well-organised, well-equipped groups. In a few days we had a horrific minor war raging throughout the area, of a kind that had probably not been seen in Europe since the days when Napoleon's troops fought the Spanish guerrillas south of the Pyrenees.

Slowly, piece by piece, we recieved new arms and new vehicles and tried to conduct a training programme for the young soldiers, but before it was running properly, our companies were deployed again, not now at the Front but in the so-called hinterland. On orders from the highest level, this new type of warfare was to be officially described as 'combating partisan activities'. It soon emerged that a good many of the groups came from villages which only last summer had welcomed the German troops with deputa-tions of honour, with bread and salt, as liberators. It could have grown into a wave of sympathy for Germany, which might have assumed historic significance, but by now the people liberated from Communist despotism had learned what German policy behind the battle front had really meant: not freedom, but new and sometimes worse oppression. The simple people in Russia had soon sensed the close relationship between Communism and National Socialism.

Then a new commanding officer arrived, a charming, friendly Austrian major who had served in the First World War as an 'imperial and royal' lieutenant – an officer of the Austro–Hungarian Empire. However, he had not the faintest notion of the ways of a Panzer division: I would have no trouble with him! Nor did he make any secret of the fact that he would much rather have worn his old 'imperial and royal' uniform than the German one. Even in war, his former uniform had always been extremely stylish.

He gathered the companies together without arms and vehicles, and introduced himself to our soldiers, mostly from Pomerania, with excessive charm. Henceforward he was nicknamed 'Moser'. The description hit the nail on the head, as I knew, having spent an evening with the great Viennese actor Hans Moser.

I was with the new Commanding Officer for only a few days. The first snow was already covering the vast expanses of the Russian countryside, but we were relieved to observe that there was evidently little danger of our second winter in Russia being as cold as the first. We were just returning from a night exercise – it was Sunday, 15 November – when I was called to the field telephone and heard the voice of my cousin Henning von Tresckow: 'So you really do still exist!' he cried, adding that he wanted to speak to me as soon as posible.

I had not seen Henning since that memorable 21 June 1941, the eve of the attack on Russia. 'I can't get away that quickly,' I said, 'because we've just got a new Commanding Officer.' Henning said he did not want to speak to me privately, it was official, and it was very urgent, an order from Army Group.

Our 'Moser' took it casually, but Major Bergengruen of the General Staff, whose aide I was soon to become, reacted indignantly: 'Now is it your cousin or is it the Ia of the Army Group who wants to talk to you?' 'Both,' I said – what else could I say? In that case he sent his greetings to Colonel von Tresckow and I was to tell him that the Army Group should do more to see that the 12th Panzer Division became a Panzer division again at last. And when I came back from Army Group Headquarters I was to report to him first.

At seven the next morning, while it was still dark, I set off in an open Kübelwagen, with my batman and two other soldiers. We were, so to speak, armed to the teeth with machine pistols and hand-grenades, because from Nevel to Vitebsk we would have to cross some 120 kilometres of allegedly partisan territory. We were stopped once or twice by German military posts and had to wait until some sort of convoy had assembled. Towards evening we reched Vitebsk, which left another 160 kilometres to Headquarters Army Group Centre in Smolensk.

At the office of the Town Commandant at Vitebsk I was told that it would be impossible to take the road to Smolensk at night. However, they were expecting a leave train returning from

Germany at half past two, which was scheduled to arrive at Smolensk at nine and was adequately armed. Leaving my faithful batman and escort behind, I joined the amazingly punctual train. Once again I was lucky, because we reached Smolensk unscathed and remarkably quickly for wartime conditions in Russia: 160 kilometres in six and a half hours. My little 1942 diary records it precisely.

Tresckow and Schlabrendorff

Headquarters Army Group Centre in Smolensk had been set up in a big house, an old villa. On 17 November 1942 I entered the outer office of Ia, the 1st General Staff Officer, on the first floor. A lieutenant-colonel on the General Staff, whom I did not know, was sitting at a desk, from which he rose to greet me in the friendliest way. He seemed to have been expecting me. This was Berndt von Kleist, 2nd General Staff Officer of the Army Group.

He began to talk to me in an unforced, natural way that I had never previously encountered in the Army between older and younger service grades. We soon discovered by what roundabout ways we were related. I could hear Henning von Tresckow's clear voice in the next-door room, where a lively discussion seemed to be going on.

In the middle of the outer office there was a chess board on a small table. I looked at the interrupted game, surprised that there were no chairs at the table.

While I was still studying the state of the game, the door to the next room opened and several officers appeared, with Henning behind them.

'Glad you've come,' he greeted me. 'I hope you had no trouble with partisans *en route*. Are you surprised we play chess here instead of working? I asked whose game this was and why there were no chairs at the table and he explained that here at Army Group headquarters they played against each other in two teams, while talking, walking past, or having a discussion. A game usually lasted a whole day, and sometimes several days.

In the restricted area of the high command there was a small guesthouse, a detached log cabin, isolated from the other buildings. Henning sent me there with a lance-corporal and told me that we would be having our evening meal there with Fabian von Schlabrendorff, who was his aide.

The lance-corporal picked up my case and took me across to my
room, which actually had a bathroom attached. First of all we ran
a little water into the bathtub, placed my case over it, removed the
contents cautiously, piece by piece and shook them over the tub.
This was because of the bugs, which had plagued me from my very
first day in Russia – and I had spent the previous night in one of
the bug-ridden leave trains. We were highly successful and our
'bag' was a sight for sore eyes. Soon I was lying in the freshly
made-up bed, fast asleep.

At the agreed hour Henning, Fabian and I met in the sitting-
room. A table had been laid for three; Henning sat on my left,
Fabian on my right and in front of me a fire crackled in the hearth.
I felt a little like a sample on the test bench, but my host soon
overcame that with his conversation, and the lance-corporal
turned out to be a master chef and waiter. We had a grilled steak
each and a good Burgundy between us.

Our knives and forks were scarcely in action when Henning
began. He wanted to know what I now thought of the war. Instead
of answering I looked interrogatively at him. He understood at
once and told me I could speak quite openly here: the lance-
corporal – unfortunately I have forgotten his name – was silent as
the grave. This was something quite out of the usual for me
because, since the beginning of Hitler's régime, we had learned to
break off any discussion of fundamental matters whenever other
ranks were present, and the habit had bitten deep.

So I began by referring back to our last conversation on 21 June
1941, the day before the offensive was launched from East Prussia
against the Soviet Union. He had said that at that time Army
Group Centre had been ordered to push ahead to the East after
taking Minsk and to take Moscow before winter; it was conceivable
that this might succeed and that Russia might collapse if the
capital, with its many centralised functions, were to fall. But unless
it happened before the onset of winter, things looked bad.

I went on to say that I had retained a very lively memory of
Tresckow's words, especially during the first months of the
campaign, and had been all the more shocked when in the summer
of 1941 we had been stopped at Smolensk and the 12th Panzer
Division had been ordered to march to Army Group North and
take Leningrad first. I asked him who had given the order.

Instead of answering he laughed and told me to guess. Who else
could have given an order of such consequence? That at least was

an unequivocal answer. I told him that on the northward march we had argued fiercely about it, making inevitable comparisons with the retreat from the Marne in France in 1914. They had had the same thoughts at Army Group, Henning commented.

Then I gave him my impressions of the situation outside Leningrad, of Tikhvin and of the disintegration of my division. The winter battles of 1941/42 had shown us that none of the operational goals we had been set in the Army orders had been achieved, despite the sacrifice of the 12th Panzer Division. I asked him how the Supreme Commander could possibly send a Panzer division into the country between Volkhov and Tikhvin without knowing that it was a gigantic quagmire.

On several occasions the entire Front had been on the brink of collapse, which made it all the more admirable that our soldiers had gone so resolutely into battle. But at the Front, the private soldier's thinking faculties were becoming blunted. In my judgement, a situation had arisen in which the war against Russia was hanging by a thread. For instance, I myself was now the last remaining officer in my battalion who had gone off to war with these troops. I was now simply grateful for every day when I saw the sun rise.

While I was speaking, Henning had only interposed an occasional brief question. Fabian had listened in silence. But now Henning interrupted to ask if the 'commissar order' had been carried out in my division. I said that as far as I knew no commissar had been shot by my battalion. In the strategic situation the soldier had no other thought than to shoot and, if possible, to survive.

I had been asked in general terms what I thought of the war and I felt my response to be rather pathetic. However, I did bear some responsibility towards my fellow soldiers. The next day or the day after I would be back with my division and my battalion, and I would be squeezed like a lemon. After all, they knew I had been ordered to Army Group Headquarters.

So I took trouble with my final comment: amid the constantly recurring doubts as to the purpose and future of this war, my hopes were still fixed on our General Staff. My faith in the German General Staff was unshaken.

Here Henning intervened. He had something vital to tell me. The General Staff was no longer worthy of the name and was only distinguishable as such by the collar patches and the crimson

stripe down the trouser leg. Clausewitz and old Moltke were no
longer consulted. Hitler – in his own words – insisted that the
General Staff Officer must be like 'a bloodhound straining hungrily
at the leash, ready to hurl himself on the enemy and tear him limb
from limb'. These words from the Führer had been an insult. All
Hitler now wanted on the General Staff was 'subservient debt
collectors'. 'Debt collectors for a capital offender!' he cried, and
repeated the words.

I must have gazed speechlessly at him during this outburst. I
had never seen Henning so passionate before. Not a muscle in
Fabian's face moved. After a pause, Henning began again. This
time he was quite calm and objective, almost businesslike: he did
not share my view that the outcome of the war hung by a thread.
The outcome was already decided: the war was lost, finally and
irretrievably lost. The last die had been cast with Hitler's insane
declaration of war on the United States of America. We might still
win a few battles, but ultimately the war was over – that was his
judgement.

After a pause I asked him if there was anything in the rumours of
SS incursions against the civilian population in the rear areas. The
rumours were true, he said, but with the rider that this was not a
matter of occasional raids but of the planned extermination of
human beings. Reliable information had reached Army Group that
special SD and SS units had been formed for the carefully
organised execution of the plan, on a scale that transcended
imagination. While we, the soldiers, were permitted to get ourselves shot at the front, the SS went about their horrifying business
behind our backs. He, Henning, saw this as a desecration of the
soldiers' willing sacrifice at the front.

I had been listening to him aghast. Then Henning said that he
was working towards the day when all this would be over. No one
could say when that day would come, but come it would, and it
would be terrible.

Then he changed the subject and explained why he had sent for
me. He had a job for me. He had had a conversation with Field
Marshal Erich von Manstein, commander in chief of the Eleventh
Army within the Army Group. The Field Marshal had asked him if
he could recommend a young officer as his personal *aide-de-camp*
and he had recommended me.

My head was spinning. I needed time to answer. I said I did not
think I could leave my battalion now, because we had just

acquired a new commanding officer who had not the faintest idea what he was doing. This made no impression on Henning: it was up to the division to find a replacement for me. Then I objected that I could not imagine how a first lieutenant on the reserve could become a Field Marshal's ADC. I knew I had been selected for training as a General Staff Officer, but I was not one yet. Henning overrode all my objections. The post planned for me was not a general staff post but a completely personal attachment to the Field Marshal, as his closest aide and escort.

Assuming that Manstein took me on, I would have an extremely important job to do, because he, Tresckow, who had worked under Manstein a lot, regarded him – after General Beck – as the most capable mind among the German generals. The objective now was to influence this Field Marshal so that at the end of the National Socialist régime he would be among those prepared to take responsibility at the highest level. I must try to come close to Manstein and support him through thick and thin. Henning thought he had known me long enough and well enough to believe that we would like each other and had already told the Field Marshal that he and his future ADC were related via his wife – though I should know that Frau von Manstein was a committed member of the Nazi party. The Field Marshal was bound to talk to me about my relationship to his wife, which provided a basis for our conversation in advance. I had an appointment to report to Manstein the next afternoon. Henning had also gone over my head and arranged for the rest of my baggage to be transferred from my battalion to the high command of the Eleventh Army.

So I had no choice. But if, tomorrow, the Field Marshal did not like my face, I would soon be back with my division, with bag and baggage. It was as simple as that.

Towards the end of that evening, Henning Tresckow became very serious and insistent again. Everything we had thought and said would come to nothing unless I took this job of my own accord and with complete conviction. Finally he told me about the military situation south of the Eastern Front, where a major offensive by the Russians was apparently in preparation. The fronts were in movement on the Volga on either side of Stalingrad and Hitler would shortly order Manstein to take his Army Headquarters there in order to be inserted as a newly created Army Group Headquarters under the name of 'Don'. So I would probably soon be witnessing an important military development.

I still had a good many questions, because I had not the slightest idea how a big headquarters was organised. The more I asked, the more Fabian began to join in the conversation. At some point I asked Henning what sort of job Fabian had with him. Henning grinned: Fabian was 'the guardian of his political conscience'. The phrase spoke volumes – though Fabian behaved as if he had not heard.

Later that evening, Henning said he wanted to give me two names, only two, but I must be careful on no account to write them down. The bearers of these two names would soon be arriving to report to Manstein and then it would be up to me to make sure that the two could be 'reliably protected' when they talked to the Field Marshal, because the personal ADC always sat in Manstein's outer office.

The first was General Erich Fellgiebel, whom I did not know personally, but as the Chief of Army Communications his name was known throughout the Wehrmacht. While many a new weapon had its teething troubles, the new communications system always functioned reliably. There was no need for me to memorise Fellgiebel's name.

However, I had never heard the second name before: Stauffenberg. I could only say that I did not know the name, but Henning said it did not matter, in fact it was a good thing. Claus Graf von Stauffenberg, a major on the General Staff, was on the organisational side of OKH. It was an easy name for me to remember, because the first three and last four letters were identical to my own. This memory system tickled me.

When I was already on my feet saying goodbye, I asked Henning what had given him the idea of recommending me in particular to Field Marshal Manstein. His answer was forthright: he was sure I was 'not scared of big game', so he regarded me as not unsuitable, with any luck. As a rule, the 'big game' were quite lonely people, grateful for a spoken word, and moreover, our common ancestor Zedlitz* (whom I had never met) had once told him that if a cause was important enough, one was obliged to appeal on its behalf to each and every man, whether previously known or not, without respect of name or rank, to serve that cause. That had been the accepted practice for many generations in Prussia.

* Robert Graf von Zedlitz und Trützschler (1837–1914), Oberpräsident in Silesia, Poznan and Hesse and Prussian Minister of Culture.

PART IV

FIELD MARSHAL
VON MANSTEIN

November 1942 – March 1944

Field Marshal von Manstein

My New Job

The next day, 18 November 1942, I reached Vitebsk and the headquarters of the Eleventh Army shortly before dark, in a car belonging to the headquarters. I had myself announced to the Commander-in-Chief with some trepidation. When I entered Manstein's study he rose from his armchair, laid aside a book he had been reading, tapped the ash from a fat cigar and accepted my posting orders. Then he shook hands and asked me to sit down opposite him.

He was wearing a white linen uniform jacket of the kind we liked to wear off duty in peacetime. For the first time in my life, I saw the golden epaulettes with the crossed marshal's batons close at hand.

He began the conversation in a very friendly, not to say charming manner. Tresckow had told him something about me, including the fact that his brother-in-law, Conrad von Loesch, his wife's brother, a casualty of the Polish campaign, had been married to a cousin of mine. So there would plenty for us to talk about.

Then he asked me about myself, and especially about my military career. I began by telling him that I had joined the 6th (Prussian) Cavalry Regiment as a volunteer in 1935 because the NSDAP in Stettin had tried to force me to become a Party Member. Without going into this point, he exclaimed with obvious pleasure that in that case I must have been serving alongside his previous aide, Specht. That was how I learned that 'Pepo', as we had called him in Schwedt, had been killed. The Field Marshal wanted to know if I had known him well and I had to say no, as I was older than he. During Reserve exercises, as an NCO, I had had to give the officer cadets riding instruction once or twice. Specht had been remarkable for sitting his horse perfectly from the first day, and had been better at all the cavalry exercises than many a veteran trooper – and certainly better than I was. The Field Marshal enjoyed talking about him and I could see how deeply Specht's death had affected him.

I also referred to the death of his eldest son, Gero – Tresckow had told me of it – and he talked to me about him. Then he suddenly reached behind him and gave me a letter from his desk to read. It came from the editorial office of the *Völkischer Beobachter*, the official party newspaper of the NSDAP. In words of contrived courtesy it informed the Field Marshal that the paper was prepared to print the notice of his son Gero's death only if the reference to the Biblical text (Acts 8, 39) which was to appear above the notice was removed. The verse ended with the words: '. . . he went on his way rejoicing.' Through this – undoubtedly perfectly inoffensive – text his wife and he had wanted to express two things: firstly, that he and his family were Christians, and secondly, that Gero had been a particularly happy human being. He would therefore tell the *Völkischer Beobachter* that the notice was to appear unchanged and with the Biblical text. After all, he had given his rank when he signed it. He looked at me questioningly.

After a pause, I asked: 'Does it have to be the *Völkischer Beobachter*, sir? The *Deutsche Allgemeine Zeitung* seems to me a more suitable place for this notice. It too is conformist, of course, but I have always noticed that "our families" prefer that paper.' He answered quickly that the *Deutsche Allgemeine* had received the notice in the same post as the *Völkischer Beobachter* and had not refused to print it. That was why he was going to insist that the *Völkischer Beobachter* should also print it in full.

At that point Manstein was obviously unaware that the *Deutsche Allgemeine* had already carried the death announcement on 7 November, having deleted the Biblical text without reference to the family. The newspaper had acted independently, in accordance with the rules of the Ministry of Propaganda for the obituaries of the fallen, whereas the Party newspaper had at least written. When writing this account, I sought out Gero Manstein's obituary in the *Völkischer Beobachter* at the Press Institute of the Free University of Berlin. It was published on 22 November 1942, without the Biblical text. So that was how the Nazi Party treated even Field Marshals.

All this lies in the past now, but it epitomises National Socialist propaganda policy, with its curious nuances, and it reveals the inhumanity and rigour of the demands it made on people. This first conversation with Manstein covered other subjects as well, and I was well aware that I was being tested. He made me report in detail on the fighting at Tikhvin and above all the battle south of Lake Ladoga, when he had led us. Quite suddenly he interrupted me. 'I'll make you an offer,' he said. 'If you like, we'll give each other a try.' I accepted at once, because I was impressed by his personality and his approach to a much younger man. I felt I could work well for him.

Then he outlined my job, of which I had only a vague idea, summing up: 'You will be my constant companion, you will be present at all my conversations, you will take brief minutes of our daily doings, in so far as they are important. You will listen to my telephone conversations, write for me and keep my files, both the military and some of the private ones.'

I interjected that I was not clear to what extent a lieutenant could share the official and other life of a Field Marshal; above all, I could not imagine that there were not some matters which a Field Marshal had to deal with privately and in the strictest of confidence. He rejected this at once, emphatically: in wartime it did not apply, at least not for him. I persisted: after all, he might be talking to the Führer. 'Then you will be there, unless accompanying officers are excluded on his orders.' Then I objected that although I could type a little, I had not learned shorthand. 'That is actually a good thing,' he said. 'I do not care for shorthand in the work of the General Staff, because the shorthand-writer records everything he hears, including trivia. I expect you to recognise what is important and what is not. The less you write, the better. I hope,' he continued, 'that I shall soon be able to dictate to you. And I expect you – though not overnight – to be able to transfer the sense of my dictation reliably to paper from your notes.'

I felt quite dizzy at what was in store for me. After a pause, during which he presumably watched my reactions, he began again, stressing something of extreme importance to him: he had worked on the General Staff in the First World War, so he knew the military hierarchy well enough to know that with each promotion a senior officer ran more risk of isolation. On the so-called path of duty, each upward step was necessarily a kind of additional filter and it was up to me to tell him important things which other people thought should be kept from him. Obviously he did not expect me to burden him with gossip, but he attached great importance to knowing what, in my view, he ought to know. What he meant, in a word, was this: 'Whatever you know I too must know, if you consider it necessary!'

I was delighted. This was a superior entirely to my taste. I was to work for a man of real consequence, who had honoured me with the greatest trust.

I then learned that the entire operations staff of the Eleventh Army (the new Army Group Don) was to move into the waiting command train that evening, to be ready to cross Russia south-ward towards Stalingrad, where the Red Army had launched a massive offensive a few days before in an attempt to pose a serious threat to the entire German Southern Front, including our Italian, Hungarian and Romanian allies. Hitler had made Manstein Commander-in-Chief of this distant section in order, as the General Staff Officer says: 'to restore the situation' or in plain language, to save what could be saved.

Whilst we waited for the orders from OKH, I made my most important preliminary visits round the headquarters, in precise order of seniority, according to custom.

General Friedrich Schulz was Manstein's Army Chief of Staff and his closest colleague since the Crimean campaign. He wel-comed me with great warmth. Word had already gone round among the staff that Tresckow had recommended me, and I had a clear sense of the reputation my cousin enjoyed. Not only that evening, but countless times in the years that followed, people would speak to me of Henning, so that I became aware of the responsibility I shouldered as 'Tresckow's man'.

I at once felt both trust and liking for General Schulz and no less so for his *aide-de-camp*, Lieutenant Otto Feil, who kept the Army's War Diary. Feil was soon one of my closest friends on that large staff.

Things were quite different with the 'Ia', the First General Staff Officer, Colonel Theodor Busse. When I went to his office, he offered me a chair facing him, turned the light of a standard lamp on me and questioned me about everything he was interested in without my being able to see his face. So there was a wall between us from the start.

The headquarters had as its mobile command post a special railway train of about 10 express train carriages. It was equipped with everything an operational department needed in war, with radio and telegraph equipment as well as its own armament. The Field Marshal had a former saloon carriage which had seen better days and which had been converted into a study and briefing room, with two large sleeping compartments next to it for himself and me, as his *aide-de-camp*, as well as compartments for the batmen. It was a wonderful old carriage, more elegant than any I had seen before. It was said to have belonged to the Queen of Yugoslavia. Precious art nouveau marquetry decorated the panelled walls and heavy silk curtains contrasted oddly with its current use.

Two days later, whilst we were visiting two of the corps still under the Field Marshal's command, the expected order arrived from OKH confirming the creation of a new Army Group Headquarters from Headquarters Eleventh Army under the title Army Group Don. The new formation was to move immediately to the South to relieve the Sixth Army, threatened by encirclement at Stalingrad, and to 'reconstruct' the defensive front on both sides of the city.

On that day (20 November), I was present at a strategic discussion of great significance. Only a very defective situation map of Southern Russia was available for the discussion, yet the sparse entries were enough to lead Manstein and his staff to the conclusion that there could be no question of a 'restoration of the former front line'.

I now realised what the 'leadership' of the Supreme Command – in other words, Hitler – really meant: it was neither flexible nor dynamic, but unimaginative, uninventive and, above all, static. I now held the key to my own terrible experiences and the destruction of the 12th Panzer Division in more than a year of battles between Leningrad and the Volkhov.

On the evening of 21 November 1942, the train left Vitebsk for Smolensk, but we did not get far. We suddenly heard a loud explosion ahead of us and the emergency brakes went on. Partisans had done their work well: we rolled back through the darkness to Vitebsk. The train left again at 8 o'clock in the morning, the German railway engineers having completed their repair work.

In Smolensk, the Commander-in-Chief of Army Group Centre, Field Marshal Hans Günther von Kluge, was standing on the platform. *'Kluger Hans'*, 'Clever Hans', as his officers jokingly called him, joined us in our carriage with General Otto Wöhler, his Chief of Staff, whom Manstein greeted with particular warmth, as a former colleague. He had brought an up-to-date situation map of Southern Russia. What Wöhler had to tell the Field Marshal sounded bad. The Sixth Army was virtually surrounded in Stalingrad and had apparently been ordered by Hitler to stand fast. I thought again of last winter in Tikhvin – so this was what the war looked like, seen from 'above'.

The conversation did not last long; we had to make haste now in order to reach the Stalingrad area as quickly as possible.

One comment by Field Marshal Kluge is still vivid in my mind, because he returned to it several times. He had some important advice for Manstein. He himself had been immediately subordinate to the Führer for quite a long time now and had some experience of his ways. Hitler's inclination was to be so much more interested in detail than in fundamental strategic thinking that he often intervened in military activities down to battalion level. Kluge's urgent advice was that any such inroads into the command structure of the Army Group should be 'blocked' from the very first day; otherwise he, as Commander-in-Chief, would soon be unable to do anything. 'And be warned,' Kluge continued, 'the Führer ascribes the survival of the Eastern Army during the great crisis of last winter, not to the morale of our soldiers and all our hard work, but exclusively to his own skill.'

I observed Manstein while Kluge was speaking. His face twitched once or twice, but he was silent.

We spent five days travelling in our special train and I had plenty of opportunity to get to know my new superior thoroughly – as he did me. I had soon discovered that he was grateful for a chance to be cheerful. We played chess and I was glad that he played better than I did. He always played an attacking game and enjoyed mating me with all the pieces on the board. In the years – just under three – I spent at his side, we played countless games, probably over a thousand, of which he won at least 90 per cent. I had a chance against him only if I succeeded – generally far too obviously – in attacking boldly from the start. Then he would sometimes get annoyed with himself and move too quickly, making irreparable mistakes.

He loved discussing music with me. Mozart was his favourite. He had a portable gramophone and a few good records in his baggage and if, for any reason, our train had to stop and wait, he would put on one of his favourite records, preferably Mozart's piano concerto in G major, Köchel number 453, in a wonderful performance with Edwin Fischer, or excerpts from *The Marriage of Figaro*.

He liked talking about his own life, about his adoptive parents, his childhood in Strasbourg, his days at the Plön and Lichterfelde cadet schools, his reminiscences as a page at festivities at the Imperial Court in Berlin. He showed me a magnificent cigarette box of solid gold presented to him by Crown Prince William of Prussia in token of his conquest of Sevastopool in the Crimea. I asked him how it was that the Crown Prince had been the one to give him such an important present. He did not know himself, he said, and invited me to open the box. The situation map of the Crimea was engraved inside the lid. I asked him if he had known Field Marshal Hindenburg. Yes, Hindenburg had in fact been his uncle by marriage. Then I asked casually which of the young Field Marshals in this war was capable, in his opinion, of becoming the 'Saviour of the Fatherland' in the event of total defeat. His answer came like lightning: 'Certainly not me.' And, in any case, there was absolutely no question of our losing the war. I persisted and asked him what he thought of Field Marshal Gerd von Rundstedt. 'He is the senior officer among us,' he said drily. 'And what do you think of Reich Marshal Hermann Göring, Sir?' I asked. 'He's a musical comedy figure. He doesn't count.' That seemed to exhaust the subject for the time being.

So we rolled through Russia, at a top speed of 20 to 30 kilometres per hour.

In the evening bridge was played at several tables in the dining-car and I received my first reprimand: 'What? You can't play bridge? What did you learn as a child besides your lessons?' – 'The violin, Sir,' I returned. 'Well, that's something, at least!' Then he appointed three of his younger staff officers to give me a crash course in bridge immediately, so that I could become a useful bridge partner, even on this train journey, and also learn to play a good 'dummy' hand. Had they understood? The grinning three confirmed their instructions.

Another day he asked me to tell him what I remembered of the months of January to March 1933, when I had been an assistant in Franz von Papen's secretariat. He listened with interest as I told him about my meetings with Hitler, Göring, Seldte, Hugenberg and others. I described my uncle Kleist-Schmenzin to him in detail, since of all those famous names, he was the one who had made the most lasting impression on me. 'Oh, so you knew all those?' he put in. I said 'knew' would be an overstatement, but I had met them and observed them. 'And what do you think of

Papen?' he asked. 'Nothing,' I said. 'Why?' he asked. 'Because he knuckled under when the SS murdered three of his closest colleagues and carried off all the people who worked at the Vice-Chancellery to Gestapo Headquarters in Prinz Albrecht Strasse, or Oranienburg Concentration Camp.' The Field Marshal knew of the murders of Bose and Jung in Berlin and Ketteler in Vienna, but the large numbers of arrests on 30 June 1934 seemed new to him, just as in general, the evils of June 1934 had been 'obscure' to him then. At OKH the events of those days had simply rolled over them. He had not seen through them at the time, and even now he was unable to analyse them.

Early in the morning of 24 November, all the officers gathered in the saloon of our carriage while the train was in motion to congratulate the Field Marshal on his 55th birthday. General Schulz made a short speech and Manstein said a few friendly words of thanks. I registered with astonishment that he was by no means a good speaker and that he did not open up in the presence of a number of people; he exerted an influence, even a certain fascination, in a small, familiar circle, and most of all à deux.

Towards nine, the train stopped in Starobielsk, a small town to the east of Kharkov, where Headquarters Army Group B was established, with Colonel-General Maximilian von Weichs at its head. There were cars waiting by the train to take us to the headquarters and now, at last, Manstein saw the situation map illustrating the latest intelligence from the area round Stalingrad. It made a catastrophic picture.

The Sixth Army and parts of the Fourth Panzer Army had been surrounded by the Russians. The best German forces on the Southern Front had been summoned to conquer the town that bore the name of the Soviet dictator. Our allies from Hungary, Romania and Italy, whose commitment to the fighting was understandably half-hearted, were deployed on their flanks. So the Russians had not had to be very inventive to turn their troops into a huge pincer.

There was the added fact that the German troops in the south of Russia had to pursue separate goals, instead of being concentrated; while the prestige goal of Stalingrad, on the bend of the Volga, was the target, Army Group A under Field Marshal von Kleist, stationed to the south of Army Group B, had orders to reach the Caucasus. The situation showed that in the attempt to achieve two goals at the same time the strength of the Soviet forces had been badly underestimated. Allowing the encirclement of the Sixth

Army had turned out to be a grave strategic mistake on Hitler's part. In Starobielsk, Weichs told Manstein how Hitler's order to the Sixth Army had been worded: 'Dig in and wait for relief from the outside!'

There is no need for Field Marshal Manstein's personal aide to describe the military events during the weeks and months that followed. There is abundant literature on the subject from more competent pens, not least the Field Marshal's own. I can therefore restrict myself to describing some experiences which are still vivid in my mind today.

The tenor of the conversation between Manstein and Weichs in Starobielsk on 24 November was one of scepticism on Colonel-General Weichs's side, while Manstein appeared amazingly optimistic. He was supported in this by Colonel Busse, with his 'It's a bad business, Sir, but we'll manage somehow!' The new Army Group had not been deployed yet and the fact that Hitler had named it 'Army Group Don' was not at all to Manstein's taste. Here was more evidence of Hitler's 'strategic' thinking: 'Don' was intended to pin the Army Group morally to this area, whereas Manstein's strategic thinking was based on the mobility of the troops. During our days on the train he had more or less taken me back to school in many of our talks. In the vastness of Russia, the commander had to operate like an admiral in the vastness of the ocean, but if 'the Supreme Command' tried to pin him down to a point on the map, it was as pointless as if an admiral were ordered to attack the enemy fleet precisely on the intersection of this degree of latitude and that degree of longitude, and nowhere else.

The military situation to the west and south of the encircled city worried us almost more than the situation of the Sixth Army and the town of Stalingrad. There was no coherent front on either side. While the armies of our allies were fleeing in more or less total disarray, the 16th German Motorised Division was operating on the Kalmuck steppe to the south, spread out over 300 to 400 kilometres, as far as the town of Astrakhan on the Caspian Sea, famous for its fine caviare.

And finally, still further to the south, there was Army Group A under Kleist, with whose Panzer group I had taken part in the French campaign in 1940. Kleist's divisions were struggling towards the passes of the Caucasus and the borders of Persia and

Turkey. Anyone was free to draw his own conclusions. If the Soviets now succeeded in destroying the Sixth Army at Stalingrad and pressing further westward to reach the mouth of the Don by Rostov, Army Group A in the Caucasus would be cut off from its base and supplies and would then have to be supplied via the Straits of Kerch, or withdraw across the Sea of Azov. Quite simply, in the situation presented to Field Marshal Manstein on 24 November in Starobielsk, there was already an acute danger of losing the war against the Soviet Union, and in short order too.

Before we left the Headquarters of Army Group B that afternoon for the area of Stalingrad, I took the opportunity to ask one of the younger staff officers for news of my uncle Hans von Wedemeyer. During my summer leave in Pomerania I had heard that he was now on Weichs's staff. I was led out of the gathering into a neighbouring room. Major von Wedemeyer was my uncle? Well, the major had simply been unable to tolerate the kind of German warfare he had witnessed here, in the headquarters of the Army Group. In August – three months ago – he had transferred as a volunteer from the headquarters to the Front in a state of absolute despair, and had fallen on 22 August as a commanding officer in the assault on Stalingrad. That was surely what he had wished.

The news hit me badly. After all, it was Uncle Hans who had got me into the secretariat of his friend Papen as an assistant in the winter of 1932/33. In January 1933 he had been among Papen's closest advisers when the point at issue was whether they could risk making Hitler Reich Chancellor. It was he who had enrolled Ewald von Kleist-Schmenzin's help in order to restrain Papen from his ambitious and risky plan with every conceivable argument. After the two of them had failed and Papen had become Vice-Chancellor under Hitler, Uncle Hans had, for a time, taken over the direction of the Vice-Chancellery. For a few weeks he had been close to the hub of political activity, witnessing the penetration of the legislative and executive arm of the German Reich by the National Socialists. I knew how greatly he regretted that he had been unable to find a solution other than Hitler in January 1933.

Then, as a reserve officer in the intelligence section of the Army Group, he had had personal knowledge of Hitler's strategic decisions. Recognising where 'both the political and the military paths were leading', he had acted in keeping with his character – a noble and a tragic decision.

Stalingrad

On 26 November we reached Rostov at the mouth of the Don, and Novocherkassk a few hours later.

The Field Marshal moved with me and our orderlies into a former tsarist villa, whose fittings no longer bore any relation to the external façade – probably the contents of the villa had passed 'into the ownership of the people' not once but many times since the Revolution. One could not have imagined more primitive furnishings.

In order to give the building the look of a militarily secure headquarters, at least externally, and for the benefit of the townsfolk, two soldiers of a type I had never seen before stood to left and right of the entrance steps – short, friendly Cossacks, with huge Russian fur caps, but in German uniforms. When we entered or left the house, they stuck out their chests and stood to attention as if for His Imperial Majesty the Tsar himself.

Our operations department was in another house, which was conscientiously guarded by a German guard company.

Without an escort, I took a walk through the town centre to see the lie of the land. The population was going about its daily affairs as if peace reigned supreme. On the corner of a boulevard I bought myself a bag of sunflower seeds, which every Russian thereabouts kept in his pocket, so that there was always a seed moving between his teeth.

It was a strange war, quite different from Leningrad. In Novocherkassk the Russians were taking responsibility for our security, and not 200 kilometres away the battle for Stalingrad was raging. And the Commander-in-Chief of the German Army Group was literally under the protection of a volunteer detachment of Cossacks.

With our arrival in Novocherkassk, my daily work in Manstein's outer office began. The connecting door to his room was almost always open and he would simply shout his orders through to me from his desk, which was quicker than using a telephone from one room to the next. It suited the Field Marshal's working pace.

More and more telephones began to gather on the left-hand side of my desk, always including one which was connected in parallel with the Field Marshal's own. He had explicitly ordered me to listen in to every conversation he conducted, often interrupting himself to say: 'Stahlberg, you hear that? Please see to it at once.'

He never used the little word 'order' to me. His 'orders' took the form: 'Would you please see to it . . . ', 'I should be grateful if you would . . . ' or 'Please connect me right away with . . . '. Genuine authority assumes obedience and mutual trust as a matter of course. Manstein was a gentleman.

On the right-hand side of my desk there were always two notepads, one for his instructions, which I took with me when he asked me to come into his room; the other stayed there for documentation purposes.

The 1:300,000 situation map was on a big table in his room which I could see from my desk. Whenever one of the draughtsmen arrived from section Ia to enter the latest intelligence, I would go in and wait. From his desk the Field Marshal then usually asked tersely: 'News?' As a rule a few key words from me were enough and he would remain seated and go on with his work; sometimes he would cross over to the map and ask what information I had when I pointed out the location of the event. And I had to be quick, or he could get quite sharp.

Like our offices, our bedrooms were also side by side, and the telephone extensions connected in the same way. The situation map of the day, rolled up on a pole, stood beside my bed.

Then there was a padlocked wooden chest, some 60 cm wide, which accompanied us day and night between office and bedroom, and whose key I carried on a chain. It contained the most important documents, especially the copies I took for the Field Marshal's files: 'Classified Document' – 'Commanding Officer' – 'By Commissioned Officer Only', the highest Wehrmacht security grade.

Everything he dictated to me or passed over in rough, I would type in clear with the usual copies. Each copy was numbered and the carbon paper destroyed. An extra typewriter with larger letters, a real monster, was kept for correspondence with Hitler.

The great man wished to be able to read such letters without the aid of glasses (especially when other people were present; a 'Great Man' in glasses was unthinkable). On this typewriter one could actually type the two runic characters of the SS with one key. So until the end of the war I typed almost everything that Manstein put on paper, including a great deal of private correspondence, as long as it fell more or less within the conventional context. It was difficult at first to take down the Field Marshal's dictation without shorthand, but in time it became quite routine. I was always fascinated when he dictated one of his memoranda to me without notes. They were divided in sections and numbered with letters and figures. Often during dictation it would happen that one of the first sections referred to one of the last, and still he would be able to give the later reference figures. He mentally visualised the layout of the entire document as he spoke, and seldom made a mistake. If he did, he could be put out to discover when he read through the document that I had not corrected the mistake myself while I was typing it.

The work became even more difficult when – after a few weeks of working myself in – he would press manucript notes into my hand crying: 'Most urgent, type immediately, original by telegraph to OKH, copies here, for all departments concerned. Most urgent!' Then I might go off to Otto Feil, the Chief of General Staff's aide a few rooms away, and ask for his help, because Manstein's manuscripts, written with a broad Mont Blanc pen, were not easy to read. Sometimes in his haste he had not written words out in full, so we had to make them up according to the sense, or else we would stand in front of the Field Marshal's situation map, searching for Russian place-names or even correcting them. Initially I would sometimes ask Manstein himself to help me identify a name, when I was overwhelmed by the responsibility. But he disposed of that briskly with: 'I think you're intelligent enough to correct my writing mistakes', or 'Have a look at the map, see if I've got it wrong.'

After a few months working with him I often had to telegraph documents of great importance typed by me in his name, but no longer read through or initialled by him. If I submitted them to him for approval he might well look at me instead of reading them, and ask: 'All done? Good, take it away then.'

One of the first officers I had to announce to the Field Marshal in Novocherkassk was Eberhard Finckh, a colonel on the General Staff. When I met him he greeted me as if we were old friends. Had someone prepared the ground for me? Finckh was Quartermaster General of the Army Group, responsible for everything connected with supplies and replacements – so he was something like a minister of transport or supply. Here he was responsible for provisions for the other armies as well as the Sixth Army in Stalingrad.

Finckh's very first talk dealt with the central question of the numerical strength of the German troops in the encircled city of

Stalingrad, which had been difficult to discover because there were so many combinations of divisions, corps and general reserve troops, both German and Romanian. In the turbulent battles of the retreat the numbers had initially been difficult to assess, but Finckh's figure stands out clearly in my memory, because it was horrifying to imagine. Finckh repeated the figure over and over again: at the time of the encirclement, 304,000 men. He confirmed this figure vigorously, because even then there were divergent estimates, lower, of course, from interested parties at the Führer's headquarters.

Reich Marshal Göring, Chief of the German Luftwaffe, had informed Hitler that he would supply the Army by air with everything it needed. That was exactly what Hitler wanted to hear, because that very summer in the Berlin Sports Palace he had shouted to his cheering party members that he no longer needed the city of Stalingrad 'because we've got it already'. But for us, hearing and reading whatever came through from the beleaguered area, it was ghastly to picture the conditions there. For me personally there was an obvious comparison betwen Stalingrad and Tikhvin a year ago. Of course, compared to Stalingrad, Tikhvin had been only a small sample, but in principle Stalingrad was the same: an irresponsible, criminal strategic error, a senseless sacrifice.

I listened in on some telephone conversations between Manstein and Colonel-General Friedrich Paulus, Commander-in-Chief of the Sixth Army. Neither Paulus nor Manstein was prepared to act against Hitler's orders as long as the Army had any chance of breaking out. When Manstein later decided to prepare for a breakout, it was too late. Equally responsible was his Ia, Colonel Busse, with his constant: 'We'll manage somehow, Field Marshal!'

On 27 November the headquarters of the Army Group, with its many command and administrative branches, was complete to the extent that it was possible to announce the assumption of command over the encircled Sixth Army and the fragmented troops on both its flanks to OKH. Early that morning the Field Marshal told me to pick up the Commander-in-Chief of *Luftflotte* 4, Colonel-General Wolfram von Richthofen, from our field airstrip and bring him as quickly as possible to our new headquarters, which he had not yet seen. Richthofen sat silently beside me in the car, having been given the truly unenviable task of supplying the Army in Stalingrad by air. I could feel his anxiety. From time to

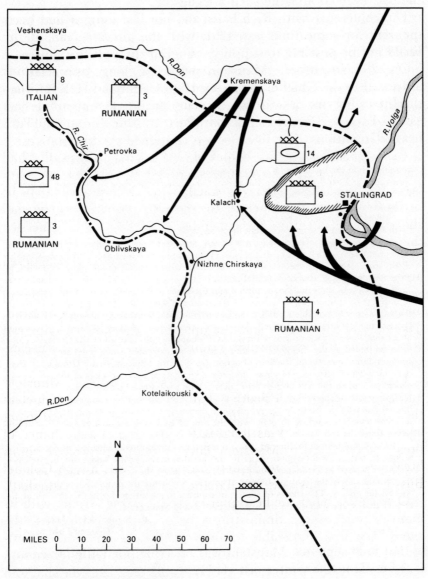

Veshenskaya

XXXX 8
ITALIAN

XXXX 3
RUMANIAN

R. Don

Kremenskaya

R. Volga

R. Chir

Petrovka

XXXX 14

XXXX 48

XXXX 6
STALINGRAD

Kalach

XXXX 3
RUMANIAN

Oblivskaya

Nizhne Chirskaya

XXXX 4
RUMANIAN

R. Don

Kotelaikouski

N

XXXX

MILES 0 10 20 30 40 50 60 70

〰〰〰 Defensive perimeter 6th Army

– – – – German front 19 November

–·–·– German front 27 November

➤ Soviet encircling attacks

Map 4. Stalingrad November 1942

time he muttered snatches of disconnected phrases: 'Impossible' ... 'even to imagine such a thing ...'.

The conference with Richthofen did not last long; it had been
apparent for some time now that, with the aircraft available, it
would not be possible to supply Stalingrad through the winter.

On 28 November, Manstein wrote a long appreciation,
addressed to the Chief of the Army High Command (OKH), that
is, Hitler. For me it was the first significant document* I had
typed: Part 1: Enemy Situation; Part 2: Our Situation; Part
3: Our Intentions. The final section contained the alternatives:

(a) ... after mustering the forces referred to above, to proceed to counter-attack ... this is
conditional on the tactical and supply situation of the Sixth Army allowing for such a long
wait (until at least 9.12.) and on the ability to execute the decision by bringing up further
forces ... under cover of the East and North flanks

(b) If developments do not allow for a wait of this length ... the Army Group must act at
the earliest possible date (perhaps on 3.12.) in order, at least provisionally, to ensure that the
Sixth Army's supply situation is kept up to strength.

(c) The prospects of success ... are largely dependent on the enemy's exhausting his
armoured forces, which constitute the chief element of his striking force, in his attack on the
Sixth Army. Herein lies the necessity for the Sixth Army to be adequately supplied with, in
particular, anti-tank ammunition and fuel ...

(d) In view of the situation, condition and problems of the Sixth Army, which may force
us to resort to solution (b), as well as the situation as a whole, the Army Group must accept
that it may not be possible to enforce an effective decision but that it will only be possible to
create a narrow link with the Sixth Army, perhaps only for a limited period .... Over and
above this, however, the crucial point is that it is not possible ... to allow the German troops
to be contained by the enemy in a kind of wedge in an extremely constricted area, while the
enemy retains operational freedom of action (vis-à-vis the adjacent Army Groups) ... over
the remainder of a frontage of some hundreds of kilometres. I do not consider that such total
dependence upon the will of the enemy over a long period can be tolerated.

If, therefore, it should not be possible to force a decision, but only to achieve a spatially
limited link with the Sixth Army, I consider it necessary to use this to bring the Army out of
its encirclement according to plan, with the aim of achieving an operational structure of
forces along the general line Yashkul – Kotelnikovo – Don – Chir – Usimko.

The abandonment of Stalingrad which this involves undoubtedly means a heavy sacrifice
in morale, but this will be made easier by the fact that in winter the Volga can, in any case,
no longer be used as a transport route and so, in exchange, the decisive aim can be achieved:
the maintenance of the fighting strength of an army and hence the restoration of the initiative
vis-à-vis the enemy. The effects of winter, in contrast to conditions in the North, will be no
greater than while waiting on the open steppes round Stalingrad.

Signed: VON MANSTEIN
General Field Marshal

In that final sentence Manstein was referring, for Hitler's benefit,
to the crisis in the winter of 1941/42.

I have reproduced this (abridged) military appreciation because
I think it is of key significance, both to the fate of the Sixth Army
and to the course of the war up to the conquest of Berlin.

A detailed inventory of the Russian troops facing the encircled

---

* The document is held in the Federal/Military Archives in Freiburg in Breisgau. See also:
Manfred Kehrig, *Stalingrad*, Stuttgart 1975, pp. 573 ff.

Sixth Army at that time was appended to this memorandum. According to Army Group Don's intelligence, they consisted of seven armies with 71 divisions and brigades as well as a further 26 divisions and brigades in reserve behind them.

Although the combat strength of the Russian formations was less than that of their German equivalents, nevertheless these figures represented an alarming Russian superiority overall.

From the days of the encirclement of Stalingrad, one officer should be remembered: the German liaison officer with the Romanian army, Colonel Walther Wenck of the General Staff. The Romanians had not withstood the Russian attacks and were in panic flight to the West. How were the fleeing men to be halted, assembled and redeployed to resist the Soviet flood?

Wenck ordered a detachment of German military police to set up signposts in the hinterland, reading 'To the Filling Station', 'To Fuel Distribution Point', in German and above all in Romanian. He had the signs positioned so that the escaping soldiers were directed to wooded areas or valley basins where they could be mustered and re-formed into fresh units. With these and other improvisations, Manstein succeeded with difficulty in building up a new defensive front on the near side of Stalingrad.

So, to leap forward a year or two, it may not be so extraordinary that in the last days of the war, in the bunker of the Reich Chancellery in Berlin, the man whose back was finally against the wall pinned his last hopes to the name of Wenck.

Hitler on the Telephone

I believe it was the night of 29 to 30 November 1942, but it may have been the next night. I can justify reproducing parts of the conversation in direct speech, because I can vouch for the sense. The content of that conversation became a key experience for me, something one does not forget for the rest of one's life.

The telephone on the chair beside my bed woke me from deep sleep. I switched on the light and glanced at my watch: it was long past midnight. At the other end a voice announced itself as General Rudolf Schmundt, the Führer's Chief Adjutant: 'The Führer wishes to speak to Field Marshal von Manstein.' I replied that the Field Marshal was asleep. 'Then wake him up and call back.'

I needed a moment to organise my thoughts, then I got up and pulled on a track suit and gym shoes. The conversation would obviously be concerned with Manstein's appreciation of the situation in Stalingrad, so I first took time to prepare the necessary background.

I unrolled the situation map of the Army Group which was standing beside my bed. On a scale of 1:300,000, it stretched from Army Group B, fighting on our left, through Stalingrad to Army Group A on the Caucasus. A map table was not available, so it had to be laid out on the floor.

A bulb hanging from the ceiling and my bedside lamp at the upper end of the map lit the scene adequately. I secured the ends of the map with my boots.

The room was unheated, so I spread out my blanket and pillow at the lower end of the map. Two telephones linked in parallel, writing tools and reading glass were set in place. Now we could carry on.

I went next door to rouse the Field Marshal, who had to be shaken by the shoulder several times before he woke up. When I told him what was happening he reacted as I had expected. He sat up: 'Is he insane?' he exploded furiously. Then, more mildly: 'So inconsiderate! To get me out of bed at – what time is it? – between midnight and morning! What does he want from me now? I need my sleep.'

I handed him his tracksuit and gym shoes, then we went next door and he lay down unprompted on my blanket; I brought in his as well, so that he would at least be covered up. After all, who knew how long the conversation might last.

So there we were, both lying on our stomachs on the floor, I on his right at an angle of 90° so that I could be of more assistance. We picked up the receivers.

I had only to touch the crank and our exchange replied at once. No wonder. Who knew how many soldiers in intelligence would now be listening in? It was only too understandable that the information services were always on the alert. So I transmitted: '*Führungsblitz*' – the highest priority – 'Führer's headquarters – the Führer personally – for Field Marshal von Manstein.'

After a few seconds General Schmundt replied and I told him that the Field Marshal was on the line and ready to speak. The connection was excellent. Schmundt said he would hand over the conversation to the Führer. Then there was silence.

No one spoke, at this end or that. I was quite excited, because I had never heard Hitler on the telephone. How would he announce himself? 'Hitler here,' or 'Adolf Hitler here'? Or even perhaps: 'The Führer speaking'? Instead of which, nothing, no one spoke at either end. It was quite understandable as far as Manstein was concerned, because he was in a very bad temper.

So I began to speak to my own receiver, giving my rank and name and repeating, as if General Schmundt were still at the other end, that the Field Marshal was ready to speak. I was keeping half an eye on him as I spoke and he at least seemed to be quite entertained by my lack of respect. But he was still silent.

Finally something happened: a deep bass voice, only too well-known to every German, intoned: 'Hello?' Manstein answered at once in his high tenor: 'Hello?' For a second time the deep bass 'Hello?' sounded from the other end.

Only after the third repetition did Manstein put an end to this curious exchange: 'Field Marshal von Manstein here.' Now came the answer: '*Heil!* Field Marshal! I have read your appreciation of the situation, Field Marshal, and I want to talk to you about it.'

For me this conversational opening was the first surprise: Hitler addressed his inferiors by rank. That was certainly 'Austrian', in fact I believe it was 'Royal and Imperial'. In Prussia the Head of State would scarcely have spoken to a Field Marshal other than by name.

Hitler came straight to the point. 'I cannot agree to your proposals. The Sixth Army will remain in Stalingrad. It has dug in on my orders and will defend this stronghold!' Manstein asked what else was going to happen.

'I want different proposals from you, Field Marshal,' said Hitler. Manstein, who had already been prepared by telephone for the refusal by General Zeitzler, the Chief of the Army General Staff, reacted at once: '*Mein Führer*, put Army Group A under my command and give me operational freedom for both Army Groups.'

Hitler's answer came just as quickly: 'That is not possible, Field Marshal!'

Then the mutual struggle began. Manstein bargained like a costermonger. At least the First Panzer Army, one of the two armies of Army Group A – if Army Group A was to hold the targets now reached in the Caucasus at all costs, it could do so with one of its two armies, that is in this case with the Seventeenth Army. But Hitler was adamant. I observed clear signs of irritation on Manstein's face, which I now knew well. Was there going to be an explosion?

But he took hold of himself, simply shaking his head briefly as if he had difficulty in keeping himself under control; after all, he was dealing with his military superior. Finally Manstein asked a crucial question: '*Mein Führer*, please tell me what Army Group A is supposed to be doing in the Caucasus?' Then I heard an answer that appalled me: 'It's a question of the possession of Baku*, Field Marshal. Unless we get the Baku oil, the war is lost.'

On hearing these words I looked straight at the Field Marshal. He made a gesture to me with his free right hand as if he were brushing something away.

Hitler repeated himself several times. He seemed to be giving the Field Marshal a lesson on the importance of oil in modern warfare. The words simply bubbled out of him: one must consider how much fuel an aircraft, a tank, etc. needed. 'If I can no longer get you the oil for your operations, Field Marshal, you will be unable to do anything.' For a few minutes there was no stopping Hitler as he repeatedly invoked the vital significance of oil to the conduct of the war.

Finally Manstein took advantage of a pause for breath the other end and said he had absolutely no doubt of the importance of Baku oil, but here and now the Sixth Army in Stalingrad came first, and then the oil at Baku. All they had to do first was agree on priorities. Finally – the Field Marshal seemed to take a deep breath – he said: '*Mein Führer*, I would like to revert to my first proposal. I would like to amend it. Put the whole of Army Group A under me and give me operational freedom, and I will give you a decisive battle in South Russia, after which you can get your oil wherever you like!'

That was bold, by God! I tried to catch Manstein's eye, but he did not look up. He was bargaining again. 'At least the First Panzer Army,' he repeated several times, but the conversation was getting nowhere – the two approaches were too far apart.

Then Manstein switched to other arguments: the enemy forces in the Stalingrad area, the Russian numerical superiority, the signs, clearly recognisable in his view, 'that the Russians are looking for final victory now, in the South of their own country.' '*Mein Führer*, the Russians have learned from us. Instead of simply pushing straight on, they are using strategy. They are beginning to feel sure of themselves.'

* Baku, on the Caspian Sea, a centre of the Soviet petroleum industry.

But Hitler did not react, he seemed to have stopped listening. He simply did not want to learn from a strategist whom he himself had promoted to Field Marshal. I no longer remember how long the conversation had been going on, but I do remember that it seemed endless to me, because it was not going anywhere. Then suddenly a new theme cropped up – at least it was the first time I had heard of it.

'Field Marshal,' said Hitler, 'I must remind you of something I have already told you repeatedly: we shall march over the Caucasus next spring. And I am thinking of handing over command of the spring offensive to you. You will then join up in Palestine with Field Marshal Rommel's army, which will come to meet you from Egypt. Then we shall march with our assembled forces to India, where we shall seal our final victory over England.'

Then our supreme commander suddenly wished him: 'Good-night, *Heil*, Field Marshal!' 'Heil, *mein Führer!*' The conversation was over.

Laboriously, stiff in every limb, we got up from the floor. I was freezing. The Field Marshal walked to his room without a word, forgetting his blanket. I took it in to him.

The Fate of the Sixth Army

On 3 December 1942 Hitler's reply to the Memorandum of 28 November arrived by telegraph from the Army High Command. Now Manstein had it in writing: 'Withdrawal . . . out of the question'. There it was, in black and white: the order for the breakthrough to Stalingrad from the South. Then came a sentence dripping with cynicism: 'At this stage it must be ensured that the attacking divisions will be immediately followed up by a large quantity of transport loaded with all necessary provisions, to be supplied immediately to the Sixth Army under armed convoy as soon as contact is established.' As if the Army Group did not know that already! This was the 'signature' of the Supreme Commander of the German Wehrmacht, who had only made lance-corporal in the First World War.

On 12 December, the Fourth Panzer Army, under Colonel-General Hermann Hoth, set off from south to north, towards Stalingrad, with all the force that could be made available. The distance to Stalingrad was about 120 kilometres and for the first two days the attack made good progress, but then the

Russians threw everything they had at it. On 23 December, Hoth's spearheads were only 40 to 50 kilometers from the encircling ring round the city. At night, the soldiers in Stalingrad could see the artillery flashes of their liberators.

In an ante-room at the telephone exchange I had listened in some days before to probably the most important of the many telephone conversations between Manstein and Paulus: 'Please, Marshal, I beg you to give the order for the breakout!' Despite the poor connection – after 12 December we had a new type of decimetre line via radio, equipped with a scrambler* – I could clearly hear the pleading note in Paulus's voice. Then came Manstein's answer: 'Paulus, I cannot give you the order. But if you take the decision independently I will do everything in my power to help you and to vindicate your decision.'

My heart contracted. Neither of them was prepared to act against the Supreme Commander.†

The Fourth Panzer Army's forces, fuel and ammunition were so depleted that Hoth could no longer advance. Then came 24 December, Christmas Eve. As the German soldiers already knew from their Christmas in Russia the year before, Germans should be attacked on Christmas Eve, when the soldiers' thoughts were not at the Front but at home with their families – at least on Christmas Eve, they need not think of the war for a few hours, but of Peace on Earth. There was no more appropriate day for the Red Army to attack.

The Russians did attack and that was the beginning of the end of the Sixth Army.

During the days that followed, Manstein's Army Group was in full retreat. The one goal now was to keep open a corridor at Rostov, without which our southern neighbour, Army Group A (Kleist) in the Caucasus, would be cut off from its communications to the rear. Above all, Manstein had to create a new defence front. If he did not succeed, the Russians would have their great opportunity to win final victory in their own country from their Southern Front.

---

* The decimetre radio connection – a linear radio beam – was a sensational novelty to us at that time. It lasted from 12 to 22 December 1942.

† See also: (a) Wilhelm Adam (Adjutant General of the Sixth Army): *Der schwere Entschluss*, Verlag der Nation, Berlin-Ost 1963, 23rd edition, pp. 191 ff. (b) Wilhelm Arnold (Chief Signal Officer of the Sixth Army): *Bericht an Fellgiebel* 1970, in the Federal/Military Archives at Freiburg, Br.

Twice a day, Manstein talked to the Chief of the Army General Staff, General Zeitzler, discussing the situation by telephone. At the peak of the relief offensive, the Field Marshal had several times suggested to General Zeitzler that he ask Hitler to come out to us in Novocherkassk and see the situation on the spot. Zeitzler accepted this suggestion very positively, but made it clear that it was scarcely conceivable. On the contrary, Hitler was so deeply committed to holding Stalingrad that for that reason alone he would not consider visiting the Front. After all, on the spot he might no longer be able to deny the disaster of his military leadership – so at least Zeitzler unmistakably indicated. Or might Hitler perhaps be afraid of entering the war zone with his rather slow-flying four-engine Focke-Wulf Condor? I put this to Manstein when we were on our own, but he did not answer. No answer is also an answer.

Manstein fought with every possible argument on behalf of the Sixth Army. In Zeitzler he had a courageous and resolute advocate and ally. All of us in the Army Group headquarters were agreed that if Hitler had given him command of Army Group A and operational freedom, the Field Marshal would have saved the Sixth Army and wrested the upper hand from the Soviets in southern Russia. It was becoming clearer day by day that one man alone was guilty of the catastrophe in Stalingrad – Hitler.

The only general whose assessment of the situation in the pocket, even before the relief offensive of the Fourth Panzer Army failed, which was to be confirmed by events right through to the defeat, was General of Artillery Walther von Seydlitz-Kurzbach. He bore the name of one of Frederick the Great's most famous generals and had been ordered by Hitler to command the encircled divisions in the northern section of the pocket. We had the impression that Hitler was now expecting the Seydlitz name, legendary in the history of Prussia, to achieve some special effect, but it was in fact the bearer of that name who had the courage to express himself frankly *vis-à-vis* the 'royal throne'. On 25 November, together with his Chief of Staff, Colonel Clausius, he composed a memorandum in which he clearly exposed the desperate situation of the Sixth Army: 'If,' he wrote, 'the Army High Command does not immediately repeal the order to maintain an all-round defensive position, the imperative duty will arise, in the name of individual conscience, the Army and the German people, to claim the freedom to act denied by the previous order and take advantage of the opportunity now available to avoid catastrophe by taking the offensive.' A great statement – a Prussian statement. It recalls Frederick the Great's words to his officers: 'Gentlemen, I did not make you officers only in order to know when to obey, but also in order to know when not to obey!'

Seydlitz had written his memorandum in Stalingrad, although it was not part of a subordinate general's job to intervene in the affairs of his superior commander. From his chief, Colonel General Paulus, he had demanded action, if not with Hitler, then without – even, if necessary, against him. True, he had not formulated it quite so 'simplistically', but it was there for anyone to read between the lines.

Paulus, it was said, had told him that he, Seydlitz, should not be doing his thinking for him; nevertheless Paulus had sent the paper on to Field Marshal Manstein.

Manstein had not received Seydlitz's memorandum via my desk but brought it back himself from a discussion with Schulz, his Chief of Staff. Through the door, open as usual, I suddenly heard him start swearing loudly. I went in and asked if I could do anything for him. He looked up in great agitation: 'Here's a memorandum from General von Seydlitz that I do not like. It's incredible the things Seydlitz pokes his nose into.'

I returned to my room. After a few minutes one of the draughtsmen from the Ia's department came in to record the latest signals on the Field Marshal's situation map. As usual, I went in with him so that I could report the news if necessary. When the draughtsman had finished and left the room, I made my report, noticing that Seydlitz's memorandum had been put on one side. I asked if I might read it and Manstein, still unusually agitated, replied with a single word: 'No!' It was the first time the Field Marshal had withheld from me a document that crossed his own desk. I read the memorandum only in published form after the war.

On 2 January 1943 – a Sunday of hard frost – my cousin Gottfried von Bismarck, the youngest of the four brothers from Kniephof in Pomerania, was suddenly standing at my desk. He was a lieutenant in the 76th Infantry Division and had been on home leave. By now his division had become one of those encircled in Stalingrad, but the daily noon 'Report from the High Command of the Wehrmacht', which broadcast all the news to the German people throughout the war, had omitted any mention of the

encirclement of the Sixth Army since 20 November of the previous
year. The Wehrmacht report had spoken only of battles *near*
Stalingrad, so it was only after his leave-train reached Rostov that
Gottfried had heard of the fate of his division. He had been told at
the local headquarters in Rostov that he should travel on to
Novocherkassk, where he would find the headquarters of Army
Group Don, to which the Sixth Army now belonged. On reaching
Novocherkassk, he had gone on asking questions, trying to find out
how he might reach his own division. Quite by chance he had seen
a staff list of the headquarters and had found my name on it. So he
had naturally come to say 'Hello'.

While he was telling me his story, the Field Marshal came into
my room and Gottfried reported: 'Lieutenant von Bismarck,
Infantry Regiment 178, 76th Infantry Division, returning to his
unit from home leave.' 'Potsdam?' asked Manstein and at once
engaged him in personal conversation. A young infantry lieutenant
from Potsdam – that was exactly what he himself had once been:
1907, Lieutenant in the 3rd Foot Guards, commissioned in 1905.
And now here was an equally youthful Potsdam lieutenant from
the next generation standing before him.

However, the conversation by my desk was interrupted after a
few minutes by the daily noon call from the Chief of the Army
General Staff, General Zeitzler. The Field Marshal asked Gottfried
to stay and went to the telephone in his room, leaving the door
open as usual, so Gottfried was able to hear everything the Field
Marshal said. That may actually have been what Manstein
intended.

The Field Marshal stressed that in his briefing session with
Hitler, Zeitzler should not forget to repeat several times the fact
that the trials of our soldiers in the pocket had reached unimaginable proportions. He, Manstein, had after all been an infantryman
at the Front in France, as had Hitler himself in the First World
War, so he must put it as clearly as this: what the soldiers were
now suffering in Stalingrad was not comparable with Verdun in
1917; it was far, far worse.

One must remember, in this context, that by 2 January there
was certainly no chance of enabling the Sixth Army as a whole to
break out to the West; the question that was constantly being
reassessed by then was whether the soldiers in Stalingrad should
be allowed to fight their way through to the West in small groups,
if necessary on foot, abandoning their heavy weapons and their

immobilised vehicles. Many would certainly not make it, but equally certainly the hundreds of thousands in Stalingrad would all be lost if Hitler's orders were followed.

After the conversation with Zeitzler, the Field Marshal returned to my room and continued the interrupted conversation. I observed the strong impression made on the older man by Gottfried's light-hearted, cheerful nature, and sensed as I listened that Manstein's thoughts were dwelling on his son Gero, who had been killed only a few weeks earlier, and on Pepo Specht, my predecessor. The conversation turned to Potsdam, to Pomerania and to Kolberg, the beautiful little garrison town on the Baltic where the Field Marshal had been a battalion commander in the 4th (Prussian) Infantry Regiment in the early 1930s. It gave him such pleasure to look back on those happy days of peace. Now he also heard that Gottfried's eldest brother Klaus was a battalion commander in that very same reigment, stationed in the North of Russia. There was much to talk about.

Gottfried was invited to the Field Marshal's round table for the evening meal, a rare distinction for the very youngest visitor I had ever seen at that table, which seated eight people at most. The talk here was frank and open – the kind of talk we could not enjoy in Germany again until the war was over. Freedom of speech at Manstein's round table was a profoundly 'Prussian' institution, which held good that evening too, perhaps precisely because we had one of the youngest lieutenants in the Army with us, who would be trying next morning to fly into the pocket in one of the few transport planes still reaching Stalingrad, to report back from leave.

All kinds of subjects were discussed, but not the one that might nowadays be somewhat frivolously described as the 'most obvious': no one questioned by a single word whether there was any sense in Lieutenant von Bismarck's flying into the Stalingrad pocket on 3 January 1943. Nor was there any direct or indirect attempt, let alone any hint from the person concerned, to suggest there might be another or even a better use for him than with the Sixth Army death squad. Gottfried had been ordered to report back to his regiment from leave, and that is what he did. Not for Hitler – Gottfried, his family and I knew each other too well – but 'because that was the law'. For so many generations: in bounden duty.

Gottfried von Bismarck is one of the survivors of the Sixth Army. Of the 304,000 soldiers in Stalingrad – I rely on the oft-calculated figures from the Quartermaster General of the Army Group, Colonel Finckh of the General Staff – about 25,000 wounded were flown out, according to the documentary evidence of the Federal/Military Archive in Freiburg. On 3 February – after the capitulation of the remaining forces – about 96,000 went into Russian captivity. Of these 96,000, about 50,000 died in the first weeks of February, most of typhus. In 1955 some 6,500 officers and soldiers were still alive in Russian camps, when Federal Chancellor Konrad Adenauer succeeded, through tough negotiations in the Kremlin, in having them released. On 9 October 1955 – more than twelve years later – we were waiting in Friedland, when from among the crowd of grey faces appeared that of the former Lieutenant von Bismarck.

Captain Behr's Mission

I have anticipated events. Before the fighting at Stalingrad was over on 2 February 1943, there were to be more weeks of death. The Russians could now see not only victory in Stalingrad but their great chance of destroying Manstein's Army Group and blocking the retreat of Army Group A in the Caucasus. Now they could justifiably believe in a victorious end to the war against Germany. Now Manstein's prediction to Hitler when he took over Army Group Don was coming true: the Russians were already beginning to withdraw the first of their troops from the Stalingrad pocket and were clearly preparing to reach the mouth of the Don at Rostov before Manstein had pulled back the right wing of his Army Group, the Fourth Panzer Army, to the West. Only now, more than a month too late, did Hitler approve the withdrawal.

The Russians also attacked Manstein's German, Romanian and Italian armies on the left wing of the Army Group and had soon created a gap more than 300 kilometres wide there. Early in January, Manstein's withdrawal operations began, justifying once again – following the brilliance of his plan of operations in the summer of 1940 against France, Belgium, The Netherlands and the British Expeditionary Force – his reputation as a great strategist. He succeeded in rescuing the Fourth Panzer Army and also – much too late – the First Panzer Army as well, northwards from the Caucasus across the Don. The Fourth Panzer Army began a great 'castling' movement behind the German defence front. In the face of grave objections from their

Commander-in-Chief General Hoth, Manstein marched them
according to the ancient rules of chess. These operations – despite
Manstein's numerical inferiority *vis-à-vis* the Soviet attackers in the
ratio of something like 1:7 – are among the most important of that
war, and moreover, in the judgement of experts and historians, are
rightly accounted one of the most brilliant expositions of the art of
warfare. At last the German armies were allowed to resume that
faculty which had once brought them their great successes in this
war, before the astonished eyes of the entire world: mobility.

While these operations were developing, Russian armoured
forces were reported on 7 January not far from Novocherkassk,
where we still had our headquarters. Their vanguard was pushing
towards us at a brisk rate. Had the Russians any idea of the spoils
awaiting them here – only 20 kilometres away?

The departure of the headquarters became an adventure. One of
our young ordnance officers assembled a group of repaired tanks
from our workshops and charged the Russians with such impetus
that the Russians turned back, so that the Operations Section just
managed to escape under cover of the encroaching night.

The next day, 8 January, we were in Taganrog, on the coast of
the Sea of Azov.

I would have loved to catch a glimpse of the sea during the days
we spent there, and also to visit the monastery where Tsar
Alexander I died, but there was no time for such sightseeing.

Novocherkassk is about 160 kilometres from Stalingrad; by air,
more than 350 kilometres separated Taganrog from Stalingrad.
The Soviets had asked Colonel-General Paulus for the capitulation
of the Sixth Army, and Paulus had reported the offer to Manstein
and to Hitler, who had decided to stay and fight in Stalingrad all
the same. In the reports from the pocket we read that, for want of
ammunition, some of our infantry were already fighting with cold
steel.

On 12 January, towards evening, Captain Winrich Behr arrived
at Army Group Headquarters. He had come on Paulus's personal
orders with three missions: first to bring the Sixth Army's war
diary to safety, secondly to hand over a personal letter from Paulus
to Manstein, and thirdly to give an unadorned and realistic picture
of Stalingrad.

Behr presented quite a dazzling appearance: of middle height,
slim and athletic, in black Panzer uniform with the Knight's Cross.
He described his experiences without any inhibitions, stressing

above all the human misery of the soldiers still fighting. He reported the famine in the pocket, he described the situation of the tens of thousands of wounded lying in the open in temperatures below freezing on the airfield he had flown from with great difficulty.

Behr spoke objectively, and so frankly that we were made vividly aware of the horrors the survivors were experiencing. He gave figures, troop strengths of divisions, regiments, companies, which he had learned by heart. The whole pointlessness of Hitler's order to hold on was exposed before us.

At the end of the report he transmitted Colonel-General Paulus's plea to be allowed freedom of action. What was meant by freedom of action was clear: permission to capitulate. All that was left now, Behr said, was to try to save human lives; the Sixth Army had no further military value.

Manstein replied that he would be pleased if Behr would fly to the Führer's headquarters next morning and repeat to the Führer at the briefing conference the report he had just made, in the same words as he had used here. He, Manstein, would telephone Zeitzler, the Chief of the General Staff, to ask for his help in having Behr admitted to the Führer.

Behr replied that General Paulus had given him the same orders. Moreover, he could see a chance of being allowed to speak to Hitler, because the Führer's Luftwaffe Adjutant, Major Nikolaus von Below, was his brother-in-law. He had already spoken to Below on the telephone.

In Behr, Paulus really had picked the most suitable officer on his staff to grasp at this one last straw for the Sixth Army.

Captain Behr was invited to the evening meal at the round table, while our liaison officer with the Luftwaffe was ordered to have an HE 111, one of the Luftwaffe's fastest aircraft, made ready for early the following morning.

Behr took his leave of us on that evening of 12 January, inspired with his mission: if he could not, at the last minute, save his entire Army from ruin, perhaps he might achieve a slim chance of survival for a large number of his fellow soldiers. When we went to our rooms the Field Marshal commented: 'Behr is fiercely determined. Perhaps he can succeed where I have failed.'

When Behr reported back two or three days later, after his visit to Hitler, he gave us a full description, but there had never been any written report by him. So I met him in June 1984 to get some precise details. He told me that he was still not planning to write his memoirs, but now, in 1987, I am glad to say that he has changed his mind and, in a detailed letter to me, has bridged what I regard as a significant gap in the Stalingrad documentation. I have handed over this document to the Federal/Military Archive in Freiburg im Breisgau.

Behr describes in this letter how, on the evening of 13 January 1943, he had waited in an outer office until Hitler came out to him from the briefing session, greeted him with a handshake and '*Heil, Herr Hauptmann*' and took him to the big situation map on the table nearby. About twenty people were there. Hitler had begun with a long exposition of the situation in Stalingrad and the steps taken to save the Army, also asking questions on the supply situation, number of incoming flights and deployment of reserves. At one or two points he had turned to Behr and said: 'Report that to your Commander-in-Chief, Captain Behr!'

After about an hour and a half Behr had had the impression that Hitler wanted to dismiss him without giving him a chance to speak, but he knew that Hitler liked to use this 'procedure' to avoid unwelcome reports. So he had asked to speak, on the grounds that Paulus had ordered him to report to the Führer personally. Then Hitler had in fact listened without interrupting, even when he reported the ever-mounting desertions by German soldiers.

Some of the participants, especially Field Marshal Keitel, on the other hand, had done all they could to trivialise and interrupt his report. A lengthy debate had followed, only to be postponed after about three (!) hours had elapsed, to the 'noon situation' the next day, 14 January. He, Behr, had been ordered to attend.

Behr writes further that even then he had had the impression that none of the high-ranking men present, with perhaps a few exceptions, now believed that the Sixth Army could be saved. Today, he writes, he suspects that at that time Hitler had inwardly already written off Stalingrad and was simply hoping for a 'heroic epic' by the Sixth Army. To judge by his comments, Hitler was then fundamentally interested in only two things: firstly, bringing up an SS Panzer corps from the West to the Kharkov area, about 600 kilometres to the west of Stalingrad, where it had already been fired on by Soviet tanks while unloading from the railway; secondly, supplying Stalingrad by air by bringing in a 'large number' of transports from Africa and Italy (sic!). Moreover, he, Behr, had been quite unable to take in just how 'out of touch' with the war Hitler was, as he operated recklessly on the situation map with formations which in many cases were down to a mere fraction of their normal strength, and were completely exhausted.

So much for the excerpts I have taken from Winrich Behr's report of October 1987. However, I personally remember that, when he stood before Manstein in January 1943, Behr seemed distinctly irritated, even at a loss, for Hitler had presented him with an extremely optimistic picture. The Sixth Army must stay in Stalingrad, because in the coming spring its position there would be vital to the outcome of the war. Then, under the command of Field Marshal von Manstein, 'the greatest battle of encirclement in the history of the world' would begin. With Army Group Don and Army Group A combined with the reconstructed and re-animated Sixth Army, a colossal offensive would be launched from Stalingrad, by the end of which all the Soviet forces stationed in the South of Russia would be destroyed. And then the victorious end of the war would be in sight.

Manstein listened aghast to Behr's report. 'Behr, do you believe all that?' he asked, and Behr replied: 'Sir, I have to believe what the Supreme Commander of the Wehrmacht tells me. Whom can I believe, if not the Supreme Commander?'

'And what will you do now?' asked Manstein. Behr went on to say that Hitler had ordered him to fly straight back to Stalingrad and report everything he had told him to Colonel-General Paulus on his, Hitler's, personal authority, and then to the generals and troop commanders throughout the pocket. He, Behr, would be responsible for the immediate execution of this order.

But the pilot of the HE 111 had not flown him back to Stalingrad, because he had no idea whether one could still fly into Stalingrad at all. And if that were still possible for an HE 111, which he doubted on the latest information, he would in any case have to land in Taganrog to refuel, because there had not been a single drop of aviation fuel available in Stalingrad for a long time now.

Behr was ordered not to fly back to Stalingrad, especially as there was by now scarcely anywhere to land. He was assigned to Hitler's 'special envoy for Stalingrad', Marshal of the Luftwaffe Milch, who was supposed to 'co-ordinate' supply traffic to Stalingrad, where there was not much left to co-ordinate. This was on 16 January, seventeen days before the remnants of the Sixth Army laid down their arms. I think Behr's mission is significant, not only as an important feature of the history of the defeat of the gallant Sixth Army, but because it illuminates Hitler's character and his ruthless method of dealing with people and disposing of the lives and deaths of even those soldiers who were blindly devoted to him.

Neither in 1943 nor today have I had any doubt that Behr approached his mission with the utmost determination. The impression made on me was so deep and lasting that even now I remember a good many details of his report, for instance the description of the difficulties experienced by the HE 111 prepared for him in taking off from Taganrog at all on 13 January. It was icy-cold and the pilot could not get the engine to start. Finally he had tried to turn the propeller by hand, but in vain. Then he had returned to the barracks, where Behr was waiting, and asked him to pull the gloves off his frozen fingers. Behr had done so, using all his strength, until he saw with horror that he had also pulled the skin off the pilot's fingers.

After that they had had to wait several hours before another pilot who could fly an HE 111 returned from Stalingrad, with the result that Behr reached Hitler that evening rather than for the 'noon situation'.

I also remember how Behr described the problems of asserting himself in the presence of Hitler and the eminent generals, when he was only a 'little' captain. How Field Marshal Keitel and General Schmundt, standing behind Hitler, had threatened him when he spoke of famine among the German soldiers, of the wounded lying untended in the open on the airfield, or of the commanding officer with the Knight's Cross who had gone over to the Soviets. Still standing behind Hitler, Field Marshal Keitel had raised his fist, his face contorted with anger.

I also remember Behr describing how Hitler, after talking again at great length the next day about the alleged purpose and aim of his order to hold on, had repeated the order to fly back to Stalingrad, though he had had a night to consider how insane that order was.

I remember how on that 16 January Field Marshal von Manstein finally led Captain Behr to the situation map. It showed all the German, and as far as we knew, all the enemy troops, the tattered sections of the Army Group's front, and – now at a great distance – the pocket of the dying Sixth Army, whose fate was sealed. By now it was no longer a matter of the soldiers in

Stalingrad but of the fate of the entire German Southern Front. Nothing had been seen of the reserves that were alleged to be on their way. Hitler had lied without scruple to the First Adjutant of the Sixth Army.

Stauffenberg and Manstein

The following entry appears in the War Diary of Army Group Don, under 26 January 1948 – eight days before the capitulation of the Sixth Army in Stalingrad.*

> 15.30–17.50 hours, Major General Schmundt, Chief Adjutant to the Führer, with the Commander-in-Chief.
> 18.15 hours, General of Intelligence Groups Fellgiebel, with C-in-C.
> 18.25–19.10 hours, Major Graf Stauffenberg of the General Staff, OKH Organisation Section, with Commander-in-Chief.

The Chief of the Army General Staff, General Zeitzler, used to telephone the Field Marshal twice a day. The first call generally came towards noon, the second early in the evening. In this way Zeitzler prepared himself for the briefing sessions with Hitler, which also took place twice daily.

At the end of the evening telephone call on 25 January, Zeitzler said: 'Field Marshal, I have another request. I have asked my Senior General Staff officer in the organisation section, Major Graf von Stauffenberg, to fly tomorrow to Army Group headquarters to give a talk on the further establishment and organisation of Russian volunteer units. I should be grateful if you would receive Stauffenberg personally, Field Marshal. So may I ask if the time is convenient?' Manstein said yes, and Zeitzler continued: 'I have a personal request to add: of the younger General Staff Officers in the Army I regard Stauffenberg as one of the most gifted, if not the most gifted of all. Since I intend to make a point of promoting Stauffenberg's career, I attach great importance to your assessment of his personality. Do you know Stauffenberg, Field Marshal?' Manstein said he did not, and had never met him. 'All the better,' said Zeitzler. 'I would be most grateful if it were possible to give Stauffenberg a little time tomorrow.' Manstein agreed.

* The original is in the Federal/Military Archive in Freiburg in Breisgau.

When I heard the name Stauffenberg on my parallel telephone, I pricked up my ears. Henning Tresckow was behind tomorrow's visit: he had told me that if Fellgiebel or Stauffenberg came to see Manstein I must make sure that each of them could talk to the Field Marshal undisturbed.

On the way to dinner Manstein told me: 'A Major Graf von Stauffenberg from the Army Headquarters is coming to talk to me tomorrow afternoon. I need some time for his visit. Please see to it that I am not disturbed. Do you know Stauffenberg?' I replied: 'I listened in to the conversation with General Zeitzler. I don't know Stauffenberg.' 'Nor do I,' he said. Then we were in the dining-room.

Later in the evening – during the bridge games – there were one or two more telephone conversations and Manstein had to interrupt play several times. But here there were no parallel telephones, so I was not listening in. Just before going to bed the Field Marshal mentioned that besides Stauffenberg, Generals Schmundt and Fellgiebel would be coming.

So the next day, 26 January, I was understandably in a state of high excitement. General Schmundt appeared first, greeting me kindly; until then we had only spoken on the telephone. I was astonished when he at once mentioned Henning Tresckow, his 'old regimental comrade'. He knew I was related to Henning and asked me to explain the relationship to him. I announced Schmundt to the Field Marshal. This time the connecting door was closed, one of the rare times that this had happened since I had come to Manstein's outer office.

As I set down these reminiscences, I am reminded by the Army Group War Diary that Schmundt spoke to Manstein for more than two hours that day. Such a long conversation with Manstein was quite unusual, but I never heard what had been discussed.

The Field Marshal's conversation with the next visitor, General Fellgiebel, was quite different. Although the connecting door was closed during this visit as well, the fact that the conversation lasted only ten minutes is significant: Manstein and Fellgiebel were friends. In later days I was often to meet them together, and in intimate circles they would address each other as '*Du*'. They were of roughly the same age, so it is revealing to read from the Army List of Reichswehr officers in 1928 what close personal relations must have existed in many units during the period of the Weimar Republic between some of the officers who later held the highest and most responsible posts. For instance:

4th Division, Dresden Garrison, 1928:

Chief of Staff	Colonel Beck
Divisional Staff	Major Fellgiebel
Divisional Staff	Captain Zeitzler
Staff of Infantry	Major von Manstein
Command IV, Dresden:	

Conclusions might be drawn from the fact that Fellgiebel was with Manstein only a few minutes before Stauffenberg, but I prefer to report the facts without speculation.

I was sitting at my desk, which was positioned in such a way that when the connecting door was open I could see the whole breadth of the table with the big situation map of the Army Group. I could not see the Field Marshal's desk, which stood to the left of our connecting door. A desk-lamp on my table was the only source of light in my room.

The building was quite silent when suddenly, without knocking, someone opened the door. The third expected visitor – it could only be he – stood in the open doorway, looked briefly round the room, came over to me in a few rapid strides, put out his hand and said: 'Stauffenberg – and you are Stahlberg?' It happened so fast that I had no time to introduce myself first, as the younger to the older man. A few conventional phrases followed, about the flight and the news. I said that the latest reports from Stalingrad were terrible, but he looked at me without answering. I was in the presence of a fascinating personality. After a brief pause, he said: 'Well then, announce me.' But before going in to the Field Marshal, and so that both Stauffenberg and Manstein could hear me, I told the courier who was still there that he could go now and I would call him in the waiting-room when I needed him.

Manstein greeted Stauffenberg and asked him to take a seat on the other side of the desk. I returned to my room, leaving the connecting door half-open as usual. This was not unwonted, since it was basically my job to listen and note what I thought important.

Before I could concentrate on the conversation next door, I realised what I had just heard: Stauffenberg had called me by name before I could tell him who I was, so someone had told him to make sure before talking to Manstein that Stahlberg was in the outer office. It could only have been Henning.

Now I devoted my full attention to the conversation next door. Stauffenberg's proposals concerned the establishment of fresh units of volunteers composed of Cossacks and Turcomans. My first impression was: excellent – he talks quickly, in fact very quickly. Like many officers of every rank, I had discovered in my few weeks with Manstein that those who spoke at length because they wanted to be particularly thorough, who repeated themelves for the sake of insistence, who were vague, in order to give the effect of talking on a 'large scale', whether staff officers or generals, were not very gently dealt with and in some cases were elegantly bowed back to my outer office.

Stauffenberg also spoke with concentration. Though unable to see them I felt that Stauffenberg's proposals were finding favour with the Field Marshal. Once I heard: 'Excellent, my dear fellow!'

Once or twice one of my telephones rang and someone asked when he could speak to the Commander-in-Chief; I had the caller transferred to our Chief of Staff, General Schulz, with whom I had an agreement. Once or twice the door to the passage opened and a courier delivered reports, so I could follow the conversation next door only intermittently. But if a written signal came in about changes in Stalingrad or on the other armies' fronts, I went in to Manstein's office to enter the new position on the situation map. For some weeks now the Field Marshal had allowed me to record such intermediate signals myself. I was working on the map from one of these reports while Stauffenberg was still sitting at Manstein's desk. When I began to draw, they both looked across at me and since I was entering a freshly-reported attack by the Russians near Stalingrad far to the East of the Army Group front, that is on the very edge of the map, both of them stood up and watched me. Manstein cast a glance at the signal lying before me and handed it to Stauffenberg. No one spoke. I withdrew to my room, leaving both of them standing by the map.

Now the talk was no longer of Cossacks and Turcomans but of the situation in the whole Army Group Don area, with the Sixth Army encircled at Stalingrad and concern for Field Marshal Kleist's neighbouring Army Group A in the South, also now in retreat, authorised far too late by Hitler. Thanks to Hitler's orders, both Army Groups were now in extreme peril. I felt that the young General Staff major had now reached his theme: 'Sir, how could the German forces in Southern Russia have been so fragmented? Trying to take Stalingrad and the Caucasus at the same time!'

He was not responsible for that situation, Manstein replied. He had taken over here when 'the baby had already fallen into the well'. Then what was the point of Stalingrad, what was it worth to us, Stauffenberg asked, and added: in the Army High Command the offensive against Stalingrad and the Caucasus had been followed with consternation from the start. If Stalingrad had to be conquered, then it had been quite wrong to position one of our best armies facing the city, leaving the protection of the flanks to the Romanians, Hungarians and Italians.

Manstein agreed repeatedly and Stauffenberg went on questioning: what was Army Group Kleist supposed to be doing in the Caucasus? Manstein: it was supposed to take Baku so that we could use the oil wells ourselves. He had told the Führer that the Sixth Army in Stalingrad was the first priority, before we could think about Baku and oil, but he had been turned down. The Führer had decided otherwise. He had begged the Führer to give him Army Group A (Kleist), or at least part of it, since our forces had been insufficient to maintain the link with Stalingrad. Had he been given operational freedom, he would have been able to save the Sixth Army.

Then Manstein quoted from that telephone conversation with Hitler early in December: 'The Führer intends to attack southwards via the Caucasus in the spring. He wants us to join up with Rommel in Palestine.' I had the impression that the Field Marshal was bringing the conversation to an end. I could see Stauffenberg clearly now, because Manstein had his back to me. He was staring wide-eyed at the Field Marshal. He had heard about that too, he said, it had been rumured at OKH, but they simply would not believe it. 'Do you really think that was my plan?' cried Manstein. 'But that's enough now, Stauffenberg!'

Stauffenberg straightened then – both of them were still standing by the map – and said emphatically: 'Sir, I respectfully beg you not to end our conversation – not yet.' 'Very well, my dear fellow,' said Manstein, 'what else have you got on your mind?'

Stauffenberg began by saying that he could not accept the fact that the Sixth Army was to be the victim of nothing but strategic errors. After all, Stalingrad had not been the first such error. In his eyes the Russian campaign had been a whole string of mistakes. Manstein agreed at once, or at least he shared the view that the offensive against Russia had been a mistake from the beginning.

Had he been asked to draw up a strategic plan before the start of
the attack on Russia, he would have seen it quite differently. Now,
however, was not the moment to discuss what his own plan for an
Eastern campaign might have been, though at least there would
not have been this constant fragmentation of our own forces.
Moreover, he had had other problems when the Western campaign
was over, because at that time he had been leading an Army Corps
which was intended for the landing on the English coast.

'One must learn, Stauffenberg, to deal with the facts as they are,
for instance with the fact that the Sixth Army in Stalingrad is lost.'

Stauffenberg responded: 'Sir, I simply cannot resign myself to
Stalingrad just like that. The sacrifice of hundreds of thousands of
German soldiers bears no relation to the purpose and usefulness of
this battle.'

The conversation was clearly entering an explosive phase,
becoming passionate. Manstein explained to the other man that an
officer's duties in time of war included resigning himself to losing a
battle. 'Name me one victorious war in the history of warfare in
which at least one battle was not lost.'

'That doesn't convince me,' Stauffenberg objected. 'Just now,
Sir, we agreed that this Russian campaign, if it had to be fought at
all, has been a string of mistakes from start to finish. Who can
guarantee that the same pattern will not continue into the future?
Since the failure of our 1941 Autumn offensive, we go from one
crisis to another; many times our armies have been on the brink of
collapse. And now, in Southern Russia, I believe we owe it solely to
the outstanding abilities of a certain Field Marshal von Manstein
that the front has not already completely collapsed.'

During this part of the argument I had to interrupt the now
vehement exchanges when more signals came in. My interruptions
did not seem unwelcome to the two men, because they allowed
time for thought. I entered the new items on the situation map,
Manstein and Stauffenberg watching me as before.

Then I withdrew, this time leaving the connecting door only
very slightly ajar, because I had the feeling that the conversation
might now become so dramatic that my presence would be a
nuisance. The door remained in that position to the end, so that I
was able to go on listening in, apart from one or two duty
interruptions.

He would like to return, Stauffenberg began, to the problem of the loss of one battle. He could not share the Field Marshal's view that Stalingrad was simply a battle lost. In his eyes Stalingrad might be the beginning of the end of a lost war, unless one began to consider the cause of all the mistakes, which he saw firstly in misguided organisation at the top. 'And secondly?' asked Manstein. 'In the Supreme Command,' the young major replied.

Manstein's response to this bold thrust astonished me: he agreed. He also believed that changes were needed in the military top ranks, at least of the Army, and, if possible, of the entire high command of the Wehrmacht. We needed a qualified military Commander-in-Chief for the Eastern Front area at the very least, and he would do everything in his power to bring that about.

His answer did not satisfy Stauffenberg, who said he thought it most unlikely that the Führer would relinquish military command. Then he switched to a still bolder line: 'Sir, you are the one predestined by ability and rank to take over the military command.

Stauffenberg's move was a clever one, because it struck at the very heart of Manstein's own thinking and action. So the Field Marshal was probably flattered; at all events he did not contradict Stauffenberg.

Stauffenberg was not going to let go now: somehow this path must be forced – but this was the threshold which the Field Marshal refused to cross. He said he was willing to discuss the question of the 'top structure' openly with the Führer at the next opportunity, but he was not prepared to be involved in illegal activities in any form, directly or indirectly.

Stauffenberg began again: if no one would take the initiative, everything would go on as before, which would mean our eventually plunging into a major catastrophe.

Manstein repudiated this vehemently: it was not his ideas, but Stauffenberg's which would lead to catastrophe. The ideas Stauffenberg had expressed would lead to the collapse of the Fronts and civil war. A war was not lost as long as it was not deemed to be lost. It might well be that our greatest military crisis was still ahead of us, and if so the Führer himself would recognise that he needed someone to restore order. One must have the strength to wait.

Then I heard a word from the Field Marshal's room which made me freeze. Stauffenberg said it: 'Tauroggen'*. There was a pause, followed by Manstein's voice, rising in indignation: Tauroggen had nothing at all to do with the present situation! Would Stauffenberg be good enough to desist from any such ideas! But Stauffenberg parried skilfully: the Field Marshal must have misunderstood him; by mentioning Tauroggen he had not remotely meant putting out feelers to the Russians. On the contrary, there could be no question of that. What he had meant was to suggest that it might be possible in some way to create a *fait accompli*. And, word for word: 'Tauroggen also involved extreme loyalty.'

The conversation became impassioned; it also grew louder. Several times I was interrupted by my telephones and had to take the calls in order to prevent anyone being connected to the Field Marshal on one of the direct lines during that time.

As I vividly remember, the conversation ended abruptly. Meanwhile the Chief of Staff of the Army Group, Schulz, had telephoned to ask when it would be possible to talk to the Commander-in-Chief. So I now reported to the Field Marshal that General Schulz had asked for an appointment. The two men were still standing by the map table and I heard Manstein saying that he had enjoyed being able to talk so openly. And he added the sentence I had so often heard him utter: 'What is the point of a General Staff, if General Staff Officers can no longer speak freely among themselves?' Stauffenberg observed the niceties and thanked him politely, but I thought I heard resignation in his voice. Probably the Field Marshal felt the same, because he quoted, apparently off the cuff, a phrase I had not heard before: 'Criticism is the salt of obedience.' He asked Stauffenberg if he knew the author of the saying. After a moment's thought Stauffenberg said: 'Clausewitz? Or old Moltke perhaps?' Manstein smiled and said he did not know either. Had it possibly sprung sponteneously from his own mind?

I left Manstein's room with Stauffenberg, he shook my hand and said a single word: 'Thanks'. His face was at once agitated and immobile.

At dinner the Field Marshal invited Stauffenberg to sit next to him. I sat opposite, as was usual at the round table. But – I remember it well even now – there was no more real conversation.

---

* The Tauroggen Convention, concluded on his own authority by the Prussian General Johann David Ludwig von Yorck on 30 December 1812, gave the signal for Prussia's abandonment of Napoleon and the Wars of Liberation.

I found the atmosphere painful, as Stalingrad moved towards its final agony. Manstein brought the meal to an end earlier than usual and Stauffenberg left at once. I made up my mind not to forget that day.

The next day, 27 January 1943, I followed the customary telephone conversation with Zeitzler particularly closely. After discussing the situation at the Front and in the Stalingrad pocket, Zeitzler asked almost in passing if Stauffenberg had been there the day before and what impression he had made on the Field Marshal. Manstein said he supported Zeitzler's judgment: he too regarded Stauffenberg as an 'extraordinary personality'. There was no doubt that Stauffenberg fulfilled all the conditions for an outstanding military career. At the same time it was clear to him that Stauffenberg had spent far too long at OKH, because he had a tendency to concern himself with matters that were nothing to do with him, so he thought it was high time to transfer him to the Front for a while. Since Zeitzler had asked for his assessment, that was his advice.

There was a pause before Zeitzler answered: 'Very well, Field Marshal, I will think it over.' I remember feeling during that conversation that General Zeitzler knew more about Major Graf von Stauffenberg than the Chief of the Army General Staff could know by virtue of his office alone.

Since our war diarist, Lieutenant Otto Feil, and I had a relationship of complete mutual trust, I told him the gist of the previous day's conversation and we discussed whether and how it should appear in the Army Group war diary. It was clear to us both that an officer of Stauffenberg's stamp was going to make his mark in the future. We could not set down a single word of the conversation, but we could record the fact that the meeting had taken place. Feil and I agreed on a form calculated as it were to rub the historians' noses in the fact that on 26 January 1943 an important conversation lasting precisely 45 minutes had taken place in Taganrog. That is how my note on 26 January 1943 found its way into the Army diary.

Soon we heard that Stauffenberg had left OKH for Rommel's army in Africa. The temporary secondment of a young General Staff officer to a field formation was quite a normal thing in itself, and it may actually have been planned for Stauffenberg already. Nevertheless it is worth emphasising that on 27 January 1943 Manstein had recommended Stauffenberg's transfer to the Chief of the Army General Staff.

On 7 February 1943, Stauffenberg became 1st General Staff Officer (Ia) of the 10th Panzer Division stationed in Africa. As chance would have it, his chief aide there was one of my closest friends from Pomerania, Captain Horst von Oppenfeld of the Reserve, and it may be worth noting that Oppenfeld, who came from the Oppenheim banking family, was of Jewish descent. For him too, joining up as a volunteer and reserve officer candidate back in 1934 had been an escape from the expected pressures of the National Socialists. Oppenfeld told me after the war about his work with Stauffenberg: 'The best chief I have ever had, either in the Army or in professional life'.

Through my brother, who as a severely disabled ex-serviceman worked in the Organisation Section, Stauffenberg's previous office in OKH, I later learned that Stauffenberg had been gravely wounded on 7 April 1943 in Africa.

A few days after Stauffenberg had faced Manstein in Taganrog, the fate of the Sixth Army in Stalingrad was sealed. The Commander-in-Chief, Paulus, promoted to Field Marshal by Hitler almost at the last minute, was taken prisoner by the Russians on 31 January. Hitler was said to have frothed with fury when he heard the news. He had wanted a 'Field Marshal who fell at the front'. On 1 February the battles died out. Army Group Don had already been forced to withdraw its headquarters to Stalino (now Donetsk) on 29 January.

At the Führer's Headquarters

Field Marshal von Manstein was called to report at the Führer's headquarters, *Wolfsschanze* (Wolf's Lair), near Rastenburg in East Prussia on 6 February 1943. Hitler sent his private plane, a 4-engine Focke-Wulf Condor, to pick him up on the day. This, the largest type of aircraft in the German Luftwaffe, had originally been designed as a long-range reconnaissance plane capable of reaching America. Another version had been a long-range bomber, intended to sink Allied shipping in the Atlantic, but it was soon apparent that the Condor was too slow for these purposes and fell easy prey to the British fighters.

When Hitler used the Condor over the European continent it was escorted by a large number of German fighter aircraft. A year ago we had observed this from the ground over Estonia and had been told that Hitler was coming to visit the Finnish Marshal Mannerheim. Our division was ordered to 'keep an eye on the sky' with its guns, which were suitable for anti-aircraft duties. The German fighters swarmed like flies round the Condor, their many powerful engines sending a tremendous noise down to earth.

Now the Condor was standing on the runway at Stalino, without an escort, of course, since today it was 'only' picking up a Field Marshal. Nor would Manstein ever have thought of asking the Luftwaffe for an escort for himself. How many flights I would be taking with him in the future! But we were never to see a single enemy aircraft while we were in the air.

The interior of Hitler's Condor was like a drawing-room. The walls were wood-panelled and the furniture upholstered in leather. A group of stewards served us attentively with food and drink as required. The china and massive silver cutlery were inscribed with the symbol of the NSDAP, but the glory of the interior furnishings was a gigantic wing-chair in the front right-hand portion of the cabin. Before the aircraft taxied off, the chief steward initiated the Field Marshal into its secrets. The upholstery of the seat actually contained a parachute, and on the right, under the window, there was a sturdy, bright red lever, secured with a lead seal. The bottom, back and sides of the chair were armoured under the leather, so anyone sitting in it would have the best possible protection against the fighters, which generally attacked from the rear. Then the use of the parachute was demonstrated and the function of the red lever explained: it was to be pulled only in extreme emergency and on no account before the parachute was attached to the body. By using the red lever the entire chair, together with part of the floor, would be released from its mountings and descend earthwards. Special care must be taken not to open the parachute by means of its release mechanism until the occupant and his armoured chair were sufficiently far apart from each other.

Manstein was hugely entertained by this contrivance and I could not resist asking in all innocence where I should find my parachute in such an emergency, but I was told that there was only one such safety device in the aircraft.

The Condor really was an interesting machine and, curious as ever, I visited the cockpit when we were in the air. Pilot Captain Hans Baur, who had already flown Hitler as a private pilot in the years before he seized power, turned out to be a simple, friendly man. We called these uncomplicated flyers 'air coachmen'. Baur handed me a throat microphone and headphones and invited me to take the co-pilot's place. Like a flying instructor, he explained the Condor's technology and instruments to me. After a few minutes he reached with his right hand into a leather holder fitted beside his seat and produced a bottle of schnapps. He took a good swig and handed it to me, but when I refused with thanks he wanted to know why. I told him that in a few hours' time I would probably be with the Führer, and that a swaying figure and a whiff of alcohol would not be quite appropriate. He simply shook his head and went on explaining the Condor to me. It was particularly important that the four engines should run at exactly the same number of revolutions. Each engine had its own throttle in the middle of the cockpit, but the four throttles were so close together that you could actually hold all four with one hand. Reading off the four revolution counters was not as important, Baur said, as having a feel for the sound and vibration of the machine. That kind of thing must be felt, not read, to keep the bird comfortable in the air. Today the revolution counters were unfortunately no longer as accurate 'as before'. Then he explained the compass, course compass, artificial horizon, and so forth to me and finally invited me to adjust my seat to my measurements and 'feel along with' his own movements on all the hand and foot-operated instruments, which were connected in parallel to his. Now and then he would reach for his bottle and take a swig. Then he set me some trivial, harmless tasks, such as flying towards this or that cloud, while keeping a constant eye on the set compass bearings.

We had good weather and I was enjoying the flight. After about a quarter of an hour I was already feeling a little more sure of myself, when suddenly I asked a question and received no answer on my headphones. I glanced at my flying instructor and was not a little startled to see that Pilot Captain Baur was asleep. His chin was on his chest and now I could hear his snores over my headphones. I wondered for a moment whether I should wake him, and turned to the radio operator who was sitting behind me at his instruments, but he only grinned, shook his head and indicated with a finger to his lips that the captain should be left to sleep.

After a few minutes Baur woke up of his own accord, glanced at the instruments and then at me, turned on to his left side and fell asleep again.

As we were approaching East Prussia he finished his siesta and dismissed me so that his co-pilot could resume his seat. Over the headphones he said: 'But you mustn't tell anyone I let you fly!'

From Rastenburg airfield a car took us to the OKH guesthouse on the Mauersee, a beautiful, gracious wooden house, which until his dismissal in December 1941 had served as a residence for Field Marshal von Brauchitsch, the Commander-in-Chief of the Army. From here, if memory serves me, we were about 15 kilometres from the Führer's headquarters, the 'Wolf's Lair'.

The evening briefing with Hitler generally began between 2100 and 2200 hours. In deep darkness, we got into a train consisting of only one or two carriages, which was waiting by the guesthouse to take us in 10 to 15 minutes directly into the innermost restricted area of the Wolf's Lair. General Zeitzler and his Ia, Colonel Adolf Heusinger of the General Staff, joined us in the darkened carriage and then we were rolling off through the darkness. There was something eerie about our journey – in fact the whole of that first evening at the Führer's headquarters made an eerie impression on me.

When the train stopped we got out cautiously, because here too it was pitch black. Then General Schmundt, Hitler's chief adjutant, came to welcome us. After only a few steps we arrived unexpectedly in Hitler's conference shelter, where the guests were standing grouped round the brightly-lit map table. Hitler's place at the centre of the long side was still unoccupied. Gold-rimmed glasses lay there ready for him.

General Schmundt appeared in the doorway and announced loudly: 'Gentlemen – the Führer.' The waiting men fell silent and Hitler gave them his angled salute without speaking. He glanced round once, then shook hands with Field Marshal von Manstein only. There was a paralysed silence in the room.

I had been eagerly looking forward to this conference, not only because it was the first I had attended, but even more because I was curious to see how – four days after the capitulation in Stalingrad – Hitler would address the Commander-in-Chief of the Army Group, who was also responsible for the Sixth Army.

What I then witnessed was a masterstroke of Hitlerian psy-chology: 'Gentlemen,' he began, 'first I would like to say a word about Stalingrad. I alone bear the responsibility for Stalingrad. And now,' turning to General Zeitzler, 'the current situation in the East, please.'

I still remember that moment vividly today, because I had

expected many things from Hitler, but not that. After all, in the past two months I had heard and read what passed to and fro between Stalingrad and OKH as well as between the Army Group and OKH, or the Führer's headquarters – and that had sounded quite different. The effect of Hitler's words, sounding almost like an admission of guilt, was then followed by a brief moment of awkward silence. Both Manstein and Zeitzler were obviously surprised.

When the conference was over and we were sitting over a glass of wine in the guesthouse on Mauersee, the Field Marshal said he was still impressed by Hitler's Stalingrad admission. He had not expected so much courage of conviction from Hitler. Even when Manstein describes the scene in his memoirs, he calls Hitler's words on Stalingrad 'soldierly'. I had felt differently about them and even today I think they were a significant example of Hitler's cold, calculating ability to prepare himself for an imminent exchange of views. It was not evidence of Hitler's 'soldierliness', it was the politician speaking, aware that he will play his part most successfully if he tells his listeners what they secretly want to hear. I suggested this – with due restraint – later that evening at the guesthouse and was then astonished all over again when Manstein agreed with me to some extent. I shall return to that evening circle at the guesthouse later.

The evening conference in the Führer's headquarters began with the dangerous situation of Army Group Don (Manstein). Spurred on by their victory in Stalingrad, the Soviets were now attacking westwards along a front of more than 700 kilometres, and it was clear that they intended to encircle the Army Group and drive it back to the Sea of Azov. Manstein's armies were in deadly peril, but the 'castling' move he had initiated behind the front from South to North was already in progress. The Russians were streaming westwards towards Kharkov with a superiority of 7:1. It was now up to Manstein to keep his nerve and penetrate deeply into the enemy's flank. But on 6 February the time for that had not yet come.

I still have a clear picture in my mind of Hitler's uncomprehending face when Manstein had the floor. There were in fact a good many expressions that Manstein loved to use, but which Hitler simply did not understand. Manstein tried to explain that our chances of success against the Russian offensive would increase in line with the extent to which he allowed the Russians to win territory. This bore a certain similarity to the Manstein Plan of May 1940, when the French and British forces were allowed to cross the Somme to the north, where they were ultimately caught in the trap at Dunkirk.

Hitler considered this 'risky'. He was no doubt remembering what he had witnessed in France in the First World War: frontal resistance, holding on 'to the last man and the last round'. For him there was really nothing but attack or defence – with that his strategic thinking was apparently exhausted. Again and again he spoke of the mineral resources of the Ukraine and the heavy industry at Stalino, which were crucial to Germany's war effort. The two of them were completely at cross-purposes. What mattered to Manstein was victory in the battle between the Don and the Dnieper, whereas Hitler's thoughts were concentrated on ore, coal, manganese and arms production. Once or twice Manstein tried to discover from Hitler how he saw the war developing in the future, in broad terms, but the question vanished into thin air as Hitler adroitly evaded it. Most of the time he stared stubbornly at the situation map, apparently without reacting.

Manstein's manner was amazingly carefree, almost as if he were facing a seminar of young trainee General Staff Officers rather than his military superior. But I remember that the atmosphere was frosty. Hitler seemed suspicious, or at least I observed in his face something that I was often to see at later briefing sessions: with his eyes still stubbornly fixed on the situation map, Hitler would clench and unclench his jaw muscles. That evening I could not decide if it was play-acting or emotion, but with the detachment of a mere observer I inclined to the former interpretation.

What I found astonishing was that Manstein, who always stood beside Hitler at the map table – I was on the opposite side – seemed quite oblivious of his facial movements.

Later, after another meeting with Hitler, I once asked the Field Marshal if he had noticed this facial tic, but my question surprised him. He had never noticed, he said, adding 'What a lot of things you do notice.' At all events, during these talks Manstein did not let Hitler impress him at all, whereas, at other conferences, I have seen senior officers – even the most senior – becoming quite unsure of themselves, almost stammering, in Hitler's presence.

For me, attendance at the frequent conferences at the Führer's headquarters was soon to become quite normal, because I knew that I was scarcely likely to be addressed. Of course, I usually had my briefcase with notepad and documents with me, but I was never asked to produce anything from it. What Manstein had to say was already in his head. I do, however, remember a later conference, at which General Zeitzler began by saying that before he embarked on the immediate situation, he must report that in the last 24 hours no fewer than three army generals had fallen at the front. Hitler, his eyes fixed on the map as usual, did not react. In the brief moment of silence that followed this shattering announcement, I heard only his: 'And then?' He neither asked for the names of the dead men nor did their Supreme Commander vouchsafe them a single word of remembrance. He also failed to appreciate that in a modern war a general's place is not normally where the fighting is but at the command post.

On the evening of 6 February, Manstein succeeded, almost without warning, in addressing the most explosive subject of all, that of the 'unified high command'. This paraphrased the dualism created by Hitler between the Wehrmacht High Command (OKW) and the Army High Command (OKH). There were in fact 'OKW War Theatres', such as Rommel's army in Africa, and the 'OKH Theatre', namely the Eastern Front – not to speak of a special instrument of power established side by side with the Wehrmacht: the steadily growing Waffen-SS, whose corps and divisions were assigned, now here, now there, to the headquarters of the Army Groups, and sooner or later withdrawn again. Not much imagination is needed to envisage the series of problems created by this system of leadership – problems which did nothing but damage to the cause in question.

With Hitler, however, the subject fell on deaf ears. He did not contradict, he simply behaved as if he had not heard the question. Nothing more was heard of the matter that evening. Both partners in the dialogue did observe the proprieties, but it seemed to me that Manstein was dismissed with distinct coolness and reserve.

Nor did I on any subsequent occasion ever see Hitler take a decision in the presence of the Field Marshal on the frequently controversial possibilities of future strategy. As a rule, he would let him go with the words: 'I wish you a good flight. You will find my decision on your return.'

The tension did not relax until we were in the OKH guesthouse on the Mauersee. We formed a little circle in comfortable chairs and, at last, the older men could also indulge in their beloved cigars. No food or drink had been offered by Hitler, whose aides even had orders to forbid any smoking in his rooms. Manstein's old friend General Fellgiebel was there too, so that for the first time I was together with them both.

The orderlies – elderly soldiers – served a snack and made sure that the Burgundy glasses were not empty. The atmosphere grew lively and tonges were loosened. Fellgiebel forced the conversation. I noticed how quickly the wine affected him, obviously making him feel that he was back in the officers' mess in the good old Reichswehr days. He simply went for his old friend Manstein as if there were no cause for restraint. Several times he claimed quite openly that his knowledge both of internal affairs in Germany and of matters at the front was far superior to the Field Marshal's, nor did he make any secret of his profound contempt for Hitler. The Chief of Army Communications was obviously one of the best-informed people in the Reich.

I listened to the conversation, worrying about the orderlies waiting on us: who were they, what were they thinking? For a time the Field Marshal made efforts to restrain his friend, but Fellgiebel grew all the more excited. I wondered how would it end. It was over quickly, and in the most natural way. Suddenly, Fellgiebel got up and headed for the door to the passage. It had scarcely closed behind him, before we heard loud imprecations from the corridor. I jumped up and ran after him. As I opened the door I saw him disappearing into the lavatory, but inside the large tiled room his anger swelled. I can still hear his furious outburst today: 'That liar! That swine! That destroyer of our Fatherland! That murderer! That scoundrel! . . .'

I jumped at him from behind and as I held his mouth closed with both hands and all my strength, I could feel him weeping uncontrollably.

Gradually the tension left his body and he became quite calm. He apologised and thanked me: 'Ah, Stahlberg, if you only knew what we signals officers hear you would not believe me. It is ghastly!'

We returned to the large sitting-room together, but when I opened the door the room was empty and the light was out. During our absence the others had gone to bed. Helping Fellgiebel into his coat, I accompanied him to the front door. The cold air felt good. I felt very close to him from that day on.

Colonel Schulze-Büttger

Since being posted to Army Group headquarters, I had been amazed to realise that the German Army Groups fighting from Leningrad to the Caucasus were only imperfectly linked with one another along this tremendous front, which stretched for more than 2,000 kilometres as the crow flies. No doubt there was some reason behind this on Hitler's part, once again revealing his distrust of the General Staff. Apparently even his chief of staff Zeitzler had orders to allow this kind of separation to be maintained.

According to my observations, it was up to individual Army Group chiefs of staff as to how often and in how much detail they co-ordinated their own military situation with their neighbours.

This was no doubt one of the reasons why Henning Tresckow, Ia of Army Group Centre, telephoned us so often. Henning's calls mostly came during the evening when we were playing bridge, so that I, being the youngest and the first to take the calls, heard his voice often.

In one such conversation with him I mentioned incidentally that changes were taking place in the operations section where I worked. Promotion to a senior field command was anticipated for General Schulz, our Chief of Staff, and I expected the former First General Staff Officer (Ia), Colonel Busse, to be Schulz's successor.

Henning arrived by air the next day from Smolensk and had a long talk with Manstein. He had previously let me know that he was going to try for the post of Chief of Staff to Manstein himself, which would have been quite an obvious step, since Manstein and Tresckow had been working closely together in the winter of 1939/ 40 at Rundstedt's Army Group in Coblenz, Manstein as chief and Tresckow as his Ia. Their joint work had resulted in the strategic plan for the Western Campaign. Even to me, Manstein had often talked of his excellent collaboration with my cousin, so to renew this link was an obvious choice.

I had realised some weeks ago that a more fateful decision was involved in this question of staff. The Busse/Tresckow alternative had politically disruptive implications. Naturally, Manstein knew that Tresckow was among the most critical opponents of the National Socialist régime, while Busse was an apparently unpolitical soldier, at a time when 'unpolitical' meant simply and solely 'obedient', come what may. The Field Marshal was thoroughly accustomed to Busse, a soldier who would present him with no difficulties of any kind. He was also possessed of great energy and above-average ability, whereas Tresckow would create a good many problems when it came to fundamental decisions. He would certainly not make Manstein a comfortable colleague.

There was yet another, compelling factor in Busse's favour: he was brother-in-law to Hitler's Deputy Chief Adjutant, General Burgdorf. Burgdorf and Busse had married sisters. General Wilhelm Burgdorf was generally regarded as a particularly committed National Socialist, known to act in accordance with the wishes of the régime in the Army Personnel Office whenever he could.

Manstein and Tresckow had a dramatic encounter behind closed doors. Before I announced him to the Field Marshal he had told me why he had come and asked me to interrupt only if particularly important signals came in.

If I remember rightly, I was in the room with them twice. At all events I can see them now, standing in front of the hearth, in a state of great excitement, Manstein shaking with agitation as I had never seen him do before, and Tresckow with tears of despair in his eyes. I had the impression that this was a kind of continuation of the Taganrog conversation with Stauffenberg, only conducted still more passionately and probably more openly on Tresckow's side.

Later I heard from Henning that Manstein had refused him once and for all. To the Field Marshal, Tresckow's ideas were quite simply appalling. It is also my personal conviction that the great strategist felt uncertain, if not positively impotent, as a political soldier. In the choice of staff – Busse or Tresckow – Busse's close link with Hitler's staff undoubtedly played a part, but for the link with Henning Tresckow's ideas, there was still the ADC, Stahlberg.

Tresckow's masterstroke in this situation was to have succeeded in inserting one of his closest friends and colleagues, Colonel Georg Schulze–Büttger of the General Staff, on to the staff of Headquarters Army Group Centre, when the post of First General Staff Officer (Ia) to Manstein became vacant. Once more my cousin's activities and imaginative resources had proved inexhaustible.

I still knew nothing of this 'substitute solution' when Schulze-Büttger joined us a little later. When I asked him where he

came from I was relieved, for now I had someone I could talk to,
and when I heard from 'Schu-Bü', as we soon called him, that
before the war he had been the last adjutant to Colonel-General
Beck, who had retired as Chief of the Army General Staff in 1938,
we enjoyed a mutual and unreserved trust which soon turned into
genuine friendship, of a kind I had not known since Heinrich
Yorck. Besides, Schu-Bü possessed an enviable gift: he could see
the funny side of the most serious things.

For Manstein as for Schulze-Büttger, the figure of
Colonel-General Beck was an object of reverence. When they spoke
of Beck the two of them often quoted old Moltke. Beck was just the
type of General Staff Officer they admired, who sees it as his chief
duty not to seek war but to prevent it wherever possible.

At that time, if one wanted to talk over fundamental questions of
strategy and policy with a friend, one arranged to go for a walk. I
was happy to do this with Schu-Bü, because a conversation with
him was always profitable. On one of these occasions we discussed
the question which constantly defeated us: when would this
dreadful war end?

Schulze-Büttger replied with one of his delightful *aperçus*: 'I can
answer that question precisely: the war will be over on the day
when the last German elementary school teacher is promoted to
major!' Then he became serious: 'As long as Hitler is Supreme
Commander of the Wehrmacht there will be no end to the war.' I
agreed, but said that I had also discussed the question with the
Field Marshal and Manstein refuted this conclusion. He gave a
great deal of thought to the conditions and possibilities of a
stalemate with Hitler. Schulze-Büttger had already heard this
theory from Manstein, who had made similar suggestions to him
when he came to work with us. 'Keep pressing that point when you
are alone with the Commander-in-Chief. Don't let go!' he added.
This was a topic we would often return to.

Three Days of Hitler

The telephone woke me up after midnight on the night of 16/17
February 1943. (By now the Army Group Headquarters had
moved from Stalino to Saporoshie). The operator asked if I was
sufficiently awake to receive a call from the Führer's headquarters.
I asked the invisible soldier at the exchange to give me a minute or
two while I got my writing things ready. Soon the telephone rang

again and Major Gerhard Engel, Hitler's Army Adjutant, gave his name at the other end: 'The Führer has just decided to fly to Army Group Headquarters in a few hours' time. General Zeitzler will be coming with him. The Führer intends to spend three days with the Army Group. Make all the necessary arrangements. Please repeat.' I repeated, and asked how many people would be accompanying the Führer. Engel's reply was: 'Expect a hundred people.' I asked when the Führer would be arriving in Saporoshie and Engel said he could not tell me yet, but we would be informed in good time. We should in any case begin at once with all the preparations. He made me repeat the instructions again and we rang off.

I considered whom to wake first and had myself put through to Colonel Schulze-Büttger. I asked him to get up and dress at once, as I had to speak to him urgently. It was important. Without asking why I had called, he said he would expect me in his bedroom.

When I reached Schulze-Büttger he was already sitting fully dressed on the edge of his bed. He offered me a chair and I reported Engel's call to him. He stared at me wide-eyed and exclaimed, in Berlin dialect: 'This is a fine kettle of fish and no mistake!' and I replied: 'Yes, Colonel, that it is.'

A long pause followed. Oddly enough I was the one to break the silence: 'Colonel, I think we're both thinking the same thing.' He looked at me again and said 'Yes, Stahlberg, we're thinking the same, but that's not the way.' Another long pause. Then he said suddenly: 'We must try to think what it means that the Führer will be under the same roof with us for three days.' We were silent again. Then another abrupt question: who else besides the two of us knew about Engel's call? I said I had not spoken to anyone else, but I was certain our telephone exchange would have been listening. General Müller, chief of our Army Group signals regiment, had once told me one must always assume that someone was listening in, especially at night; this applied in particular to a conversation with the Führer's headquarters.

Schulze-Büttger said: 'You know, Stahlberg, any spontaneous action would be irresponsible. If we really want to play for such high stakes, all the consequences will have to be thought out beforehand. What we're both thinking of now can only be a starting-pistol, but once that is fired all the runners in the race must be on their marks already.'

For us, that dealt with the subject we had never named. Now we had to prepare for the arrival and accommodation of our 'guests'. First we considered how and where we should house Hitler. Schulze-Büttger had an excellent idea. The Operations Section of the Army Group had its offices on the top floor of an administration building which, as far as I remember, had three floors. The offices of the other sections were on the floor below and those of our guard company on the ground floor – we were in the middle of quite a big town. All the offices of the operations section must now be transferred to the rooms below them. Only the guard company would have to move to tents or barracks beside the main building. Hitler and his hundred-strong escort would have the vacated upper floor. Even if it was a little cramped for them, they would have to put up with it. After all, we were at war. Since only the offices of our operations section were housed in that building – bedrooms and messes were in other premises – Hitler and his escort would be alone in the house with the guard at night.

We considered the security problems and at once – it was obvious – came to the problem of possible air attacks on Saporoshie. True, our high command had never been attacked by the Russians from the air, but if Hitler was really going to spend three days in Saporoshie as announced, Schu-Bü and I could scarcely believe that Moscow would not be informed of his presence with us by at least the second day. But Schu-Bü dismissed the subject at once, since air defence was the Luftwaffe's responsibility, not ours. Nevertheless, we both thought it wise to obtain the highest level blessing, if possible, on accommodating the Head of State on the top floor of a primitive, detached administration building.

So I had myself connected with the Führer's headquarters, asked – not without a certain *schadenfreude* – for Major Engel to be woken up, and handed over the conversation to Schulze-Büttger. He expressed himself diplomatically, speaking of moving the individual sections of our staff around inside the building, and also mentioned that there were air raid shelters in the gardens surrounding us.

Engel seemed to agree, but before the conversation was over I asked for the receiver again. I had considered the Führer's accommodation, I said, and was thinking of suggesting that the Field Marshal vacate his own offices for the Führer, but I asked them to remember that our accommodation here was very primitive and very 'Russian'. So could he please prepare the Führer for this.

Engel said he would, but told me it would be wise to expect that during his stay with us the Führer would very probably look into other rooms in addition to those prepared for him. If so, there must not be the slightest possibility of his seeing a single piece of furniture in another room that was better than a comparable object in his own rooms. Schulze-Büttger, who was now listening in, clapped his hand to his mouth to suppress a snort of laughter.

Then we went to work. I undertook to inform the Field Marshal, and Schulze-Büttger suggested that if Manstein agreed to our plan I might personally undertake the transfer of his three offices to the same rooms immediately below, as well as the fitting-out of our three rooms for Hitler.

But before we separated I asked him why Hitler – for the first time in this war as far as I knew – should be leaving his headquarters to spend three days with an Army Group. This was just what had been worrying him from the first moment, Schu-Bü said. He thought the answer could be found in our situation map. The tip of the Russian offensive to the north of us was a few kilometres from Dnepropetrovsk, and further to the south, less than 100 kilometres from our own headquarters at Saporoshie, whereas Manstein's counter-offensive on the Russian's southern flank was only just beginning to roll. According to our operational plans, our attack would become effective in three days' time. Zeitzler had apparently described Manstein's plans so convincingly that 'the greatest commander of all time' saw a chance of representing Manstein's operation as his own in the event of its foreseeable success. Nevertheless, Schulze-Büttger was not happy at the thought that Hitler might interfere in operations yet again at the peak of the anticipated battle, as he had repeatedly done in the past, contributing nothing but damage and unnecessary losses to the German cause.

Back in my room, I knocked at the connecting door to the Field Marshal and entered the dark room when I heard his voice. I reported everything that had happened in the last hour and what Schulze-Büttger and I had arranged. 'Did you have to wake me up for that?' was his first comment. I said I had thought it my duty and asked if he agreed to the transfer of his offices. 'Yes, naturally,' came from the darkness, 'when will he be here?' I told him that we had not been given a time yet but I would make sure he was woken up in time. Just as I was leaving he asked: 'Tell me, Stahlberg, what does Effendi really want here?' (When Manstein was in a bad mood, he liked to give Hitler this oriental title.) I said I had already been over that question with the Ia, but it was not for me to judge. Then, as if he were already half asleep, I heard him say: 'Yes, yes, Effendi often has a nose for a propaganda coup.'

I sent for a car from the pool to take me to the operations section building. The town was silent and empty, but when we turned in through the iron garden gates the place was teeming with soldiers. The outer guards had already been reinforced many times over and the inside of the big building was like a startled hive of bees. Soldiers were carrying furniture up the only staircase, so that I had difficulty in reaching the top floor. When I looked out of the window lorries were already arriving at the house with beds, chairs and tables – brand-new furniture – taken from a field hospital depot.

For three days I said goodbye to our shabby old leather armchairs, which had probably seen service in the days of the Tsars. The Commander-in-Chief's three rooms at the eastern end of the long corridor became a suite for the Supreme Commander.

Manstein's office became Hitler's bedroom, my outer office became Hitler's office, and the third room, our conference room, retained its usual function. I ferreted through the lower floors for furniture several times, finding clothes' stands, washstands, etc. Then came my first problem: there was no water supply to those three rooms; the 'comfort station' was on the other side of the passage, where there was in fact an extremely large lavatory, but this room – if you will forgive me – stank indescribably. The sanitary arrangements were very far from sanitary. There was a cabin with water closet for officers, but it was a water closet without a wooden seat. There were no water closets for other ranks, merely a hole in the floor.

I solved the problem quite simply by sending for a large can of carbolic. Carbolic was the tried and tested disinfectant for field hospitals. Of course, carbolic also gave off an infernal stench, but it was said to be a very effective disinfectant. I had it used in abundance to make it universally apparent that we had done our best. The lavatories still stank vilely, but only of carbolic.

Then came another problem: I did not succeed in chasing up a wash-basin. All the enamel bowls brought to me were damaged and I did not want anyone telling me that surely I could at least have been able to organise a decent washbasin for our Führer. So I commissioned my batman to scour out my own brass washbasin with sand. The basin had a history for me: in a village to the south of Leningrad, a Russian woman had come up and presented me with this beautiful old basin, about 50 cm wide. 'Bread!' she had repeated several times, and I had given her several army loaves. Now I hoped the beautiful basin would still be there when Hitler left and (to anticipate) it was, and I have it still.

Schulze-Büttger made a tour to see how my preparations were progressing. He also glanced into the lavatory opposite, but started back: 'A bit much carbolic, phew!' he exclaimed, and escaped, chuckling.

By then we knew our exalted guest's arrival time. If I remember rightly, it was to be at noon, so I woke the Field Marshal at the normal time and met him as usual in our breakfast-room. Breakfast and afternoon tea were our retreat times, when I was virtually always alone with him. He got me to tell him about my 'night shift', but one question was still unanswered: where was his secret box to live over the next three days? This wooden box, for which I was responsible, always stood beside my bed at night and by day it remained in my outer office. It also stayed in the outer office during lunch or any other absence, because there was adequate security there. Now I asked the Field Marshal if the chest should still stay in my outer office at lunchtime. His decision was as I had expected: for the next few days the chest would not be left in the operations section building at any time when we were absent.

I asked him if he wanted to see the three rooms for Hitler, but he was not interested.

Towards noon a long column of cars began to move across the town for the arrival. Saporoshie had two airfields, one to the east of the town, the other west of the Dnieper. The streets were virtually empty. Manstein sat with me in the back of his big official car with the roof and sides closed. Sergeant Sakolowski was at the wheel.

Looking at his driver, the Field Marshal said suddenly: 'Well, Sakolowski, you'll have to come back in one of the other cars. Lieutenant Stahlberg will drive this car, leaving the other front seat free for the Chief Adjutant, General Schmundt, or General Busse. The Führer will sit at the back on my right.'

I looked at the Field Marshal in astonishment, but he did not react. So I was to drive Hitler! My stomach muscles tightened. Me, of all people.

What had made the Field Marshal order this seating plan? Was it considerations of protocol, or did he want to discuss things on the journey from the airfield to headquarters which, according to security rules, could not be discussed in the presence of a sergeant?

On the airfield the cars were ranged according to rank and station. I sat experimentally at the wheel of the big official car and adjusted the driving seat. After a few minutes two Focke-Wulf Condors flying nose to tail appeared on the horizon and came in to land. While I was still wondering in which of the two planes Hitler would be travelling, the square standard of the German Head of State was flown from the cockpit of the front plane. Manstein left our group and stood on the airfield a few metres in front of us. I took my place 'back left', as I had seen on newsreels and great state occasions.

The pilot of Hitler's plane had recognised the Field Marshal from a distance and put the machine down so precisely that there were no more than a few steps between the two. The door opened above us and a ladder was heaved down. The first people to appear were two SS men, who climbed down and posted themselves at its foot. Hitler kept us waiting before appearing in the doorway. The two SS men reached up to support him, so that he should not have to climb down the ladder backwards. This had obviously been rehearsed and worked extremely well. The Supreme Commander was wearing a dark leather coat and Manstein saluted him with his field baton.* Only Manstein was allowed to shake hands; all the rest received Hitler's bent-arm salute.

For a few minutes Hitler made no move to walk over to the cars waiting about 30 metres away, but began a conversation with the Field Marshal and his Chief of Staff, Busse. I kept at a little distance and, thanks to the strong wind, was unfortunately unable to hear a word. Then my eye fell on the second Condor and I saw quite a large group of SS men moving towards our column of cars at the double. The cars taken over by SS men disappeared at top speed towards the town – in other words, the delay in our departure had quite obviously been planned.

Only an hour later I heard the reason for this manoeuvre from Schulze-Büttger, who had stayed at headquarters: the SS men had turned up at the Operations Section building, cleared out the rooms I had arranged for Hitler down to the last piece of furniture,

---

* In the field a Field Marshal did not carry the marshal's baton but a slender ebony baton with a silver head and band.

upended every bit of it in the passage and searched it inside and out before replacing it in its orginal position.

After about a quarter of an hour, accompanied by the Field Marshal and the rest of us, Hitler at last walked slowly over to our column of cars, headed by the Field Marshal's car, instantly recognisable by the standard with the gold embroidered crossed marshal's batons on the front right wing. All four doors were open, Sakolowski had already started the engine. Then something unexpected happened: when the four of us, that is Hitler, Manstein, Busse and I were about to get into the car at the same time, I felt myself being grasped urgently by the left arm and rudely jerked backwards. I turned and looked into the face of an SS officer. All he said was: 'I drive this car!' And the Field Marshal's car was off, without his ADC. I just managed to jump on to another car, also already in motion, which was exclusively occupied by SS guards.

On the one hand I was thoroughly relieved to escape the burden of having once been Hitler's chauffeur; on the other, the manner and style of this abrupt changeover were in very poor form. He could have introduced himself to me, and I would certainly not have put any difficulties in the way of Hitler's chauffeur. But Erich Kempka – it must have been he – had probably not been very well tutored in such matters.

The column then moved off at a moderate pace towards the town, where a fresh surprise awaited us when we reached the first houses.

In a word: Saporoshie was on its feet. The population lined the roadsides and among the Russian men, women and children I actually saw a good many German soldiers. The news of Hitler's coming must have run like wildfire through the town in the last hour, because when we had driven to the airfield the streets had been practically empty. Hitler was sitting on the right beside Manstein in the car ahead of me and even though the plastic side-windows had been put in place – Sakolowski had always taken care to have good transparent windows – the occupants were easily recognised. I was able to observe the reactions on either side of the street quite clearly. The Russian civilian population was silent, while the German soldiers saluted with their hands to their caps, which was still the rule at the time. But I also saw some soldiers giving the Nazi salute – contrary to regulations – which meant that they had recognised Hitler.

We reached our headquarters without incident, the cars driving round the circle between entrance gate and main building until the first car stopped before the steps. I was able to catch up with Hitler and Manstein as they entered the house and to follow them up the stairs. Manstein gave me a friendly nod, as if to say he was glad I had got through.

There were already SS men with machine-pistols at the foot of the stairs to the top floor. So this was where our dominion now ended.

Manstein and I took Hitler to the rooms prepared for him. Behind us, still on the stairs, appeared an SS officer with an Alsatian on a lead. So this was the famous bitch so often photographed with Hitler over the years – a splendid specimen! On entering the rooms intended for Hitler, the bitch was let off the lead and welcomed her master by jumping up and licking his hands.

The Field Marshal now also had an opportunity to introduce his ADC. Hitler gave me his hand, but this was no handshake, his hand felt like a sponge. He said he already knew me. Eleven days earlier he had perhaps seen me across the map table in his headquarters, but had not spoken to me. I was pretty sure that he would not have remembered me with Papen in January 1933.

Then he unbuttoned his leather coat and allowed me to take it from him, and at that point I discovered with a shudder that Hitler had very bad breath. As I took his coat there was a savage outburst from the Alsatian bitch and I admit that I was not too happy, faced with her bared teeth and her crouching posture, ready to spring. But once again she turned out to be an extremely well-trained animal. 'Down, Blondi, down!' her master shouted, and Blondi obeyed at once. I hung the coat on the clothes' stand and I could have sworn that in the pockets – just as in January 1933 – there were two pistols. Alternatively the coat may have had a bullet-proof lining. At all events it was unusually heavy.

Manstein and I were then dismissed, to be greeted in the passage, now teeming with officers and SS men of all ranks, by the men waiting there: Manstein by Hitler's Chief Adjutant, General Schmundt, and I myself by a very corpulent, grubby-looking man, who had not shaved for days, wearing a grey made-up uniform. He introduced himself to me as Professor Morell, the Führer's personal physician.

Theodor Morell wanted me to tell him if there was a slaughterhouse in Saporoshie; he needed a calf today, from which he would extract certain glands while the carcass was still warm. If necessary a calf would have to be slaughtered specially, because he needed the fresh glands for a treatment which must not be interrupted. I asked Morell to be patient until I was back with the Field Marshal in his offices one floor below. From there I would make enquiries for him by telephone.

I had scarcely spoken when something else unusual occurred: a large, dark-coloured wooden chest was moving towards us from the staircase. It must have measured about a cubic metre, with handles at the four corners. Four SS men were carrying it, with a fifth walking ahead who asked the Field Marshal and onlookers to stand aside for a moment to allow the chest to pass. Then the fifth man opened the doors to the lavatories and while a cloud of fresh carbolic billowed out at us, the bearers and their burden disappeared into that sweet-smelling area of the top floor. When the door shut again Manstein asked General Schmundt: 'What on earth was that?' Schmundt told him rather awkwardly that it was the Führer's new dry closet.

The time seemed to have come to leave this strong-smelling area of passage, so we moved towards the stairs, where the traffic was as brisk as an underground station. Boxes and baskets were being carried upstairs in large numbers, and Professor Morell explained that they were full of equipment and supplies for the Führer's private kitchen, adding with a trace of pride that the entire kitchen and its personnel were under his supervision.

Arriving in our new offices, I first tried to solve the problem of 'Morell and the calf glands'. I had myself connected with our Senior Quartermaster, Colonel Finckh. 'Colonel,' I began, 'this is a very important matter. I have with me Professor Morell, the Führer's personal physician, who needs for his treatment, today . . . '

At first Finckh did not answer, then he asked me to repeat it all over again. I did so, word for word. Then he asked if the professor's problem was being dealt with by his staff. When I said no, he said this really was a very important matter and I should send the professor to him at once, as he was most interested in the affair and would like to meet the professor personally. I apologised for turning first to the Senior Quartermaster of the Army Group for advice on this request, but: 'No, no,' Finckh responded, 'I am exactly the right person for such an important event. Where the health of our Führer is concerned, the highest authority is just adequate!' Even then I knew Finckh well enough to be aware what he was thinking behind the ironic teasing.

That got rid of the personal physician, who was grateful for my help, while I was still enjoying Finckh's dry humour.

Then there was much coming and going in my room, and Lieutenant Feil, our War Diary keeper, also put in an appearance. He was the first to tell me that all hell had broken loose in the building in our absence. What had happened was that a host of other aircraft had landed on the second airfield on the far side of the Dnieper, so that the numbers of the entourage by now far exceeded 100. It looked as if the Führer's entire headquarters had been transferred to Saporoshie.

Feil and I were standing at the window, watching still more bags and boxes being carried into the house, when the passage door opened behind us and a rather stout general entered. 'My name is Choltitz,' he began, and asked me to announce him to the Field Marshal. He was on his way to take over a new command. When I made a move to go in to Manstein he stopped me. He had plenty of time and would very much like to have a word with the two of us beforehand.

'Tell me, gentlemen, what are you in such a state about here?' he began. I said that Feil and I were not in a state. 'No, I don't mean you two, but the whole house is in a state – what's going on?' Since I had no idea what kind of person I was dealing with, I played the innocent and said that up to now I had not observed anything out of the ordinary. 'Now look here! What is the SS doing? Or perhaps you'd like to tell me if I've come to the wrong house. This is Headquarters Army Group South ('Don' had now become 'South'), isn't it?' 'Undoubtedly, Sir,' I told him, and the Commander-in-Chief is next door.' 'Then please explain to me,' Choltitz went on, and now there was a hint of steel in his voice – why General Choltitz has just been challenged by the SS to show his pass on the way to see his Commander-in-Chief?'

I was shocked and asked him to allow me to report this to the Field Marshal at once, because it was news to us. 'Leave it, I'll tell him myself,' Choltitz retorted. 'In any case, I'm not the only soldier here being checked by the SS. But you still haven't told me what all the excitement is about.' I said it was probably the presence of the Führer which had given rise to a certain amount of tension. 'Just as I thought!' Choltitz exclaimed, 'I heard something about that. So it's really true. But tell me – what was your name? – tell me, Stahlberg, where is the Führer?' I said the Führer was probably exactly over our heads at that moment, as his office was above this room.

The moment had come for Dietrich von Choltitz to display his gifts as a kind of court jester: 'What an uplifting sensation!' he cried. 'The Führer directly above General Choltitz – incredible!' Then he asked me if I had yet seen the Führer face to face. When I said yes, he said: 'I haven't. Please help me to meet him. One is always hearing about his brilliant blue eyes and how wonderful it is looking into them!' When, keeping my face as immobile as possible, I described that kind of 'help' as rather a lost cause, he suddenly went to the window and said he had an idea: did I know when the Führer took his walk? I said I had no idea, and could scarcely imagine that the Führer would go walking here in Saporoshie. But Choltitz was getting more and more fun out of his fool's rôle. 'Do you see that pedestal down there?' It was a white pedestal, of a type that stood in front of official buildings in every Russian town, supporting a plaster bust of Lenin. Wherever German troops appeared, the pedestal was at once relieved of its bust, as it had been here. 'You know, Stahlberg, nature frowned on me, alas, and made me short of stature. So I beg you to let me know in good time when the Führer leaves this building. I'm sure you'll know soon enough to give me a chance to climb on the empty pedestal before the Führer leaves the house. I want to be standing up there when the Führer comes. He won't be able to overlook Choltitz there!'

Still evasive, I said I thought two conditions would have to be met first. Firstly one would need a ladder, because the pedestal was too high to be climbed just like that, and secondly one must have a head for heights. He looked at me cheerfully: 'We should be able to find a ladder, but unfortunately I have no head for heights.' With that he gave me a friendly pat on the shoulder and said that I could now announce him to the Field Marshal. An unforgettable meeting with an unforgettable man.*

* As German town commandant of Paris, General Choltitz was ordered by Hitler on 23 August 1944 to reduce the city to a pile of rubble before the Allies arrived. He handed over Paris unscathed.

Conferences at Saporoshie

We had five conferences with Hitler in those three days. On our office floor, one floor below Hitler's rooms, a large room had been equipped for these sessions, with the usual map table in the middle, round which the participants gathered. As at the Wolf's Lair, the Reichstag stenographers sat against the left-hand wall of the room; I stationed myself in their corner so that I could see the major participants diagonally across the table and had the window light behind me.

The first conference took place soon after Hitler's arrival on 17 February, when General Zeitzler had also reached Saporoshie. Manstein was standing with him at the door when General Schmundt arrived to announce Hitler. The ceremonial was the same as in East Prussia.

Although I had already seen Hitler that day at the airfield and when he was shown his rooms, now, when he was standing a few metres away from me with the midday sun shining on him from the window, his appearance shocked me. His skin was slack and yellowish, he was unshaven and the lapels of his double-breasted grey uniform tunic were spotted, apparently with food stains. His stance made a disturbing impression on me: his head hanging forward from his shoulders, his stomach projecting without restraint. Hitler looked like a used-up man, a sick man.

When Manstein began his presentation without looking at anyone – as was his wont – regardless of who was listening, and moving his hands casually over the map to illustrate his ideas, Hitler continued to stare doggedly at the table. Once again Manstein was so preoccupied with his description of the military situation and his operational plans that I felt the world around had vanished for him. I looked again at Hitler, whose eyes were still directed at a single fixed point and remained there, though the Field Marshal's hands were indicating positions right across the map. Once again Hitler's jaw muscles began to move, not once, but for minutes on end, and as it seemed to me, more and more vigorously. It looked almost as if one of his choleric outbursts was on the way – we had often heard that Hitler was capable of wild excesses of fury.

However, nothing of the kind occurred. While I observed the scene intently – determined never to forget it – Manstein continued unconcernedly with his presentation and Hitler, beside him, never stopped exercising his chewing muscles. Having now seen this twice within a few weeks, I realised that it was a psychological tactic which had become routine. Once again I mentioned it to Manstein that evening, but once again he had noticed nothing.

When the presentation was over, Hitler cleared his throat and made one or two indifferent comments, such as, yes, that was interesting, but it all seemed to him very risky. Manstein was familiar with this objection and the short dialogue that followed proved yet again that Hitler was not capable of strategic thinking. He simply would not see that in view of the massive numerical superiority of the Soviets our only chance was to shift decisively to mobile warfare. What constantly astonished me was Hitler's incapacity to learn from such an outstanding military expert as Manstein. I saw Hitler ultimately as a small-minded man, riddled with complexes.

With all his undoubted intelligence, his thinking was confined to the retention of his position as Supreme Commander and only his memory for figures was still astounding. He tried repeatedly to divert the conversation to the theme of Russian mineral resources, whose possession he regarded as indispensable, juggling figures like a virtuoso. The briefing on that first day in Saporoshie ended with a certain sense of relief: at least Hitler had not interfered with operations. That alone was a success in Manstein's eyes.

In a discussion of the military situation with the Supreme Commander of the Wehrmacht one would also have liked to hear something about the other theatres of war, for instance the battles in Finland, the situation in North Africa, where the German troops were apparently at the end of their tether, and not least the battles in the Pacific, which had expanded to unusual dimensions. But there was nothing.

So the front line in Russia was not supposed to be reminded that by now Hitler's war had expanded into a world conflagration. Even a Field Marshal should kindly confine himself to his own sphere. That was my impression. When Manstein was back in his office with me I had the idea that he might ask Hitler by telephone to send one of the many officers in his retinue to give a briefing on the other theatres of war. Manstein refused. That would once have been a matter of course, he said, but such a request would simply have the effect of making Hitler suspicious. Hitler had in fact been profoundly suspicious of generals and the General Staff for years now, and it would make the necessary co-operation even more difficult.

I made another suggestion: should we not try inviting Hitler to a small dinner so that we could sit round afterwards and exchange ideas? Manstein revealed that he had issued just such an invitation to Hitler on the drive from the airfield to headquarters, but Hitler had said it was unfortunately out of the question, because he would have to work late into the night.

In the afternoon there was suddenly a commotion throughout the building: on Hitler's orders, we embarked on an exercise that verged on the farcical. Coats and caps were borrowed from officers of every rank from the offices, and in the corridors soldiers and NCOs of the headquarters guard company were dressed up as generals and staff officers. As many generals' overcoats with red flashes as possible were called for. I even had to make my old leather coat available, but refused to hand over the Field Marshal's coat – there must be some limits to this play-acting. General Busse thought it a splendid idea; Manstein cloaked himself in silence.

At the same time a good many of the vehicles that had fetched Hitler from the airfield at noon drove up to our office building. One after another the illustriously disguised soldiers left the house as darkness fell and vanished into the cars. The population of Saporoshie was to see that our distinguished visitors were already leaving the town. This piece of theatre was a great success. Hitler's two Condor aircraft were soon taking off and flying low over the town towards the west, where they could land again at the second airield on the far side of the Dnieper.

I found the whole manoeuvre shameful. Did it mean that Hitler was – to put it bluntly – a coward?

I went down the corridor to Schu-Bü's room to talk it over. He felt the same as I did, having been rendered speechless when this 'Führer's order' reached him. We stood by his situation map, showing one of the Russian spearheads still 100 kilometres away. At least the Russians could not be in Saporoshie tonight.

We moved on together to section Ic a few rooms off, where all the intelligence about the enemy came in, to find out if there was any evidence that the Russians had got wind of Hitler's presence in Saporoshie. Nothing useful came up, but we agreed that it was at least highly probable that Hitler's presence was known to the Soviets.

I reported Ic's views to the Field Marshal and asked if he would allow me to check the surroundings of the house where our bedrooms were and get a clear idea of the position of the air raid shelters. He looked up briefly from his reading, tapped the ash off his cigar and said I had a vivid imagination. I asked him if my worries were not realistic, but he said they were quite the opposite. He had already given some thought to the problem and had reached the opposite conclusion: 'My dear Stahlberg,' he began, 'listen carefully. In this war Stalin and Effendi are not going to hurt each other, I am quite sure of that. Well, and if I should be wrong and you right, then you have already solved the problem of our security without my assistance, because you and I are sitting here under Effendi's rooms!'

His answer surprised me and I could not help commenting that this was the first time I had heard such a highly political utterance from him. He ended the conversation with an 'Enough – and as far as I am concerned, off you go and check on your air raid shelter.' Aha, I thought, but I did not say it.

At headquarters we had considered the possibility that, apart from the conferences, if Hitler really intended to spend three days with us as announced, he would also want to spend an afternoon or an evening with the Field Marshal and one or two other staff officers. He had already turned Manstein down for the first evening, but we thought it scarcely conceivable that Hitler would really stay in his room for several days. We were wrong. Hitler left the top floor only for the conferences on our floor, and to the best of our knowledge not once did he leave the house until his departure two days later, on 19 February. Only Blondi was taken out now and then by one of the SS body servants. Both nights passed without incident, nor was there an enemy air attack, so Manstein had been right.

The next day, 18 February, there were to be two sessions with Hitler. With Manstein's permission I took my film camera, a 16 mm Siemens, to the noon session. I carried it as inconspicuously as possible in my left hand, because even I knew that Hitler allowed himself to be photographed only by his own cameramen, and insisted on seeing the photographs before they were distributed. I took up my former position, where the light was ideal. I wanted not only to catch Hitler and Manstein in discussion, but to try to snap Hitler with his glasses on. No such picture of him had ever been made public. The camera was set, and I waited like a hunter for his prey, with 15 metres of film ready for the shutter release, and more rolls of film in my trouser pocket. Hitler made the same impression on me as the day before. There was something horrifying about his slack stance and the uniform, which was still dirty in spite of the batmen present.

Manstein began with the situation, which had developed dramatically following the Russian breakthroughs, while Manstein's counter-offensive had not yet begun. For anyone who had ever witnessed the development of a battle on a military situation map, the tension in the room was indescribable.

Once again I had the feeling that Hitler scarcely followed the Field Marshal's presentation, although this time he did interpose a question now and then. Two or three times he picked up the glasses left ready to hand and put them on, only to take them off again immediately afterwards. On the second or third occasion I raised my camera, matching my movement to Hitler's hand, but Hitler at once lowered the hand holding the closed glasses, concealing them in his palm. He seemed to do it without looking at me, apparently quite intuitively. I repeated the game two or three more times without success, and finally let the film run while Manstein was speaking and Hitler was silent. So at least I had that, and I began to put in a new film behind the broad back of one of the stenographers.

But I had no chance. General Schmundt, standing behind Hitler, came round the table to me and whispered indignantly that I was to stop filming at once for God's sake, because the Führer had expressly ordered that only those with special permission could photograph him. I whispered back that it was very disappointing not to be able to capture such a highly important meeting on film. Schmundt agreed at once and sent one of his 'junior aides' out to get a cameraman. One appeared a few moments later and I beckoned him over. Now my few metres of film had a sequel from the same position, and of course the professional photographer was using a much more efficient camera. I whispered to him: 'With glasses on!' But he shook his head and whispered in my ear: 'Forbidden'. When he stopped filming I whispered: 'You owe me those pictures. Let me have a copy.' He nodded, and I still have the film today.

Meanwhile Manstein and Hitler had embarked on a really lively discussion. The Field Marshal was clearly trying to get away from his own counter-offensive and use the opportunity to learn Hitler's further plans, but without success. Once again he asked for operational freedom, at least in the area of his own Army Group, but once again his questions fell on deaf ears. When Manstein spoke of operational freedom, Hitler talked about personnel and material planning, exchanging exhausted troops in the East for fresh ones from the West, or about his plan to release another age group soon for call-up. Then he told Manstein that in France a new 'Sixth Army' would be set up, which would keep alive the tradition of the Stalingrad army. The debate was endless, but once again they were talking at cross purposes.

Finally Hitler concluded the conference and we went off to lunch, Hitler and his entourage to their upper floor, the rest of us driving off to our lodgings. As agreed, I took the Field Marshal's secret chest with me during the lunch-break. One never knew.

On the short drive, I mentioned Hitler's questionable physical condition to Manstein and he agreed with my observations. He said he had also talked to Schmundt about it and the General had said that it was probably a result of the military situation in Africa: things were going badly for Rommel's army.

A second conference had been called for that evening, with the blackouts over the windows in the conference room and powerful electric light blazing down from several ceiling lamps.

For me, the listener and onlooker, able to devote myself wholly to my observations, Hitler's entry into the conference room was a totally unexpected revelation: a completely different Hitler came in, in no way comparable with the man of earlier today and the day before. The drooping, failing figure was suddenly transformed into an upright, brisk and vital apparition. He was freshly shaved, his skin had colour and he was also wearing a clean tunic. What had they been doing to him? Morell, his personal physician, had arrived in Saporoshie with him the day before and later his second physician, Karl Brandt, was there too. General Schmundt had introduced me to him and described him as the Führer's 'surgeon'. (Brandt was in fact wearing SS uniform.) We knew that Hitler liked to sleep late in the morning and generally went to bed hours after midnight, but such a transformation could not simply be attributed to the time of day. Drugs must have been at work here.

Late on the evening of 18 February 1943, Field Marshal Ewald von Kleist, Commander-in-Chief of Army Group A, joined us on Hitler's orders. Army Group A now consisted almost exclusively of the Seventeenth Army. Its withdrawal from the Caucasus had been approved by Hitler, a month too late. Instead of coming to the aid of the Sixth Army in Stalingrad in December, it had not been allowed to leave the Caucasus until January. It had retreated with heavy fighting to the Kuban Peninsula by the Strait of Kerch. With its back to the sea, it was in a far from enviable position, because soon its only salvation would be for the small German naval forces to carry it across the sea to the Crimea. Hitler was in the process of adding the further sacrifice of the Seventeenth Army to the senseless sacrifice of the army in Stalingrad. It was becoming unbearable to watch this hair-raising method of conducting a war. The supplies for Kleist's troops already had to be transported by sea. Had the sacrifice of the Sixth Army in Stalingrad not been enough?

Manstein and Kleist sat together after the evening meal, preparing their thoughts for the joint presentation before Hitler the next day. I sensed that the two Field Marshals, with their different temperaments, did not like each other. Kleist, the elder, seemed to be jealous of the younger Manstein and the evening passed coolly. But naturally enough, the exchange between them was worth listening to. Just as, with Manstein, Hitler had always returned to the mineral resources between the Don and the Dnieper, so for months he had spoken to Kleist of little but the oil reserves on the Caspian Sea and, for 1944, new offensives planned again Persia, Palestine and India. During the Stalingrad crisis, Hitler had told Manstein that he would probably be the one to lead the Indian campaign – and made precisely the same advances to Kleist. The two Field Marshals looked at each other in consternation.

Then they talked about Papen, the German Ambassador in Turkey. Kleist had had a visit from a young diplomat sent by Papen to 'make contact' with him. Typical of Papen, I thought when I heard it, but I held my tongue. Manstein, with a gesture of rejection, thought it a waste of time to agonise over the Near East – there at least the two agreed – but Kleist insisted that Hitler was still attached to the idea and that was why the Kuban Peninsula was to be held, as the 'springboard' for a campaign across the Caucasus. Hitler's generalship was becoming more unrealistic all the time.

For me the most astonishing thing about that evening was the fact that two Field Marshals were sitting together exchanging views, while their Supreme Commander kept his distance, only a few hundred metres away. Had Hitler possessed the merest hint of greatness, he could easily have taken the opportunity to sit with the two Field Marshals and inform them fully, or have them informed by a third party. But the opposite happened: he avoided any exchange of ideas, presumably spending those hours sitting in one of his three rooms, surrounded by his four undistinguished ADCs.

Perhaps that evening he had also had himself connected by telephone with Field Marshal Rommel, the shattered remnants of whose Army Group had been thrown right back to Tunisia. In a few weeks Rommel would be dismissed 'on health grounds' and the rest of the German troops in Africa would capitulate to the British and the Americans.

But perhaps Hitler had also telephoned from Saporoshie, using one of his personal lines, separated from our intelligence connections, to his propaganda minister Goebbels, who on that very evening was proclaiming 'total war' to rapturous party members at the Berlin Sports Palace, certainly not without permission from the very highest quarter – in Saporoshie.

At breakfast the next morning Manstein asked me about Papen – how from my knowledge of the military situation I would assess Papen's personality as an ambassador in Turkey. He wondered why, when Kleist had mentioned the Ambassador the night before, I had not joined in the conversation.

But since I had told Manstein weeks ago about my experiences with and of the Reich Chancellor, I preferred now to reserve my personal judgement of the German Ambassador in Turkey.

Naturally the Field Marshal understood, but he insisted on an answer.

Very well then, I thought, let's talk about Papen. In my eyes, I said, he was a man who despite all his gifts, over-estimated himself. He was driven by ambition. Of course politicians needed ambition, and also the ability to switch off their own conscience, but if one proceeded from the assumption that the German Ambassador in neutral Turkey was probably better informed on the south side of the Black Sea about the entire war situation than the Field Marshals to the north, then one must also assume that former German Reich Chancellor Papen had been considering for quite a while what he would do if World War II continued as it had been over the past few months. So I would not be surprised if Herr von Papen had been dreaming of his own renaissance for some time now. At all events, I thought him capable of the most astonishing about-turns.

Manstein was pleased with our breakfast-time chat and seemed almost to have forgotten that he still faced a potentially difficult conversation with Hitler later that day.

At the noon meeting that 19 February, Hitler still gave an impression of freshness (in spite of the 'early' hour, for his lifestyle) in no way comparable with the shocking picture he had presented only 24 hours ago. I once again joined the two stenographers, who in view of the far larger number of participants that day, asked me to give them the names of the speakers as they took the floor. Their pencils flew over the stacks of paper, putting down whatever reached their ears. I had to whisper only the names of the speakers, as far as I was able. What a muddle there might be later on, when reliable minutes had to be produced from the shorthand texts! When researchers are studying the minutes of Hitler's conferences, it is worth bearing in mind that names may have been taken down or ascribed wrongly in shorthand.

That day Hitler had one Field Marshal on his right and one on his left. I had the impression that he enjoyed being the centre of such a distinguished group. It was extraordinary, I thought, how different this man could look – no sign of the ridiculous jaw flexing today, either.

The two Field Marshals reported on their situation one after the other, both quite obviously avoiding controversial material. As on the two previous days, General Zeitzler was also visibly restraining himself. On the military side, people were taking care not to provide Hitler with any opportunity to interfere in the current operation – until something totally unexpected happened: Hitler interrupted, took one or two steps back from the edge of the table so that the two Commanders-in-Chief were now standing in front of him and had to turn towards him, and declared tartly: 'Gentlemen, I observe that there is little point in continuing this conversation, as you have agreed among yourselves. Previously, whenever I have spoken to you individually, your reports and proposals have been mutually opposed, whereas today you speak with one mind.'

Embarrassed silence. Then Manstein repudiated the accusation and asked for examples, to which Hitler replied coolly and objectively that he was thinking of the tug-of-war over the First Panzer Army in December. Manstein had demanded it for his Army Group, whereas Kleist had declared over and over again that in view of the instructions he had been given, he could not hand it over. This 'example' amounted to perfidy. Both Field Marshals positively exploded, arguing against each other, both speaking at once, and both very agitated.

Once again Hitler took a step back, leaving the two Field Marshals confronting one another like fighting cocks, until Hitler said, with smiling superiority: 'That's enough, gentlemen. You see how necessary it is for me to be the one to decide. Please stop quarrelling in front of me now!'

I was appalled by these tactics, which had just given us a profound insight into Hitler's psychology. What an instructive scene!

The conference ended soon after that, without any mention of what Manstein and Kleist had agreed the night before, namely to get Hitler to disclose the broad lines of his ideas and plans for the future conduct of the war. On a short walk with Schulze–Büttger the next day, we agreed that Hitler undoubtedly had no overall plan at all – unless it was to defend and gain time, but for what?

A few hours after that conference, Hitler left Saporoshie. Once again, the column of cars moved off, travelling through the town and to the eastern airfield, where his two aircraft were already waiting. Once again, I drove in one of the cars behind Hitler, and the streets were almost empty. Not until we turned into the restricted area of the airfield did we meet with about 100 onlookers, mostly members of the Luftwaffe.

There were long goodbyes in front of Hitler's Condor, with yesterday's cameraman catching the farewell scene for the news-reel. He was kind enough to add this piece of film to mine. Talking incessantly, Hitler shook hands with Field Marshal von Manstein, holding on to Manstein's hand for exactly 35 seconds. (I timed it on my film with a stop-watch.)

Finally two of his SS men took him to the ladder of the aircraft and both held him up from behind so that he should not slip. This too I have on my film. As German fighters appeared in the distance, the two Condor aircraft disappeared in a westerly direction.

'And you didn't shoot him?'

A few days after Hitler's visit to Saporoshie, Henning von Tresckow appeared in my office. 'What brings you here so suddenly?' I asked, and his answer 'called me to order' at once: 'Now listen to me, my dear fellow. If you have been discussing the military situation here for several days with our Supreme Commander, surely it's obvious that the Ia of your neighbouring

Army Group should want information? What we at Centre receive officially from South is by no means sufficient.'

Before I announced him to the Field Marshal he said he wanted to talk to me on our own before he flew back to Smolensk at dawn. He was going to ask Manstein to release me for half an hour for a personal chat, because he did not want to give the impression that he was talking to me behind the Field Marshal's back. And with an almost cheeky look he said that I should please keep the connecting door to the Field Marshal closed as long as he was there; in any case, I knew what he had to discuss with the Field Marshal.

After about half an hour he came out of Manstein's room and said at once: 'Come along, the Field Marshal agrees.' I asked him if I should order a car so that we could be undisturbed somewhere. That wasn't necessary, he said, he had decided on the place for our talk before he came into our office building.

Then we were at the entrance and without another word he stepped on to the circular driveway before the building, which I remember as being about 30 to 40 metres across, and took it, as I still recall precisely: 'On the left hand'.

We walked round at least once without speaking. I could feel his mind hard at work. Finally I was the first to speak, describing to him, rather disingenuously, the meeting with General Choltitz, up there by one of those windows, one floor below Hitler's office. He listened in silence and when I finished the little episode he commented drily that he was glad to observe that I had apparently learned 'our language' very well and he was also glad to hear such news of Choltitz. Even such an innocent-sounding story was important, because one could deduce a great deal from it which might one day be significant.

By now we had already made several rounds of the forecourt and I said that down here we could be observed by practically the entire operations section of the high command. 'Observed, yes, but not heard,' he retorted, and went on: 'I will explain: I have already spoken to Schulze-Büttger on his own in his office, but the Field Marshal's ADC, who as everyone knows is my cousin, I address in full view of everybody. And I hope Busse can see us here too, as well as the Field Marshal.'

Then he went straight to the subject I had been expecting: Hitler's visit to us.

'So you had Hitler here in this building for several days. What I want to know now is whether you would have had a chance to shoot him?'

I had been expecting all kinds of questions, but not this one. My heart was pounding as I tried to answer. Then I said: 'Yes, Henning, I would have had the chance, not once but several times.'

At this he stopped, turned to me and looked straight into my eyes: 'And you didn't do it, although you could have done it?' We walked on a few paces before he stopped again and repeated, 'And you didn't shoot him!' Then he resumed our walk, the words now pouring out of him with increasing passion: 'We have been looking for an opportunity for months! Waiting for it, longing for the day when we can kill this scoundrel who is destroying our Germany! The day never comes! Each time, it's no use! Each time, something goes wrong! And you here in Saporoshie, who see things the way we do, you let the chance slip!'

We must have walked round again at least once in silence. I needed some time to recover after these terrible words. Then I said: 'Did you talk to Schulze-Büttger the way you've just spoken to me!' 'Yes, I did,' he replied, 'and Schulze-Büttger also told me that the night before Hitler's arrival you did at least have the courage to approach him about this, but the two of you decided that you should not do anything.'

After another pause he continued: 'Now I'm going to ask you some hard questions and I want absolutely clear answers. I have asked Schulze-Büttger the same questions, by the way. After spending three months at Manstein's side and seeing the way we're conducting this war, do you now agree that Hitler is not merely a military dilettante, but also a criminal?' I replied: 'Without reservation, yes.' Henning continued: 'And so, once again: why didn't you kill the man?' I answered: 'Firstly because I don't yet know what is supposed to happen when Hitler is dead.' 'And secondly?' he asked at once. I said: 'Because I haven't the strength for this kind of job. I have taken part in plenty of attacks with my division. I also have the assault badge. But I have had the great good fortune never to have had to shoot a man face to face.' ' I won't buy that,' Henning retorted, but I went on: 'Only a few days ago I was standing opposite Hitler for hours during the conferences. I wondered once or twice if I could manage to shoot him down across the table, because it would have been easy for me to bring my Walther PP in, ready to fire, in my right trouser pocket. But I was sure I would have been so nervous that I would definitely have missed. And I did and do believe that one could theoretically remove Hitler, as a single agent, but that all one would end up with would be Göring or Himmler taking command immediately. And in my eyes they are just as villainous as Hitler.'

After another pause Henning said: 'You asked me earlier what was going to happen when Hitler is dead. I'm not avoiding the question – we think about it all the time. I won't give you any details, but I can assure you that many highly qualified people are ready to assume responsibility after Hitler's death.' 'Henning! You do bear in mind, don't you, that there are dozens of commands, ministries and so on, which would not give up without a struggle?' 'Of course we know that,' he said. 'We have set up an outfit at "Centre" to deal with partisans. In fact it will be flown into Berlin at the crucial moment. You should know that we have two brothers called Boeselager who command it. They are both our people. Remember the name.'

Then he asked me what I thought of Manstein. I said that he fiercely rejected any suggestion that we might lose the war. His theory was that when one day 'the water was up to his neck', Hitler would remember him and be prepared in his hour of need to hand over command to Manstein to save himself. Henning listened quietly, then he said: 'That's one of Manstein's typical illusions, but it won't be long before even a Manstein is unable to help!'

We were still circling the front drive when Henning said: 'So you agree that Hitler must go?' I said: 'Yes. But how?' As if looking for something, he fixed his eyes on the path. 'We think about it all the time. We have many friends who agree on the end, but there are the most varied ideas about the means, some so naïve that it would be a sheer waste of time to consider them. Force is the only solution, and it has to come.' 'Did you speak as frankly as that to the Field Marshal just now?' I asked. 'Yes, why do you think I was with him?' he questioned, with a trace of annoyance.

'I'm sorry, Henning, I have to know, and so does Schulze-Büttger,' I said. 'We both have a commitment to Manstein, we're on that footing with him. But Schulze-Büttger and I have often wondered if the time is really ripe to get rid of Hitler. We are inclined to think that the war will have to be going a great deal worse before the German people start to think.'

Then I asked what he thought about Hitler's relationship with Stalin. In view of the 'slip-up' with the population in the streets when Hitler arrived in Saporoshie, we had assumed that Stalin must have known by the next day at latest that Hitler was staying with us. Henning was silent for a time. Then, 'I agree with you,' he said. 'Stalin must have known, and probably there were two reasons rather than one why he did not send bombers to Saporoshie. Firstly, the Russians must have known for a long time that the German Wehrmacht is very badly led. Remember that the Russians have undoubtedly been questioning Field Marshal Paulus and the other generals of the Sixth Army intensively, and are still doing so. In other words, the Russians would have to be complete fatheads not to have realised that the German armies would be far stronger adversaries without Hitler in command than with him. So it would be logical for the Russians to do all they can to spare Hitler – for the time being.

Secondly, if the German and Russian fighting forces should one day have torn each other to pieces to such an extent that both are impotent, while the Western Allies have not landed a single soldier on the European continent, Stalin and Hitler might get the idea of sitting down at the same table after all and totting up their mutual interests. Let me remind you that they did precisley that in 1939.'

I was startled. I agreed with the first theory, but not with the second. 'The second theory isn't something I want,' Henning replied, 'but I'm sometimes afraid that two mutually hostile criminals might be capable of some astonishing *volte-face*. In any case, it's worth thinking about, and I would consider it proper for you to discuss such matters with the Field Marshal.'

He ended our conversation – he wanted to reach Smolensk in daylight – on a conciliatory note: 'Please don't be angry with me for treating you like that just now. Actually I doubt if I would be capable of shooting and killing a man face to face myself. And as far as "afterwards" is concerned, Schulze-Büttger and you are quite right. There is still a lot to be done.'

Correspondence with Colonel-General Beck

One day – I can no longer remember the exact date – Manstein called me into his office, where he was busy sealing a letter. The red sealing-wax was dripping on to the envelope and he had taken his signet ring off his finger in readiness.

After sealing the letter, he asked me to shut the door to my room and sit down.

This was a letter to Colonel-General Beck, he began, and he would like me to take it personally to Berlin. 'But you will not enter

Colonel-General Beck's house and you will not meet him anywhere else, either,' he said.

This was an exciting mission. I did not know the former Chief of the Army General Staff personally, but for many years now his name had been so much a household word that I could almost believe I knew him well. Beck had retired from his post in 1938 because he refused to go along with Hitler's war policy. He was regarded as the outstanding mind on the German General Staff as a whole, and through my friends Achim Oster and Heinrich Graf Yorck von Wartenburg I knew a great deal about Beck. I also knew that he had been a member of the secret opposition to Hitler for years, and was one of its leaders.

'Have you any idea,' the Field Marshal continued, 'to whom you could entrust the letter in Berlin so that it reaches Beck? It must of course be someone absolutely reliable.' I thought for a moment, then I said – feeling as if I were diving off the high board: 'Major General Oster, Sir.' 'How do you know him?' Manstein responded at once. I said: 'I've known him for years; his son Achim is one of my best friends, we were in the same division in Poland and France and Frau Oster and my mother were jointly in charge of the people's kitchen of the Evangelical church in Eisenzahnstrasse in Berlin.' 'Agreed,' said Manstein, 'and give General Oster my regards!'

Now it was my turn to be astonished. Did the Field Marshal know what manner of man Oster was? I went back to my room and reserved a bed for myself by telephone in the sleeping car of the night courier to Berlin. Every night there was a train connection for the Army Group in both directions. Then I thought over my unusual mission again in peace and quiet, went back to the Field Marshal and said that I still had some questions about it. Firstly, I asked him to tell me if the letter was urgent. If so, I could try to get a connection by air through the air fleet. No, he said, and added, without my asking, that the Colonel-General had sent him 'a classical situation appreciation'. The letter he had given me contained his response. A day here or there did not matter.

Secondly, I asked to whom I should hand over the letter if for some reason I was unable to meet General Oster in Berlin. 'Make a suggestion!' he replied. 'Admiral Canaris,'* I said. The reaction was prompt: 'Do you know him too, then?' 'No sir, but I've heard a

---

* Admiral Wilhelm Canaris, Chief of the Overseas Office (Intelligence) of OKW, was Hans Oster's superior officer.

lot about him and I would be very interested to meet Admiral Canaris personally.' 'Excellent, Stahlberg! Very well. If you don't meet Oster, let it be Canaris.'

I left the train next morning at Friedrichstrasse Station in Berlin and walked across Unter den Linden, through the Brandenburg Gate and the Tiergarten, to the Wehrmacht High Command (OKW) on the Tirpitzufer. I had myself taken to General Oster's office but did not find him there. General Oster had gone to see the Admiral, the ladies in the front room told me, and I could sit and wait. They seemed rather surprised when I told them that suited me very well, as I wanted to speak to the Admiral too.

Canaris's offices looked out over the Landwehr Canal. When I entered the outer office I was startled to hear loud shouts from the Admiral's room on the left. Someone in there was in a fury. 'For God's sake, what's going on?' I asked the secretaries sitting by the window. Both of them indicated their own shock without speaking. Someone was still screaming next door, as if it were a matter of life or death, but the words were incomprehensible. The door was probably padded on the other side. I was still standing in the middle of the room as if rooted to the floor.

Then the door was flung open from within and General Oster stood before me. 'Stahlberg, where have you come from!' he cried, and I saw that he was still in a state of high excitement, breathing hard. He took me in to Canaris who was sitting at his desk and introduced me to the Admiral as 'Field Marshal von Manstein's ADC'. Canaris rose, gave me a friendly handshake and asked Oster and me to sit down. 'What brings you to us?' he asked. 'I have a letter from the Field Marshal to Colonel-General Beck,' I said and told him what I knew about it. Canaris asked at once what was in the letter, and though I was unable to tell him, he felt that the mere fact that they were corresponding was extremely interesting. Then I told him that the Field Marshal had forbidden me to give the letter to the General myself, but had agreed to my suggestion that General Oster should act as 'postman'. 'There you are then, Oster,' cried the Admiral, amused. 'Congratulations on your new "post"!' 'It gets better, Sir,' I told him. 'Again at my suggestion I have the Field Marshal's express permission to offer you the post of deputy postman, Admiral. And I am to give you both his regards.' There was some laughter and the noisy emotional outbursts of a few minutes since were apparently forgotten for the time being. The Admiral still had some questions

about Manstein, and I had the impression that both Canaris and
Oster had been informed by Stauffenberg about his conversation
with the Field Marshal at Taganrog, but I said nothing until Oster
suddenly interjected that I was closely related to Tresckow.
Canaris's eyes brightened. 'That's good,' he said, 'we greatly
respect Tresckow.'

Oster took me to his office, which was on the same floor; it
looked out on the courtyard. I gave him the letter to Beck and he
looked at it from both sides as if trying to weight it up. Then he said
he would take it that very day.

He changed the subject: 'I'm afraid I sounded very loud in the
Admiral's room just now.' I said he had, but that no words had
been distinguishable from the outer office. 'I may as well tell you
the reason, Stahlberg,' he said. 'This is it, have a look at this.' He
handed me a thin file. I opened it – and froze as I read. I held in
my hands one of the copies of a summarised report from SD
'Einsatzgruppen' on the liquidation of Jews in the Reichskommissariat Ostland (an administrative unit in the Occupied Eastern
Territories), neatly and clearly laid out, broken down by regions,
summarised according to numbers executed – tens of thousands of
them, adding up to six figures.

I handed the report back to Oster, too stunned to speak. 'This
arrived this morning. Now you will understand what I was feeling.
Do they know about these things at the Army Group?' I said I had
heard rumours; but only Tresckow had told me privately a few
months ago about organised campaigns of murder in conquered
territories. Oster said: 'You must tell Manstein. Although this
report does not affect the "rear military zone" of the Army Group,
he should be informed.' I promised to do so, and asked him if any
of the Russian losses in partisan fighting might possibly appear in
these reports. Oster denied that emphatically. Reports of partisan
losses were combat losses. The figures from the Reich Security
Head Office were reports of executions. When he left, Oster said
very gravely: 'One day this will come back on us all.'

When I left OKW I had to pause to draw breath. What I had
just learned was so appalling that I was still unable to take it in.
This was far worse than war, it was sheer murder, the planned
murder of thousands of innocents – men, women and children.
And my great-grandfather Heckscher had been a Jew.

On my return I reported to Manstein that General Oster had
promised to give his letter to Beck, and I also told him about my

brief meeting with Admiral Canaris, and finally that Oster had shown me a report which had just arrived from the Reich Security Office (RSHA) on the mass executions of Jews by the SD in the 'Reichskommissariat Ostland'. He listened in silence. He made no comment at all.

It was years after the end of the war, on 5 Februry 1968, when Field Marshal von Manstein wrote to the editor of the journal *Alte Kameraden* about Beck's letter and his own reply:

> Beck's letter ended with the warning that the operations should be conducted with the utmost economy of forces, with a view to the further development of the war, which was what I always tried to do. For myself, I wrote that a war was not lost until one was forced to admit to oneself that it was, but that in my view we had not reached that point at that time. On the contrary, I am convinced that after our successful counter-attacks on the Dnieper and at Kharkov in March 1943 we would still have been able – under reasonable leadership – at least to fight our way to a stalemate.
>
> In his letter Beck did not say a word about his plan to remove Hitler or to stage a *coup d'état*. I wrote to Beck again after he had sustained a serious stomach operation. He thanked me very nicely, but still without mentioning anything of a political or military nature.*

I have nothing to add.

Meetings

Sometimes the Field Marshal's outer office was like Piccadilly Circus. Lots of generals and general staff officers taking over a new command at the front reported to the Army Group's Commander-in-Chief on their way through. If Manstein was interested in the visitor, or actually knew him, conversations could grow from these official reports, but if not, the Field Marshal would say curtly, or even more than curtly: 'Thank you for your report.' And the visitor was out.

One day – it was early in 1943 at Saporoshie – an early pre-war acquaintance appeared, Ulrich de Maizière, a friend of my brother's since they had both served with Infantry Regiment 50 in Landsberg an der Warthe. Maizière had been a regimental adjutant when my brother Hans-Conrad was first posted there as a lieutenant. They had enhanced life in the small garrison town in an unusual way, by giving concerts with Maizière at the piano and my brother on the cello, playing sonatas by Beethoven and Brahms.

Maizière was now a General Staff Officer. He came straight to the point of his visit: he had just heard from Colonel von Werder, our Chief of Officers' Personnel Affairs, that he was to be

---

* From: Rüdiger von Manstein and Theodor Fuchs: *Manstein, Soldat im 20. Jahrhundert. Militärisch-politische Nachlese* (Manstein, A 20th Century Soldier. Military-political Gleanings), Munich 1981, pages 208/09.

transferred to the Waffen SS, but he had absolutely no intention of becoming a member of the SS.

I knew that the Supreme Command had ordered transfers of Army General Staff Officers to the Waffen SS because the SS losses had been inordinately high, thanks to poor leadership. I suggested that Maizière should be admitted to the Field Marshal at once so that he could tell him personally how he felt, but Maizière stopped me. He had not met Manstein before and preferred me to put the matter to Manstein myself. Then he said a hasty goodbye and left the room at once.

I went straight in to the Field Marshal and told him – as 'personally' as possible – about Maizière's visit. Manstein listened to my account and after a brief pause, as if he were considering the many aspects of the problem, he said, as if speaking to himself: 'A young General Staff Officer, who will not tolerate being transferred to the SS.' 'Exactly, Sir,' I confirmed. 'Right, telephone Colonel von Werder and tell him I would like Major de Maizière to be struck off the SS list. And if the transfer has already been posted, he must ring General Schmundt, and tell him I have asked him to set it aside, because I might need de Maizière myself.'

I telephoned Werder and heard that the transfers had not yet been posted, so the Commander-in-Chief's wishes could be taken into account. Moreover, he had another list with the names of General Staff Officers who had expressed a wish to be transferred to the SS when places were available. A few days later, Werder actually showed me the list, and I was staggered by some of the names I saw on it.

I often had cause to look back on the 'Maizière case' later on, because it showed that there actually were ways – at least for an officer – of escaping the clutches of the SS. The episode also shows that there was a good deal of ambitious careerism in the Army at that time, because word had gone round, long ago, that one could rise more swiftly to higher ranks in the Waffen SS.

It was also in Saporoshie that the Waffen SS put in a personal appearance at our headquarters one day. Hitler had assigned an SS Panzer Corps to the Army Group. It had come from greener pastures – from France, where it had been equipped with the latest weapons.

Manstein was pleased that the army corps, which was of great military value, was also commanded by an experienced officer. The acting Corps Commander was a former Reichswehr officer,

SS-*Obergruppenführer* Paul Hausser, whom he knew from his days in Dresden.

The Divisional Commander of the '*Leibstandarte* Adolf Hitler', which had now become a Panzer division, was quite a different matter. This unit had once 'taken care of' the suppression of the Röhm *Putsch* and had 'proved itself' in the liquidation of political undesirables between 30 June and early July 1934. Now its commander since those days, Sepp Dietrich, was here as a divisional commander. I was ashamed to have to shake hands with him.

Hitler had 'released' the SS Panzer Corps for the Eastern Front in order to save the Sixth Army in Stalingrad, but it turned out that though an army corps could quite well be transferred from France to Russia, it could not be done overnight. By now there was no longer a Sixth Army. Instead there was a similarly 'popular' tactical objective: Kharkov, the capital of the Ukraine. Sepp Dietrich, already grown somewhat plump over the years, was positively burning with zeal to become the reconqueror of Kharkov, and Manstein had to take some pains to prevent him from making a frontal attack on the big town. The idea of achieving military targets with as few casualties as possible was apparently unfamiliar to the SS.

At Manstein's briefing session with the SS commanders, it was obvious that Sepp Dietrich had difficulty in reading a big situation map. He was ignorant of numerous military symbols, especially when they were entered on the northern margin of the map and were therefore upside down for the men standing on that side. Without a second's hesitation he flung himself on the map table from the 'southern margin' on his stomach, which in turn was extremely damaging to the entries.

Had the matter itself not been so serious, it could have been as entertaining as a cabaret turn.

At a later date – it must have been between March and April 1943 – Colonel Schulze-Büttger came to my room and introduced me to the officer with him: Lieutenant-Colonel of the General Staff Rudolf-Christian Freiherr von Gersdorff. Gersdorff brought me greetings from Henning, and Schulze-Büttger remarked in passing that he and Gersdorff had worked together in the Operations Section of Army Group Centre. This was the usual method of signalling how the person one was talking to should be 'classified'. We had a brief conversation *à trois* and Gersdorff said that he had not come on Tresckow's behalf but on the orders of Field Marshal von Kluge, Commander-in-Chief of Army Group Centre. He wanted to explain the situation at 'Centre' to Manstein, but he also wanted to discuss the issue of the upper structure, the cover phrase for the concerns of the military resistance, which allowed one to withdraw as soon as the discussion became fruitless, or even dangerous.

Schulze-Büttger left us before I announced Gersdorff, and Gersdorff said he would like to be alone with the Field Marshal, so I closed the door behind him.

I remember having the feeling that Gersdorff was not the right man to impress Manstein. At that time, of course, I did not know what I read years after the war in Gersdorff's memoirs: a few days earlier, he had attempted to blow himself up with Hitler in the Berlin arsenal.

I have no doubt that Gersdorff's conversation with Manstein was as he described it in his book. I remember distinctly that the two men were talking loudly and excitedly, but I was unable to catch the words. Gersdorff writes that the conversation was dramatic, and that he quoted to Manstein the story of General von Yorck in Tauroggen, which – whether deliberately or unconsciously – made the Field Marshal suspicious, because the code word 'Tauroggen' had already been used to Manstein by Claus Stauffenberg on 26 January 1943 at Taganrog. Stauffenberg had probably told both Tresckow and Gersdorff about it. Gersdorff also describes how Manstein sent him packing, with 'Prussian Field Marshals do not mutiny!' Manstein had once used the same phrase to me.

Hitler in Saporoshie Again

On 21 February 1943, two days after Hitler had left our headquarters, the success of Manstein's offensive between the Donetz and the Dnieper became clear. In the North our troops were approaching Kharkov, capital of the Ukraine. It was to be the last victorious operation in the East. At the height of the action, on 10 March, Hitler once again appeared at Saporoshie. Schulze-Büttger and I saw his sudden arrival as a propaganda coup, because although Saporoshie was more than 200 kilometres from Kharkov it was there that the heart of the offensive was beating, so that at corps and divisional headquarters it might seem

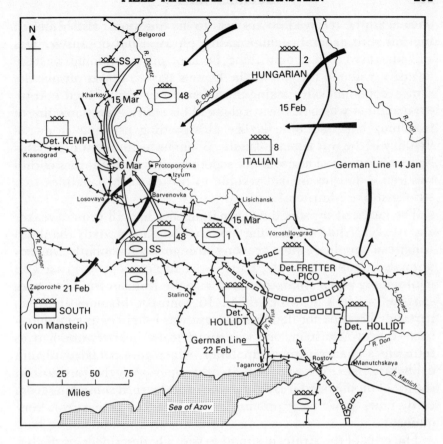

Russian attacks

Manstein's preliminary redeployment

The Counter Stroke

MAP 5. Von Manstein's Counterstroke – Kharkov March 1943

that 'the greatest commander of all time, Adolf Hitler' was responsible for the outcome of these last successful operations in the East.

To achieve this effect, Hitler needed to spend only a few hours rather than days with us. He had Manstein explain the situation to him on the map, adopting a knowledgeable expression. His gratification at the fact that his SS Panzer corps and his SS *Leibstandarte* had taken part in the operation was clearly visible.

At the conference Manstein's thoughts were less with the battle now ending than with the future planning of the war in Russia, but once again he received no answers to his questions. Hitler fobbed him off with general, uninformative phrases, but no answer was still an answer. The only thing he kept on mentioning was the 'decisive value to the war of the Donets basin'. It was always the same, economic policy taking precedence over victory by the Army – a maxim to which he always clung. This entirely irrational line of reasoning had undoubtedly been his guiding principle from the first day of the war against Russia. When he lectured away like this he reminded me of a secondary school master facing a class of dull children – and he did not scruple to preach such banalities to a strategist like Manstein!

The fact that by now the German armies had all grown weaker and weaker, while at the same time the Russians – partly thanks to American supplies – were growing stronger by the month, was not discussed. Quite obviously, Hitler's defence concept was based on maintaining equal strength right along the Russian front, in order – as he put it – 'to avoid risks'. In contrast, Manstein tried to persuade his superior that this concept was infinitely more dangerous. If, said Manstein, one was numerically inferior, one had to seize one's chance through mobility, which meant taking certain deliberate risks. We were still greatly superior to the Russians in the art of mobile warfare, though they had learned something from us by now, as we were proving in the Kharkov area at this very moment.

The crux of the strategic situation is easily described: on the left wing of Army Group South the Russians had won a significant salient. To the west of the town of Kursk a 'balcony', as the Field Marshal called it, now existed, which would serve the Russians as an ideal springboard for a new push far to the west or south. Another point in favour of dealing with the balcony was that the German defence lines could thereby be shortened by about 400 kilometres, allowing us to build up reserves – but this had to be done at once, before the Russians could provide the salient with a strong defence system.

However, Manstein had another alternative to offer, which actually appealed to us younger men more: he suggested that Hitler might perhaps leave the Russians the 'upper hand', that is, allow them to attack in order to drive deep into their flanks at a given moment. It was very probable that in either case this would remobilise the entire Southern Front, which was what Manstein wanted. He sought movement, while Hitler shunned it. What

Manstein wanted was decisive military action, whereas Hitler was trying to avoid or delay that very thing. So no conclusion was reached.

At lunch all those present went to our mess, where a horseshoe-shaped table had been laid. Manstein showed Hitler to the head of the table and the rest of us took our seats according to rank all the way down it, until it turned out that there was no chair left for Lieutenant Stahlberg. That suited me. I stood with my back to the free wall facing Hitler and Manstein, as if I were responsible for the safety of the highest-ranking officers, and was thus able to view the entire scene. It was the ideal place for me, and I would certainly be able to find some lunch somewhere later on. For now it was unimportant.

As was our custom, the orderlies carried in a stew, but no one began to eat because nothing had yet been served to the highest-ranking officer of all – until, finally, two servants dressed up in SS officers' uniforms appeared with several dishes and accompanied by fat Professor Morell, the personal physician. Standing behind Hitler and Manstein, the doctor tasted a sample from one of the bowls, with ritualistic solemnity, moving the sample to and fro conscientiously between his cheeks. Only then was Hitler's dish placed before him, but even now he did not begin to eat, because one of the SS servants then appeared with a bottle of Fachinger, which was not opened until it had been presented to the Head of State. Byzantinism on the classical pattern.

To watch Hitler eating was still more edifying for me. His left arm rested on his left thigh while his right, the elbow propped on the table, moved the spoon to and fro along the shortest possible route between bowl and mouth. Conversation at the table was muted, as if we were at the start of a funeral feast. As far as I could see, there was no conversation at all between the two central figures.

That evening, when the distinguished visitor had left, I asked Manstein what Hitler could have been eating from his special dish. 'A thin vegetable soup,' he said, and that was all he would say.

On 14 March Kharkov was reconquered, the German defensive front was once again running along the Donets, and troops were immobilised by the thaw, which had turned all the roads into quagmires.

During those weeks, Manstein drew up a memorandum, addressed to the 'Führer and Supreme Commander of the

Wehrmacht'. I copied it from his handwritten draft on the machine with the large typeface.

The conclusion of the comprehensive appreciation of the situation was that although there was no longer any point in hoping for absolute victory in the East, a military stalemate should be sought. In other words: a military 'non-decision' should create conditions for the 'political leadership' to end the war by negotiation.

I found the idea of a stalemate quite unreal. After the document had been dispatched I asked the Field Marshal about his stalemate theory over afternoon tea. He gladly expounded on it and, on my own with him, I had no difficulty in speaking freely and openly.

If I had understood his memorandum correctly, I began, he was assuming that Hitler would be placed in a situation where he could sit down together at one table with Stalin, Churchill and Roosevelt to negotiate a great compromise. Manstein nodded. In simplified terms, that was his view. I said I thought it was an illusion: at public Party rallies, broadcast by radio, Hitler had described Winston Churchill as a 'whisky-bibber' and the President of the United States as a 'paralytic'. That alone meant that Hitler had irrevocably blocked any possibility of political dialogue. Then, even before the outbreak of war, Hitler had broken treaties which he himself had concluded only a short time before. In my eyes he therefore no longer had any negotiating, let alone contractual capacity. And finally, in the territories we had occupied, acts had been committed on the German side since the beginning of the war which were incompatible with international law.

Manstein let me talk without contradiction, but when I paused he said that although he did not dispute my arguments, nevertheless I was wrong. In politics such arguments were insignificant in the last analysis, and above all it was not the job of soldiers to argue about political morality. Germany still held a good many trumps which had not yet been played. For instance, not one Allied soldier had yet landed on the continent of Europe. Of course he now expected the Americans and the British to land in Italy or the Balkans, or on the Atlantic coast in the foreseeable future, and then we Germans could, if necessary, retreat on to the Alps, which could be defended with very limited forces. We still had unsuspected reserves, but reserves were useful only if they were established in good time and if strategic plans were developed in good time. Our argument ranged to and fro. It would be to Hitler's advantage to leave the planning and operations to him, Manstein, because it was only if things went on as wretchedly as they had recently that the situation would one day become critical – but we had not yet reached that point.

Meanwhile, fairly predictably, Hitler had ordered the 'lesser solution', the removal of the Russian 'balcony' to the west of Kursk: under the code name 'Citadel', Army Group Centre was to attack Kursk with its right wing from the North and Army Group South with its left from the South. Preparations were in progress. The Field Marshal urged that the operation should begin as quickly as humanly possible, but more than two months were still to elapse before Hitler approved the attack. Our 'leader' had become a 'laggard', no longer daring to make effective decisions.

At that time Manstein was having increasing problems with his sight. We flew in our Ju 52 from Saporoshie to Liegnitz* and he had his eyes examined at the University Optical Clinic at Breslau.† Professor Dieter – in SS uniform under his white doctor's coat – diagnosed cataract and prescribed a treatment surprising to the layman: a tonsillectomy, to arrest the cataract. The operation took place and I was able to take a few days' leave.

After I reported back to Liegnitz at the beginning of May we did not return to Saporoshie but to Munich. Hitler, who was staying at Berchtesgaden, wanted to discuss the imminent Operation Citadel with the Commanders-in-Chief concerned.

Hitler's Berghof at Berchtesgaden

A large, open 7.7 litre Mercedes with an SS driver took us to a new, splendidly extended road from Berchtesgaden up to Hitler's mountain refuge at Obersalzberg. We passed through a number of barriers and stopped at a broad stone staircase built against the rock face. At its foot General Schmundt, Hitler's Chief Adjutant, was waiting to lead us up the steps and then into the hallway of the house on the right.

The first impression was one of astonishing magnificence. To the left was a cloakroom lobby on the three walls of which at least fifty people could have hung up their coats. Then came the first surprise for me, because it was in total contradiction to everything that the press had been telling the public since 1933 about the simple, unpretentious lifestyle of the 'Führer and Reich Chancellor', who

* Now Legnica.
† Now Wrocław.

had actually waived his salary as Head of Government: in front of the tall cloakroom glass were a massive comb, brush and hand-mirror heavier than any I had held in my hand before, made of solid silver, almost too cumbersome to use.

The objects were marked with their owner's initials, but not by an engraver: a goldsmith had made the eagle with the oak leaf wreath and swastika in gold and soldered them on to the silver handles. On either side of the wreath were the Latin capitals A and H, also in solid gold.

Still in the hall, came the second surprise: there was noisy barking from the upper floor and suddenly two Scotch terriers were racing down the long stairway towards us, barking at the top of their voices. Manstein turned in amazement to General Schmundt to ask if there were no longer any German Shepherds here and the Chief Adjutant replied rather awkwardly that the two dogs belonged to Frau Dreesen from Godesberg who had recently come to run the house. 'The hotelier's wife?' asked the Field Marshal. Schmundt told him that Frau Dreesen had taken over the housekeeping at the Berghof from the Führer's sister. (Years after the war was over I learned that General Schmundt had been telling a white lie: the Scotch terriers belonged to Eva Braun, Hitler's ladyfriend.)

General Schmundt led us past the foot of the stairs to a sitting-room at the end of the hall on the right and asked the Field Marshal to wait. There were good oriental carpets on the marble floor; the room was dominated by a big tiled stove, round which a wooden bench invited guests to sit down. The Field Marshal lowered himself gratefully on to it, while I began to study the contents of the open bookshelves to right and left of the French windows on to the large verandah. Dictionaries and quantities of German classics were here, and there was even Shakespeare, in the Schlegel-Tieck translation.

All the books in this extensive library were bound in leather, with the author's name and the title printed in gold on the back, and at the bottom were the owner's initials in gold – the symbol I had seen in the cloakroom recurred in gold everywhere.

After a few minutes, an SS officer appeared, opened a portière that had been closed until then and led us down eight steps into the 'Great Hall'. This was an impressive room, recognisable from pictures in illustrated journals, because it was the showpiece of the Berghof. A single, sash window offered a view of the Berchtesgaden countryside, across to the Unterberg Massif. The window must have been about nine metres wide and six metres high, but today it was open and the temperature in the room was only a few degrees above freezing. The SS servant had withdrawn at once, no one was worrying about the visitors. Manstein and I began to look round at the pictures and tapestries, all apparently of high quality. I was struck by the portrait of a woman, a beautiful, dark woman, hanging in a position of honour. I would have been prepared to bet that she was Jewish but, on a later visit to the Berghof, General Schmundt told me that this was one of Anselm Feuerbach's masterpieces, a portrait of his beloved Nanna. A large Bechstein concert grand piano stood near the painting.

The Field Marshal and I were beginning to feel cold, and I decided to do something about it. On the right-hand side of the enormous window I found a large handle behind the curtains and began to turn it. It was a poor design and I had to use force to move the window. But after I had gained only about a metre someone suddenly tore open the entrance door to the hall and rushed over to me, telling me to stop at once, it was his duty and his alone to look after that window. I told him it was too cold to stay in here any longer, but the uniformed caretaker explained that the room must never reach a temperature above 16° Celsius; those were the Führer's orders.

So Manstein and I returned to the much warmer sitting-room with the stove in it and closed the portière behind us. It was an outrageous affront to keep a Field Marshal waiting so long and to let him freeze into the bargain.

But at last things began to happen. Several officers arrived to prepare the way for the no doubt imminent arrival of the master, including one, also in uniform, who set out in both rooms a number of gold-rimmed spectacles in open cases, two on the large marble table by the window, one each on the grand piano, the round table before the stove and in front of the books in the living-room. The positions seemed to have been planned and laid down in advance.

I shall have to dispense with a detailed description of the conversation during this, my first visit to the Berghof. I was at the Berghof five or six times, accompanying Field Marshal von Manstein, but I cannot undertake to give details of the talks from memory. The reader will find plenty of information in the contemporary literature, so I shall restrict myself to one or two completely personal reminiscences.

On these visits to the Berghof it was always uncertain until just before the sessions began which of those attending would be directly involved. Sometimes it would be: 'Accompanying officers please stay in the living-room!' Then the adjutants and ADCs would be left standing on the far side of the portière, listening in silence; we did nevertheless manage to keep the curtain open by about a centimetre.

On another occasion – it must have been in March or April 1943 – Field Marshal von Kluge, Commander-in-Chief of Army Group Centre, was called to the Berghof as well as Manstein. Kluge had with him as his ADC Rittmeister Eberhard von Breitenbuch, one of my regimental companions before the war in Schwedt.

Shortly before the conference began, it was suddenly: 'No ADCs today.' Both Kluge and Manstein were rather put out and pointed out to General Schmundt that their ADCs had the situation maps in their briefcases. (It was not the done thing for a Field Marshal to carry a briefcase under his arm.) But it was no use: Schmundt said that the Führer had expressly stated that at this particular conference he wished to see the Field Marshals on their own, so the two of us stayed outside with our briefcases. An SS man was ordered to take Breitenbuch and me to the Platterhof guesthouse, but instead of going into the house, some 200 metres away, we stayed on the terrace, since it was fine and the view over the massif was magnificent. While we were enjoying the panorama I noticed that Breitenbuch was no longer reacting when I spoke. His forehead was beaded with sweat and his hands were shaking. I asked him if he was ill and if we should order a car to take him to a hospital in Berchtesgaden, but he refused help and said he would be better soon. He would not even accept the chair I brought him.

A few years after the war I visited Breitenbuch in Coppenbrügge on the Deister, where he was the forestry commissioner, and asked him what had been wrong with him that day on the Platterhof terrace. He told me that he had been assailed quite suddenly by a recent memory – a moment when, with a pistol in his right-hand trouser pocket, he had considered shooting Hitler in the Berghof. Tresckow had given him that mission previously, but he had not met Hitler then, because he had been excluded from the conference, just as we had this time. I told him that I too had been reproached by Tresckow in Saporoshie for failing to take advantage of several opportunities to shoot Hitler. Now we both admitted that, had we shot, we would very probably have missed, though we had not been bad shots when we were trained at Schwedt. 'The fact is,' I said, 'we are no Brutus and Cassius.' He entirely agreed.

I shall give a detailed account of two of my later visits with Manstein to the Berghof because, having been chronologically checked, they deserve to be recorded for their particular significance in the course of events.

Danger!

Time and again Hitler deferred the date of Citadel, the assault on Kursk. The reasons for the postponement were always different. In reality – or so we joked over a glass of wine in the evening – somebody 'up there' was not keen to burn his fingers. But when we discussed it in earnest, we all agreed that the delays would be paid for in blood.

Nothing much was going on along the fronts, so Manstein sent to Silesia for his saddle horses so that he could spend at least an hour a day in the saddle. There was a stretch of steppe country south of Saporoshie that positively invited a gallop. The Field Marshal rode a rangy, thoroughbred grey in the prime of life, and the horse I was given was also a sheer joy to ride.

On one of our rides my mount plunged into an overgrown hole at the gallop and pitched forward. I had managed to keep the reins in my hand and was soon back in the saddle, but where was the Field Marshal? Wherever I looked, I could see neither the grey nor his rider. Manstein had probably ridden on without noticing that I had been thrown. Since my horse had been slightly lamed in the fall, I gave him the reins and rode slowly on. After a few hundred metres an extraordinary black colossus loomed out of a hollow in front of me. At first I took it for an oil tank, but at a closer view it turned out to be the wreck of a river steamer. And then the Field Marshal appeared too, having inspected the monster from all sides.

How could such a ship have arrived out on the steppe, we wondered as we rode home. We decided in the end that the flood-wave from the Dnieper dam torpedoed by the Luftwaffe less than a year before had swept the ship miles inland. By now, of course, our field engineers had repaired the dam as far back as Dnepro-petrovsk, over fifty miles away, the river had become a lake again and the turbines at Saporoshie were supplying electricity – an impressive achievement.

About a week later, Cousin Henning visited us again. After a talk with the Field Marshal we took our customary short walk together, but this time he surprised me by asking if it was true that the Field Marshal had recently been riding out with me in the afternoons. I asked him where he had heard about it. 'At the Führer's headquarters,' was the astonishing answer. I must have shown my amazement, because he went on to say that he had something very important to tell me. 'Lately Hitler has flown into a violent rage several times when Manstein's name has been mentioned.' According to his information, this kind of thing generally happened only in Hitler's immediate circle, usually after midnight, when the evening situation conferences were over and the company had been dismissed. Henning told me he had heard a description of these outbursts, in which Hitler sometimes completely lost control. Often they were real fits of frenzy, when Hitler screamed orders to 'his people' that were definitely criminal. 'A few of his entourage,' Henning went on, 'are so much in his thrall that they immediately pass the orders on and have them carried out.' There was more: Hitler had the private life of his Commander-in-Chief watched and wanted to know the smallest and most intimate details of the results of this surveillance.

I asked Henning where his information came from, but he said he could not tell me. However, his informant was very sympathetic to Field Marshal Manstein and stressed the urgency of warning him. Hitler knew that the Field Marshal was in the habit of riding out with his *aide-de-camp* in the afternoons, so that — and he repeated Hitler's own words — 'it would be an easy matter to have a partisan ambush get rid of them both'.

I asked Henning what he would advise me to do in response to such appalling news, and he said that the Field Marshal must on no account be told. He would dismiss the warning as quite incredible and refuse to pay the slightest attention to it. Manstein would never entertain the absurd notion that a Head of State, in the small hours, might toy with the idea of having one of his Field Marshals murdered. In any case, he, Henning, had already warned Schulze-Büttger, so that for the time begin I should first try to make sure that the rides did not take place. Should I fail, which was more than likely, Schulze-Büttger and I would have to invent reasons that made it urgently necessary to have our rides covered by our own military police.

I talked to Schulze-Büttger the same night, adding that I had difficulty in taking Henning Tresckow's warning very seriously. On the contrary, he said, he had always found Tresckow's information to be reliable, and in any case he did not see why Hitler, who had had Generals Schleicher and Bredow murdered back in 1934, should not have Field Marshal von Manstein and his aide killed in 1943.

Our delightful solitude on the steppe was at an end. When, on our next ride, we came across a number of respectfully saluting, motorised military police, who at times even followed us at a decent distance, Manstein, riding beside me, asked me who on earth had arranged all this. I had, I said, because I had heard there were some shady characters hanging around. 'That's your vivid imagination again,' he said. 'But still, it may be a good idea.' The matter was closed.

A year or two after the end of the war, Fabian von Schlabrendorff told me who Henning's informant had been: none other than Hitler's own aide, Chief Adjutant General Schmundt. The two of them went back to the old German Army days of the 9th (Prussian) Infantry Regiment in Potsdam. Schmundt was not the brightest of men, and he was literally under his Führer's spell.

It undoubtedly never occurred to him that Henning had been sounding him out and that he had unwittingly been the source of so much information for the greater good.

A Show for the Turks

From the weeks of waiting for the order to attack in Operation Citadel, I remember one peculiar order that reached the army group from the highest level. A high-ranking Turkish military delegation was to be shown a warlike manoeuvre with the most up-to-date weapons, behind the front.

Kempf's Army Detachment Kempf*, with its Chief of Staff Major General Speidel, was entrusted with the planning. The Turkish officers, headed by their Chief of the General Staff, Colonel-General Toydemir, were taken to a hilltop from which it was possible to observe an attack the like of which had not occurred in this war. We felt as if we were on one of Frederick the Great's observation hilltops. Heavy and light artillery opened the

---

* Translator's note: An Army Detachment was a tactical headquarters equating in scope to an Army. In operation 'Citadel' Army Detachment Kempf had two Panzer Corps and one Infantry Corps under command.

'battle', reconnaissance Panzers roared to and fro across the
terrain, engineers with flame-throwers set part of the prairie grass
alight, armoured personnel carriers rolled along, spewing out
crowds of soldiers firing non-stop in all directions; the high spot
was the arrival of several companies with the latest AFVs, who
gave an artistic display: some of the Panzers had their turrets
traversed sideways through ninety degrees.

Infantrymen jumped from cover on to the long gun barrels of the
moving tanks and clambered on top of the colossi as they rushed
past. It was a splendid show – using blanks, of course.

After that there was stew at long tables in the open with Turkish
and German military flags for decoration and the 'old
Turkish-German brotherhood in arms' of World War I was
toasted with gusto.

We had been performing for the Turks what we as young
soldiers in time of peace called a 'Turk', or a bluff. It was obvious
that our show was politically motivated, but on what grounds?

Late that evening – our guests had already moved on – we
discussed it with Manstein. I said I would take a bet that Franz
von Papen, the German Ambassador in Turkey, was behind it.

At that time we had no idea that Papen had concluded a 'Treaty
of Friendship' between Germany and Turkey the year before.
Until then Turkey had pursued a policy of neutrality; in fact, as
one can read in Papen's memoirs, Hitler had actually arranged an
exchange deal with Turkey: two Panzer divisions to be equipped
against supplies of chrome. (So the Turks had presumably received
the equipment for which my old, shattered 12th Panzer Division
had waited in vain.) We in the Operations Section of Manstein's
Army Group knew that Hitler had planned a German attack on
Turkey via the Caucasus and at that time there was still one army
of our neighbouring Army Group to the South stationed on the
Kuban peninsula, which – in Hitler's own words – was to be the
'springboard for an attack via the Caucasus'. Had not the German
Government once concluded Treaties of Friendship with Austria
and a year or two later with the Soviet Union, only to invade those
countries soon afterwards? The faces of the Turkish military who
came to visit us had been impassive, and they had joined 'happily'
in the toasts.

My Turkish story is not over yet, however. A few weeks later I
received an imposing letter by courier. I read, on elegant paper,
the unexpected name of the sender: the German Amabassador in

Turkey was writing to Manstein's personal ADC. 'My dear Stahlberg,' he began. He had heard by chance of my recent attachment to Field Marshal von Manstein . . . and so forth. He, Papen, would be delighted if we were to resume our old acquaintance, of which he had such excellent memories. And he hoped to hear from me very soon . . . with best remembrances . . . etc. etc.

I read through the letter once or twice, wondering what it could mean. Then I went in to Manstein and put Papen's letter on the desk in front of him. When he had read it he looked up at me and said: 'What will you do?' I took the letter and tore it across and across, until only scraps of paper were left in my hands. 'Why so?' asked Manstein. I answered, not without emotion, and when the words were out I was surprised to have said them: 'Because I no longer want to have any connection with a man who accepted the murder of three of his closest colleagues by the National Socialists without doing the least thing about it.' For a moment Manstein stared at me in amazement. Then he said, simply: 'Good!'

Operation Citadel

Hitler kept on postponing the attack. One of the reasons was the expectation of new AFVs: the intention was to deploy more tanks for Citadel than ever before in the history of war.

Early in May, we received the signal that Citadel had now been postponed to 10 June, but when June came nothing happened, the front remained quiet. On 30 June, however, there was something new: all the Commanders-in-Chief and commanding generals, in so far as they were involved in Citadel through the two Army Groups, Centre and South, were summoned to Munich for 1 July. At first we thought we must have got it wrong: to Munich? Yes, to Munich.

When Field Marshal Manstein and I reached the Party premises of the NSDAP on Königsplatz, the scene was rather like a state reception. We were led to a big room on the upper floor, but we looked for a map table in vain. Hitler had no intention of discussing the situation with his two Field Marshals, Kluge and Manstein, and the many other generals. What was the point? They had been studying their orders for Citadel in detail for over two months and were only waiting for the 'starting pistol'. But then, after we had waited for some time, General Schmundt appeared and asked those present to form a large circle on the empty parquet floor of the room. Slightly surprised, the generals did as they were asked, their Adjutants and ADCs taking their places behind them. Then Schmundt left the room, to return a few seconds later, announcing loudly as he looked round the circle: 'Gentlemen, the Führer!'

Hitler appeared, saluted once, and then remained standing in the centre of the room. No one spoke. Starting from the left, Hitler scrutinised every single man present intently. I regarded this as nothing but a pose, the military leader's pose of a man who was no military leader. Then he began to speak. The Citadel attack would begin on 5 July, he said, and from that day on the fate of Germany would be in the hands of the generals summoned here to Munich.

That dealt with the purpose of the journey to Munich, and everyone drove back to Riem Airport. Plenty of interested onlookers had gathered on the Königsplatz and in the streets: scarcely ever had so many generals been seen all at once. Such an ostentatious method of 'briefing' was not likely to escape the notice of the Allies to the East and West. The news of an unusual military action by the Germans must surely even have reached Moscow on that same day.

By issuing his orders in Munich in this way, Hitler had probably been cherishing some illusion connected with the old etchings of the life of Frederick the Great: 'Address by the King to his officers before battle'.

In that case the place for it should not have been Munich, but some headquarters near the Russian front. This performance at the Munich Party Headquarters was nothing but a farce.

We flew back to our own headquarters at once, only to set off again the very next day, this time for Bucharest. Hitler had thought up yet another demonstration: on the anniversary of the conquest of Sevastopol, Manstein was to hand over to the Romanian head of state, Marshal Jon Antonescu, a ceremonial gift, a special issue of the 'Crimea Shield', which all German and Romanian participants in the conquest of the Crimea wore on their left sleeve. General Busse and I stood behind Field Marshal Manstein as the solemn music played and he laid a wreath on the memorial to the fallen of Bucharest. Then we drove with an extravagant escort to Antonescu's private house, where the handing-over ceremony took place, followed by a delicious meal.

That evening there was a huge state banquet, but before we sat

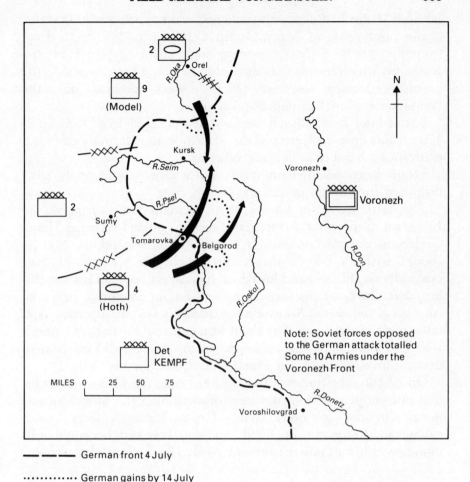

MAP 6. Operation Citadel – Kursk July 1943

—————— German front 4 July

·············· German gains by 14 July

➤ Planned German Thrusts

down we each received a beautiful order appropriate to his service, with a kiss on the cheek from the War Minister and a certificate. When we arrived at our royally furnished hotel rooms, our night-time security had also been taken care of: before each bedroom door stood a double guard in ornate peacetime dress uniform.

Back at our headquarters on 4 July we at once ordered our command train and moved up to the Front, where Manstein wanted to conduct his two army offensives on the spot.

On 5 July the battle for which we had all been waiting since April began. I remember that I did not feel happy about it, because Hitler had designed the operation in such a way that our armies and those of Army Group Centre would have to drive frontally into a defensive system long since prepared by the Russians, which meant that our soldiers would have to attack the enemy's strength instead of his weak points. But the Commanders-in-Chief had acquiesced.

I read later in published works that a total of 1,081 tanks and 376 assault guns took part in the attack on the German side – an enormous assembly of fighting vehicles.

We doubted whether our visit to Bucharest could really have disguised the date of the attack.

The battle raged for a week. With so many tanks engaged, the Inspector General of Armoured Troops, Colonel-General Heinz Guderian, was also present. It was quite understandable that he should wish to take a direct interest in the weapon he had originally established and for which he now had overall responsibility, but since, as an inspector, he had no authority over the conduct of the battle, Manstein regarded his visit as superfluous, if not a positive nuisance. The Field Marshal sent me to the General, who was waiting by the command train, where I did my best to detain him until the Field Marshal had time for his visitor.

On 12 July, the Soviets threw in fresh reserves. Our own armies had not yet achieved their target of encircling the Soviet formations. On the contrary, Army Group Centre's forces were exhausted; however, the Field Marshal believed he could still mobilise sufficient power from our Army Group South for victory.

Rommel and Kluge

Had Operation Citadel already failed, or was the outcome soon to be decided? That was the question, when on 12 July, the order arrived from the Führer's headquarters that Field Marshal von Manstein should report for the midday conference with the Führer on 13 July, together with Field Marshal von Kluge, Commander-in-Chief of Army Group Centre.

Manstein was furious. This, by God, was not the moment to make the Commander-in-Chief take a 'trip to East Prussia' at the very height of the battle – but there was more to come.

When, on the morning of 13 July, the Field Marshal and I landed at Rastenburg airfield and travelled to the guesthouse on Mauersee, General Schmundt informed him by telephone that the noon conference would not take place and the Field Marshal was expected for the evening conference. This change of plan had just reached Kluge before his flight left Russia, but not us.

Manstein accepted this incredible situation astonishingly quickly – it was not his responsibility. So what should we do now? At least eight useless hours stretched before us. First he put through a call to his own headquarters to get the latest news from Busse, then he told me: 'Do you know what we're going to do now? We're going to have a bathe.'

'Wonderful!' I said, 'but I didn't have our swimming trunks packed, Sir.' That didn't matter, he said, since there were not likely to be any members of the female sex here, in the restricted area of the Army High Command. We would undress in our rooms and throw our uniform raincoats over our shoulders.

No sooner said than done, and we left the guesthouse together and walked along a broad wooden footbridge through the reed-beds surrounding the Mauersee, meeting no one on the brief walk. Soon we were both swimming happily, naked as the day we were born, towards the middle of the lake.

Only someone who knows the beauty of the East Prussian lakes can judge how good we felt. Nothing but fields and forests round the shores, not a village or even a house to be seen.

Somewhere in the centre of the lake we turned back, our footbridge now far away. We must have been 200 or 300 metres from our goal when I saw people on the footbridge. The Field Marshal asked me if there were any women among them, but we were still too far off for me to tell. When we were closer to the bridge I reported that I could see officers, but had not yet spotted a woman's dress – and I could see some 'red trousers', as well. 'Which red?' he asked. 'Both reds!' I said. (Generals' red and general staff officers' red.) Finally we reached the two sets of rungs leading up to the landing stage.

I tried to see if I knew any of those who were now hanging sailor-fashion over the railing, and, yes, I thought I recognised one among the many faces. 'I believe, Sir,' I began, 'that that is Field Marshal Rommel!' and back came a voice from above: 'You're right, my dear fellow, this is Field Marshal Rommel!'

Then there was a big hello from below and above, and Manstein shouted: 'So we meet at last!' It was true: Manstein and Rommel had never met until that moment. One had been a General Staff Officer and the other a dedicated front-line soldier – two completely separate careers. Rommel spoke again from above: 'Well, gentlemen, why don't you come up?' And Manstein called back: 'Yes, why not?' And so, mother naked, we climbed the rungs until we were standing before the well-dressed officers.

But this bathing story is not yet over, because before I reached the footbridge, I noticed that our coats had disappeared! At that the joke was over, for me at least, and I shouted to one of Rommel's young officers to deliver up the coats to me immediately. Meanwhile Rommel was still savouring the scene, behaving as if he had not even noticed my 'interpellation' and pretending that he was about to introduce his officers to us. Of course the coats were then produced and we covered our nakedness. After much joking and laughter the two men began to talk easily together.

What, Manstein began, was Rommel doing here at Headquarters – had he been given a new command? Rommel replied, word for word: 'I am here for a sun-ray cure.' 'Sun-ray cure?' asked Manstein, 'whatever is that?' 'Sun-ray cure,' Rommel repeated, but although his mind was so quick, Manstein still did not understand and asked again: 'Sun-ray cure?' Rommel put it more plainly: 'I am soaking up sun and faith!' At last Manstein understood. That's good,' he said, and repeated, 'That's good.' Would they meet again that evening, he asked, and Rommel said: 'Of course – under the sun-ray lamp.'

We pulled our slippers on and returned to the house. Manstein commented that he had had a completely different idea of Rommel – he liked him. Manstein liked people with a sense of humour.

As usual we did not arrive at the Führer's headquarters for the evening conference until after dark. With three Field Marshals – Kluge, Manstein and Rommel – we sat in the darkened carriage and of course 'Ball Lightning' – the nickname of the Chief of the General Staff Zeitzler – was with us too. The conversation during the short drive turned on some shocking news: three days ago American and British troops had landed in Sicily from Africa and the Italians had done virtually nothing to defend the island. Zeitzler reported what he knew about it. The four of them were sitting in a four-person compartment of the old third-class carriage, while I stood in the centre aisle, listening. So now we had the Western Allies in Europe, Manstein remarked drily. Zeitzler emphasised that fundamental decisions must now be taken with regard to the further progress of the war, but apart from scanty briefings, the Army General Staff had been completely excluded from events. Kluge vigorously backed Manstein and Zeitzler; only Rommel was silent.

Rommel was also silent during the conference, the subject of which was not Sicily but the heavy fighting at Kursk. Nevertheless, a decision had to be taken as to which should have precedence: the Eastern Front or the Mediterranean area. That session was probably the last opportunity to form a unified high command to save what could still be saved for Germany.

But the decision was too far-reaching and fundamental for Hitler. He was looking exhausted, groggy and tense again this time, just as he had months ago in Saporoshie. He would concede nothing. Once again I saw his jaw muscles grinding away, but now the reaction, which I had regarded as a pose months ago in Saporoshie, looked as if it might be genuine.

So no clear decision emerged, but one sensed that Hitler would break off the offensive against Kursk and also that he would withdraw some of their forces from the Army Groups, who would be left to think up some way of fulfilling their missions, even with reduced forces. Though it was not made explicit, the line of reasoning was obvious.

At the end of the appreciation, the Field Marshals were left to themselves again. The guesthouse had a fine, big room where snacks could be served and people could go on talking in comfort. The three Commanders-in-Chief were sufficiently experienced to foresee that the knell of the war was being sounded for Germany by events on the Eastern Front and in Italy, but as to when and how and where it would end, their views differed. Manstein maintained his theory of the possibility of a stalemate, but Kluge and Rommel were disinclined to comment. There was good French red wine and gradually tongues were loosened. Finally Kluge was the first to decide that it was his bedtime, and Manstein and Rommel both rose politely to their feet as well. As the three stood together I heard Kluge say something momentous: 'Manstein, the end will be bad, and I repeat what I told you earlier: I am prepared to serve under you.' Manstein thanked him as one thanks a friend for a charming compliment. He was friendly, courteous and non-committal.

Soon only Rommel, Manstein and I were left in the room. We stayed with the same wine, and suddenly it was out – Rommel had said it – the end of the war would be a total catastrophe. If the Allies were also to land in the Balkans and finally on the Atlantic coast, the whole house of cards would collapse.

Manstein countered that we had not reached that point by a long way. Hitler would give up the Supreme Command before the crash came. Rommel remained obdurate: 'He will never give up the Supreme Command. I obviously know him better than you do, Herr von Manstein.'

Manstein rose to say goodnight and at once Rommel was standing beside him. 'I too am prepared to serve under you,' he said. 'Good night,' said Manstein, and headed for the door to the hall. Just before it, when Manstein was already outside, Rommel caught at my sleeve. 'Your Field Marshal is a strategist of genius,' said Rommel. 'I admire him, but he is cherishing an illusion. Make sure he doesn't forget what I've just told him.'

Vinnitsa

Citadel was to be the last German offensive on the Eastern Front. With its failure, the initiative passed irrevocably to the Soviets, but there would be a long string of defensive battles before Berlin was taken. Citadel had meant extremely heavy losses to the Russians as well as to us. On the evening of 13 July 1943 Field Marshal Kluge had spoken to Hitler of 20,000 casualties in his Army Group Centre. Field Marshal Manstein later estimated Army Group South's casualties at 20,720 men, 'including 3,330 dead'. He estimated the total Soviet casualties at 85,000 – and we were then only at the beginning of the avalanche of horror.

The Russians had succeeded in holding the 'balcony' at Kursk, and now this mighty salient had become exactly what Manstein had predicted in both written and oral warnings to his Supreme Commander: the basis for their own offensive. They won back Kharkov and took Orel from Army Group Centre. Final victory was now in sight.

Early in October 1943, Army Group South moved its headquarters to Vinnitsa, at least 500 kilometres back towards the West.

Only a few months before, Vinnitsa had been Hitler's own headquarters, from which he had directed the attack on Stalingrad and – simultaneously – to the Caucasus. Our Operations Section took over the blockhouses built for Hitler in a patch of woodland north of the town. From the outside they were simple and rustic, but every comfort was provided inside.

With me and our two batmen, the Field Marshal took over Hitler's former residence. The architect who had built this house had designed it with great skill. From the pathway leading to the house it appeared modest, with only two groups of windows on either side of the front door. The two left-hand ones belonged to the Adjutants' room, which I now took over, and the right-hand ones to a living and briefing room which in fact extended backwards like an unfolded towel.

Consequently the many photographs of Hitler in front of his house had never had to be touched up in order to show him off to the public before his 'modest little cottage'.

In fact, the house had an inner courtyard. Its ground-plan had been borrowed from the classical atriums of the ruined city of Pompeii. I had a bath to myself. Hitler's suite at the back of the house contained a beautiful living-room and study, bedroom and bathrooms.

I inspected the interior with the utmost interest. All the walls were panelled in pine and there were a great many pictures in Hitler's suite, now occupied by the Field Marshal. The study contained a series of idyllic Spitzweg prints, but it was the picture in Hitler's bedroom that I found particularly revealing. It was hung in such a way that the eyes of the person in bed were inevitably drawn to the portrait.

It was a reproduction of a drawing in red chalk, showing a young, allegedly Pomeranian woman, who was neither beautiful nor interesting.

When, later on, we had to evacuate Vinnitsa in the face of the advancing Russian troops and our engineers stood ready to blow up the 'house of the Führer' on express orders from on high, I sprinted back to take the picture from Hitler's bedroom as a souvenir. I still own it today, but it is now hung where it can scarcely be seen at all, high under the ceiling in a dark passage.

Field Marshal Manstein used the 'Führer house' only to live in, keeping our offices in one of the other houses and using Hitler's big room to sit in with his 'small circle' only in the evenings. We often had a fire in the hearth and it was obvious that we were the first to do so. An interesting sheet of cast-iron had been let in to the fireplace, representing the devil in the fires of hell. We deliberately brought this decoration to our visitors' notice, occasioning either chuckles or astonished silence.

As I write I remember the Field Marshal's reddish-brown, long-haired dachshund, an attractive and entertaining dog called 'Knirps'. At mealtimes Knirps would always appear at my side and sit up and beg without being asked. I taught him another trick: at the phrase 'What does the brown* dog do?' He had to raise his right paw before he was given a titbit. So we had a dog that could give the Hitler salute. Manstein was amused by my success as a trainer, but I promised to put on my dog-show only in the presence of really good friends.

It will be remembered that Colonel Eberhard Finckh of the General Staff was the Senior Quartermaster of our Army Group. In Vinnitsa the Quartermaster's Department was in the town, a few kilometres from our forest camp. When Finckh came in to report I would leave my work to listen to his precise, intelligent accounts and far-sighted judgements, which fascinated me.

One day he told the Field Marshal that he had tried to calculate with the Senior Quartermasters of the other Army Groups and the relevant offices in the Army High Command how much the war was costing us now. Manstein asked what his reference points were, probably thinking of the financial costs. Finckh replied that it would be quite impossible for him to work out the financial side – he wanted to find out how many men the war was now costing. According to his calculations it was about 3,000 per day. He was doing this in order to indicate the orders of magnitude within which we were now operating: about 3,000 men per day – impossible to imagine.

Another day I received an unexpected telephone call from Finckh in Vinnitsa. He had to talk to me, he said, it was important. I asked the Field Marshal for an hour off after lunch and told him that Colonel Finckh wanted to speak to me personally. He agreed.

I drove into the town and had myself announced to Finckh, who told me at once that this was a very bad business and the Field Marshal must be informed, but he wanted to discuss it with me first. That morning he had been visited by two General Staff Officers passing through, who quite by chance had witnessed a mass execution of Jews in our Army rear area. It had taken place in a wooded region which came under the responsibility of our Army Group. The executions had obviously been planned and well-organised, and the executioners had been wearing SD or SS uniforms.

* 'Brown', used to denote Nazi storm trooper, or 'Brown Shirt'.

I asked if he knew how many Jews had been murdered and he said the two witnesses had told him that according to one of the SS officers it was by then already a matter of more than 100,000.

I already knew from my visit to General Oster in Berlin that the SD and SS were systematically exterminating Jews in occupied Poland, and I had reported this to the Field Marshal at the time. But it was new to me that murders were now also being committed in our own rear area, now withdrawn in a westerly direction.

I asked Finckh why he had told me first, instead of reporting at once to the Commander-in-Chief, and he said that he would go and give him the news at once if he wished – he could be with him in an hour.

We continued to discuss the significance of this information. The SS units did not answer to the Army Group but only to their chief, Heinrich Himmler, from whom the orders must have come. But Himmler's only superior was Hitler. Without the Führer's approval not even Himmler could have carried out mass murder on this scale. So there was not the slightest doubt that the 'responsibility' lay at the 'highest level'. Geographically, however, it concerned the Army Group, so the Field Marshal must be informed.

On the drive back to the forest camp, I thought about the forthcoming tea-break with Manstein. I set out our chess board: a game of chess could help in potentially explosive conversations with him.

Scarcely had tea been poured out and the orderly left the room, when he said: 'Well, what did Colonel Finckh want you for?' 'A bad business,' I began: 'in our own Army Group's rear area SS units were engaged in the mass murder of Jews.' He demanded angrily why Finckh had told me first, instead of coming to him personally to report.

I told him that Colonel Finckh had expressly asked me to say that he would come at once in answer to a telephone call and make an official report.

There was a pause and we began to play chess. Then he made me tell him exactly what I knew. When I had finished he said: 'A hundred thousand, did you say?' 'Yes, sir.'

Then came a violent reaction: 100,000, that was absolutely unbelievable. Given that 100,000 Jews had really been killed in one area of woodland, would someone kindly tell him how one could make 100,000 corpses disappear? This kind of incredible statement

just went to prove that I and 'your friend Finckh' were the victims
of a dirty propaganda plot. He, Manstein, had come across this
kind of incredible enemy propaganda as a young staff officer in
World War I, and it was all the more important not to fall for such
tricks now. The two of us, Manstein and I, had been talking
recently about the opening celebrations of the Olympic Games of
1936 in Berlin, which both of us had attended, and where there had
been more than 100,000 people in the Stadium. Visualise that, and
then explain where one could dispose of that many corpses in order
to conceal their murder. In short, I should tell my 'friend Finckh'
that he must put such fairly-tales out of his mind – or else come
and make his report in person.

When at length he paused, I said that I too found it inconceivable that 100,000 people could have been murdered at once and
their bodies made to vanish from the face of the earth. My mind
was completely incapable of grasping such a thing – and yet I had
to repeat that it was Colonel Finckh who had told me about it and
that his two informants were General Staff Officers. I had too
much respect for the German General Staff to entertain any doubt
of its trustworthiness.

We made a few moves and then I asked if I should telephone
Colonel Finckh, but the Field Marshal said he must run over it all
in his mind again first.

We both made one or two more remarks and then I suddenly
had what I still think was a good idea:

'Sir, I must take this opportunity to tell you that I had a great-
grandfather who was born a Jew and as far as I know was not
baptised a Christian until he was eleven years old. So I feel
involved with the fate of the Jews quite personally, as well as on
principle.'

The Field Marshal was not sorry that, without changing the
subject, I had introduced a new element into our dispute. Why had
I not mentioned this before, he asked, and made me tell him in
detail what I knew about the delegate for the town of Hamburg to
the preliminary parliament of 1848 at the Paulskirche in Frankfurt.
'Really, Reich Minister for Foreign Affairs?' he asked. 'Yes, Sir,
and before that Reich Minister of Justice, and he played a leading
part in drafting the German Constitution of 1848.'

I had to repeat my great-grandfather's name several times,
because he had not heard it before: Wilhelm Moritz Heckscher.
Later on I had other opportunities to talk about my great-

grandfather, because the Field Marshal was very interested in history. And now I actually thought I had the conversation well enough in hand to embark on a further variation:

'Sir, I shall never forget one evening in Saporoshie when, after a few glasses of wine, you surprised us at bridge with the story of the origins of the Lewinski* family, the story of your great-great-grandfather Lewi, who – just possibly – may have been Chief Rabbi in Warsaw ages ago.'

'Oh, did I tell you that?' he cried. 'Yes, Sir,' I replied. 'Well that must have been very late at night!' 'It certainly was,' I said, and asked again whether I should now call Colonel Finckh in to see him. 'Not today,' he said. He had to sleep on it.

Finckh was called in the next day and when I announced him the Field Marshal greeted him as kindly as ever, for he liked and respected him. I closed the door behind him. This time I did not want to listen, because I knew the subject of the conversation and its consequences in advance. What could the two of them have done to stop the SD and SS thugs from committing organised murder a few hundred kilometres to the west of us? A criminal prosecution should have been brought against the man who had ordered these atrocities, and that, after all, could only have been one man.

A year later, in the summer of 1944, Colonel Finckh was Senior Quartermaster West in Paris. On the evening of 20 July he played a prominent part in the attempted *coup d'état*. That night, a total of 1,200 SS and Gestapo functionaries were arrested in Paris. They actually allowed themselves to be arrested without a shot being fired. On 30 August 1944, Colonel Finckh was condemned to death by the People's Court in Berlin and hanged. He too had been unable to do anything to prevent the murder of the Jews to the west of Vinnitsa.

Albert Speer, Armaments Minister

I am not sure of the date, but I believe it was on our visit to the Wolf's Lair, Hitler's East Prussian headquarters, on 9 November 1943, that one of Hitler's adjutants informed the Field Marshal, who had arrived punctually, that the beginning of his presentation would be 'somewhat delayed'. We were taken to Hitler's outer

---

* Manstein was born von Lewinski, the tenth child of his parents, and was adopted by his uncle, von Manstein. The King of Prussia approved a new name: von Lewinski, known as von Manstein.

office, where there was a round table and some deep armchairs scattered about.

To our surprise, a visitor who had arrived ahead of us was already in there: Albert Speer, Hitler's architect and now his 'Reich Minister for Armaments and War Production'.

Manstein was in a very bad mood. After all it was, at the least, in very poor taste to leave a Field Marshal waiting in the ante-chamber. But there was nothing to be done, the Field Marshal sat in the armchair furthest removed from Speer, having barely shaken hands with him. It really was no fault of Speer's, so I sat between the two of them and tried to keep up a conversation. I was also interested in seeing something of Albert Speer, who now responded willingly to my questions, since – as we now learned – he, the Armaments Minister, had been waiting for over an hour. His appointments diary for that day had been reduced to chaos.

Faced with such frankness in the Dictator's outer office, I now engaged a 'higher gear' and asked him if when attending on the Führer he stood or was allowed to sit. He gave an astonishing answer: he sat down as a matter of principle, before being asked to take a seat, except for the part of the talk when large plans had to be unfolded. But he knew from his many years of experience that he achieved more sitting than standing.

Now Manstein was beginning to take an interest in our conversation. Encouraged, I asked another question:

'What do you do, Minister, if the Führer interrupts your presentation and does not give you another chance to speak?' Speer's reply came promptly: 'I let him talk and take a sketch-pad from my brief-case' – it was standing on the floor beside his chair – 'and begin to draw. It is never long before the Führer asks me what I am drawing and I have the floor again.'

Then I asked Speer what he did if it happened again – after all, one could not repeatedly use the same technique. 'For that I keep at least two books from my library in my brief-case. I take out one of them and turn the pages as if I were looking for something.'

I asked if he could show me the book 'for today'. He at once took from his briefcase a large, leather-bound album with a bourgeois family coat of arms resplendent on the cover, and handed it to me. The album contained a collection of menu cards, made over generations for family parties, engagements, weddings, christenings and so on.

The conversation with Speer was more relaxed by now, but as we had already been here for over an hour, the Minister had been waiting for more than two hours.

Suddenly Manstein rose and went to the door; I followed him into the corridor, because his eyesight made it difficult for him to find the right place in strange houses. After I had found the door he wanted, I returned at once to Speer. Now we were on our own, he asked me, almost as if it were urgent, if the Army Group received one of the original copies of the routine production lists of tanks, weapons, munitions, and so forth from his ministry, or as information from the Wehrmacht High Command. I was able to tell him immediately that I had seen these monthly lists many times and read them with interest, but had never seen one with the letterhead of his ministry. 'Then please would you see to it,' said Speer, 'that these lists are read with great suspicion, and please pass this on to your Senior Quartermaster. Our figures are in fact manipulated at OKH!'

On the return flight I told the Field Marshal. 'Speer told you that?' was his reaction, almost disbelieving. After a time he said he thought I ought to tell Colonel Finckh and Finckh must think out a way of getting hold of the original figures. Finckh knew enough people in Berlin to do that, said Manstein, shaking his head several times.

'Total War'

We had news from home over the official telephones of extremely heavy bombing raids on Berlin on the nights of 22 and 23 November 1943 and I had received a call from my home town, Stettin, to let me know that our oil factory had been virtually obliterated by precision bombing. The Field Marshal offered me a few days' leave in Stettin and gave me a letter to one of his sisters in Berlin, because the post was not yet in operation again. Her address was in Brückenallee, in the Hansa quarter on the western edge of the Tiergarten, one of Berlin's most prestigious residential districts.

I walked through the badly battered city to the Landwehrkanal to look up my father at Corneliusstrasse 10a, opposite the Zoological Gardens. The house no longer existed. There was a note at the entrance: 'Herr Stahlberg is safe and well and living at Misdroy, Wollin Island, on the Baltic. Address . . .'

I walked on into Brückenallee by the Tiergarten railway station. The inferno I saw there reminded me of the battlefields on the Volkhov. I had to pick my way over corpses to reach the house to which I had been directed. No wounds were visible on the dead: the Allies had begun to use land mines, a new weapon, and when I reached the house I found myself facing a burnt-out ruin.

I walked on to Stettin station at the end of Invalidenstrasse, but there were no trains to Stettin. The station lay in ruins. Somehow I managed to make my way along the Stettin line to a station with the beautiful name *'Gesundbrunnen'** where a goods train was awaiting the departure signal. I went up to the engine and asked the driver to take me with him to Stettin. He agreed and I climbed up to join the two railwaymen. The train was proceeding 'by eye' and we took many hours to reach Stettin. Then it was only a few hundred meters to our factory from Pommerensdorf goods station.

What point is there in describing what I found? The factory no longer existed. All that had been built, developed, modernised and expanded since my great-grandfather's day in 1841, now lay smouldering a little here and there. A number of fire engines from Berlin had actually been brought in along the new autobahn, but had returned to Berlin a few hours later, having accomplished nothing. The oil tank plant had been burnt out, the extractor reduced to scrap metal, the refinery was a chaos of iron; a mountain of 6,000 tons of sunflower seeds from the Ukraine, once protected by a vaulted roof, was still burning and would go on smouldering for more than five weeks. Only the beautiful new power station in the Oderwiesen and the seed cleansing plant on our little harbour were almost undamaged.

Our managing director asked me to come with him to the town hall. It would help to have a uniformed junior director with him. In the town hall we sat facing a number of the brown-uniformed Party Members whom we called 'golden pheasants' because of their splendid uniforms. We were handed a non-negotiable cheque on the Deutsche Reichsbank for a sum I had never had in my hands before, and we were promised effective help, because the Stahlberg oil factory had a quota of 10.5 per cent in the planned economic system of the German Reich.

I had a couple of telephone conversations, with my father in Misdroy and my grandmother in East Pomerania, who told me that Uncle Hans-Jürgen had 'gone away' again, this time to

* Translator's note: Literally, Fountain of Health.

Prinz-Albrecht-Strasse in Berlin*. Grandmother was brave – or careless? – to say such things on the telephone. Our managing director had just told me that his wife had been 'called up'. She was on duty at the 'research office' in Berlin. All unsuspecting, I asked what they researched, and learned that hundreds of employees sat there doing nothing but tap in to the post office telephone network, in three shifts, right round the clock and record what they heard on their shorthand pads. The 'research office' was under the jurisdiction of Reich Marshal Hermann Göring.

I returned to Berlin as I had come, thankful for the mixture of smoke and fresh air on the engine.

* * *

Aryanisation became a technical term in National Socialist Germany, having power over life or death. Jewish firms, Jewish businesses, Jewish medical or law practices were 'Aryanised' by 'exchanging' their owners or managers for non-Jews. In rare cases Jewish people were actually Aryanised. As Hermann Göring announced: 'I decide who is Aryan.'

Back in Berlin I had trouble finding an intact telephone booth and reaching the right subscriber. When I finally succeeded and Tatiana Gsovsky, the famous ballet mistress answered, her assistant Inge Schweitzer also came to the telephone and we agreed to meet at a restaurant on the Kurfürstendamm.

Inge was looking pale and careworn. 'They've taken Mareile!' she began. 'What do you mean, taken?' I asked, and Inge told me.

Mareile, the elder sister with whom she lived, had had to give up studying medicine a few years ago because of her Jewish descent; later she was one of the unfortunates who had to wear a yellow star marked 'Jew', were allowed on the street only after dark and whose food rations were far below the norm. Then she had been 'called up' and was working – night-shifts only – in an electrical goods factory.

One morning she had not come home from work. Inge had gone to the factory at once, to be told that all Jewish women workers from that department had been taken away in closed vans after midnight; they were no longer in Berlin.

Inge had done all she could to find out where her sister had been taken and – improbable as it may sound – after a few days she had succeeded.

* The Gestapo prison.

The chain of information began with the BVG, the Berlin Transport Authority. The streetcars ran 'special services' when normal traffic was over for the night, from the western quarter of Berlin to the Grunewald Station, where goods trains were waiting beyond the ordinary passenger platforms for their human freight. At the end of the chain were the engine drivers who had to drive the empty trains back to Germany.

'And where did they take Mareile?' I asked. 'To Auschwitz,' she said. At that time I had never heard the name Auschwitz and asked where and what it was. Inge could not believe that I knew nothing about Auschwitz. When I assured her that I did not she said: 'Auschwitz is one of the many concentration camps in Poland. It is near Cracow. No one has yet returned from Auschwitz.'

'Yes, but what about you?' I asked. 'You don't wear a yellow star, and you're still allowed to work with Tatiana Gsovsky?'

Inge opened her bag and took out a well-filled envelope. After looking round to see that there were no undesirable onlookers, she opened the envelope and put some documents on the table for me to read.

They were declarations on oath. In the first, a friend of her father, now living in America, declared that he and not Dr. Schweitzer was the father of Fräulein Inge Schweitzer. In the second document Frau Tatiana Gsovsky, ballet mistress of the State Opera, declared on oath that before Dr. Schweitzer had left Germany he had disclosed to her that his old friend, and not he himself, was Inge's father. Tatiana Gsovsky's declaration had actually been confirmed by a Berlin court. Then came a geneticist's opinion. He declared that the ear lobes of the sisters Inge and Mareile Schweitzer were so different that they could not have had the same parents. Another declaration came from the famous pilot Ernst Udet, until recently Colonel-General and general technical director of the German Luftwaffe. Ernst Udet declared that it was he himself, not Dr. Schweitzer, who was the extra-marital father of Inge Schweitzer. Udet was no longer alive, having shot himself in November 1941 when Hitler and Göring blamed him for the failure of the German air attack on England in the summer of 1940.

I asked Inge which of them had really been her father, but of course she did not know. However, there was no doubt in her mind that it had been Dr. Schweitzer himself. Udet had been a friend of her parents. Her mother had died young and, before he emigrated, her father had asked Udet to look after both his daughters if he was unable to return to Germany. Udet had been unable to claim the 'paternity' of Mareile, because the sisters really were so dissimilar that the declaration for Inge would have lost all credibility had Mareile been included. What a ghastly fate!

My train was not due to leave for a few hours yet, so I accompanied Inge to Fasanenstrasse, where Maria Kalamkarian, whom we called Maika, was still the piano accompanist. She played classical and romantic works by heart, as if she were a musical encyclopaedia. I sat beside her and enjoyed hearing and watching the work of the master class, but no atmosphere was created. Basically, this was no time for ballet dancing. I asked Maika to play some Bach and she began at once with pieces from *The Well-Tempered Clavier*. By now no one was dancing. Johann Sebastian Bach was a help on a day like that. Finally Maika said: 'There, now I'll play another piece for Mareile and that will be all for today.' And we listened to the final chorale from the St. John Passion.

When it was dark the three of us, Maika, Inge and I walked down Lietzenburger Strasse to Nollendorfplatz. Quite suddenly Maika said: 'Listen, it's nice walking with you, because you're wearing a decent uniform and actually carrying a pistol.' I didn't quite understand what she meant. She said that with me there, she was safe against being 'chatted up'. I wondered who would chat up plump little Maika out in the street, and asked her to explain. There were police patrols, she said, who were always asking her why she was not wearing a yellow star. I had not known that Maika was an Armenian, not a Jewess. She had a German passport as a 'stateless' person.

Maria Kalamkarian had already been bombed out once and now had a basement flat in Mackensenstrasse. She opened a door to the right which led directly from the pavement into the basement. We groped our way down the dark stairs and walked into a windowless room to the left, in which the furniture consisted of virtually nothing but mattresses, crates and one or two carpets. In fact it was actually pretty cosy down there.

I hung my coat up on a hook and asked for a certain room. Yes, she had that too, but before I went she must first 'clear the way'. A married couple, friends of hers, were living there and if they came across me unexpectedly in my uniform in the meagrely lit basement, she could not answer for the consequences.

Maria Kalamkarian was truly one of the heroic women to whom Jewish citizens of Berlin owed their lives, though she herself made no fuss about it. (Maria Kalamkarian lived in the University town of Tübingen as a piano teacher until her death in 1988.)

With the customary hospitality of East Europeans, she made tea and produced something to eat from her scant supplies. Suddenly she asked me when this terrible war would be over. I must know, she felt, because I was working in such a superior military position. She was horrified when I said I could see no end to it within the near future. Then she said that there really were no 'sensible people' left in Germany who still believed in final victory for Germany. Was there no one, the two ladies asked incredulously, who would 'put an end to this business by force'?

What was I to say? Inge shook me still more by saying that there was a group of senior officers in the Berlin High Command who were planning a *coup d'état*. I said I knew nothing about that and I doubted it. What else could I say? I begged them not to pass on that kind of talk.

Then came something still more astonishing: there was a general feeling that there were a lot of people in headquarter posts who spoke as I did, because they had more information than most, though evidently none of them had the guts to act.

I could not answer, so I tried to change the subject: what, I asked, was ultimately to become of the two people hidden down here in the basement? Now it was the two brave ladies' turn to be stricken. I gave them two addresses, for an extreme emergency, which I had from my mother. First, the Swedish Protestant church between Kaiserallee and Landhausstrasse, where one could knock on the door at night, and second, the Swedish Embassy in the Tiergarten quarter. The Swedes had twice granted asylum to relatives of ours (Achim von Rohr-Demmin and Ewald von Kleist-Schmenzin).

I also gave them the name and address of my grandmother, Ruth von Kleist-Retzow, Klein-Krössin, Kreis Belgard in Pomerania, but I begged them to memorise the names and addresses without writing anything down.

It was a depressing evening, just as depressing as all my days in Berlin and Stettin had been. It was terrible to be unable to help. What could I do? Just in time I remembered the supply of food ration cards which I had 'organised' for myself from our staff for such emergencies.

I walked through blacked-out Berlin, past the Bendler block where I had met Canaris and Oster, through the Brandenburg Gate to Friedrichstrasse Station. Everywhere I saw ruins; by night the city seemed dead. At the station the courier trains to the various Army Group headquarters in the East were waiting, and one had to be careful not to get into the wrong train in the darkness or one might wake up at Leningrad instead of in the Ukraine. I was almost ashamed to be travelling in such a comfortable sleeping car.

Back at headquarters, I had to report in detail to the Field Marshal. I described the state of Berlin to him, the hellish image of Brückenallee in the Hansa quarter. I gave him back the letter to his sister, told him about Stettin, my journeys on the goods train engines, and above all I did not spare him the name of the concentration camp, Auschwitz, from which no one had yet been known to return. His face twitched. He was silent. I added a reminder of his instructions to me: anything I knew, he must know too. I withheld only my visit to the basement of the house in Mackensenstrasse – I owed that to the people down there.

I took care to report objectively, without emotion, and I had the impression that he was finding it hard to listen to me. He was silent. Should I continue to report, I asked him. 'Yes, of course,' he replied.

An Interjection

Early in 1944 Army Group South was involved in fierce rearguard actions. Our headquarters had been moved back more than 100 kilometres west of Vinnitsa to the town of Proskurov. On 4 January, Manstein flew to the Führer's headquarters with me again, because Hitler was constantly frustrating the operations of the Army Group. 'Positions to be held to the last round!' was the extent of his strategic thinking. Manstein was determined to urge Hitler once again to give up the supreme command, still intent on his theory that it must be possible to fight through to a military stalemate. Once that was achieved, Hitler could negotiate a political peace compromise through diplomatic channels. The Field Marshal therefore undertook to bring about a stalemate as soon as Hitler transferred the supreme command to him. General Busse, his Chief of Staff, supported him.

No one but General Zeitzler was present at that part of the

meeting with Hitler when Manstein made his attempt. Manstein describes the conversation of 4 January in his memoirs and often discussed the subject with me before and after he had seen Hitler. My view was that neither he nor anyone else would ever succeed in getting Hitler to forgo even a fraction of his power, but Manstein disagreed. The sheer weight of evidence would force Hitler to relinquish a part of the means at his disposal in order to save himself. For me personally there is no doubt at all that on this issue General Busse exerted a decisive influence on the Field Marshal's thinking.

The Commanders-in-Chief in Russia and a large number of generals and admirals had been summoned to the Führer's headquarters for 27 January 1944. I knew only that Hitler intended to give a crucial address. I had witnessed only one such previous gathering, when Hitler had announced the date of the Citadel offensive in Munich, so there was probably something important in the wind this time as well.

The Field Marshal and I did not fly directly from Proskurov to Rastenburg in East Prussia on 27 January. Instead, we left a day early, at 10 in the morning, for Liegnitz, where Manstein's family was living at 10 Holteistrasse, his official residence before the war.

The account of what happened on the days from 26 to 28 January 1944 became significant to historians some years after the war was over, so I am lucky that in the military section of the Federal Archives in Freiburg there is a copy of the document which I myself typed and signed at the end of this journey for the War Diary of the Army Group.

Years later, some imprecise testimony led to the dissemination of the story that on 25 January 1944 Manstein took part in a 'National Socialist Command Meeting' in Poznan, at which both Goebbels and Himmler spoke. In fact, on 25 January, Manstein was not in Poznan but at his own headquarters in Proskurov.

As far as Manstein's personality is concerned, I must say that his presence at such a meeting would have been quite unthinkable, since he fundamentally rejected the institution of the *'NS-Politruks'*, because it undermined the authority of the senior officers of the Armed Forces. Moreover, as a Field Marshal, he scarcely ever took part in any assembly under the control of General Hermann Reinecke of the OKW, a high-ranking Nazi official and assessor at Freisler's People's Court.

What is far more significant in my view is that, on the day before the predicted speech by Hitler, Manstein wanted to talk to his wife. So on the morning of 27 January 1944, we flew in our Ju 52 from Liegnitz to Rastenburg. For the War Diary of Army Group South* I recorded under 27 and 28 January:

27 January
09.45 hrs From Liegnitz to Rastenburg (12.00 hrs), drive to Führer's Headquarters.
14.00 Commanders-in-Chief of the Eastern Front Army Groups and a number of Army Commanders-in-Chief, Corps Commanders and Divisional Commanders lunched with the Führer.
15.00 Address by the Führer.
20.00 Commanders-in-Chief of the Army Groups dined with the Chief of the Army General Staff.
23.00 Conference with the Führer at his headquarters. Present: Chief OKW, Commanders-in-Chief Army Groups A, South and Centre, Chief of the Army General Staff, Commander-in-Chief of the Navy. (Ended 01.10 hrs) Spent the night in outer building.

28 January
01.40 hrs Resulting from the conference, the following radio signal from Field Marshal von Manstein to Army Group South: First Panzer Army: Continue attack by III Panzer Corps and XXXXVI Panzer Corps with all available means. Then, after dealing with enemy forces there, proceed north-east with III Panzer Corps and Leibstandarte SS AH to rear of enemy forces attacking in area of VII Army Corps. Hold position at VII Army Corps, if possible maintaining current position of Corps Group D, until 24th Panzer Division, to be brought up, or 8th Army troops relieved by it, can bring enemy troops under control if and where they have broken through. (Via Lieutenant Stahlberg to Captain Mast.)
09.00 Depart Rastenburg for Proskurov (11.25 hrs)
(Signed) Stahlberg

Field Marshal von Manstein dictated this signal to me in the large room with the stove at the Mauersee guesthouse ('outer building'),

* In the Federal/Military Archive in Freiburg im Breisgau.

without either situation map or notepad, walking up and down, while I sat at the table in front of the stove taking dictation. Then he asked me to read it out, wished me good night and went to his bedroom, while I telephoned the signal through to Army Group from my notes.

But now to return to the most important event of that day, Hitler's speech to the generals. It took place in a large hut, divided by a frosted glass wall. Before entering the front part all the accompanying officers were separated from the rest. Hitler's Adjutants showed us to the rows of chairs in the back section, where we had to be content with a view of the frosted glass. I could hear Hitler speaking, but it was impossible to make out what he said. What I could clearly hear was that Hitler's voice was becoming louder and louder.

Suddenly someone tore open the glass door from the inside and Field Marshal Keitel hurried past me – almost running – down the central aisle, followed at once by Hitler, also in great haste. General Schmundt appeared behind him. Then, for the time being, nothing.

Something unusual must have happened. I remember having time to think of Field Marshal Keitel's nickname, 'Lakaitel'* because he was said to run ahead of the Führer to open the door for him. I had seen with my own eyes that it was true to life.

Manstein appeared with most of the other generals, walked with me to the car waiting outside the hut and, in a state of high excitement, told me on the way to the guesthouse what had happened. He was shaking with anger.

What they had just had to put up with had been 'unbelievable'. The Führer had spoken as if his listeners were totally oblivious to obedience and loyalty, and as if he had forgotten that we had all sworn an oath to him. When he had finally begun to paint an apocalyptic picture of his vision of a final battle – he, the Führer, at the centre, surrounded by his last, faithfully devoted Field Marshals and generals – then he, Manstein, could 'not stand it any longer'. He had shouted: 'That is how it will be, *mein Führer,*' because he found Hitler's words 'insulting'.

Still extremely upset, the Field Marshal – paying no attention to the strange driver in front of us – went on talking: it had been unbearable. Finally 'there had been nothing for it' but to interrupt the Führer, and now he was wondering if he should 'take his leave'.

* *Lakai* = lackey.

I replied at once that that was what I would do in his place. He looked at me for a moment and then said he would think it over in peace and quiet. It was perfectly clear to me at that moment that nothing of the kind would happen before he had discussed the problem with his Chief of Staff, General Busse, whose response was quite predictable. Many years later, I was asked if I thought it was conceivable that, whilst he was among so many people who had been at the earlier meeting at Poznan all waiting for the start of Hitler's speech on 27 January 1914, Manstein might not have learned from somebody there that Himmler had made the first public mention before the generals assembled in Poznan of the mass extermination of the Jews. My answer is that I do not know. Manstein was not what we might now call 'a good mixer'. He was uncertain of himself with people he did not know personally, and his wife or accompanying officers, myself in this instance, saw to any new contacts. If I was not immediately beside him in a crowd I often saw him standing as if quite alone.

On 27 January 1944 Schmundt noted in his official diary:*

> The Führer speaks in a very seriously worded address to field marshals and generals from all three arms of the Wehrmacht at the conclusion of a meeting of leading National Socialists. During the address Field Marshal von Manstein makes an interjection.
>
> Following this interjection and the various tensions in recent times, the question of replacing Field Marshal von Manstein as commander is reappraised.

Manstein's signal, dictated to me on the night of 27/28 January 1944, clearly reveals the extent of the Russians' prowess in adding further victories to their colours after their successful offensive across the Dnieper. To the west of Cherkassy they had encircled two of our Army Corps, the 42nd and the 11th. Once again Hitler had given the order to defend the pocket. A second Stalingrad was on its way.

Now, however, Manstein was determined that on no account would he allow a repetition of Stalingrad. His last conferences with Hitler and his open clashes with him had obviously – at last – given him more detachment and resolution.

To be closer to events at the Front, our Operations Section had taken to the command train again. Thanks to the frequent

---

* *Tagebuch des Generals Schmundt* (General Schmundt's diary, 1985, p. 126).

alternations between frost, thaw and snow, the roads were in any case so muddy that the railway was more reliable. As the pocket of encircled divisions narrowed steadily in the wake of Russian attacks, Manstein decided – without getting Hitler's approval – to order a breakout. We breathed sighs of relief.

On the night of 16 to 17 February, when the breakout was due to take place, it was my turn to be 'duty officer'. I was sitting by the telephones after midnight in great suspense, when suddenly the signals came in. Tens of thousands of our soldiers had overrun the enemy with savage determination, though the heavy guns had apparently been left behind in the deep mire. After I had passed the signals on to OKW I woke the Field Marshal and reported the news to him, with my congratulations, in the darkness of his sleeping-car compartment. Through his independent decision, counter to Hitler's orders, he had saved the lives of thousands of German soldiers.*

Next day the members of the Operations Section of the Army Group were silently wondering how Hitler would react to Manstein's high-handedness. Well, he did not react at all. He approved Manstein's order – after the event.

The 'Oath of Allegiance'

Cherkassy was simply an episode – a significant one for Army Group South – but how was the war against Russia to continue now? Again and again Manstein tried to bring the subject up in discussion, repeating that 'the Supreme Command' was thinking three or at most four days ahead, whereas in a war against Russia one had to think at least three to four months ahead.

In Manstein's own memoirs* there is a brief note of a telephone conversation on 18 February 1944 with Zeitzler, the Chief of the Army General Staff, which is instructive and which I quote because I wrote it myself. Manstein had drawn Zeitzler's attention to the relative strengths of our forces and those of the Soviet Union and asked again how the next step was seen at the highest level. I quote:

---

* According to later calculations some 54,000 German soldiers had been encircled. More than 30,000 of them escaped in the breakout.
* Manstein, *Verlorene Siege* (Lost Victories), Bonn 1955, pp. 590/91. (English translations by Methuen (1958) and Arms and Armour Press (1982)).

Zeitzler: '*I have had another long conversation with the Führer about that, and about its consequences, but once again was not received with open arms.*'

Manstein: '*Then how does he see the future of the fighting in our area?*'

Zeitzler: '*He says that some time or other the Russian will finally have to stop attacking. Since July last year he has been continuously on the attack. It can't go on for ever. I asked him:* Mein Führer, *if you were a Russian what would you do?* He replied: Nothing at all! I said: I would attack, towards Lemberg!*'†

The nature of the military situation on the Eastern Front in the Spring of 1944 could scarcely be more aptly summed up than in this brief record. Hitler was presumably turning over quite different problems in his mind – or had he already given up the war for lost?

About the middle of March, his Chief Adjutant, General Schmundt, came to see us. Soon after he left, I found out the reason for his short visit: Manstein had been asked to attend a meeting of all Field Marshals in Berchtesgaden on 19 March.

We flew off on 19 March 1944 in our Ju 52 to Munich; General Busse was also of our party. At a station not far from Riem airfield, Hitler's own train was waiting to pick us up. For the first (and only) time I entered this showpiece of luxury and comfort. It was some time before the Field Marshals were assembled, because they had flown in from every point of the compass and from great distances. As far as I remember, they included Kleist, Busch, Rommel, Weichs and above all, Rundstedt.

An elegant compartment had been allocated to each of these senior officers and his escort. We had scarcely entered our coupé when General Busse suggested to the Field Marshal that he might take this unique opportunity to pay a call on Field Marshal von Rundstedt. Manstein might ask him, as 'doyen of the Field Marshals', to act as their spokesman, asking Hitler to hand over supreme command of the Army, at least on the Eastern Front, and make one of them Commander-in-Chief or Chief of Staff. Manstein agreed to Busse's proposal at once and we set off to find Field Marshal Rundstedt's compartment. When we were already in the corridor, Busse again turned to Manstein and suggested that he should make the visit without me. Manstein agreed to this too, and I thought it perfectly proper, because there is really no place for an *aide-de-camp* in a dialogue of such a potentially explosive nature.

† Now L'vov.

The train was already moving when Manstein returned without Busse. I asked him how the conversation had gone and he said that in principle Rundstedt had agreed with him, but he had refused to be the Field Marshals' spokesman. Rundstedt believed that such a proposal, no matter from whom it came, could only cause trouble. He himself had often broached the problem of the leadership structure to Hitler, but each time he had been 'sent off with a flea in his ear'. Hitler had no intention of giving up even a fraction of his power. Moreover, Manstein told me, Rundstedt had become a tired, impotent man, in no way comparable to the Rundstedt under whom he had once been Chief of Staff. Whatever Busse and he had proposed, Rundstedt had simply turned down.

There were a number of large 7.7 litre Mercedes standing at Berchtesgaden station. None of us would have thought it possible that Hitler kept so many of these expensive cars. During the drive to the Berghof, clouds of artificial smoke began to veil the entire valley round the Berchtesgaden district about half-way up the mountains. When we asked what this meant, we were told that the Berchtesgaden area had recently been camouflaged in 'fog' as soon as enemy aircraft were detected *en route* for Southern Germany.

As usual, General Schmundt received the Field Marshals at the foot of the steps to the Berghof. Even when such a distinguished gathering of eminent visitors was expected, the master of the house did not come to the entrance to welcome his guests.

Hitler's four Adjutants, and with them the recently appointed fifth, *SS-Gruppenführer* Hermann Fegelein, did the honours. The Field Marshals were led into the large hall and all the other officers – even generals like Busse – were accommodated in the living-room, which was now rather crowded. No one said a word, because everyone hoped, acoustically at least, to gather something of what was going on behind the portière eight steps down. The portière was left a hand's breadth open so that one could at least pick up a few hints of the proceedings in the large hall.

Schmundt asked the Field Marshals to stand in a row. As the 'doyen', Rundstedt stood at the right-hand end. Schmundt gave him the paper that those present had already signed on Schmundt's tour a few days earlier. Hitler appeared and Rundstedt read out what the paper contained: an oath of allegiance.

But what was the reason for organising such an extraordinary demonstration? General von Seydlitz, a former Corps Commander in Stalingrad, who was now in Russian captivity with many other captive German officers in the prison camps, had founded a 'National Committee for Free Germany' and drawn up proclamations with black, white and red borders calling for the overthrow of Hitler. These proclamations had been dropped over the German lines and had evidently affected Hitler so much that he had followed Schmundt's advice in seeking renewed assurance by this means of the unswerving loyalty of his Field Marshals, in writing as well as by word of mouth.

The whole event was quickly over, someone opened the portière behind which all the rest of us were standing and everyone proceeded past us on to the glazed terrace, where little round tables and chairs had been set out. People seated themselves according to rank and station, and a number of SS servants appeared and served coffee, apple pie and whipped cream.

I had not seen any whipped cream for years, so I tucked in happily, still finding time to admire the heavy silver teaspoons and dessert forks with their solid gold, soldered-on initials of the master of the house, like those I had already seen in the cloakroom.

Absorbed in a lively conversation with one of the other ADCs, I suddenly felt a hand on my right shoulder. When I looked up it was into the face of the master of the house. I tried to stand but he pressed my shoulder and said: 'Stay where you are, *Herr Oberleutnant*. Enjoying the pie?' I praised the apple pie. Then I was glad when he moved to the next table, because his breath was foul.

This was a strange occasion. On my many visits to Hitler's headquarters, I had never before been entertained; for the first time I was seeing Hitler as a sociable host.

That day Hitler took leave of his guests in his front hall, standing in the centre of it, flanked by two SS men, while people put on their coats in the cloakroom and buckled on their pistol-belts. The servants standing on either side of him each held a large rectangular silver tray. On the trays lay open cigar boxes from the firm of Boenicke in Berlin, with big cigars in metal tubes. Manstein, ahead of me, took one of the fattest. Never having been allowed to smoke in Hitler's house, he at least intended to enjoy that pleasure on the journey home.

Then it was my turn and I hesitated for a moment, being a non-smoker. 'Take one, *Herr Oberleutnant!*' Hitler encouraged me. '*Mein Führer*,' I said, I'm a non-smoker, but I know my father would be glad to smoke such a beautiful cigar again, and I also have an

uncle for whom "the fat Boenicke" is the finest possible smoke.'
And with the affability he had been showing all afternoon, he
replied: 'Then take two, *Herr Oberleutnant!*' I took two cigars in
metal tubes, the like of which had not been seen in Germany for
years. Then I received the spongy handshake. Three steps further
on Manstein was waiting for me. *'Donnerwetter,'* he said, as we
walked down the long flight of steps to the cars, 'I've only got one
and you've got two!'

The next day I provided myself with wrapping material and
stamps. Two packets were painstakingly made up and addressed
in capital letters, one to my father in Misdroy on the Baltic, the
other to my Uncle Hans-Jürgen von Kleist-Retzow, currently a
prisoner, care of *Geheime Staatspolizei*, Berlin. Neither packet bore
the sender's name, of course.

I posted them in two widely separated letter-boxes so that the
addresses of the recipients could not be connected. My father
received his packet, my uncle did not.

Reichsführer SS Heinrich Himmler

As I remember it, we were on one of our Bergohof visits in
March 1944 when, after a morning conference, General Schmundt
suggested to the Field Marshal that he should show us the house
on the peak of the Kehlstein. The Kehlstein is 1,837 metres high
and anyone who climbed it in the old days was rewarded with a
truly majestic view. None of us had heard the faintest hint that
since 1939 the peak could be reached by car and lift, because it was
in the restricted area. The house on the peak, built of marble
blocks, the bold sweep of the mountain road, asphalt footpaths and
rock tunnels, and the 120-metre lift shaft inside the mountain had
been secretly built for the Führer, Schmundt told us, in 1938/39,
as a 'birthday present'. More than 2,000 workers, including many
Italian experts, had worked day and night shifts so that it could be
'handed over' for Hitler's 50th birthday. The total cost had been
'little more than thirty million marks', 'only' seven labourers had
lost their lives in the building, the initiator of the whole thing had
been Martin Bormann, the Führer's secretary.

It was extraordinary to hear the Chief Adjutant talking so
frankly, even naïvely. During the drive up he told us that later on
Bormann had also thought of having the Führer's profile carved in
relief several hundred metres high in the massif of the Untersberg,

but since this could not have been done in secret he had had to ask the Führer's permission, which had been refused 'for the duration'.

That day we had heard the din of pneumatic hammers below us during the situation conference at the Berghof. When Manstein asked what was going on down there Schmundt told us that a gigantic system of tunnels was being built, deep in the Obersalzberg.

He spoke of 'kilometres of subterranean passages, workrooms and living rooms big enough to accommodate the entire leadership of the Reich "in the event of a crisis".' The tunnels were designed in such a way that they could be reached by a direct subterranean route from the Berghof and would be proof against air raids of any kind. They were also built so that they could be effectively defended against penetration from the outside, so that when the building work was finished the entire Obersalzberg would be one gigantic, impregnable underground fortress.

So – I thought as I listened – had Hitler's apocalyptic vision of the 'last battle', on 27 January, in his speech to the generals which had provoked Manstein's interruption, been a slice of reality after all? While we were flying back to our own headquarters I put this notion to the Field Marshal, who did not dispute it. The fact that the Obersalzberg was being converted into a subterranean fortress disturbed me, and a day or two later I sought out my friend Schulze-Büttger in his office and described what General Schmundt had told us. Our interpretations coincided: Hitler's strategic thinking was now entirely concentrated on delaying the end of the war, and with it his own end.

When Field Marshal Busch was summoned as well as Manstein to conferences at the Führer's headquarters, I often met my former regimental comrade Eberhard von Breitenbuch, who held the same post with Busch as I did with Manstein. He had been one of our circle in Schwedt even before the war.

At the Berghof there were occasions when Schmundt gave the order: 'No escorting officers today'. We would usually stay in the so-called living-room, hoping to pick up a little of what was going on in the big hall on the other side of the portière, but sometimes we were sent out to the Platterhof, the nearby guesthouse, where Breitenbuch told me on the terrace, when no one could hear us, that he had heard from Tresckow that many hundreds of millions of marks had already been invested in the Obersalzberg houses. But this information predated any subterranean building works, so however much the development of the Obersalzberg might have cost up to now, one had to assume that Hitler was using private resources for it – or had he been drawing on the public purse? Only the Reich Minister of Finance could answer that question, but Breitenbuch had other information: Tresckow had once said that for every stamp with his picture on it issued by the German post office, Hitler was paid a percentage. Without knowing the amount of the percentage, the sums received must certainly be enormous. (*After the war, it turned out that Hitler really had collected a percentage on stamps.*) Perhaps the building works on the Obersalzberg were insignificant compared with the stamp 'royalties'. It was said that Hitler had anonymously invested a huge fortune in Switzerland.

At the end of another midday analysis at the Berghof, in the second half of March, Manstein and Schmundt went off to a corner of the front hall to discuss something which I was obviously not intended to hear. I waited by the cloakroom.

When we subsequently drove to Berchtesgaden – with an SS man as chauffeur – Manstein told me we would not be spending the night as planned at the Hotel Berchtesgadener Hof, but at Schloss Klessheim near Salzburg. It was, I was told, a beautiful old Baroque castle, converted by Reich Foreign Minister Ribbentrop into a guesthouse for official visitors.

At first I took this to mean that we might be spending the evening with Ribbentrop, and was already beginning to wonder what was ahead of us, when the Field Marshal said quite matter-of-factly: 'We shall be spending the evening with Reichsführer SS Himmler.'

The brief phrase struck me like a thunderbolt. All I could say was: 'With Himmler, Sir?' But something inside me began to reel. I could say nothing, with an SS man sitting in front of us, but I told him to stop at the Berchtesgadener Hof, cancelled our rooms and sent for the cases we had already left there. We drove on towards Salzburg, with me sitting in the back beside the Field Marshal without a word to say, but my head was whirling. The end of the war was in sight, we were facing the unimaginable – and this was the moment Manstein chose to get in touch with Himmler? Or was it the other way round? Who had more blood on his hands than this monster? Manstein had once told me that he had never seen Himmler, let alone spoken to him.

It was almost dark when the sound of gravel crunching under the wheels of the heavy Mercedes recalled me to reality. SS servants took our bags, SS officers saluted us with loud 'Heil Hitlers!' Our suite was on the ground floor, and here we were, surrounded by marble and silk – and in the hands of the SS.

When the orderlies had left the room I repeated softly: 'With Himmler, Sir?' 'Why not?' he said. 'What is there against it?' 'Everything, Sir,' I replied. He embarked reluctantly on something like an apology: it was never a bad thing to meet people personally, nor could we predict even now when it might be useful.

We dropped the subject.

SS orderlies rolled in a laid table and served us a dinner of several courses. Then an SS officer appeared and announced that the Reichsführer SS was at home and expected the Field Marshal upstairs. When we were alone again I asked Manstein if I had to attend the meeting. 'Of course,' he said, and asked me why I obviously did not wish to. I said as quietly as possible that it would be hard for me, and suggested telephoning the headquarters of our Army Group for a situation report. Then I would follow him up and report any changes in the situation. He agreed, and I asked the exchange to send an officer to fetch him.

I extended my telephone conversations with our headquarters as long as I possibly could, talking to General Busse, our Chief of Staff, and most lengthily to Schulze-Büttger, the Ia. Each time I began by saying that we were 'in *Reichsführer SS* Himmler's guesthouse'. It was important for them to know that before we spoke.

Finally I walked up the big staircase to the upper floor. There were SS men all over the hall and stairs. Himmler took good care of his safety!

The central reception room of the castle was dominated by a great round table with eight or ten deep armchairs. Manstein and Himmler were sitting side by side, but all the other chairs were occupied by senior SS officers. A great many more SS officers stood chatting in casual groups round the walls of the room.

I reported to the Field Marshal and told him in a few words what Busse and Schulze-Büttger had passed on to me; there was no news of particular significance. When I had finished the Field Marshal turned to Himmler and said he wished to present his ADC, Stahlberg. Without rising, Himmler gave me his hand, practically forcing me to bow to him, when I saw to my astonishment that his cheeks were made up.

Manstein encouraged me to sit with them and I walked round

the big room, as if in search of a chair. No one greeted me or involved me in conversation, and it suited me to remain a stranger here. I took up a position where the Field Marshal could see me, and stood there.

The conversation between Manstein and Himmler seemed to be restricted to conventional matters, although I knew how lively and sparkling Manstein could be in intimate conversation. So it was not long before the Field Marshal rose, took his leave of the officers round the table and came over to me.

The next morning a lavish breakfast was brought to our suite and soon we were back in the big 7.7 litre Mercedes of the previous day. The driver had opened the roof, although it was a cold morning. Was it done from malice? On the almost empty autobahn to Munich the SS chauffeur did his best to show us what he and his car were capable of. More than once we were on dangerously icy surfaces. It was a horrific drive and both the Field Marshal and I were freezing. It was not until we were saying good morning to our pilot, Captain Langer, by his Ju 52 in Riem that the tension relaxed.

I have often wondered about the motive and background to Manstein's meeting with Himmler, but I never mentioned it to the Field Marshal, because I wanted him to sense my revulsion. I did talk to my friend Schulze-Büttger about it and once again our views coincided. The initiative was not likely to have come from Manstein, but most probably from General Schmundt, because by then Manstein's star was fading in Hitler's staff policy planning. In fact, Hitler dismissed the Field Marshal only a few days after Klessheim. Again, I cannot really imagine that Hitler himself initiated the visit. True, the star of Heinrich Himmler and his SS was in the ascendant, but it seems to me improbable that Hitler was thinking of a Manstein/Himmler combination.

However, there is another possibility which seems to me worth serious consideration. We know that in 1944 Himmler too regarded the war as lost and was thinking hard about the end. By now there are also many clues to indicate that in 1944 Himmler was seriously toying with the idea of having his friend Hitler killed by his SS. I shall have more to say about this supicion later on. So I think it quite conceivable that Himmler had put out feelers in Klessheim and been 'brushed off' by Manstein, just as he had turned down both Tresckow and Stauffenberg months before.

Manstein himself suppressed all memory of the meeting with

Himmler: there is not a single word about it in his memoirs.

In June 1944 I described the meeting to my cousin Henning Tresckow in our last conversation in Babelsberg near Berlin. Henning listened attentively and finished by ticking me off: 'You were undiplomatic,' he said, 'you should have listened in to the conversation between Manstein and Himmler from beginning to end.' I said I could not have done it, so great was my loathing for Himmler.

The Dismissal

On 30 March one of Hitler's Condor aircraft landed at the airfield near Lemberg, where Army Group South now had its headquarters. Field Marshal von Manstein, Colonel Schulze-Büttger and I welcomed Field Marshal von Kleist and his entourage in the cabin. The two commanders-in-chief already knew that Hitler had summoned them to Berchtesgaden to announce their dismissal, and their successors' names were known, too: Manstein would be replaced by Colonel-General Walter Model, who had a reputation for preferring to 'lead' through his personal presence with regiments and battalions rather than from his headquarters.

General Ferdinand Schörner (Mountain troops) was known to the Army as a fanatical National Socialist. It was said that on his visits to the Front, German soldiers who were not able to report clearly to him on whose orders and for what purpose they were in that particular spot, were hanged out of hand from the nearest tree.

The mood in the Condor was sombre. Manstein sat down on the right-hand side and looked out of the window, not responding to my attempts at conversation. Kleist sat on the left-hand side, busy with a new cigar. He drew me into conversation, explaining that a good cigar took as long to prepare correctly as it did to smoke. Since he knew that my mother was a member of the Kleist family, I was asked to explain our exact relationship. I had to pass.

Eventually I went forward to the cockpit, but Hitler's pilot, Captain Baur, was not there. Instead there was a taciturn pilot who had no bottle of schnapps hanging by his seat. So I sat with my friend Schulze-Büttger at the rear of the big cabin. The two of us always had plenty to talk about.

As usual, General Schmundt received us at the foot of the big steps in front of the Berghof. He took us first to the living-room, where he left us standing and vanished. After a few minutes he reappeared and invited Manstein alone into the Great Hall, where, as the portière opened, we could see Hitler already waiting. Then the curtain closed and we could not hear a single word of what passed within, though we could hear Hitler's voice, making an unexpectedly long speech. Suddenly the portière reopened and Schmundt asked Schulze-Büttger and me to come and join Hitler and the Field Marshal. That was how we heard Hitler's last words to Manstein. He wished him good luck in his forthcoming eye operation and concluded by telling him to hold himself in readiness to come back into service as Commander-in-Chief West (a post still occupied by Field Marshal Rundstedt). Salute – finish. General Field Marshal von Manstein, with his first General Staff Officer and his personal ADC, left the Great Hall through the direct door to the front hall, without having to walk through the living-room where the others were waiting. In the front hall they did, however, meet their successors, Model and Schörner. The niceties were observed, they greeted each other coolly.

At the Berchtesgadener Hof the three of us sat down in a corner of the hotel lobby and ordered something to eat. The Field Marshal was relaxed now, and with all the liveliness of the 'old days' he readily told Schulze-Büttger and me what we had been unable to hear at the time.

Hitler's speech had been 'like a necrology'. Or 'not a necrology', rather 'a laudatio'. Above all, he had praised the operational plan of the French campaign in 1940, which 'would go down in history'. Hitler had mentioned all the further stages of Manstein's military career, especially the defeat of Sevastopol. Schulze-Büttger asked – rather mischievously – if the Führer had also mentioned Stalingrad, and the Field Marshal grinned. The name Stalingrad had not come up. But there had not been a word of the criticisms of past months, no mention of the many differences over strategic problems, nothing about the accusations of the last few weeks. What there *had* been – he took it from his pocket and laid it on the table before us – was the little case containing the 'swords with oak-leaf cluster of the Knight's Cross'. We congratulated him.

When we asked if Hitler had given any reasons for the dismissal, the Field Marshal told us something quite incredible. Yes, he had given reasons.

The 'days of operations' were now over, he had said. Now there was no longer any question of 'operations', only of defending, 'to the last man and the last round.' And for this Model was the right Commander-in-Chief, because he 'whizzed all over the front, when things got hot!' Model was now 'the right man' for the Eastern Front. Schulze-Büttger and I looked at each other. We did not ask any more questions.

While we were eating, a large, cheerfully noisy group came into the hotel. The men were wearing SS uniform and I seemed to recognise some of the faces; the girls were 'lightning girls'*. They all sat down at a round table diagonally across from us. Whole bottles of schnapps were put out at once and the group became rowdy. Soon they were singing soldiers' songs and bawling, some kissing their girls – one of whom was already sitting on her host's lap.

Our waiter shook his head, he could do nothing, the table had been reserved 'from above'. 'From above?' we asked. 'From above' meant the Obersalzberg. It was the birthday of one of the men.

That was how the day of Field Marshal Manstein's dismissal ended. He got to his feet earlier than usual, and I arranged to have another bottle of wine with Schulze-Büttger. Then I accompanied Manstein to his bedroom door.

After that Schu-Bü and I sat on with our bottle, still rather dazed by what the Field Marshal had told us: 'The day of operations is over,' Hitler had told him. The man who had not even made sergeant between 1914 and 1918 had the audacity to make that outrageous remark face to face with the most important strategist of the war. The man who, according to the General Staff's calculations, was sacrificing an average of 3,000 Germans a day was not ashamed to make such a pronouncement. No one knew better than he did that his war was long since lost. Before the war Schu-Bü had been Adjutant to Colonel-General Beck, Chief of the Army General Staff, and knew what he was talking about. Even in 1938, Beck had predicted that Hitler was a man without conscience, a brute incarnate. 'This war will not end as long as Hitler lives,' said Schulze-Büttger.

And we spoke of Manstein, the commander whom the majority of all General Staff Officers regarded as the greatest strategist of our time, the Field Marshal under whom I had heard Field Marshals Kluge and Rommel declare themselves ready to serve, the man who had not dared to decide against Hitler. And why not?

* 'Lightning girls' was the name given to the uniformed telephonists who wore a lightning symbol on their sleeves.

Because 'Prussian Field Marshals do not mutiny', as he had repeatedly said among his intimates. What tragedy governed his life! There was still time for a fundamental change; there was still not a single enemy soldier on German soil. Germany was still capable of some sacrifice for great gain.

That talk with Schulze-Büttger was to be our last. On 13 October – barely six months later – his life would end at the hands of the executioner in Berlin-Plötzensee.

PART V

THE LAST YEAR OF THE WAR

3 April 1944 to 6 May 1945

The Last Year of the War

Liegnitz–Dresden

On the night of 3 April 1944 the daily courier train was waiting at Lemberg Station for the signal to leave. A special express train carriage had been attached to the end of the train for the departing Field Marshal Manstein, not a saloon car as before but a special accommodation carriage belonging to the *Reichsbahn*. Colonel Finckh of the General Staff had organised this after I had told him that the Field Marshal had been ordered by Hitler to hold himself in readiness for the post of Commander-in-Chief West. Finckh caught on at once: 'Then he needs a carriage with an office and several sleeping compartments. You make sure the carriage stays in Liegnitz and is at his disposal whenever he needs it.'

I had asked Manstein what was to become of me, now that he had been dismissed, and he said he would like me to stay on with him. An adjutant was always made available to a Field Marshal for his lifetime, and since the time of Frederick the Great – or even earlier – a Field Marshal was never 'retired'. He would remain a Field Marshal as long as he lived. So I was no longer an ADC but 'Adjutant to General Field Marshal von Manstein'.

All the officers of the Operations Department were standing on the platform to bid him farewell. They would never again work under a commander of his calibre, and were already dreading the thought of their newly-appointed chief – of two days' standing – General Field Marshal Model. Finckh and Schulze-Büttger had already applied to OKH for transfer, but General Busse, as Chief of Staff, stayed on with Model. Those two might not get on too badly together.

Then the train rolled off into the night. Our carriage would be detached at Liegnitz.

That evening I sat up for a long time alone with the Field Marshal, drinking a good Burgundy and making use of the opportunity to suggest how my job with him might look in the

343

future.

I wanted to try to keep him better and more fully informed on
the further course of the war than had previously been possible.
Since the battle of Stalingrad I had realised the extent to which the
Commander-in-Chief of an Army Group was kept in the dark
about what was happening outside his own area of command.

He asked me how I proposed to put this into action, and I said
that with his approval I intended to travel a great deal. I was
already well known as his ADC at many senior headquarters and I
was certain that their doors would be open to me now, as his
adjutant. He agreed.

In Liegnitz I was very kindly and hospitably received in the
Manstein home, and while Manstein went into the University Eye
Hospital at Breslau I began on my information tours. First I got in
touch with my brother, who had been wounded no fewer than eight
times at the front and was now serving as a severely disabled officer
in the organisation department of OKH, where Major Graf
Stauffenberg of the General Staff had worked as Head of
Department II up to January 1943. One could still sense the spirit
of Stauffenberg in that department, where he had had an unusually
powerful influence, but my brother also saw to it that I met the
officers working in the Foreign Armies Department. For the first
time I saw from their situation maps and statistics the extent to
which the war unleashed by Hitler on 1 September 1939 had
expanded into a world-wide holocaust.

I was also shown the situation map of Italy, which Manstein had
never seen, and I noted the German armies, corps and divisions
fighting under Field Marshal of the Luftwaffe, Albert Kesselring.
The German Army Groups in the Balkans and Italy were not
subject to the Army High Command (OKH) but to the High
Command of the Wehrmacht (OKW). I paid particular attention
to the Allied landings in Italy – successively in Sicily, Calabria and
the Gulf of Salerno, as well as the murderous fighting at Cassino,
because Italy had become a political as well as a military theatre of
war. In July of the previous year, the Italians had overthrown and
imprisoned Mussolini and replaced him with Marshal Pietro
Badoglio. In September, Hitler had freed his friend Mussolini in
an SS commando operation, since when Italian soldiers had been
fighting on the side of the Allies as well as on the German side.

By now Manstein had had his operation at the University Eye
Hospital in Breslau. When we picked him up, the Professor of

Ophthalmology accompanied his prominent patient to the car, his white doctor's coat open to show off his SS uniform.

During his convalescence in Liegnitz, complications set in, the Field Marshal was in great pain and could not bear any light. I brought the results of my military researches to his darkened room, and whether I was describing the war in the Pacific or the battles in Italy I was astonished again and again by his geographical knowledge. All the maps from the geographical atlas were in his head – he could have been a champion at 'blind' chess, had he so wished.

My account of the war in Italy excited him greatly and I had the distinct feeling that he had no time at all for his fellow Field Marshal Kesselring. But the Allied Commanders-in-Chief did not get off lightly, either. 'Those gentlemen in Italy command like pipsqueaks!' he cried. 'They are squandering their troops. One should not wage war with modern weapons in Italy at all – destroying the art treasures and spilling the soldiers' blood. If they think they must fight in Italy, they should look for one decisive battle in the Po Valley. If I were an Allied Commander-in-Chief I should hold the Germans down in Southern Italy with minimum forces and land my main forces in Genoa to cut off Kesselring's entire Army Group from its base. Then Italy would fall into my lap like a ripe fruit!'

I asked Manstein how he would conduct the war in Italy now, and he said he would withdraw all German forces from Italy to Germany, if possible, too quickly for the British and Americans to catch up with them. We could defend the Alpine passes with only a few troops and the mobile units of Kesselring's Army Group should then be rehabilitated at home and prepare for action as strategic reserves.

I wanted to know if, in the event of the expected Allied invasion, he would give priority to the East or the West in our defensive strategy, but the answer I received was not one I could accept. It was a political decision, he said, and the soldier was the servant of policy. We should confine our discussion to military matters and not rack our brains over political problems. I protested; however, he had no intention of dropping the subject.

In these conversations I gained an ally in the person of Manstein's sister-in-law, Dorothea von Loesch, who lived in the same house. This beautiful, intelligent and clever lady from Salzburg was the widow of Frau von Manstein's brother, who had died as a dive bomber pilot in the Western campaign. We all respected her.

Fortunately every discussion has an end, because our arguments were sometimes quite explosive, and since out of consideration for our patient we had to argue in the dark, many of our talks teetered, according to the rules of the day, on the brink of legality. The darkness of the room helped. Manstein and his wife insisted on loyalty to the sovereign power, while Dorothea von Loesch and I argued for the limits of obedience. As soon as argument and counter-argument seemed to be repeating themselves, we would stop without any disharmony.

Another mental pastime for the sufferer in that week or two was to get me to read to him by the light of a shaded lamp from an important work: Wilhelm Dibelius's *England*, in two volumes. I did it gladly, especially as I also benefitted. Volume I was almost finished by the time he could see again.

In May the Field Marshal, together with his wife, son and daughter-in-law went to the Weisser Hirsch Sanatorium near Dresden for his convalescence. I was taken along as well. We had two cars, the big BMW drophead coupé, and a Volkswagen jeep for me. I had got myself this nippy little cross-country buzzbox in order to stay independent and mobile.

I had met my friend Achim Oster in Berlin and obtained fresh information on the situation at the auxiliary quarters of the Wehrmacht High Command in Zossen. Achim had been summoned to the Personnel Office about his father, who had been suspended from his post with Admiral Canaris a year earlier. The Reich court martial found against him, the Gestapo and SS having become suspicious that a conspiracy was afoot in Admiral Canaris's headquarters. I got Achim's father's address from him: he had retired to his family house in Dresden.

Back at the Weisser Hirsch, I reported what I had heard in Zossen to the Field Marshal and asked him if he would allow me to visit Major General Oster to obtain more details. I could wear civilian clothes and take public transport for the visit. 'You visit him in uniform, give him my regards and take the BMW,' was his reply. I telephoned General Oster and we arranged that I should pick him up in the car the following afternoon for a drive.

When I stopped in front of his house next day he came out at once, wearing a grey raincoat and hat. This was the first time I had seen him in civilian dress. 'My God!' he cried, 'you've come in

Field Marshal von Manstein's car; anyone can see from the front right wing (with its painted "Crimea badge") whose car it is!' 'I have another suggestion, General,' I said. 'I'll open the roof, so that everyone can see that General Oster's and Field Marshal von Manstein's adjutant's consciences are as clear as a bell.' He laughed and helped me to fix the roof.

I asked him where we should go. 'I'd like to drive along the left bank of the Elbe towards Meissen,' he said. In glorious spring weather we drove across the famous Augustus Bridge, past the Semper Opera House and the keep, enjoying our outing. 'What a wonderful day!' he cried several times.

At the same time, words were positively bubbling out of him: his agonised doubts over the tragedy of our Fatherland, his profound loathing of Hitler and his 'clique of murderers', and now his own fall. 'Stahlberg, you have no idea how far the organised crimes of Hitler and Himmler have gone by now!' Then he asked me to what extent Tresckow, Finckh, Schulze-Büttger and I had kept the Field Marshal informed about the extermination of the Jews. I said I could only answer for myself and that Manstein found the news of Auschwitz and other extermination camps 'so incredible that he refused to accept it'. And Oster had spoken of Tresckow, Finckh and Schulze-Büttger – how well informed he was about us!

More than once we turned to the subject of 'the Field Marshals'. They included some whom he could only despise, because they had become 'enslaved' by the 'Lance-Corporal' against their better judgement and for the sake of their careers. I said that this was not how I saw Manstein. A 'Moltke' by temperament, he could not resign himself to the fact that his knowledge and talents had been abused by Hitler. He was still waiting for 'his moment'. The fact that he had sent his adjutant to General Oster today spoke volumes, I thought.

Oster fell silent. At Meissen we crossed the river and drove back to Dresden and at the last minute I remembered a little pleasure I had wanted to give him. In a showcase on the north side of the Kurfürstendamm in Berlin, only a few metres from the corner of Joachimsthale Strasse, I had seen a portrait photograph of General Oster only a few days before. The Tita Binz photographic studio had apparently not heard, I thought, that the subject of the portrait had 'fallen from grace' a whole year before. 'Oh, she has,' he said. 'Frau Binz knows all about it. That's precisely why she's showing the picture on the Kurfürstendamm.'

That was my last meeting with Hans Oster. A few weeks later he was imprisoned. He died on the gallows shortly before the end of the war, on 9 April 1945, with Dietrich Bonhoeffer, Admiral Canaris, Judge Advocate General Karl Sack and others of like mind, in Flossenbürg concentration camp.

Major General Henning von Tresckow

By some means, I no longer remember how, I heard that Henning had become a general. I tried to reach him by telephone to congratulate him, but without success. I was told Tresckow was on leave in Berlin.

I suggested to the Field Marshal that I should drive to Zossen and ask the 'Foreign Armies West' department to let me see the enemy situation map of England with the preparations for the Allied invasion. One of my brother's friends worked there as a staff officer.

The Field Marshal agreed and when I told him that I also wanted to visit Tresckow, who was said to have become a general, he asked me to convey his congratulations and kindest regards.

My journey went as planned, although I did not succeed in seeing the enemy situation map of England. However, I did learn in conversation that armies numbering millions were standing by.

In Zossen it was easy to find out where Tresckow was at that moment: in Babelsberg near Potsdam, Strasse der SA 25 (formerly Kaiserstrasse).

I reached Babelsberg on the *S-Bahn* and was soon standing outside the house. I rang the bell, the door opened surprisingly quickly, and Henning's wife Eta stood in the doorway, her face pale. 'Please don't come in, please take a walk' – she pointed out the way – 'and Henning will catch up with you.' I began to stroll in the direction indicated and it was not long before Henning overtook me. He was wearing civilian clothes. I congratulated him and passed on Manstein's regards, but I did not ask him why Eta had told me not to come in. She would have her reasons. We began to discuss the military situation at once.

Henning was no longer at Headquarters Army Group Centre; he was now Chief of Staff of the Second Army on the southern wing of his old Army Group. At present the Eastern Front was quiet, but there were many indications that not only invasion from the West but also the decisive major offensive in the East were imminent. Our numerical inferiority to the Soviets was now greater than ever before. Our front was like a string of beads, Henning said; strategic reserves were virtually non-existent, now that Hitler had transferred the strongest of the remaining German units to France.

This brought us to the first question: did that mean that defence in the West was to be given priority over repulsing the enemy in the East? Henning's answer was shocking: he was deeply suspicious that 'when the water was up to his neck' Hitler would reach an accommodation with his arch-enemy, Stalin. 'Crooks like those two are capable of anything,' he said. It seemed inconceivable to us, the consequences unthinkable.

My next question was how he assessed the coming invasion by the Allies in the West. Henning expected extremely heavy fighting when they landed.

I added another question: when would the assassination of Hitler finally take place? Henning stopped, looked at me and said: 'The assassination will come, and soon. Everything is ready. It's been decided who will do it.' I asked another question: where would he be when Hitler was dead? 'I shall come straight to Berlin,' he said. 'That has been organised as well.'

I asked if the *coup d'état* which must then follow had also been organised – after all there were far more serious problems than simply killing Hitler. 'The *coup d'état* has also been organised,' said Henning. I asked if he thought there was a chance of its succeeding and received an answer that shook me: 'There is every likelihood that it will all go wrong.' 'But nonetheless . . ?' I asked, appalled. 'Yes,' he said, 'nonetheless!'

As we walked he went on talking, as if he were on his own. One had to imagine how history would judge us Germans in later generations, if there had not been at least a handful of men in Germany prepared to spike that criminal's guns. As yet, only a few Germans knew what unspeakable crimes were being committed by the Nazis – it was known only to the highest military authorities – but one day everyone would know, and then they would rightly condemn those who had known and done nothing to stop it. 'That is why Hitler must be killed, *coûte que coûte*!' As he spoke I saw a hardness in his face that I had never seen in him before.

I asked why the assassination had been left so late, and he referred his answer directly to me: I had been at conferences in the Führer's headquarters often enough to know how easy it was to say, but how difficult to do. 'We couldn't find anyone prepared to do it among the people who still have access to Hitler. Now we have someone,' he said.

I said I did not like the thought of Hitler being killed before the Western Allies had reached the continent of Europe, but Henning told me that there had been considerable controversy over 'before or after the invasion'. He himself supported 'before the invasion', because the British and Americans would be more prepared to negotiate without the sacrifices attendant on an invasion. But the argument had remained purely theoretical as long as there was no one prepared to carry out the assassination.

Finally he asked me if Manstein knew about the crimes against the Jews. 'Yes,' I said, 'but he regards them as so incredible that he refuses to "take note of them". On the other hand, he is sending me to you now, just as he sent me to Oster a few days ago, although it's over a year since I told him about the progress report of the SS task forces* in the Occupied Eastern Zones, which Oster showed me.'

Henning was startled when I said I had been in Dresden with Oster. 'You know,' he said, 'that Oster is being investigated, he's in great danger?' I confirmed that I knew that from Oster's son, Achim. 'You should avoid any more visits now,' he said, 'unless they are absolutely essential.' I promised. He asked about Manstein again and I described the Field Marshal's precepts of loyalty and obedience, appealing for sympathy for the man to whom the oath of allegiance was so absolutely binding. We discussed Manstein's lack of knowledge of human nature and his inability to recognise that Hitler was not simply a strategic 'zero', but a man completely devoid of character or conscience.

Then Henning asked: 'Where does Manstein stand when Hitler is dead?' I said I was sure he would stand where the law prescribed. 'For a Field Marshal, that's not enough,' he said.

By now we were on our way back to Babelsberg Station and when we were already in sight of the building he stopped again. We had taken so many walks together since my youth; before saying something he regarded as of the highest importance he always stopped and turned to me, as he did now: 'You too wear the shirt of Nessus.† God protect you.' He shook hands with me and turned to go. I began to ask him what the shirt of Nessus meant. 'Look it up in the dictionary!' He left me and I watched him walk

---

* The notorious '*Einsatzgruppen*'.
† According to Greek mythology, Hercules died tortured by the flesh-eating shirt of the Centaur Nessus, which his wife had sent him as a love-charm.

away. I would never see him again.

He ended his own life on 21 July 1944.

Ambassador Herbert von Dirksen

How should a Field Marshal dismissed by Hitler pass the time? Manstein first visited his friends in the area, most of whom he had not seen since the beginning of the war.

Herbert von Dirksen, who had been German Ambassador in London up to 3 September 1939, the day on which Great Britain declared war on Hitler, invited us to dinner at Gröditzberg. At the foot of the mountain, with its ruined fort, a relic of the Thirty Years' War, stands the three-winged Baroque castle, a princely seat. The great central doorway gives access to the reception hall, where the coaches had once stopped to allow the guests to enter the residence dry-shod. The carriages then left the castle through the gateway to the park, where they turned and re-passed the reception hall on their way along the broad avenue to the stables and coach-houses.

The diplomat received us with the gracious air of a man of the world, a master of social form – after all, his father had been an imperial envoy to Japan, and the son had represented the German Reich for five years in Moscow, then in Tokyo and finally in London.

Of course, in 1944, the guests' carriages no longer halted within the building, but a magnificent marble table had been placed at their previous stopping place. Like a Bible on the altar of a Gothic cathedral, an immense guestbook lay open ready to receive the names of those invited, but as the open page had to be turned first, the guest was inevitably transfixed with awe. Yes, indeed, the leading figures of the Third Reich had passed in and out of these doors before the war. It was only now that I remembered old Berlin gossip about the 'Führer' and the present master's late mother.

The guests were agreeably few in number: Manstein, his wife, his sister-in-law and his adjutant. The two older men kept the talk going and I listened with interest as Dirksen took up his favourite topic.

On 31 March 1939, when Hitler, in breach of the treaty, had

occupied the rest of Czechoslovakia and the German Government had subsequently uttered threats against Poland, Great Britain and France had guaranteed their support to that country. A few weeks later the German Ambassador in London had drawn up a memorandum on the basis of extensive intelligence and sent it to Reich Foreign Minister Ribbentrop 'to be handed on to the Führer and Reich Chancellor'. In this document, Dirksen said, he had urged the Reich Government not to attack Poland on any account, as Great Britain was firmly resolved to stand by her pledge and to come to Poland's aid in the event of a German attack.

Dirksen told us that neither Ribbentrop nor Hitler had responded to his memorandum, so that Great Britain's ultimatum and the declaration of war on 3 September 1939 had been inevitable. Hitler simply had not recognised that Prime Minister Chamberlain would react so toughly, no doubt believing that the British Government would be prepared to compromise a second time, as it had done in Munich in September 1938, when Hitler had threatened to attack Czechoslovakia.

The former ambassador's chief concern, however, was that after the outbreak of war he had not been called upon to make his 'final report'. He had asked several times for an appointment, but neither the Foreign Minister nor the Head of State had granted him an audience. This had caused deep offence to Dirksen, the correct diplomat.

It became an unusually interesting evening. To some extent Manstein's and Dirksen's careers were similar: both had served their country in important posts; the downfall of both had been a dictator who observed the rules of protocol only as long as they suited him. Both – so it seemed to me – were living in the 'wrong' generation. Both were apparently unwilling to see that so many assumptions of the 19th century were no longer valid in the 20th.

Manstein still insisted that although the war could no longer be won, it should by no means be given up for lost. Dirksen suggested that Stalin was 'approachable': as Ambassador in Moscow, he had had several talks with him without an interpreter. Both Manstein and Dirksen were only waiting for their hour!

In the course of the evening it emerged that Dirksen was inadequately informed about the military situation, so after that, every time the Field Marshal's adjutant brought a new military situation map to Liegnitz, he had then to report on it at Gröditzberg as well.

Offensives from the West, South and East

On 6 June 1944 the Allies landed on the French Channel coast. I still remember exactly what I felt when the news reached us: 'Thank God, the curtain has risen on – let's hope – the final act!'

Had I still been with my old Panzer division that day, and had fate ordained that I fight the invaders on the coast of Normandy, I and my companions would have done our bounden duty 'according to the law', though sore at heart, because there was a difference between fighting the Soviets and fighting Englishmen, Americans and Frenchmen who had gone to war to free the world from this monster and his policy of world domination.

Now, however, I was no longer at the Front; I was one of those who 'knew', and that knowledge meant responsibility. I was conscious of Henning von Tresckow's admonition to me back there in Schwedt: 'You share the responsibility.'

I went to Berlin several times and collected information. The fighting in Normandy was fierce. I heard a young staff officer at OKH say how astonished they were at the Americans' unexpected combat morale. The Allies held their bridgeheads and two artificial harbours had been assembled on the coast. They were building up their strength from day to day, while fighting off the counter-attacks of the German divisions. The remnants of the German Luftwaffe were practically out of action. It was clear that the landing was successful.

After only three weeks, the Americans, who had broken out of their bridgeheads, took Cherbourg, which meant that by the end of June they already held a major harbour for further landings. Our defeat in the West seemed imminent: while the German forces were wearing themselves out, the Allied strength was growing all the time.

In Italy resistance was maintained as the German armies continued to retreat step by step, until the opposing sides were now halfway between Rome and Florence. Hitler had no intention of relinquishing Italy and moving out, so an entire Army Group continued to be tied up there, when it was needed more urgently than ever in the East.

There, a front of well over 2,000 kilometres had to be defended against the Russians. When I showed Manstein the situation map for the East, he groaned, foreseeing the approaching catastrophe at a glance. He asked me if it was possible that the draughtsmen had left out a few German units on the map, but I knew that 'the Supreme Command' had actually withdrawn forces from the East in recent weeks and transferred them to France.

I got on the train and travelled to the headquarters of Manstein's former Army Group, no longer called 'South', but 'North Ukraine', a change of name devised by Hitler to attach it somehow 'morally' to the Ukraine – that was what our Supreme Commander understood by 'tactics'. We had already seen it for ourselves when Manstein's Army Group had been named 'Don' in that winter at Stalingrad.

Back in Liegnitz, we learned of the start of the major Russian offensive in the sector of Army Group Centre. A few days later I went to Berlin again to have a copy of the situation in Russia drawn for me at OKH. Army Group Centre had been smashed. The Second Army, on its right wing, had been able to retreat in time to a shorter line of defence, but to the left there was no longer a coherent front. Corps, divisions and regiments had taken up all-round defensive positions on Hitler's orders. By far the greater part of the Army Group area had turned into mere islands, between which the routes to the West lay open.

A 'culprit' had already been found: Field Marshal Busch had been dismissed (at the end of June 1944) and replaced by Model, who now had the dubious honour of taking over the overall command of the remnants of Army Group Centre in addition to Army Group North Ukraine. We counted them up together: of the 40 divisions of Army Group Centre about 28 were left. The losses in men could only be estimated at present – not less than 300,000, I was told. Minsk, which we had taken three years ago, was lost, the forward units of the Red Army were now scarcely more than 200 kilometres from the East Prussian border.

After Manstein had studied the map closely, I asked him how he assessed the situation and he said that it was lucky for us that although the Russians could certainly fight, they did not know much about the art of leadership. They would probably soon stop again to bring up their supplies. When I reported on the situation map in Gröditzberg there was no response – Dirksen's face was expressionless.

The Field Marshal had asked me to drive on from Gröditz* to a military camp – called Neuhammer, if I remember rightly. Field Marshal Busch had telephoned him from there, and he had

* Now Grodzisk.

already warned Busch that I would be coming.

I found the Field Marshal in the commandant's house. My regimental companion Breitenbuch was still his ADC. I unfolded the situation map on a big table while Busch sat down to study it in peace. When he saw what had become of his Army Group in the few days since his dismissal, he clapped both hands to his face, gave a loud cry and flung his massive body across the map.

Berchtesgaden, 11 July 1944

While in the East the Russians' offensive had gained them about 300 kilometres in a few days, in the West, in Normandy, the battle for every foot of ground was still hard-fought. But since the Cotentin Peninsula, with the port of Cherbourg, was in American hands, the Allies were able to reinforce their troops virtually unhindered from day to day. I heard on the telephone from my brother that the Allied forces in France were already estimated at over a million. In one such conversation, I heard almost incidentally that Hitler had sacked the Commander-in-Chief West, Field Marshal von Rundstedt, and appointed Field Marshal von Kluge in his place. Manstein was thunderstruck when I told him: after all, on 30 March Hitler had told him to hold himself in readiness to become Commander-in-Chief West. The constant interchange of Field Marshals was evidence of the desperation at the top.

On 10 July I took the train from Liegnitz via Berlin for Berchtesgaden. Hitler was back at the Berghof, so that at Berchtesgaden I was able to find all the departments of the military high command I needed in order to obtain information.

I reached the Berchtesgaden barracks area late on the morning of 11 July and went first to the Organisation Section of OKH to see my brother. I bumped into Major General Hellmuth Stieff, head of the department, who asked me how Manstein was and whether there was anything new to report about him. I said no. He seemed to be in a hurry and said we would see each other at lunch.

After that I went on to the Operations Department, found the draughtsmen's section and asked, as so often before, for copies of the situation maps of the Western, Southern and Eastern theatres for Field Marshal von Manstein. I sensed an extraordinary tension in the building – doubtless because of the very difficult situation at the Fronts. I went back to my brother's office and asked him about this purely instinctive feeling, and he confirmed it, though even he was unable to explain it. We agreed that I would pick him up later for lunch.

Then I crossed the barrack square to the building with the initials HN (for *Heeresnachrichtenwesen*), the quarters of the Chief of Army Communications, General Erich Fellgiebel.

I always enjoyed talking to Fellgiebel, first because he was a personal friend of Manstein's, secondly because he always had a great deal of information and lastly because, since I had once calmed him down a little 'forcibly' in a rather uncontrolled outburst of rage at the headquarters in East Prussia, he had trusted me. Since then he had sometimes referred to me jokingly as his 'saviour in time of trouble'.

When I had myself announced, he came to meet me in his outer office and took me, with obvious urgency, into his own room. I was scarcely sitting down when he began: 'Stahlberg, you have come just at the right moment. Stauffenberg is at the Berghof with the bomb in his briefcase. Manstein will be free of his oath at any moment. He must know now. When will you be seeing him?'

At first I was incapable of speech. My heart was suddenly racing with excitement (an awful trait, which I was born with and which has frequently bothered me at critical moments). When I had myself under control I could only say the one word: 'Stauffenberg?' 'Yes, Stauffenberg!' he cried, much too loudly, I thought. 'Can you think of anyone else, anyone better, who still has access?' No, of course I knew of no one, but I said that I had heard that Staffenberg now had only one eye and one arm, and only three fingers on that hand.

'My God,' I burst out, 'how can this man bring it off?' Fellgiebel said a man's inner strength was what mattered at a time like this and Stauffenberg had it.

Then I asked for details. It was possible, he told me, that Stauffenberg might bring the bomb back with him unexploded. This was in fact the second time he had taken it in to a conference, but he was waiting for one at which Göring and Himmler were present as well as Hitler. The explosive charge was calculated to kill everyone standing round the table.

Then Fellgiebel changed the subject. He asked again when I would be seeing Manstein and I had to promise to speak to the Field Marshal as soon as I got back to Liegnitz. We agreed that all he had to know was that Hitler's death, if it did not take place today, would happen in the next few days. I asked about the preparations for the *coup d'état* and was told that the advance warnings had gone out. Stauffenberg himself, now a colonel on the General Staff and Chief of Staff to the commander of the Reserve Army in Berlin, would be the organiser. Then Fellgiebel suddenly asked if the Field Marshal ever travelled by plane nowadays. Surprised by his question, I said he travelled only by car, at which Fellgiebel said he had asked for a particular reason: as Chief of Communications he had a few close confidants who listened in on the telephone lines now and then, and he had a very strong suspicion that 'the Berghof had had a hand in the game' when Colonel-General Eduard Dietl (German Commander-in-Chief in Finland) died. I asked for more details and was told that on Dietl's last visit to the Berghof there had been a noisy dispute with Hitler, at which Dietl had been dismissed with abusive language. On the return flight, Dietl's aircraft had crashed, for mysterious reasons, soon after take-off. 'If I told you,' he concluded, 'what staggering crimes are ordered from the Berghof, you would not believe me!'

Then I picked up my brother for lunch. As we crossed the barrack square together to the officers' mess, I commented that all hell was let loose here today. I took it for granted that my brother had known for longer than I had what was going on, but I heard from him after the war that he had known absolutely nothing about the assassination attempt, though he was sitting in the middle of one of the centres of preparation. It was an iron rule that no one should know more than was absolutely necessary to enable him to carry out his allotted task. But on the short walk to the mess, my brother told me that General Stieff was among Hitler's most fervent enemies. Once again, it was clear to me why Hitler's real enemies were precisely where people were experiencing directly how Hitler governed and commanded: not among the fighting troops but in OKH and OKW.

On the first floor of the mess building, we went into the dining-room, which had a large, round table surrounded by armchairs on the left and on the right a table laid for 20 to 30 people, where most of the chairs were already occupied. I went round saying 'Hello' and then sat at the window end of the table with my brother on my left and Rittmeister Hans von Herwarth on my right. So, in fact, I was in the ideal place for a view not only of the table but of the entire dining-room. The table conversation was muted.

Suddenly the door opened and Stauffenberg appeared. For a moment he stood where he was, looking round as he had done in my room at Taganrog in January 1943, but at his appearance something happened that startled me. About half of the generals and staff officers at our table jumped up, hurried over to Stauffenberg and surrounded him. Herwarth, my brother and I were still sitting down and I was horrified at the reaction of most of the others to Stauffenberg's arrival. Who already knew what I had known for the past hour? Which of them knew nothing?

Most of the men standing round Stauffenberg did not return to our table, but went over with him to the round table on the other side of the room, where they sat down. There were not enough armchairs, so some of the younger men sat on the armrests.

We had finished our meal by now and I told Herwarth and my brother not to wait for me, because I wanted a word with Stauffenberg. They left the room and soon afterwards the men at the round table also got to their feet. I stood up at once, very anxious to have a brief word with Stauffenberg.

I met him in the middle of the room and introduced myself, but he remembered our meeting at Taganrog. I wanted him to know that my thoughts were with him. 'Thank you, I'm in need of that.' Then he asked: 'Are you still with Manstein?' When I said I was, he continued: 'That's good. Any news?' I said: 'No.' He wished me a good journey home and gave me his crippled hand.

I had to walk round the barrack square once or twice before my pulse returned to normal. I had been talking to the man who was prepared to risk everything to free our Fatherland, indeed the whole world, from that monster. What strength of mind this man must have, to decide, in the presence of the criminal chiefly responsible for this terrible war, to delay the assassination attempt. Delay, because the other chief culprits, Göring and Himmler, who were meant to die with him, were not there.

This was to be repeated a third time, on 15 July 1944, when the headquarters had been transferred to East Prussia. Once again Stauffenberg carried the bomb away with him from Hitler's conference room. The deed was not done until 20 July 1944.

On the Autobahn between Liegnitz and Breslau

I took the train overnight but got scarcely any sleep. I was still quivering inside. What nerves Stauffenberg must have! I too had so often been at Hitler's situation conferences, so often felt the cold, mistrustful eyes of the SS men. How easily one of them might suddenly have decided to look in my briefcase, containing the Field Marshal's plans.

So Stauffenberg wanted to get rid of Hermann Göring and Heinrich Himmler at the same time as Hitler – Göring because Hitler had appointed him as his successor in the German Reichstag at the beginning of the war, and Himmler because he was Chief of the SS, which since 30 June 1934 had carried out the murders ordered by Hitler and which, in the course of the war, had turned into SS Divisions, SS Army Corps and even SS Armies. And now, it had long been rumoured in Germany, the guards in the concentration camps and organisations for the planned extermination of the Jews were also wearing SS uniform.

I thought over in peace and quiet my forthcoming conversation with the Field Marshal, when I would have to be alone with him, and above all without the ladies. So the conversation would have to take place outside the house.

General Stieff, Chief of the Administrative Section of OKH, had asked how Manstein was getting on, and Stauffenberg too had asked after Manstein, which must mean that they wanted to talk to him as soon as Hitler was no longer alive. General Fellgiebel, Manstein's old friend from the days of the Reichswehr and the Weimar Republic, had put it still more clearly: the Field Marshal will be free of his oath at any moment now.

I myself had heard Field Marshals von Kluge and Rommel – independently of each other – telling Manstein that 'at the end' they would be prepared to come under his orders. By now Kluge had become Commander-in-Chief West instead of Manstein and Rommel was commanding Army Group 'B' in Normandy. Did all this mean that Manstein had not yet been 'written off' by Stauffenberg and his friends for their future plans?

I reported back at Liegnitz at breakfast time and when the meal was over, I spread out my maps and gave an account of new events. The ladies listened as well and put questions, but when I folded up the plans, I said in front of them all that before I went over to Gröditzberg I would like to discuss a personal matter. Manstein reacted at once: 'Right, then drive with me today to Breslau. I want to look in at my bank, and we'll leave the driver here.'

Sergeant Sakolowski had already brought the big Mercedes coupé round to the door. It was one of the wonderful '540 K' type from the last year of peace, and he looked glum when he was told he would not be needed that day. All he could do now was to ask me not to drive too fast on the autobahn, as the quality of the fuel had become so poor that it would be easy to ruin the engine of this splendid car.

Sakolowski had no need to worry: I had other things on my mind besides delighting in a big supercharged Mercedes. Scarcely had we reached the autobahn when the Field Marshal began: 'Now, fire away. What's troubling you?'

I still remember this exchange word for word, not only because it was important, but because it was brief.

'Sir, I feel it is my duty to report that today or within the next few days the Führer will be killed.'

Pause. Long pause. No answer. After a time which seemed to me an eternity an answer came: 'Say that again!' I repeated my own words.

Another long pause. I did not look at him at all, glad of the many pheasant cocks and hens populating the autobahn which demanded my full attention. I hate running over game. After another 'eternity' came the question I was expecting, the answer to which I had spent long hours thinking over the night before.

'Who gave you this information?' I replied at once: 'General Fellgiebel'.

After yet another pause he made me repeat my answer: 'General Fellgiebel'. After a silence which lasted over many kilometres, I felt that the time had come to ask the Field Marshal a question: 'Sir, I would like to ask if it would have been better not to make this report?' His answer came very quickly: 'Of course not! It was your duty to tell me!' I breathed again.

After another long silence the towers of Breslau were rising in the distance when the Field Marshal suddenly broke the silence and said: 'Stahlberg, what the two of us know now is quite something.' A heavy weight fell from my heart, but all I said was: 'Yes, Sir.' On the drive back to Liegnitz, Manstein did not say a word, and when we reached his house he went straight up to the bedroom floor. To whom would he pass on my report to him? Or would he say nothing to anyone?

During lunch he asked me out of the blue if I knew of some nice house on the Baltic where we could all take two or three weeks' leave. I gave him the name of the hotel pension 'Seeschloss' in Bansin on Usedom Island.

Frau Karow, the owner of the Seeschloss, was overjoyed when I telephoned. 'Oh, a Field Marshal, and Field Marshal von Manstein into the bargain!' she cried, adding that for the next evening she would invite her resident guest, Wernher von Braun* from Peenemünde. It would be a great pleasure. Frau Karow was difficult to stop, and I had to repeat several times that we wanted only rest and refreshment.

Then I drove to the main station and decided on the route the Field Marshal's special carriage would take that night from Liegnitz to the Baltic spa of Bansin – without touching Berlin or Stettin, because of the nightly bombing raids.

Manstein gave me a thorough dressing-down when I told him when and how we were going to travel. Would I kindly not turn him and his household into a royal progress! I said that it was quite possible that he might receive a call from the highest level when he was in Bansin and have to hurry to Paris as the new Commander-in-Chief West, and that was why we had the special carriage. He laughed and in fact was really quite amused to be going on holiday in this fashion. Neither he nor I spoke of our real concern, which was to construct an extremely conspicuous alibi for himself and for me for the days ahead.

Thanks to the many shunting stops, our night was not exactly comfortable – coupling and uncoupling from one train to another is, after all, a noisy business – but on the morning of 13 July we stopped in a siding at Bansin. Manstein's BMW and my VW jeep were ready for us to pick up.

20 July 1944

I still had the battery radio that Antoinette Esher had given me in London in 1934. At my request, Frau Karow had given me a room where I would not disturb anyone, but in reality I wanted to be somewhere where I could listen to London at night without running the risk of being denounced for listening to 'enemy' radio. A box radio could be taken under the bedclothes at night, but any ordinary citizen who was denounced for this offence faced the death penalty. I listened regularly to the German news by day and the English news by night.

We rejoiced in the sea and sunshine, and once I visited my father on the neighbouring island of Wollin, where he had rented a furnished room in Misdroy. There was only one other person I

* German engineer, designer of the V-2, later US designer of Apollo.

knew among the guests at the pension Seeschloss: Helga von der Forst, wife of the former captain of the despatch boat 'Grille', which had been at the disposal of the German Head of State in peacetime whenever the Navy was to be inspected. Hitler had taken a fancy to the naval officer and summoned him to his side as a liaison officer. The Forsts now lived in Berchtesgaden. So there were a few interesting chats, and that was all.

But on the evening of 20 July, the announcement suddenly came through: an assassination attempt had been made on the Führer by a bomb in his headquarters in East Prussia. The Führer was unhurt and would address the German people over the radio that very night.

I no longer remember the time of that announcement, but it may have been about seven o'clock. At all events we had not yet dined.

I went to the Mansteins to report what I had just heard. The Field Marshal asked if I had heard who had made the attempt, but since this had not yet been announced, he told me to telephone General Fellgiebel at the Führer's headquarters at once to ask for further details. I confess that when he gave me the order I felt my heart miss a beat.

On the way to my room I met Frau von der Forst in the front hall, where she had been waiting for me. 'Have you heard,' she cried, 'an assassination attempt on the Führer . . . I must talk to you at once!' I asked her to be patient, as I had to make a telephone call first.

In my room I arranged for the call via the post office telephone: '*"Führungsblitz"* (highest priority) for Field Marshal von Manstein – Führer's Headquarters Wolfsschanze – General Fellgiebel, Chief of Communications.' The telephonist asked me to hold on, I heard some connecting noises, and after ten seconds at most came the voice I knew so well: 'Fellgiebel'. I gave my name and said I was calling on behalf of Field Marshal Manstein. We had just heard the announcement on the radio and the Field Marshal wanted detailed information. After a pause, as if to draw breath, he said: 'Everything is as you have just heard on the radio. I have nothing to add. My regards to the Field Marshal. And farewell!'*
Immediately after that last word the receiver at the Wolf's Lair

---

* As part of the preparations for the *coup d'état* General Fellgiebel had undertaken to have all telephone lines to the Führer's headquarters disconnected immediately after the assassination attempt. On the evening of 20 July he was one of the first to be arrested by the Gestapo. This telephone conversation may have been his last.

was apparently replaced – at all events the connection was broken. Fellgiebel's voice had sounded profoundly sad.

On the way to the Field Marshal's room I met Frau von der Forst yet again and asked her to wait. Then I described to Manstein my brief conversation with Fellgiebel, passed on his regards and said I would go back to the radio and report to him as soon as there was any news.

But first I went out on to the promenade with Frau von der Forst. She began at once: Did I know who had carried out the attempted assassination? I said I did not. But she did, she burst out excitedly, she knew exactly. It had been the SS. That wasn't mere suspicion, the SS had been planning an assassination attempt on the Führer for a long time. The SS had worked it out in every detail.

When I could finally get a word in I said I could not believe that, because the SS were after all 'the truest of the true'. I played the innocent, the naïve onlooker, but she would not give up. She had been living in Berchtesgaden with her husband for years, knew lots of people there, she and her husband had lots of friends there, not only in the Navy but also in the Diplomatic Service, and in the SS, too. I brought the conversation to an end by saying that I must go back to my radio.

After midnight I heard Hitler's speech* with the other guests in the hotel foyer. Now the public knew too: it had been Stauffenberg.

Then I went to the Field Marshal's room and knocked at the door. He had not yet gone to bed and was sitting at the table with his wife. I reported that Hitler had spoken and announced that it had been Stauffenberg. For a moment he looked at me as if stunned, then he began to shout in a way I had never known him to do before. He raged: 'Has he gone crazy? How could he do such a thing!' repeating the words again and again. When he was calmer,

---

* Text of Hitler's speech on all German channels on the night of 20/21 July 1944:
'German *Volksgenossen* and *Volksgenossinnen*! I do not know how many times an assassination attempt on me has been planned and carried out. I am speaking to you today for two reasons: firstly, so that you can hear my voice and know that I myself am unhurt and in good health. Secondly, to give you details of a crime unequalled in German history.

   A tiny clique of ambitious, ruthless officers who were also criminal lunatics forged a plot to get rid of me and together with me virtually to wipe out the staff of the German Wehrmacht Command. The bomb, which was placed by Colonel Graf von Stauffenberg, exploded two metres to my right. It very gravely wounded a number of dear colleagues, one of whom has died. I myself am completely unhurt, apart from some very slight grazes, contusions and burns. I regard this as confirmation of my mission from Providence to pursue my life's goal as I have done up to now . . . The circle represented by these usurpers is extremely small. It has nothing to do with the German Wehrmacht, nor above all with the German Army . . . This time the account will be settled in accordance with National Socialist practice!'

I asked if he had any further orders for me. Then I wished him good night.

As I went downstairs I found myself wondering whether that emotion had been genuine. I could not shake off the feeling that it had been principally for his wife's benefit.

In the hall, the guests were still sitting in front of the radio. I invited Frau von der Forst for a second walk and asked, when we were on the promenade: 'And what do you say now?' But she still insisted that the SS had originally planned the attempt. After all, even the SS could not be prevented from thinking about the end of the war, and Frau von der Forst suspected that they must have got wind of Stauffenberg's intentions and had perhaps only then called off further plans, in line with the age-old historical experience that the first revolutionary activists come to grief, while their successors reap the harvest.

It took me a long time to get to sleep that night. My thoughts were with Stauffenberg – was he still alive? What would now happen to the many like Henning von Tresckow and Fabian von Schlabrendorff, like Fellgiebel, who had done the preliminary thinking and planning, or been actively involved? And what would happen to the many who knew of the plans?

My thoughts also went back to that evening at Schloss Klessheim near Salzburg. Had Himmler really been sounding Manstein out on that occasion?

The remaining days in Bansin passed in dejected mood. Stauffenberg and three other officers had been put in front of a firing squad on the night of the attempt. Field Marshal Rommel had been gravely wounded in a low-flying attack a few days earlier in France. Colonel General Beck had turned his gun on himself. As Tresckow had feared, the *coup d'état* had failed.

There were many changes overnight. Hitler appointed SS leader Himmler as Commander-in-Chief of the Reserve Army. Colonel General Guderian, Hitler's unqualified admirer, replaced Zeitzler as Chief of the Army General Staff. What Clausewitz, Moltke and Beck had once created, a General Staff admired as a model for the whole world, was in the hands of the Nazis. Goebbels, the Propaganda Minister, was given the additional title of 'Reich Plenipotentiary for Total War Effort', though no one knew what responsibilities this martial title entailed. The confusion of responsibilities was turning inevitably into chaos, the process of inner dissolution had begun.

Finally there was an outward change as well: the soldiers of the Wehrmacht would no longer give the 'military' salute by raising a hand to their caps, but would have to give the 'German salute'. From now on we would have to salute like the Nazis and the SS.

I made no more trips to high commands and headquarters. Everywhere people were being replaced, arrested, 'purged'. One never knew which old acquaintance one would still find in the offices of OKH and OKW and one could easily lay oneself open to suspicion by asking for someone who was already in one of the Gestapo's prisons. All I would risk was a run out to Zossen, the auxiliary quarters of OKH, because my brother, who had had himself transferred from Berchtesgaden to Corps Headquarters in Stettin, had given me some tips on those to whom one could still talk in Zossen and those who were best avoided.

On 24 July I heard this sentence in the OKW's report: 'An Army Chief of Staff, Major General von Tresckow, has met a hero's death in the front line.' I froze. Henning was not the kind of chief of staff who would have abandoned his post in the Operations Section of an army in order to fight 'in the front line'. The harder an army has to fight, the more the chief of staff must be at his post. If Henning had really left his headquarters to move up to the Front, it could only mean that he had wanted to die.

Henning had been the chief organiser of the military resistance to Hitler. He had told me that he had been busy weaving a net across headquarters and the various high commands for a long time. After Hitler's removal there would be a new beginning. Now that Hitler had survived the attempt to kill him, he would take his revenge as soon as the network was discovered. They knew Hitler well enough to know that his revenge would stop at no one, whether lieutenant or Field Marshal.

The wording of this single sentence in the OKW report of 24 July 1944 did show, however, that the network had not yet been discovered at the highest level. Hitler did not yet suspect that on 20 July 1944 there had not simply been 'a tiny clique of ambitious, ruthless officers, who were also criminal lunatics', but precisely, and word for word, the opposite.

But now Stauffenberg's liberating action that had promised peace had failed, and there was no doubt that Henning von Tresckow had sacrificed his own life in order to save what could still be saved. He himself had been consumed by the 'shirt of Nessus'. From then on his only concern had been the survival of those whom he had recruited and who had trusted him.

I had obtained a large map of the European continent for myself, on which I entered anything I could still discover about the military situation, but since I had to assume that the map might suddenly fall into the 'wrong' hands, I was at pains to mark only what I could deduce from the Wehrmacht reports. I showed my map of Europe to the Field Marshal as often as possible and asked for his views.

In the days that followed 20 July there was still not a single enemy soldier on German soil. On the contrary: Norway was still occupied by our troops, and in the Arctic North there was still fighting at Murmansk. In the South of Finland the Soviets had penetrated to the West. Leningrad had been liberated by the Russians, but in Estonia, Latvia and Lithuania our Army group North was still fighting desperately, its back to the Baltic. In Poland, the Red Army had reached Brest-Litovsk and in the south of the country they were to the east of Lemberg. Romania and Hungary, Bulgaria, Greece, Albania and Yugoslavia were still in German hands. In Italy the adversaries still faced each other south of Florence. There was still heavy fighting in Normandy where 1,500 Allied bombers had just dropped a 'carpet of bombs' on German units, and there could be no possible hope of driving the invading armies off the continent of Europe. But the whole of the rest of France was still in the hands of the German occupying forces, as were Belgium, The Netherlands and Denmark.

Was this not a positively classical set-up for armistice negotiations? A German government without Hitler would still have plenty of negotiating strength. I was preoccupied with these ideas after 20 July and one day I asked Manstein if this pan-European situation did not coincide with the ideas he had dictated to me in 1943, in his memorandum to Hitler on the subject of a 'stalemate'.

Naturally the Field Marshal immediately scented the provocative background to my question, so I did not receive a straightforward answer. He repeated the words he had so often used before: as long as they were wanted, stalemate and compromise were possible, always and in every way. But to want them was the politician's job, not the soldier's.

I could not know then that this very question I had put to Manstein was central to the thoughts of the planners who held positions of command in the military resistance. I could not know, but I suspected it, because the question was obvious.

When Hitler had dismissed the Field Marshal he had told him he could count on becoming Commander-in-Chief West quite soon, but meanwhile Field Marshal Kluge had been given the job instead. Even the post of Chief of the Army General Staff, which Manstein had had an eye on, presumably as a way of compelling Hitler, at a given moment, to create a Chief of the Grand General Staff after all, had now been taken by Guderian. Manstein's thoughts had often revolved around the topic of a Chief of the Grand General Staff, but with the appointments of Kluge and Guderian any such ideas had become pointless.

I was quite glad of all this. From countless discussions with the Field Marshal I knew that as supreme commander Manstein would conduct the war in Europe very differently from Hitler. His repeatedly expressed view that the German Army Group fighting in Italy should be withdrawn northward across the Alps to form a strong operational reserve would alone have created completely new situations, both in the West and in the East. Equally, Manstein often pointed out that the German Army Group in the Balkans should have been back in Germany long ago. Even now, the 'greatest commander of all time' had completely failed to understand that one cannot wage war without reserves. Apparently he was still waiting for a miracle. So, as I say, I was reassured to know that Manstein would apparently not be given a new command. Of course he would have been a far better leader than the Germans had had up to now, but with Hitler as his superior he could only have extended a war which was already long since lost.

At the Tannenberg Memorial

In August a 'wanted' poster was published throughout the country: the wanted man was the former Leipzig Lord Mayor Dr. Carl Goerdeler, for whose capture a reward of one million Reichsmarks was offered – more than had ever been offered in our country before.

I knew now that the 'network' had been discovered. General Oster had told me in Dresden that Carl Goerdeler would be the future German Reich Chancellor, and Manstein commented at table in his family circle that the year before 'someone' had once suggested that he should let Dr. Goerdeler come and talk to him, but his instinct had been right when he refused.

We were far more affected by the news that the Führer had ordered the establishment of a 'Court of Honour' of the German Wehrmacht; the chairman was Field Marshal von Rundstedt. Field Marshal Keitel and Colonel-General Guderian were also members. The task of the Court of Honour was to reduce to the ranks and expel from the Wehrmacht any officer justifiably suspected of participation in or knowledge of the planned *coup d'état*. The suspect would then be handed over to the Gestapo and the People's Court. By this means members of the Wehrmacht would be removed from the legal jurisdiction of a court martial – what utter contempt for justice and the law this order revealed!

The names of the first to be 'degraded by the Court of Honour and expelled from the Wehrmacht' were published at the same time: Field Marshal von Witzleben, Colonel-General Hoepner, General Fellgiebel, and General Stieff. This 'honour' had also posthumously befallen General von Tresckow. The men thus demoted were immediately brought to trial, condemned in Berlin Plötzensee and executed by hanging.

To look at the newspapers in those weeks was unbearable. Papen had left his post as Ambassador to Turkey because the Turks had now entered the war against Germany after all. Hitler had awarded Papen the Knight's Cross of the decoration appropriate to his office. SS Chief Hermann Fegelein, Himmler's personal representative with Hitler, whom I had met so often at Hitler's headquarters, and who had married the sister of Hitler's friend Eva Braun in June 1944, had received the Knight's Cross with oakleaf cluster (for what, one wondered). Everywhere decorations were positively raining down on the Germans. Suddenly the almost forgotten former Commander-in-Chief of the Army, Field Marshal von Brauchitsch, wrote to the newspapers, to say how greatly he despised his former comrade Witzleben and his friends, and how humbly he desired to pay homage to Hitler. The papers also announced a new tank, named the Royal Tiger, now in mass production. V-1 rockets were being fired off daily at London, in 'reprisal' for the invasion of Normandy. The 60-hour week was introduced in German factories.

I was acutely aware that Manstein was growing uneasy. One day he said that he would like to buy a piece of land and a farm now, if possible in East Pomerania, where he had friends who would make agreeable neighbours. The beauty of Pomerania had captivated him since he had been a battalion commander in

Kolberg. I questioned whether it might not be better to look for somewhere in Schleswig-Holstein or Westphalia and said something about the 'westward shift of Poland', but he retorted that if Pomerania were lost, we were all lost.

So I picked up the telephone and began to search. First I spoke to Alexander von Quistorp, head of the Prussian *Zentrallandschaftsbank* on Wilhelmplatz in Berlin. He was friendly, but obviously reserved. Then I asked to be put through to a Dr. Hagemann, a widely respected agricultural expert in Pomerania, unequalled in his knowledge of East Pomeranian agriculture. Manstein and I took the car and made appointments for several viewings. Driving across Pomeranian fields with Herr Hagemann was instructive, but there was something against every place we saw. Only failing enterprises were available, the owners of flourishing farms were not thinking of selling. One old gentleman to whom I was related told me roundly that he had no intention of selling his property, even if cash to several times its value were put on the table before him.

Herr Hagemann also explained that nothing could be done without the approval of the Gauleiter, Franz Schwede-Coburg, in Stettin, even if vendor and purchaser agreed. So I asked for an appointment with the Gauleiter and next morning we were sitting in his outer office. After he had kept his visitors waiting for more than half an hour we left the building. I was glad not to have had to talk to that man.

Early in October came the news that General Schmundt had died as a consequence of the assassination attempt on 20 July; on 7 October the Field Marshal was expected to attend the State ceremony in the Tannenberg Monument in East Prussia.

On 6 October we drove to Berlin, avoiding travelling in the dark because of the prescribed blackout hoods on the headlamps. We reached Berlin in daylight, but the special train to East Prussia was not due to leave Friedrichstrasse Station until late that evening.

In one of the hotels on Unter den Linden – I think it was the Adlon – we took a table in the foyer. While the Field Marshal ordered tea I chased up information on entertainments in the capital to which one might go that same evening.

And, in fact there still was something: a symphony concert at the State Opera Unter den Linden: Bruckner's Eighth Symphony, conducted by Herbert von Karajan. I asked the hotel porter to get me two tickets, but he shook his head. I took my wallet from my pocket, in vain. I got on the telephone to the opera management: nothing left, I was told. I suggested putting two chairs in the centre box in the front row – no good. I would not give up. Being familiar with the theatre, I asked about the two proscenium boxes beside the stage. Well, yes, in the left-hand one, the theatre manager's box, two extra chairs could be brought in behind the seats that were already sold. I should report early to the box office.

Manstein was shocked when I told him of my success. 'My God – Bruckner!' he groaned. 'Why not Mozart?' I did not tell him that I had only obtained proscenium seats, or the whole visit would have been at risk, but in the mood I was in at the time I wanted to hear Bruckner – Bruckner in particular.

When the Field Marshal arrived at the Opera House the public stood aside for him. After all, how often did one meet a Marshal with orders, decorations, baton and all, accompanied by his adjutant, at a Karajan concert? Several times I heard Manstein's name, which was familiar from the newspapers and journals.

We had scarcely sat down on the chairs put out for us against the back wall of the box when the orchestra arrived. I realised with a shock how much it had been augmented – and there we were, sitting immediately behind the eight horns, their bells all facing in our direction. Not having heard a symphony concert for years, I was not in the least disturbed by our unpromising position, but when the brass began on a triple forte, the Field Marshal beside me covered both his ears. However, when pianissimo came round again, I could see how much Herr von Karajan's beautiful conductor's poses amused Manstein.

At Friedrichstrasse Station many prominent figures were assembled by the special train. When the Führer invited you to a State occasion you could not – or would not – fail to go. Especially not when the funeral service for the Chief Adjutant was taking place where Field Marshal von Hindenburg's coffin stood – Hindenburg, victor of the Battle of Tannenberg in 1914 and last President of the German Reich. Probably many of those who joined the long sleeping-car train were also trying to create something like a *post facto* alibi for themselves, following 20 July.

When the special train stopped towards noon of the next day, we were directly before the wide entrance to the mighty tower-encircled octagon of the 'German National Memorial'. An icy wind met us as we left the train. Opposite the tower housing the coffins of Hindenburg and his wife stood, rather forlornly, the coffin of

Hitler's Adjutant, covered with the military flag. What a dispro-
portion of size and significance! Surrounded by the symbolism of
German and Prussian history, built in the days of the Weimar
Republic, now destined to be the backdrop for a demonstration
against those who had dared to try to save the German Reich from
downfall!

They took their positions according to rank and station. I
remember Field Marshals Busch and Keitel, Colonel-Generals
Schörner and Guderian, General Burgdorf, Schmundt's successor
as Chief Adjutant (in a few days he would be the one to take the
poison pill to Field Marshal Rommel on Hitler's behalf and compel
him to commit suicide); I remember the Reich leader of the
NSDAP, Martin Bormann, politically the strongest and most
dangerous man in the darkness surrounding Hitler; I also remember Graf Lutz Schwerin von Krosigk, the Reich Minister of
Finance (a post he had occupied ever since he had been a member
of the Papen cabinet in 1932). I also remember a snappily-dressed
young colonel, who announced the funeral procession assembled
for the state occasion to the Field Marshals in an over-loud, ringing
voice. (I discovered on our return journey in the train that night
that his name was Remer; on 20 July, as a major and commander
of the guard battalion, he had proved loyal and reliable.) Having a
good musical memory I also remember the music, played by a
band, which echoed across the broad arena of the monument: they
began with a piece from Wagner's *Götterdämmerung* and ended with
Beethoven's hymn *Die Himmel rühmen des Ewigen Ehre*. Everything
ran according to somebody's plan. Only one person was missing:
the Führer and Reich Chancellor, the Supreme Commander.

So the funeral oration was not given by Hitler. Instead, Field
Marshal Busch spoke, probably selected because he had once been
Schmundt's superior in Potsdam as Commander of the 9th
(Prussian) Infantry Regiment. But it was not a Prussian speech; in
fact, I remember that Busch's speech was an ovation of unalterable
allegiance to him who was not present.

After the coffin had vanished into a carriage coupled to our
special train, Manstein told me to reserve a table for four in the
dining-car that evening. It was a long evening. Manstein and
Colonel-General Guderian, the new Army Chief of the General
Staff, sat opposite me, his Adjutant on my right.

At first the conversation turned on the military situation. The
Soviets had reached the Baltic coast at Riga, thus cutting off Army

Group North. Once again Hitler's orders to halt had led to a catastrophic defeat, but this time his strategic incompetence had led not only to the loss of a division, a corps or an army: he had manoeuvred an entire Army group off the rails. Thanks to the presence of their two Adjutants, the commanders facing us could only hint at their criticism of the 'Supreme Command', but the two young officers had long since learned to read between the lines.

In the area of Army Group Centre, close to East Prussia, the Russians were approaching the German border. Almost in passing, Manstein asked Guderian what would become of the Tannenberg Monument; perhaps the fate of the two coffins of his Hindenburg relatives was on his mind. At all events, we learned that the Hindenburg coffins were to be brought to the West in good time, but the monument itself was being prepared for demolition.

The conversation after the meal became more relaxed over a bottle or two of wine. Manstein spoke suddenly: 'Tell me, Guderian, I hear you've got yourself an estate in Posen province. How did you do it?' And Guderian told him quite uninhibitedly that he had been given a list of fine Polish estates which he had viewed over a few days, before deciding on the most suitable property. Manstein was taken aback and asked if the Polish owners had still been living there. When Guderian said they had, he asked what had become of them. Guderian said he did not know, when he had taken over his estate the Poles had gone and he had no idea what had become of them. Manstein was speechless. His face twitched once or twice, and I knew him too well to be unaware what it meant: that method of coming by an estate was not his style.

The next morning, Berlin's Friedrichstrasse Station also had its military ceremonial. Then the column rolled through the ruined streets behind the gun-carriage bearing the coffin to the Invaliden cemetery. Among the graves of the great military leaders of the Kingdom of Prussia, the Adjutant, promoted by his Supreme Commander to General of Infantry on his deathbed, found his last resting-place.

The funeral guests included Admiral of the Fleet Erich Raeder, the Commander-in-Chief of the Navy, who had been dismissed back in 1943. When the ceremony was over, Raeder asked the Field Marshal to come for a walk across the cemetery. The paths between the rows of graves were just wide enough for two people walking side by side, and I followed as close behind as possible. I

was passionately interested in what the two men in front of me
were discussing. They plunged at once into the subject of operation
'Sealion', the German invasion of the south coast of England,
planned by Hitler in the summer of 1940. Manstein had then
commanded a corps whose divisions were supposed to land at
Beachy Head in the first of three sorties from Boulogne, then to
join the troops scheduled to take London by encirclement from the
West.

Now Raeder asked Manstein why he had 'made so many
difficulties' at that time. Manstein was astonished. He had never
thought of difficulties – on the contrary, he was convinced that he
could take his corps successfully to the British Isles, on condition
that the date of the assault was not delayed. But then, it was that
senseless war in the air, initiated by Göring, which had given the
British time to prepare carefully and effectively for the defence of
their coasts. An air force was, after all, no more than modern
artillery, and to conquer a country one still needed the infantry.
However, there was no question of his having wanted to make any
difficulties for the Navy.

Without contradicting him, Raeder explained that the invasion
of England might have been feasible, but the British Navy had very
soon cut the channels of communication to the British Isles, and
the German naval forces had been too weak to prevent it. So
ultimately a German invasion would have been doomed to failure.

So the two strategists argued together, observed the proprieties
and parted in friendship.

Late that afternoon, Manstein took me with him to visit the
Reich Minister of Finance, Graf Schwerin von Krosigk, in his
offices on Wilhelmplatz. His big study was so heavily blacked out
that only a small table-lamp was left to cast a meagre light on the
centre of the desk. The scene reminded me of a stage set by the
great director, Max Reinhardt. The figure of the Minister was
absolutely out of keeping with the group who had been responsible
for the fate of the German Reich for the last 12 years.

Incidentally, he too had no idea how to go about purchasing a
country seat.

Towards the End

In August 1944 a personal difference arose between Manstein
and me. He had asked me why I was still a First Lieutenant and I
had said the answer must be that I had not yet been promoted. He

laughed and told me to request a form for promotion proposals from the Army Personnel Office.

When the form arrived on 28 August, I filled it in, in so far as my personal data were concerned, and submitted it to him so that he could dictate his answer to the question about the assessment of the candidate. He wrote me his assessment in rough on a piece of paper, answering the question on political affiliation quite simply with the words 'National Socialist'.

I typed the assessment on the form, leaving out the answer to the question on political affiliation.

When I submitted the application to him for signature, he immediately asked me why I had not copied the words National Socialist. I said: 'Because I am not a National Socialist'. He said he knew, but in that case I certainly would not be promoted. I said that in any case I attached little importance to my promotion; being his Adjutant meant more to me than promotion to captain. Then he grew serious: if the proposal said nothing about my political stance, I would be disavowing him. Still I did not give in, because I could not bear the thought of appearing in my personal files at OKH more or less *ex officio* as a certified Nazi. I said nothing about the fact that I also thought it quite superfluous, following 20 July 1944, for my personal papers to be taken out of the cabinet in the Personnel Office and submitted to the new chief, General Burgdorf. The Field Marshal put a brusque end to the *contretemps*: 'That's enough. You will add the missing words, and that's that!'

I returned to my room, but instead of putting the printed form back in the typewriter I wrote a fresh application on a plain sheet of paper. The addition might have been unduly obvious. When I reached the final entry that went so sadly against the grain, I felt ashamed to read it.

This time Manstein signed the form at once. I asked him if he would also sign the copy in full, for me personally. He did so. I still have the paper today.

When we returned to Liegnitz after the ceremony in the Tannenberg Monument, my promotion to captain had arrived in the post, signed by General Burgdorf.

A few days later, I was in Berlin again briefly, in search of information on the military situation. I met my friend Achim Oster, who told me that he had been called to the Personnel Office, where General Ernst Maisel, Burgdorf's deputy, had summoned him and ordered him to 'renounce' his father, General Hans Oster, in a written declaration. When Achim demanded to know the reason, Maisel refused to answer. So Achim was waiting for the next order from the Office. It was quite clear that Achim Oster was in extreme danger.

He had yet another, no less alarming piece of news from a friend: Field Marshal Erwin Rommel, gravely wounded on 17 July in France, who had allegedly died as a result of his wounds on 14 October, and whose corpse had been publicly honoured at Hitler's behest with a ceremony in Ulm, had in fact been forced to commit suicide, on Hitler's personal orders. Generals Burgdorf and Maisel had been accomplices in this shameful act.

The day before Christmas Eve the Field Marshal pressed two letters into my hand, almost as if they were a Christmas present. Since they affected me, I could keep them, he said. I turned numb as I read them. The sender was the Chief of the Army Personnel Office, General Burgdorf.

In the first letter, dated 16 December 1944, Burgdorf referred to his own letter (unknown to me) of 24 October 1944 and 'proposed First Lieutenant von K. to the Field Marshal as successor to First Lieutenant Stahlberg'.

The second letter, dated 22 December 1944, ran as follows:
'Dear Field Marshal von Manstein,
I received your letter of 15.12. today. Of course Stahlberg can stay on there. I shall inform the office that his appointment is provisionally extended to 28.2.45. Unfortunately I see no possibility of a meeting with you at present, since our quarters (the Führer's headquarters) have been moved, and owing to the events in the West I shall not be coming to Lübben, Berlin or Zossen in the foreseeable future.

With best wishes for a pleasant Christmas and a Happy New Year, which we hope will bring a victorious end to this war for us all, with respectful greetings and

Heil Hitler
I am,
Yours sincerely,
Burgdorf.'

What was the real background to this correspondence? Had they chanced on my close relationship with Henning von Tresckow? Hitler's 'Court of Honour' had posthumously expelled him from the Army after 20 July. Or was it because of General Fellgiebel? I had telephoned him on the evening of 20 July, though I had no idea at the time that I was one of the last, if not positively the last person to speak to him. Immediately after that he had been arrested, condemned to death by the People's Court and hanged on 4 September in Berlin-Plötzensee. Whatever the reason, General Burgdorf had wanted to take me away from Manstein, but Manstein had made up his mind to keep me with him; after all, on 12 July, through me, he had shared the knowledge of the imminent attempt on Hitler's life. Since he had not had me arrested immediately, it must now be in his interests not to let me go. We were dependent on each other.

In October, events followed thick and fast. On the 17th the press and radio had published and broadcast, quite without reason, the oath of allegiance sworn by the Army Field Marshals on 19 March before Hitler at the Berghof. Why now, after six months? Manstein had not given me the text to read, but now it was in all the papers:

> We, the General Field Marshals of the Army, have now received, to our profound grief and anxiety, the certain news that General of Artillery Walther von Seydlitz-Kurzbach is committing base treachery against our sacred cause . . . He has forfeited the right to wear the officer's uniform in which nearly 50,000 Army officers have sacrificed their lives in this war for you, your ideals and the German people united under you . . . He has trampled on the sacrosanct tradition of German heroism. He has sullied the memory of the fallen in this war . . . More than ever will it now be our task to anchor the high ideals of your philosophy in the Army, in order that every soldier may become a more fanatical warrior for the National Socialist future of our people. We know that only an Army grounded in National Socialism will withstand the tests of endurance that still separate us from victory. Accept, *mein Führer*, this declaration by your Field Marshals, as evidence of our unswerving loyalty.

On 11 October 1944, the Soviets invaded East Prussia and began to wreak vengeance. The old men, women and children fled before them, resulting in a mass migration such as the European continent had not seen since the fourth century. From now on, we constantly saw them passing us along the roads, and in the coming winter months there would be millions of them.

On 19 October, Hitler announced the creation of the 'Volkssturm'*.

All males between the ages of 16 and 60 were now – even without uniforms, hence as partisans – to defend their towns, villages and houses, and Goebbels as Minister for Propaganda sent the German people on their way with the line with which the Prussians had risen against the conqueror Napoleon in 1813: 'Now people rise and [let the] storm break forth!'

In the West too, the Americans and the British were advancing. The German Town Commandant of Paris, General von Choltitz,

---

* Translator's note: Equivalent to the British Home Guard.

had long since handed over the city to the enemy undamaged, contrary to Hitler's orders.

On one of my journeys of discovery, I met my mother in Berlin. She had been transferred to the Board of the German Red Cross as a 'staff leader'. Now she asked me whether she should get me tickets to the sessions of the People's Court; the German Red Cross Board had been encouraged by the Party to help with the distribution of tickets. I shuddered. What sort of people, I asked her, would want to look on while that tribunal showed its contempt for law and justice?

Since 21 October, the Western Allies had been on German soil, at Aachen. This was when the official propaganda began to intensify stories about the imminent deployment of the German 'wonder weapon', which would be the decisive turning-point in the war. Had there really been a wonder weapon, we would have known about it. A German rocket (V-1) had been fired at Britain for some months now – 'in reprisal', they said. Since September the V-2 had been added. Was that the wonder weapon? Some people seriously believed it.

On 16 December, the world listened. In the West, the Germans had begun an offensive in the Ardennes. Field Marshal von Rundstedt had been given a front-line command again; Hitler had presumably clutched at this straw, remembering Manstein's strategic plans of 1940. Manstein set me straight to Berlin for a copy of the strategic plan. As he leant over the map the next day he asked me about the reserves.

I told him that I had entered everything I had found out at OKH. He straightened up: 'Effendi thinks it's that easy to launch an offensive and break through into the heart of the enemy without reserves!'

For a day or two, the Wehrmacht report boasted of 'overwhelming' successes. Then it was the Sixth SS Panzer Army, in particular, which saw the German attack faltering on the third day after very heavy losses. By Christmas Day the last German offensive had failed. 'If General Eisenhower launched a determined attack now,' Manstein commented, 'he could end the war in a few weeks.'

Another Wedding

Had he possessed the merest whiff of a genuine sense of responsibility, Hitler would have asked our adversaries for an armistice at Christmastime 1944 at latest after the failure of the Ardennes offensive. By so doing he could still have saved millions of Germans from death; but he did the opposite. On 1 January 1945 he, Göring, Dönitz, Guderian and Himmler, each individually, issued exhortations to victory to the German people. All they had to do now was to stand fast, then final victory for us all was certain.

During those days it was my brother who provided us with a distraction. Thanks to his severe disabilities, he had gone to see the supposedly excellent ophthalmologist in SS uniform, in Breslau, had met one of Frau von Manstein's nieces and had immediately fallen head over heels in love with this beautiful, charming and extremely intelligent girl. Taking the proverb about the early bird to heart, they soon fixed a wedding date. Relations and friends were invited to Lorzendorf in Silesia on 18 January, as if we and the world were at peace. Lorzendorf lay right on the old Reich frontier between Silesia and Poland. As we in Liegnitz had not received any precise details of the situation reports yet, on the day before the wedding I got into my jeep to take a look round the area. In the Army the manoeuvre would have been called a 'reconnaissance'.

I drove through Breslau to the district town of Namslau. In the market place I saw in front of a large building – probably the town hall – a sign indicating the command post of an army corps. I parked my car at the roadside. I would certainly be able to obtain enough information from an army corps to find out how far the Russians had advanced.

When I entered the building, I was surprised to see no sentries anywhere. Odd, I thought, an unguarded corps command post?

On the first floor I found a room bearing the sign 'Ia'. A staff officer was sitting by a field telephone trying to get through, while a younger officer was leaning over a situation map.

I introduced myself as Field Marshal von Manstein's Adjutant and asked him to show me where the divisions of the corps now stood. The two officers looked at me as if I had come from the moon: 'We have no divisions left. We just have the ruins of regiments. The front is open to the East.' I asked what the corps' job was and was told that a new defence line was supposed to be constructed along the former frontier, but this was simply theory, because the corps no longer had a single intact battalion left.

I enquired about the enemy situation and heard that the

continuous efforts to obtain reconnaissance reports via radio and telephone were producing only meagre results. Refugees from the former Polish areas had talked of Russian tanks. It seemed that the Russians were mustering their tanks in a large forest six or eight kilometres north-east of Lorzendorf.

I drove immediately to Lorzendorf, where young and old were as busily engaged in wedding preparations as people usually are before wedding days. Nevertheless there was no real question of a pre-wedding atmosphere.

The next morning – and what a memorable day 18 January was in the history of Prussia – I first drove back to Namslau, where I hoped to meet the Field Marshal and report the little I had discovered about the military situation here. I did indeed meet him, with the Commander of the corps that was supposed to be fighting here, but had no divisions left, standing beside his car reporting what I already knew.

In Lorzendorf, in the person of Sergeant Sakolowski, Manstein's driver, we had at least one soldier who would ensure that, if the worst came to the worst, we would leave the house in time, jump into the cars and escape. Apart from him I did not see a single German soldier, either in or near Lorzendorf. We took care to have the guests' cars parked in the courtyard in such a way that chaos would not ensue if we had to leave in a hurry.

We soon left the manor house in a well-organised wedding procession for the chapel across the park. The atmosphere could have been memorable, because in the distance we could hear the sounds of the harmonium on which my mother was playing first Mendelssohn's *Wedding March* and then some Bach chorales. But at the last minute Sergeant Sakolowski reported that the Lorzendorf *Volkssturm* was about to start blowing up embankments, culverts and bridges in the direction of the old frontier. From the explosions already echoing across the park anyone who had not been told might easily have thought that enemy tanks had already reached the edge of the park and were firing off their cannon.

I left my place in the bridal procession and hurried forward to reassure my mother at the harmonium. She was sitting at her instrument, deathly pale, playing as bravely as if we were facing the Last Judgement. Without interrupting her performance, she listened to my explanation of the warlike din. She shook her head, thanked me for trying to reassure her, but told me she knew that it was not the *Volkssturm* but the Russians, and she would go on

playing as long as she could. Then I spoke to the pastor, awaiting
the bridal couple in the open doorway. He at least believed what
my mother would not.

I can say nothing about the proceedings in church, because I
stayed in the park, listening hard for the sound of tanks from the
East. I had experienced many an enemy tank attack with my 12th
Panzer Division, and knew the sound that travels several kilometres ahead of advancing Russian tanks when the wind is in the
right direction. That is why I remember the East wind that day; I
could actually hear the all-too familiar rumble of the Soviet tank
tracks. It was uninterrupted, which probably meant that not one
but many AFVs were approaching. I estimated the distance at
about 10 kilometres.

The Soviets were obviously mustering in the wood I had been
told about, before launching their attack on the old frontier of the
Reich. They must have taken it for granted that the Germans
would offer fierce resistance at this point, though if their military
reconnaissance had been better they would have known that the
road to Breslau and the Oder lay open before them.

The wedding banquet, with all the candles lit, was festive, the
food good and abundant, but conversation was muted and the
speeches were terrible. Nevertheless, Lorzendorf maintained its
style. In place of the bride's father, killed in the Polish campaign,
the young bride's respected old grandfather, Stephan Graf
Zedlitz-Trützschler, uttered words that became a funeral oration
for his beloved land of Silesia. His voice choked on the words and
he was unable to finish his speech.

Immediately after him the Field Marshal, sitting next to my
mother, rose to his feet. I can see him before me now, magnificent
in his dress uniform. The end was not yet, he cried, not yet!

The meal was scarcely over when the whole company left the
house, as if in flight. A happy few still had cars of their own, but
those whom we could only transport, shuttle fashion, to Namslau
Station were in utter despair. I saw the platform under its blacked-
out lamps, too small for the numbers who had been waiting hours
for a train. A terrible fate was in store for many of the women and
girls.

The Manstein family and I took the road via Breslau. It was
bitterly cold and the road was covered with ice. We would have
made better progress on skates than by car. I kept my Volkswagen
close behind Manstein's BMW so that I could drive without lights

and left the roof of the little car open – you never knew.

We passed through Oels, where the outlines of the last German Crown Prince's castle to the left of the road stood out like a spectral kccp against the sky. We must have been about five kilometres from Breslau when I heard above me the deep organ note of aircraft. I signalled to the car in front and we pulled up at the roadside. A dreadful drama began to be played out before our eyes: Breslau was being bombed. The aircraft came through in several waves, not from the West but from the East. No German night fighters flew in to drive the enemy away. Were the Russians, we wondered, already capable of bombing German cities? At that time we did not know that the American and British air forces were already able to attack Germany from the air in a 'shuttle service' between West and East.

Anti-aircraft searchlights raked the sky, the German anti-aircraft guns fired where they could, but we saw no hits.

We made a detour north of Breslau on small roads, reaching Liegnitz after midnight. Here Manstein asked me to do him a personal service. He did not order me – he never gave me an order – he asked me if I would drive back to Lorzendorf, wake up all the residents and send them across the Oder to the West at once in a group. And would I also arrange for the neighbouring Hennersdorfers to set off for the West. The Field Marshal's mother-in-law, the 'old Frau von Loesch', was living in her 'dower house' at Hennersdorf.

Everyone in Silesia knew that the Nazi Gauleiter Karl Hanke had forbidden the population, on pain of death, to abandon their homes. The people were not to take flight; the Party district leaders were to ensure, by force if necessary, that people defended their houses. I was prepared for some excitement.

Manstein's sister-in-law, Frau von Loesch, offered to come with me. I was thankful for her company – such a personality could only be helpful. I equipped the Volkswagen with as many drums of petrol as possible and the ladies put up provisions for several days and thermos flasks of coffee or tea, enough to share with other people. Frau von Loesch appeared with a hospital pack of 'Pervitin', the awful 'wake-up' drug which she had kept after the death of her dive-bomber husband. Above all I did not forget to take my machine-pistol, with as much ammunition as I possessed. I had got the armoury to supply me with it only last October – I felt safer with it than with a simple pistol.

We took the route via the autobahn to Breslau, zigzagging our way through the burning town. The inhabitants were on the streets, trying to put out the fires, recovering the wounded and the dead. Now we had the 'total war' announced to the German people over all channels by Goebbels from the Berlin Sports Palace.

At first light on 19 January we were in the courtyard at Lorzendorf. The women were just coming from the village to milk the cows, the manor house was still asleep. I knocked at the front door, rang and knocked again, but no one opened. I found a stick and broke in the first window to the right of the front door.

There I switched on the light and went up to the first floor. The doors to the main bedroom had once been the double doors of an antique Baroque cupboard – a curiosity I had seen before. I opened them and began waking people up as if I were NCO of the day at the barracks. I glanced into the dining-room, where the wedding feast of the night before had not yet been cleared away.

In a few moments the house was like a disturbed ants' nest. I ran across to the cow byre, where the women were sitting among the cows on their milking stools. I shouted loudly into the peaceful sound of the milk spurting into the pails: they must stop milking at once, even if the cows had not yet given all their milk. They must run back to their hosues and begin to pack up for the trek to the West. The carts were being prepared outside the manor house. The trek must be ready to move off in a few hours – the Russian tanks were not far away.

I was surprised how quickly and quietly the women obeyed me – they apparently had more faith in an army officer than in the district Party leader.

Then we drove on to Hennersdorf, about three kilometres away, though I was paying more attention to the snowy fields to our left than the icy road, because the old frontier of the Reich ran parallel to the main road and the Soviet tanks might come from there. So I managed to skid the car off the road on a left-hand curve, but together we succeded in getting it back again – what a good thing there were two of us!

Hennersdorf was already on its feet, because telephone calls had been made from Lorzendorf. The 'old Frau von Loesch' was standing on the terrace of her little manor house, with the German men and women workers and the few prisoners-of-war gathered round her, while she issued her orders like a good commander before the battle, the tone of her voice wonderfully clear and calm as she distributed her protégés among the various vehicles.

Then the old lady took me on one side. She wanted to know if it was really her son-in-law, the Field Marshal, who had sent me. We must expect serious difficulties with the local Nazi group leader, because of the prohibition against leaving. The man was a fanatical Nazi. I promised to be in Hennersdorf when the time came for them to leave.

Back in Lorzendorf we found chaos. Everything that had been clearly and calmly organised in Hennersdorf was in a state of hectic muddle here. I could only be glad that the Russians had not yet attacked.

I had a little time to spare now and drove to Namslau, hoping for more news about the enemy situation from the corps staff. What I learned was reassuring for the moment, but the next day, 20 January, they were definitely expecting the major Russian offensive to be launched. They agreed with me that the trek should not pass through Breslau but should head for the town of Brieg* on the Oder. It could be confidently assumed that the road to Breslau would be completely blocked by the next day, but on the way to Brieg the trek would make more progress on lonely woodland tracks.

When I got back to Hennersdorf at the time agreed, the various farm carts and other vehicles were just assembling on the village road. At the manor house everything was ready for departure. The little old lady was back on her terrace and in a firm voice she cried 'Hennersdorf – farewell!' to the departing people. She was the last to get into her ancient carriage. I shall not forget that great woman.

I attached myself and my Volkswagen to the end of the column. There was still room in my car for any stragglers. I had barely reached the village street when the procession ahead of me stopped again. I called out to find out why it was not moving, and the answer was passed back from vehicle to vehicle: 'The district group leader won't let us go! The district group leader won't let us go!'

From that moment on I acted almost automatically. I took my machine-pistol from its mounting, loaded it and slipped two more magazines into my coat pockets. Then I walked forward along the left-hand side of the column, nearly as far as the exit from the village.

And there indeed, two party functionaries in their brown

* Now Brzeg.

uniforms, with red swastika armbounds and with pistols in their brown belts, were standing in front of the first car. They were hefty, well-fed men of peasant build, and of an age to have been serving at the Front in accordance with the conscription laws in Germany. I stopped about two metres short of them and ordered them to clear the road. The elder said loudly: 'Orders from Gauleiter Hanke in Breslau: no resident to leave the village!'

Suddenly I was overcome with rage. Releasing the safety-catch of my pistol, I aimed it at the Nazi's chest and shouted, loudly enough for most of the people waiting behind me to hear: 'And this is an order from General Field Marshal von Manstein: leave the road at once, or I fire!'

Still they hesitated. I took a step closer to the older man and shouted: 'This is my last word: leave the road at once, or I fire!'

Still rather hesitantly, both men then raised their hands. Good Lord, I thought, two Party functionaries put their hands up for an army captain! 'We yield to force!' cried the elder. Then both men stepped aside and vanished hastily inside one of the houses.

I asked the first car to drive on and stayed where I was until the last had passed me by. Many of the people gave me a friendly nod. Slowly, step by step, like a funeral procession, the refugee train left the village.

Then I went back to my Volkswagen, standing alone in the road. The engine was still running and I stepped on the accelerator, keen to leave the village as quickly as possible. I would not have liked to take the two party members along as 'stragglers'. They would have to look after their own escape. Then I rejoined the end of the column at walking pace.

When I reached the curve from which I had flown off early that morning I could hear hoots and jeers coming from the vehicles ahead of me. At first I was puzzled, but then I saw two men in dark, civilian clothes running across the snowy field towards the middle of our procession. They had probably picked the shorter but far more laborious path across the fields in order not to meet me a second time.

These two party functionaries had really been in peril for a few seconds – I would, by God, have been quite prepared to shoot them both. But even they had only been doing their duty and carrying out the orders of their Gauleiter.

In Lorzendorf everyone was now ready for departure, and the two village treks joined up. I gathered the responsible people together and advised them on no account to take the road to Breslau from Namslau, explaining that the wagon train would most probably not be allowed to pass through Breslau but would be employed building tank-traps. The vital thing was to cross the Oder by the shortest route, which meant getting to Brieg. We agreed on the route and I told them I would drive ahead to find out if it was possible to use the Oder bridge. If the horses held out, they should try to keep going throughout the night, and I would return from Brieg along the agreed route to give them any further information.

Then the carts set off. Once again I waited until the last vehicle had left the village, but in contrast to Hennersdorf, no uniformed local group leader showed his face here. Nor was there a glimpse to be seen, far or near, of the Lorzendorf *Volkssturm* which had been creating such a row here only yesterday. The tears of many of the women and children were heartbreaking, and from the big cow byre came the loud complaints of cows suffering from the pain of swollen udders.

Without lights our progress was so slow that we did not reach Brieg until dawn. The administrative offices were in uproar, having just heard that the Russians had now crossed the old Silesian-Polish frontier – so the poeople of Lorzendorf and Hennersdorf had escaped just in time!* I was told that the Oder bridge had been opened to traffic, but Breslau was to be defended. We drove back towards Namslau, meeting the Lorzendorfers halfway. They were just feeding their horses. I confirmed our route via Brieg, and then old Frau von Loesch took me aside. She had heard over the foreign radio of an 'Oder-Neisse line' and she wanted to know which Neisse they meant – Silesia had three rivers of that name, the Glatzer Neisse, the Jauersche Neisse and the Görlitzer Neisse. For her and her train this was an important question, but I could not answer it. I advised her to assume the 'worst case scenario' for us Germans, the Görlitzer Neisse.†

A Sinister Journey

Since 20 January 1945 Silesia had become a theatre of war. Despite all the Gauleiters' orders, the westward-fleeing stream was

* Years after the war I discovered that some old people had been left behind in Hennersdorf and Lorzendorf, unnoticed during the departure. Those who were left were, without exception, shot by the Russians on 20 January 1945.
† The treaty eventually signed at Görlitz (now Zgorzelec) in 1950 confirmed the author's prognosis.

swelling uncontrollably. The Mansteins were expecting the Russians to reach Liegnitz before long.

The Field Marshal told me to enquire at OKH whether Achterberg, the country house to the West of the military training area at Bergen near Celle, would be available to him and his family as a residence if necessary. The last person to live there had been the former Commander-in-Chief of the Army, Colonel General Freiherr von Fritsch, who had died in the Polish campaign in 1939.

Achterberg turned out to be free, and Manstein decided to leave Liegnitz and move there. I drove to the main station and gave instructions to prepare our living compartment for the journey to Dorfmark near Soltau. The departure was fixed for 25 January, to Frankfurt-on-Oder, transport number 7291775.* From there we should reach our destination by a detour round Berlin and Hanover, in view of the constant air attacks by the Allies on the big cities.

For the last time I drove to Gröditzberg, to tell the former Ambassador von Dirksen what I knew of the military situation in Silesia. I advised him urgently to prepare to move to western Germany himself, but Dirksen repeated what he had hinted to me before: he would stay in Gröditzberg. When the Russians arrived he would demand to be taken to Moscow as quickly as possible for personal discussions with Stalin on all matters concerning the future of the German Reich, in so far as they were relevant to foreign policy. He was certain that Stalin would receive him – there would be a future and Germany would be part of it. He was planning his own return to the diplomatic service after the war.

I must have looked astonished, because Dirksen reminded me that he had once represented the German Reich in Moscow, in Tokyo and in London – who better than he to recreate the ties with the Soviet Union?

Years after the end of the war, I heard the sequel to this story: Dirksen really had waited for the Russians to reach Gröditzberg, and the Red Army officers had been so astonished by his demand to be taken to see Stalin that they allowed him to remain in his castle to await the answer from Moscow. Just then Hitler, receiving the report of the situation in Lower Silesia, had suddenly seen the name Gröditzberg on the map and, having been a guest there before the war, had asked where Herr von Dirksen was now. The next day he had been told that the former ambassador had

* I had destroyed my diaries for 1943 and 1944 in July 1944, but I still have the 1945 diary.

apparently not fled but remained in Gröditzberg, and was there-fore in Russian hands. Hitler had at once ordered an undercover commando raid to remove Dirksen from Gröditzberg. No sooner said than done, and not long afterwards Dirksen was back in German hands.

The Dirksen episode is illustrative of Hitler's style of leadership: at a time when there was no longer any hope for him and his war, the Supreme Commander still took time to concern himself with an ultimately quite insignificant detail. Or, plagued by suspicion as he always was, had he perhaps intuitively realised that Dirksen on the Russian side could still be a danger to him?

In those January days the Mansteins made a few visits to their neighbours around Liegnitz. On one such trip we had a devastat-ing experience. We had to stop the car at a crossing because the road was filled by a long procession of women in prison clothes. A dreadful scene unfolded before our eyes. Half-starved bodies, many bent double, with livid and yellowed faces, were dragging them-selves over the crossroads with the last of their strength.

Uniformed women, with pistols in their belts, drove them forward with loud shouts. Some of them were swinging leather whips.

I got out, walked forward and asked for an explanation. The answer I was vouchsafed was brief: 'Prisoner transport Grossrosen Camp'. I reported this to the Field Marshal, whose face was rigid. His wife had covered her eyes with both hands. I had never heard the name of Grossrosen before.*

Terrible though the sight of the captive women was, I felt the ghost of a sense of satisfaction that we had been eye-witnesses to something that I had been told was 'unbelievable'.

For the journey to Achterberg the family and household were divided into two groups, some to travel in the special railway carriage with the majority of the luggage and cases, the others in the BMW and the Volkswagen. The railway compartment would be attached on 25 January at 4 p.m. to train P 250 for Frankfurt on Oder and the cars would leave Liegnitz on the evening of the following day.

In the midst of the sorting and packing on 25 January, there was a ring at the door. I went to the glass door of the lower floor and opened it. Before me stood a plain man wearing a black leather

---

* There had been a concentration camp at the village of Grossrosen, 20 kilometres south of Liegnitz, since 1940.

coat. He held out an official pass and said: 'Secret Police!' (Gestapo). I asked him what he wanted. 'We have heard that Field Marshal von Manstein intends to leave Liegnitz. As you know, Captain, that is forbidden!'

I remember going hot and cold all over. Who could be responsible for this? I thought of the rumours passed round by word of mouth in recent months about the arrests and imprisonments in Berlin and was surprised how quickly I reacted: 'Leave us in peace,' I said. 'The Field Marshal has been ordered by the Führer to send his family to West Germany at once and hold himself in readiness for a new posting.' 'Then please excuse me, Captain,' said the Gestapo man. 'We did not know. Heil Hitler!' As suddenly as he had appeared, he left the house.

I drove at once to the station to find out if the Gestapo had intervened in the travelling arrangements, but they had not. All the same, I was glad when the train left Liegnitz according to plan. The Manstein family and I reached Berlin by car on 27 January.

The Agony Begins

When on the morning of 29 January 1945* I went to Berlin-Steglitz to fetch the Field Marshal and his wife from the house at 31 Munsterdamm where they were staying with friends, Manstein came out on his own. We got into the BMW and I asked where we were to go. 'We're driving to the Reich Chancellery. I want to speak to the Führer.' I thought I could not have heard correctly and asked: 'Vossstrasse, Sir?' He replied: 'No, Wilhelmstrasse,' I reminded him that as far as I knew the main entrance to the Reich Chancellery had not been in Wilhelmstrasse since 1939, but was in the new side-wing in Vossstrasse. 'Right,' he said, 'then we'll drive to Vossstrasse.'

During the drive I wondered what Manstein might want to discuss with Hitler. If Hitler had summoned the Field Marshal, Manstein would have given a different answer, saying, as so often before, that the Führer wanted to speak to him, or something of the kind. But I had never before heard the Field Marshal say that he wanted to speak to the Führer. I saw a second possibility in the sentence we had so often discussed over the last two years: 'When the water is up to his neck he will call me . . .' But in that case Manstein would scarcely have concealed his triumph from me. My

* Hand-written diary entry: 'Reich Chancellery', 29.1.1945, by Frau Dorothea von Loesch.

third idea was connected with that interjection on 27 January 1944
– almost exactly a year ago – at the Führer's headquarters in East
Prussia: the apocalyptic vision of Hitler and the last battle, with
the Field Marshals gathered about him; Manstein had interrupted
Hitler and shouted: 'That's how it will be, *mein Führer!*' was
Manstein's visit to be a sign of his readiness for that 'last battle'?
Not a very alluring prospect for me, as Adjutant, if I had to be one
of the party!

In Vossstrasse we stopped in front of the central main doorway
of the 400 metre-long neoclassical façade. The two SS men on
sentry duty outside the main entrance were not at the 'present', as
in the old days, but had their machine-guns slung at the ready.
Sakolowski was asked to wait there. We strode straight towards the
passage between the two sentries. The SS men looked irresolutely
at the unexpected visitors for a second, then clicked their heels and
came to attention.

The main door was not closed and in a few strides we were in the
centre of the long hall, which architectural gigantomania had
endowed with exaggerated proportions. Now the irresolution was
on our side. A cold wind was blowing towards us through the many
shattered windows on the garden side. Was it possible that no one
was going to appear to all to receive us and ask what we wanted?

We waited, and no one came. Finally the Field Marshal asked
me whether we should turn left or right. I thought it over. I had
never been inside the Reich Chancellery, neither the 'new' nor the
'old' one on Wilhelmstrasse, but it had been rumoured that Hitler
now worked and lived in a bunker deep underground in the garden
of the Reich Chancellery. Where might that bunker be? To the
right, the Wilhelmstrasse direction, seemed improbable, so I
suggested we go left. (I discovered after the war that Manstein and
I had gone in the wrong direction.)

We had to weave our way through, because the ceiling, some 10
metres high, had been hit by bombs in several places, leaving
metre-wide holes open to the sky; the rubble underneath had not
been cleared away.

At the western end of the hall we came to a high door, which I
opened. We entered a large room – still no one. I opened another
door opposite, to a room even bigger than the first, but on the other
side, at a table by yet another door, sat two SS men, the first people
we had seen in the eerily empty building. They rose and saluted,
and the Field Marshal responded with his field baton: 'I am Field

Marshal von Manstein. Please announce me to the Führer.' One of
the two asked: 'Have you an appointment, Sir?' Manstein said he
had not, but he had come on an important matter. We were asked
to sit down and wait. There was an ante-chamber sofa near one of
the windows. One of the SS men left the room and we sat down.

We were kept waiting there for at least half an hour, while the SS
man who was still with us scrutinised the Field Marshal and me
with unconcealed curiosity. No one spoke.

Finally the other returned. 'I have orders to inform you that the
Führer is not receiving,' he reported. 'Have you told the Führer or
one of the adjutants who I am?' asked Manstein, and I could tell
from his voice he was having difficulty in controlling himself. 'I
have, sir!' 'Then I wish to speak to one of the adjutants.'
Manstein's voice was now a shade louder. 'I regret, Sir, I have
orders to admit no one.'

The Field Marshal rose speechlessly and left the room without
saluting. We wound our way silently through the long hall, while
the thoughts went round and round in my head: not even one of the
adjutants had come to welcome Manstein – it could not be worse –
it was the equivalent of an insult. No General Burgdorf, no
Admiral von Puttkamer, no Army Adjutant, no Luftwaffe Colonel
von Below, not even SS Gruppenführer Fegelein, all of whom were
working here. For Field Marshal von Manstein there was no one
left to speak to.

The SS sentries at the main gate clicked their heels again.
Sakolowski opened the car doors. We picked up Frau von
Manstein and left Berlin on the autobahn to the West.

We had left Berlin just in time. A few days later there was
another air raid on the city, this time by more than a thousand
bombers.

Achterberg, a country house on the western edge of the military
training area at Bergen, turned out to be idyllic. While all around
us the whole of Germany was heading for eclipse, here one could
still abandon oneself wholly to the beauties of nature. A friendly
old gentleman appeared from the nearby district town to introduce
himself as the provisional district magistrate – it is proper to make
a formal call on a Field Marshal. His 'brown' predecessor had
already left his post.

The news our caller brought us from the other side of the
training area was hair-raising. There, between the towns of Bergen
and Belsen, stood a concentration camp where the number of

arrivals – half-starved prisoners, men and women – was increasing from day to day. He also spoke of 'uniformed females', who performed their duties as guards with pistols and whips.

After thirteen days' meandering from Liegnitz to Dorfmark, the special Reichsbahn accommodation carriage also arrived – with that, there were no real official duties left for me. I was allowed to travel about again as I had the year before, to gather intelligence on the situation and possibly to give a hand here or there.

I drove first to Berlin, to look for my mother's flat at 28 Brandenburgische Strasse. The house had not gone up in flames but had 'only' been blown up by one of the new landmines. The bearing walls were still standing and in the ruins of the furnishings I found, almost undamaged, my mother's string quartet lamp, on the shade of which Heinz Boese had once painted the four stages of Andersen's fairy-tale *Of heavenly music* at the Academy of Art on Steinplatz. There was nothing else to be saved here, but it was only as I left the flat that I saw my mother's handwriting, in the place where the door had once been: 'We are at Red Cross headquarters in Schloss Wiesenburg, Mark Brandenburg.'

I drove to Fasanenstrasse to ask after Tatiana Gsovsky's assistant Inge Schweitzer, and was told that Inge, after being buried alive under a house opposite the Städtische Oper in Bismarckstrasse, had left Berlin and was thought to be in Freiburg.

With a great deal of luck I found an hotel. The Savoy was almost intact.

The next day I drove along the autobahn to Stettin. When I got out of the car I could clearly hear the thunder of Russian artillery in the distance. I found my brother at corps headquarters, organising refugee transports where he could. Our oil factory, laboriously rebuilt after its first bombing, was still working.

Then I drove via Altdamm to Misdroy on the Baltic, to see our father, who had not been able to make up his mind to escape. Where could he go now? We arranged for friends in Hamburg to give him shelter.

My brother had news of relatives in Pomerania: Uncle Franz-Just von Wedemeyer and all the male inhabitants of the village had been shot by a Red Army commando on his estate of Schönrade in the Neumark. Only his stud master had escaped, having succeeded in hiding in the hay-loft, from where he had seen everything through a hatch. Our uncle had not even been a member of the Nazi party. Uncle Hans-Jürgen von Kleist-Retzow, whom we knew to have been in Berlin's Moabit prison since 21 July 1944, together with his cousin Kleist-Schmenzin, had telephoned my brother one day in Stettin. The Gestapo had released him without giving reasons and now he wanted to try to make his way to Kieckow.

The refugees trekking to the West were pouring across the Oder bridge at Stettin – the migration was at its height. As soon as anyone reached the west bank of the Oder, they felt safe, but Uncle Hans-Jürgen was moving eastward against the tide of refugees, his first concern being for his wife, his mother (my grandmother) and the Kieckow workers' families.

Later we found out what had happened. He had, in fact, reached Kieckow and set off for the West at once with his group of refugees, but they were soon stopped in a wood by a Soviet tank company. When a Russian officer discovered on checking the passes that this was a Herr von Kleist, he cried: 'You Field Marshal!' The news that the Field Marshal was a very distant relative did little good – one could not really blame the Russian officer for his mistake, because my uncle actually looked very much like a military commander. So even if he was not the Field Marshal, he was still under suspicion by the Russians of having been released by the SS only in order to work against them as a German spy. They took him by plane to Moscow and locked up the man who had just been released by the SS in the Lubianka, Stalin's infamous prison. A year in the Lubianka, with its unlit cells, where the prisoner did not know if it was day or night, undermined his health and when the Russians released him in 1947 he returned to Germany an old man, though still unbroken in spirit.

Back in Achterberg, Field Marshal von Manstein asked me to try to get through to Silesia again and find his mother-in-law, old Frau von Loesch. I was to try to bring her to the West. She and her column were said to be in a village not far from the Sudeten mountains.

On the road to Hanover the engine of my Volkswagen suddenly went on strike. Bearings rattling, I found an army workshop, where a friendly mechanic had one new engine in his store. After an hour or two I was able to drive on, with the warning 'Don't drive too fast, Captain, the new bearings won't take it!'

I reached Dresden, the most terrible example of a ruined town that I had ever seen. The inner city, that jewel, was a heap of rubble. In a square near the famous church the dead had been stacked to form a bonfire and street-cleaning teams were trying to keep the fire going to burn the corpses.

From Achterberg I had discovered by telephone where Army Group Silesia's headquarters now were: in Kolin on the Elbe, where Frederick the Great once lost a battle. I drove from Dresden to Prague and from there to Kolin, where a young lieutenant at the Headquarters of Army Group Centre answered all my questions willingly without knowing who I was. Colonel-General Schörner was the Commander-in-Chief here and on the other side of the Sudeten mountains was the Seventeenth Army, with its headquarters in Bad Salzbrunn. I about-turned quickly: I had no desire to bump into Herr Schörner.

On the way I remembered: Army Group Centre – Field Marshal von Bock – Henning von Tresckow – and now Schörner, the most fanatical Nazi of all Hitler's generals. And the Seventeenth Army: before Stalingrad, Manstein had fought to get this army, in order to save the encircled Sixth Army, but Hitler had wanted to use it to win the Baku oil on the Caspian – and then to march to Palestine – and then to India.

In Bad Salzbrunn I went into the outer office of the Ia, as it had occurred to me that my friend Otto Feil, who had written up our War Diary, had now been posted here. I asked for him. He had been shot yesterday on a reconnaissance tour, I was told. Otto Feil who, like myself, had discovered since we began serving in a senior command headquarters the senselessness and criminality of Hitler's conduct of the war and who, thanks in part to his work on the War Diary, had come to hate Hitler for his scandalous abuse of the trust of all those soldiers who had gone to their death for him; now he too had died 'for the Führer' after all, not long before the end.

There was little enough information about the situation in Silesia. The Russians were already on 'our' side of the Oder, Liegnitz had fallen, Breslau, declared a 'fortress' by Hitler, was encircled. The town was not commanded by an army general but by the Nazi Gauleiter.

Not far from Bad Salzbrunn I actually found the old lady I was looking for, but she refused to be parted from her people; she was determined to stay with those for whom she was responsible. It was her duty, she said.

On the way back I drove via Schreiberhau in the Sudeten mountains to look up my sister, whose husband was medical

director of the municipal hospital there. He and his wife had
decided to stay: a senior consultant could not run away.

April 1945

In retrospect, events in Germany at that time seem unreal.

The British and American Armies have long since crossed the
Rhine and penetrated deep into our country. In many places our
troops are no longer offering any resistance. Elsewhere German
units are still fighting the Allies with self-sacrificial devotion. It is
almost incomprehensible that many German divisions in the West
should be resisting as fiercely as others in the East. Again and
again, vital bridges and strategically important viaducts are being
blown up in the West to delay the Allies. Surely the most
important thing now is who reaches Berlin first? After all, what
matters now is the future of Germany after Hitler.

While the Western Allies have already reached the Weser, an
entire Army Group under the command of Field Marshal Model
has been surrounded in the Ruhr. On 10 April, in Achterberg,
when we hear that the American advance guard has already
reached Hanover, Field Marshal von Manstein decides to leave
Achterberg. He has no desire to present himself to the enemy
troops as a 'prize' until an armistice has been declared.

Our first goal is a village near Bad Oldesloe in Holstein. The
drive there in our two cars on 11 April is arduous. On the roads we
are met by horse-drawn refugee columns from Pomerania and from
East Prussia. The Manstein family, its escort and the luggage are
distributed between two cars. I drive the BMW. As I make way for
the refugees, I am often forced to take the 'summer road'. Many of
the draught-horses have lost nails from their shoes and consequently several punctures follow, one after the other. With rolled-
up sleeves, I change wheels and mend inner tubes.

On 13 April, in Oldesloe, we hear of the death of the American
President, Franklin D. Roosevelt, but none of us feels that his
death will alter the course of events in Germany now. On 16 April,
we hear that the Soviets too have now launched their assault across
the Oder. On 18 April, Army Group Model capitulates in the Ruhr
pocket. Model, of whom Hitler had said to Manstein that he
'whizzes all over the place with the troops', which was more
valuable than simply continuing to 'operate', shoots himself. But
nowhere do we hear that anyone in Berlin is considering that the

time may perhaps be ripe to put a stop to the fighting and the senseless bloodletting.

The Field Marshal asks me to find out by telephone where the Army Group headquarters responsible for North Germany is now quartered. On the morning of 19 April, he drives with me to Hamburg. In the Wohltorf district, near Bergedorf, we find the Headquarters of Army Group North-West, in a big old house. For a few days now it has been commanded by Field Marshal Busch, the same Busch who broke down in front of Breitenbuch and me last summer when I had to announce the destruction of his Army Group Centre. He has since been rehabilitated by Hitler, who has no doubt been told with what loyalty and devotion Busch had spoken by Schmundt's coffin in the Tannenberg Monument. His new job is the equivalent of being appointed a gravedigger.

Two Field Marshals now stand before the situation map. Their opponent here is the British Field Marshal Bernard Montgomery. It is clear to see that Montgomery will not make a frontal attack on Hamburg, but will circle to the south of the city, cross the Elbe and probably work towards the Baltic near Lübeck. For Manstein, this means that he will have to move from Oldesloe yet again, to avoid being taken prisoner before the end of the fighting.

The two Field Marshals discuss the hopeless situation of the Army Group. Suddenly I hear Busch asking if the Kiel Canal on either side of Rendsburg should be prepared to defend the Southern Front. It takes an effort of will to listen.

I take the opportunity for a private word with Busch's new ADC, whom I know personally. He has taken the position with Busch that Eberhard Breitenbuch used to occupy. I ask him if he can advise me where to find a new refuge for the Manstein family further to the North, in the province of Schleswig-Holstein. He does not need to think for long: the widow of SS *Obergruppenführer* Reinhard Heydrich, murdered in Bohemia, lives on the Baltic island of Fehmarn, in a very beautiful and sufficiently large house with guestrooms, and the lady of the house is charming. One could certainly stay with her 'until the military crisis is over'. I could mention his name to Frau Heydrich. My response could only be silence.

Suddenly the door opens and the Reich Minister for Armaments and Munitions, Albert Speer, stands before us. He has come from Berlin, he says, and spoken to the Führer 'for the last time'. We sit down and listen tensely.

He had flown to Hamburg to persuade the Gauleiter Karl Kaufmann there, against the Führer's orders, not to have the bridges across the Elbe blown up. The two Field Marshals listen, dumbfounded. 'Against the Führer's orders . . . ?' Speer confirms: 'Yes, against!' The Field Marshal and Commander-in-Chief of the Army Group – the only person with military responsibility here – hears the news after the Gauleiter of Hamburg! So chaos has already spread through the chain of command.

Speer describes his last visit to the underground bunker at the Berlin Reich Chancellery: in the office a trembling, wasted wreck of a sick man sits under the portrait of Frederick the Great, scarcely listening to his visitor. He is clutching the bundle of writing and drawing implements from the desk tray in front of him in one hand and driving them incessantly into the table top, until the points are broken and the table top deeply punctured. Beside him lies an issue of the *Völkischer Beobachter*, now only a few pages long. It lies open at the final part in the series of 'Personal reports by Frederick the Great from the Seven Years' War'. Only one book, a volume of Thomas Carlyle's *The History of Friedrich II of Prussia, Called Frederick the Great*, lies nearby.

Speer speaks of the two army leaders on whom the Führer's last hopes rest: Generals Wenck and Busse.

We sit up: Wenck? – Busse? – Is it pure chance that two General Staff Officers from the school of Field Marshal Manstein should be the ones to rise to the rank of Army Commanders-in-Chief at the eleventh hour?

Wenck, on whom all eyes turned in November 1942, when he succeeded by a trick in 'capturing' two Romanian armies fleeing westward from the Stalingrad area, a coup that had brought him promotion from Colonel on the General Staff to Major General. And Busse, Manstein's former Ia and later – in preference to Tresckow – Manstein's last Chief of Staff: had not General Fellgiebel and our Army Group Communications Chief Major General Ernst Mueller warned me in 1943 to be careful in Busse's presence, because he telephoned his brother-in-law, General Burgdorf, at the Führer's headquarters almost every night? Now Burgdorf was Hitler's Chief Adjutant and Busse had been chosen to defend his home town of Frankfurt-on-Oder as Commander-in-Chief of the Ninth Army, and when that was lost, the capital itself.

Speer speaks of the situation around Berlin: they are now

expecting the city to be encircled in a matter of days. He asks the Field Marshals if they think it possible that Wenck could push through from the South-West as far as the capital. No answer.

Speer reports frankly that the Führer has ordered him to ensure that all major factories in the German Reich are destroyed before the arrival of the enemy. Under these auspices, he has been travelling from factory to factory for weeks now, urging the directors not to carry out the order. The two Field Marshals remain silent, shaking their heads.

Our programme for this 19 April is not yet finished. Field Marshal von Manstein takes me on one side and asks if I know of a first-class restaurant in Hamburg where one could at last have one more good lunch. I suggest the 'Ehmke' in Gänsemarkt, which looked to me as if it was still open when I drove by. Ehmke also had elegant private rooms on the first floor. He asks me to reserve a private room and to let Frau von Manstein know.

In fact the Ehmke restaurant is still standing and the food is even now like an excursion into 'the good old days'. On that April day, too, Ehmke justifies its fine reputation. While we are celebrating the gastronomic arts of old, we speak freely, as soon as the frock-coated waiters have left us, about Albert Speer and his unexpected disclosures. Scarcely anyone had ever before spoken so freely and openly before two of Hitler's Field Marshals at once.

We are unaware that at this moment Speer is already on his way back to Berlin – after all, he has only just told us that he has been with Hitler 'for the last time'. He certainly had the courage to speak up unequivocally against Hitler in front of two Field Marshals, but he had not dared to say that he wanted to revisit Hitler that very day, to 'see him once again'.* So Albert Speer is not yet free of his lord and master, who sits in his underground bunker, surrounding himself to the last with 'Frederick the Great', revealing that the tyrant has never understood, but has only 'used' and hence abused, Prussia and her great king.

From Oldesloe I drive northward on my own at random to find new accommodation. My old friend Irmgard Georgius, Germany's best woman equestrian competitor in the 1930s, gives me some tips in Waldhof. Most of the estates are already overcrowded with refugees from the Eastern provinces and in one of the manor

---

* Albert Speer, *Erinnerungen* (Recollections), Berlin 1969, pages 472/73 and note 10 (pages 591/92).

houses the door is shut in my face. 'And now a Field Marshal on top of everything! Wouldn't think of it!'

On the roadside two naval officers wave to me, asking to hitch a ride. One, a U-boat captain, is wearing the Knight's Cross. They want to go to Plön and I am happy to have someone to talk to, though I find it difficult to believe that a U-boat captain, who can steer his submarine through minefields to the East coast of America, is incapable of finding his way on the map through Schleswig-Holstein. However, the other proves to be an extremely useful aerial observer, as British fighter aircraft sweep along the roads, hunting for prey.

For three days I drive from place to place without finding anything suitable. In the twelve years of the 'Third Reich' one has developed a nose for whether the house one is entering is a 'Nazi house'. I do not wish to spend the end of the war in a house with a National Socialist bias.

And then, after all, I find the goal of my desires. In Weissenhaus, on the Baltic, not far from Oldenburg, I meet the owner and his wife: Graf Clemens Platen invites me in at once for tea, so that we can talk things over together.

We walk through the lovely, big house, its ground floor stuffed to bursting with furniture and cases: the stocks of the Kiel Landesmuseum. Almost buried under cases of paintings is a black concert grand. I open the lid over the keys, pick up a lovingly-worked piece of embroidery and read the music of a theme from Humperdinck's *Hansel and Gretel*. The Platens explain: Humperdinck composed that wonderful opera on this piano. Weissenhaus will be our quarters when the end of the war comes. On 30 April we move in.

Hitler is Dead!

In the attics of the Weissenhaus manor four carpets are hung up for me as a substitute for four walls. A mattress, a box or two – and I have a comfortable 'room'.

The next day – it is 1 May 1945 – I switch on my radio to the first notes of the second movement of Bruckner's Seventh Symphony on the Hamburg radio. 'Very solemnly and very slowly' the tubas and violas join in. I think I know the recording: Furtwängler with the Berlin Philharmonic. It does me good to be listening to this symphony again after all this time.

Suddenly I am seized with suspicion. Why are they broadcasting Bruckner's Seventh today? When the movement ends I know the answer: in an emotional voice the speaker announces:

'It is reported from the Führer's headquarters that our Führer, Adolf Hitler, died this afternoon for Germany at his command post in the Reich Chancellery, fighting to his last breath against Bolshevism. On 30 April the Führer named Grand Admiral Dönitz as his successor.'*

It is not easy to describe what went through my mind at that moment. 'Thank God! – I feel as if I have been saved from death myself.' The tension and burden of more than nine months since 20 July 1944 have suddenly slipped away. And the end of the war is near.

I need a few minutes to draw breath, and lie down on my bed to think. My first reaction is to feel the perfidy of the abuse of this movement of Bruckner in association with the death of that monster. 'Fighting in the Reich Chancellery?' – how does that coincide with Albert Speer's last report? And 'Dönitz as his successor'? Not Göring, not Goebbels, not Himmler? I am beginning to suspect that only one item in the radio announcement can be true: the death of Hitler. Dönitz as Head of State? What is Dönitz but a naval officer?

One floor down I knock at Manstein's door. He is sitting at a table with his wife, reading a book. I report: 'Sir, the Führer is dead.' For a few seconds he looks at me without moving a muscle. Then comes a cry from his wife: 'No! That can't be true!' For the first time since I have been the Field Marshal's aide a little of my self-control slips and I say: 'Yes, madam, the scoundrel is dead!' The words are scarcely out before I regret them. The Field Marshal hurries round the table to look after his wife.

I report the rest: 'Fighting in the Reich Chancellery', 'Dönitz as successor'. I ask if he has any further orders for me, and leave the room.

I go to the Platens' flat and find that, like myself, they have heard about it on the radio. We discuss the news. Platen gets a bottle of wine from his cellar.

In the next few days, Manstein busies himself with contacts, first with Field Marshal von Bock, who commanded Army Group Centre at the beginning of the Russian campaign, but then joined

* In reality Hitler had committed suicide on 30 April 1945.

the many Field Marshals who, for one reason or another had – as we used to put it when we were boys – been 'kicked into the turnips'. In view of the military situation, Bock has retired to the Lensahn area. Admiral of the Fleet Dönitz, our new 'Head of State', is governing from Plön naval college. He too wants to speak to Manstein. We drive to Plön, but shortly before us the SS Reichsführer, Himmler, has been with Admiral Dönitz – at all events the squabble over the post-Hitler period is obviously already in full swing. Previously it had been known that Dönitz wanted Manstein to take Field Marshal Keitel's place as Chief of the Wehrmacht High Command (OKW). But of course neither Keitel nor the SS Chief agrees to that. All in all, Manstein finds it far from appealing to be ranked now with the crew of gravediggers.

On 3 May a tragic event occurs: Field Marshal von Bock had arranged from Lensahn to come and have tea at Weissenhaus. I am already standing outside the manor house to welcome the visitor, when I see British fighters in the distance. I can already hear the chatter of their machine-guns. Half an hour later I telephone Lensahn, moved by a feeling of unease. Bock's limousine has in fact been hit by one of the aircraft and Bock is lying gravely wounded at Oldenburg hospital. His wife and daughter are dead. Manstein drives to the hospital with me. Before us, unrecognisably swathed in bandages, lies the wounded Field Marshal. When a senior physician tells the patient who is standing by his bed, we can hear only a few words – the last Bock ever spoke: 'Manstein, save Germany!' On the return journey to Weissenhaus the thought runs through my mind again: once more I have been a witness to the words of an older Field Marshal who, directly or indirectly, regards the younger as '*primus inter pares*': Kluge, Rommel and now Bock as well.

At that very moment Admiral Dönitz's envoy, Admiral Hans Georg von Friedburg, is negotiating an armistice between Great Britain and Germany with Field Marshal Montgomery at the British headquarters near Lüneburg.

Field Marshal Montgomery

On 4 May we hear on the radio that Admiral von Friedeburg, on behalf of Dönitz, named by Hitler before his suicide as the new Head of State of the German Reich, has signed an armistice agreement at Field Marshal Montgomery's headquarters not far from Lüneburg. Only four days after Hitler's death, here at least the war is over.

The next day, Field Marshal von Manstein asks me to compose a personal letter to Montgomery, giving his address and putting himself at the disposal of the English Commander-in-Chief.

On 6 May – a Sunday – I am sitting at the wheel of the Field Marshal's big BMW before dawn. Graf Platen, the owner of Weissenhaus, is travelling with me, wearing hat and Loden coat. He comments that this is the first time he has had any contact with the events of the war: a lifelong eye condition had prevented him from becoming a soldier.

For good reason, we have opened the roof of the coupé. Everyone must see from a distance that our intentions are entirely peaceful, since the Lüneburg armistice has apparently been effective only since yesterday.

We creep through the darkness at bicycling speed. The blackout caps on the headlamps give a wretched light, through a slit measuring one centimetre by ten, as prescribed since 1 September 1939.

Now we are on the road to Bad Segeberg. Where, we wonder, shall we meet the first British soldier? There is no sign of the German Army, not a soldier whom we could ask about the armistice line, not a single one.

It is about half-past four – dawn is just breaking in the East – when ahead to my right, half-hidden by a tree bordering the avenue, I discern the outlines of an armoured car. I drop down to walking pace, and see the muzzle of a light cannon trained on me (which does not trigger off pleasant emotions in a former Panzer Division officer).

I stop in front of the armoured car and wait; the muzzle is still trained directly on me. An English soldier climbs out of the side hatch of the vehicle and comes over to me; he is a sergeant. He asks me where I am going and I tell him in English that I have been ordered to carry a letter from Field Marshal von Manstein to Field Marshal Montgomery. I have to repeat it once or twice – he has probably not come across anything like this before. Then he goes back to his vehicle and takes out a microphone. He too has to repeat himself several times.

After a few minutes he returns and asks if he may travel in my passenger seat: the other gentleman will please sit in the back. As he gets in, it occurs to me that he has apparently forgotten to buckle on his pistol-belt, and as if by thought transference he mutters, before sitting down: 'Excuse me,' returns to his vehicle and retrieves belt and pistol.

After a few hundred metres' drive, we reach a village. At the first farm he asks me to turn left into the big farmyard, where a young lieutenant is apparently waiting for us. He salutes and asks me to repeat what I have already told his NCO. Then he invites Platen and me into the farmhouse, where we enter a large room to the left in which a long breakfast table is already laid.

I introduce Graf Platen to the young officer. 'Count?' he asks, 'a real count?'

We hear that the commander has already been woken, but has sent a message that it is still too early in the morning to get up, so will we please wait, because he would like to breakfast with us. Almost apologetically, the lieutenant adds that as they 'celebrated the victory' the night before, it was not long since they had gone to bed. The lieutenant helps Platen and me out of our coats – yes, really, an English officer helps us out of our coats! He hangs them up on a stand, together with my belt and pistol, gets us one or two English newspapers and disappears. We are left alone for an hour or two.

Suddenly the room is filled with officers. I am given a seat halfway down the table and told that we are the guests of the officers of a parachute battalion.

While the orderlies serve a classical English breakfast, a free and frank exchange of views quickly – and almost incredibly – develops among us. I immediately seize the opportunity to stress how inaccurate it would be to equate all Germans with National Socialists. The entire table listens attentively. When I ask in passing if by any chance anyone present knows my cousin Lionel Brett, someone calls across from the far end of the table to ask if I mean the architect. When I say yes, the exchange – unfortunately – turns into question time, and with my trip to London 10 years behind me, my vocabulary has serious deficiencies. I am asked about my experiences with the Russians. A very young lieutenant declares himself a convinced Communist, which for him is the weightiest reason for fighting the Nazis. I reply that in my view National Socialism and Communism are closely related. The officers are silent. I can sense their surprise.

In the end it is I who have to ask to be allowed to drive on, because I hope to be with Montgomery that same day.

Now a young English major is sitting in the car beside me. He must be younger than I am. I ask if he knows Field Marshal Montgomery and he says he does not – that is apparently the reason why he has been given the honourable job of taking me to his Commander-in-Chief. What interests him most is the BMW. I tell him it is a 1939 prototype and after a few kilometres he says: 'I like this car. It will be mine.' As calmly as possible, I retort that I cannot stop him, but he has now obliged me to report this personally to Field Marshal Montgomery.

When we are approaching Hamburg I ask him if he knows the city, and he says no, adding that he has not yet seen a single big town in Germany. His unit's operations have always made a detour round the larger cities. I ask the major where we are going in Hamburg and he tells me that it's to the Hotel Atlantic, so I drive him on a big detour through the shattered eastern parts of the city. This is the first bombed city my English companion has ever seen. He is silent. Only once I hear him murmur: 'My God!'

I stop at the main entrance to the Hotel, which is almost undamaged, and has apparently become the military headquarters in Hamburg. I drop the car key rather ostentatiously into a pocket of my uniform. From the hotel foyer, Platen and I are led to one of the banqueting halls on the right, where lunch is already over. We are the only guests at a long table. An orderly sets a dish of food before us, together with a carafe of red wine. Our young major has vanished from our sight. It soon turns out that his dream of meeting his Commander-in-Chief is already over.

A young captain appears, speaking German without an accent. As we approach the Elbe bridge, I ask him: 'Intelligence Service?' 'Yes,' he says.

A barrier has been set up in the middle of the great old iron bridge. No German is allowed to cross the Elbe, nevertheless a German lorry has halted ahead of us, with a black coffin on the platform and wreaths beside the coffin. A group of black-clad mourners are negotiating with a British officer, who finally allows them to pass.* Our car is next; the captain beside me shows his official pass and we are through.

Now the road to Lüneburg lies open. Hesitantly, even suspiciously at first, the captain beside me starts to ask questions. Soon I ask him, as directly as possible: 'You are German?' He *was*

---

* Years later I discovered that the trick with the coffin (minus body), wreaths and mourning clothes, was for some weeks the only way for a German to cross the Elbe at Hamburg.

German, he says. Then he asks me if I have seen Bergen-Belsen? – 'Yes'. The next question follows immediately: 'Did Field Marshal von Manstein know?' I do not answer. For a time no one speaks. Then I try to steer the conversation to our conflict between duty and conscience, telling him of close relatives and friends who have been killed by the National Socialists. The answer I receive startles me: 'We know that. We already have information about you, too.'

In Lüneburg white flags are flying from many houses, though only a week before, to hoist a white flag in Germany meant the death penalty without trial.

On the southern edge of the town I have to stop. In front of us a unit of armoured engineers is leaving the barracks with pontoons and other bridging materials of a size completely unknown in Germany. I guess that what is emerging from the barracks in front of us is a bridge to cross the Lower Elbe. I ask the English officer beside me if the equipment is English or American. 'The US gave it to us.'

A few kilometres south of Lüneburg we turn left off the road. Another surprise: we are driving on an artificial road across the fields. Never before have I seen such military equipment. After a few hundred metres, and still rolling along the steel carpet, we reach a lightly wooded hill; then the stand of young trees opens up and we stop on the hilltop. We are in the middle of a large tented camp. 'This is the headquarters of the Army Group,' our companion explains, and asks us to wait. Then he disappears, leaving us alone.

Now Platen and I have some time to ourselves. So this is the place where the armistice was concluded between Great Britain and Germany two days ago. In which of the big tents round us had it happened? There is not a sign to be seen, no indication of who is in which tent. How many German headquarters had I seen, all of them accommodated in big houses, often in old castles, never in tents. These headquarters tents have probably already been used in the Sahara. 'In England everything is different' – here is fresh confirmation!

Now and then a soldier or an officer crosses the clearing, but no one is interested in us. We feel unobserved. No one has come to take my pistol from me. It is as if we belonged here. The hours pass.

Suddenly the scene changes. The captain who brought us here appears and asks me to station myself at a spot indicated by him.

Graf Platen, whose exact function he has vainly attempted to clarify, is instructed to stand slightly to the rear. Then, as if at a word of command, the tents around us open and a large number of officers and soldiers of all ranks appear. A small, wiry, athletic figure in an open-necked uniform shirt, displaying no badges of rank or decorations, stands in front of the rest, a few metres from me. I guess who he is.

To my left a staff officer steps forward and asks me in German to report. I report my name, rank and position, and add a request to know in whose presence I am. The staff officer replies: 'You are in the presence of His Majesty's Commander-in-Chief of the British troops, Field Marshal Montgomery.'

Only then does the Field Marshal begin to speak, not to me, but to his officer. I am to report my message. I reply that I have to hand over a personal letter from Field Marshal von Manstein to Field Marshal Montgomery. Montgomery: 'Tell me what is in the letter.' I say that I have no orders to interpret the letter, only to hand it over and ask for a reply.

Then the interpreter steps forward, I hand over the letter and he gives it to Montgomery. The Englishmen all disappear. Platen and I are alone again.

Once again the hours pass, and it is long after dark when the staff officer to whom I handed the letter is suddenly beside us. The content of the letter has been communicated to Allied Headquarters and the British Government, he says. Field Marshal von Manstein is requested to stay at Weissenhaus until further notice and await any other news there. The troops have been informed, and we can rest assured that there will be no unauthorised infringements. I can now drive back to Weissenhaus.

I remind him that I am hardly likely to be able to travel the roads unhindered, and above all, to cross the Elbe. He will get a pass written out for me, he says, and disappears. After a few minutes he is with me again, and by the light of the torch I read the brief English text: 'The two occupants of this car:- Hauptmann STAHLBERG, and Graf PLATEN have taken a personal message from Field Marshal VON MANSTEIN to Field Marshal MONTGOMERY. They are now returning and will be granted passage.' (For original see plate 38.)

I thank him and he wishes us a good trip.

The engine of the BMW is already running. Then the staff

officer knocks on my side window. I get out again and the Englishman says: 'I forgot to tell you that the blackout has been lifted today. You can take the caps off your headlamps.'

My God, I think, how we had longed for the day when we could turn on the lights again!

I have to get out the toolkit, as the blackout caps are secured under the metal rims. While I begin on one of the headlamps, the English officer suddenly takes a second screwdriver from the toolbox and begins to work on the other. I look across at him, touched by his action.

When it is all done, we stand face to face again, ready to say goodbye. Then the Englishman does something quite 'un-English': he shakes my hand.

Name Index

Adenauer, Konrad 233
Albers, Hans 21–2
Albrecht, Prince 82
Alexander I, Tsar 234
Anastasia, Grand Duchess (Anderson, Anna) 49, 101
Antonescu, Jan 304

Badoglio, Pietro 344
Bäumer, Gertrud 86
Baur, Hans 249–50, 337
Beck, Ludwig 90, 95, 203, 241, 258, 283–7, 339, 364
Becker, Heinrich 91–2, 116, 121–8, 131, 136, 142–3, 153, 156, 159–62, 164–5, 174–6, 179–80, 187–8, 192, 195–6
Behr, Winrich 234–8
Below, Nikolaus von 235
Bentz, Beatrice 86
Bergengruen, Major i. G. 195, 198
Bielski, Prince 125–6, 128–9, 146
Bismarck, Gottfried von 230–2
Bismarck, Hans-Otto von 148
Bismarck, Herbert von 7, 9–10, 33–6, 101–2
Bismarck, Klaus von 9, 107, 109, 232
Bismarck, Otto von 25, 28, 88
Bismarck, Ruth-Alice von (née von Wedemeyer) 107
Blaskowitz, Johannes 148
Blomberg, Werner von 18, 31, 44, 46, 48, 87
Boes, Heinrich (Heinz) 391
Boeselager, Georg Freiherr von 282
Boeselager, Philipp Freiherr von 282
Bock, Fedor von 156, 159, 399–400
Bonhoeffer, Dietrich 82–4, 193, 348
Bormann, Martin 332, 371
Bose, Herbert von 22, 39, 45, 46
Brandt, Karl 275
Brauchitsch, Walther von 182, 251, 368
Braun, Eva 296, 368
Braun, Gretl 368
Braun, Otto 22
Braun, Wernher von 361
Breitenbuch, Eberhard von 298, 333–4, 395

Bredow, Ferdinand E. von 44, 46
Bredow, Maria Gräfin von 13, 17, 46
Brett, Lionel 58, 402
Brüning, Heinrich 4, 7–8
Burchard-Motz 40
Burgdorf, Wilhelm 257, 374–6, 396
Busch, Ernst 32, 333, 354–5, 371, 395–7
Busse, Theodor 210, 215, 220, 256–7, 263–5, 272, 323, 327, 329–30, 335, 343, 396

Canaris, Wilhelm 84, 95, 284–7, 346, 348
Carlyle, Thomas 396
Caulaincourt, Armand Augustin 161
Chamberlain, Arthur Neville 91–2, 94–5, 99, 105–6, 142, 352
Chemin-Petit, Hans 86
Choltitz, Dietrich von 268–9, 280, 376
Churchill, Winston Leonard Spencer 95, 105–6, 142, 294
Clausewitz, Carl von 129, 202, 246
Clausius, Colonel 229
Cleve, Frieda 191–2
Colvin, Jan 104

Daladier, Édouard 92, 94
Dibelius, Wilhelm 346
Dieter, Professor 295
Dietl, Eduard 357
Dietrich, Sepp (Joseph) 289
Dirksen, Herbert von 351–2, 354, 386–7
Dirksen, Viktoria von 351
Dirksen, Willibald von 351
Dönitz, Karl 378, 399–400
Dollfuss, Engelbert 81
Dovifat, Emil 5
Duesterberg, Theodor 4, 15

Ebert, Friedrich 46
Eisenhower, Dwight David 377
Elizabeth, Duchess of York 56–7
Elizabeth, Princess 56
Engel, Gerhard 259–61
Engelhardt, Helmuth 169, 172–3, 176, 179–80, 183
Esher, Viscountess Antoinette (née Heckscher) 48, 53, 55–8, 143
Esher, Viscount Oliver 48, 53, 55–8

Falkenhayn, Erich von 32
Fegelein, Hermann 330, 368
Feil, Otto 210, 219, 247, 268, 393
Fellgiebel, Erich 204, 239–41, 255, 356–7, 359–60, 362–4, 368, 375, 396
Finck, Werner 101–2
Finckh, Eberhard 219–20, 232, 267–8, 312–15, 317, 343, 347
Fischer, Edwin 212
Forst, Helga von der 362–4
Franco, Francisco 188
Freisler, Roland 105
Friedeburg, Hans Georg von 400
Frederick II (The Great) 30, 96, 396–7
Frederick William I, King 30
Fritsch, Werner Freiherr von 87, 386
Fürsen, Angelica (née Stahlberg) 58
Fürsen, Antoinette 58
Furtwängler, Wilhelm 3, 143

Gaulle, Charles de 135
Gempp, Walter 25–6, 36
Gerdsdorff, Rudolf-Christoph Freiherr von 289–90
George VI 56
Georgius, Irmgard 41, 397
Goebbels, Joseph 6, 21, 24, 30–1, 41, 88, 147, 277, 364, 376
Goerdeler, Carl 367
Göring, Hermann 9, 24–6, 31, 33–6, 45, 148, 154, 213, 220, 282, 319, 356, 358–9, 378
Grimm, Hans 17
Gsovsky, Tatiana 86, 114, 319–20, 391
Guardini, Romano 5
Guderian, Heinz 306, 364, 367–8, 371–2, 378

Hagemann, Albert 369
Halder, Franz 93
Hammerstein-Equord, Kurt Freiherr von 18
Hannussen, Jan 25
Hanke, Karl 381, 384
Harpe, Josef 161, 180
Hausser, Paul 288
Heckscher, Johann Gustav Wilhelm Moritz 40, 61, 88, 314
Henderson, Neville 104
Herwarth von Bittenfeld, Hans 357–8
Heusinger, Adolf 251
Heydrich (Widow of R. Heydrich) 395
Hilton, Jack 55
Himmler, Heinrich 282, 313, 332, 334–7, 356, 358–9, 364, 368, 378, 399–400
Hindenburg, Oskar von 18, 31
Hindenburg, Paul von Beneckendorff und von 3–4, 7, 9, 11–13, 17, 20–2, 25, 31–2, 46, 48, 66, 213, 370

Hitler, Adolf 3 passim
Hoepner, Erich 368
Hoesch, Leopold von 54, 57
Hoth, Hermann 227–8, 233
Huch, Ricarda 86
Hugenberg, Alfred 14, 17

Joachim, Joseph 86
John, Archduke of Austria 61
Jung, Edgar 45–6

Kalamkarian, Maria 114, 321–2
Karajan, Herbert von 369–70
Karow, Frau 192, 360–1
Kaufmann, Karl 396
Keitel, Wilhelm 236, 238, 326, 368, 371, 400
Kempf, General 301
Kempf, Wilhelm 86
Kemka, Erich 265
Keppel, Major 184
Kesselring, Albert 344–5
Ketteler, Wilhelm Freiherr von 89, 214
Kleist, Berndt von 199
Kleist, Ewald von (Field Marshal) 131, 214–15, 242, 275–9, 337
Kleist, Ewald von 16–19, 22, 64, 88, 94–5, 101, 104, 213, 216, 322, 392
Kleist-Retzow, Hans-Friedrich von 170–1
Kleist-Retzow, Hans-Jürgen von 94, 170–1, 192–3, 332, 391–2
Kleist-Retzow, Jürgen-Christoph von 170–1
Kleist-Retzow, Konstantin von 148
Kleist-Retzow, Maria von (née von Diest) 193
Kleist-Retzow, Ruth von (née Countess Zedlitz and Trützschler) 81–4, 148, 170, 192–3, 322
Kleist-Schmenzin, Ewald von see Kleist, Ewald von
Klemm, Richard 119
Klepper, Jochen 86
Klingler, Karl 86
Kluge, Günther von 211–12, 290, 298, 303–4, 306–10, 339, 355, 359, 367
Kohlrausch, Eduard 4

Lenin, Vladimir Ilich 269
Lenski, Arno von 67
Leverkuehn, Paul 101
Lewinski, Captain von 63, 66, 71–2, 75
Lloyd George, David 95, 105
Loesch, Amaly von (née von Schack) 381–3, 385, 392
Loesch, Conrad von 207
Loesch, Dorothea von (née Strakke) 345–6, 381
Loesch, Maria von 378

Lubbe, Marinus van der 25, 36
Luther, Martin 84

Maisel, Ernst 374–5
Maizière, Ulrich de 287–8
Mannerheim, Carl Gustav von 179, 249
Manstein, Erich von 195, 202–4, 207
  passim
Manstein, Gero von 208, 232
Manstein, Jutta Sibylle (née von
  Loesch) 203, 399
Manstein, Rüdiger von 287N, 346
Meissner, Otto 18, 46
Model, Walter 337–9, 343, 354, 394
Molotov, (Skrabin) Vyacheslav
  Mikhailovitch 154–5
Moltke, Helmut Karl Bernhard Graf
  von 129, 202, 246
Mommsen, Ernst-Wolf 27–9
Montgomery, Bernard 395, 400–3, 405
Morell, Theodor 266–7, 275, 293
Mueller, Ernst 396
Müller, Ludwig 259
Mussolini, Benito 91–2, 99, 145, 155, 344

Napoleon I Bonaparte 98, 161, 183, 197
Neurath, Konstantin Freiherr von 87
Nicholas II Tsar 49
Ninow, Klara 49–1, 79

Oppenfeld, Horst von 248
Orsenigo, Cesare 31, 37–8
Oster, Achim 90, 93, 118–19, 147–8, 284,
  346, 350, 374–5
Oster, Hans 84, 90, 95, 284–7, 313, 346–8,
  350, 374
Owens, Jesse 79–80

Pacelli, Eugenio (Pope Pius XII) 37
Papen, Franz von 7–20, 22, 24–6, 29–32,
  38–9, 41–8, 81, 88–9, 213–4, 216, 276–7,
  302–3, 368
Papen, Frau von (née von Boch) 18–19
Paulus, Friedrich 220, 228, 230, 234–7,
  248, 283
Planck, Max 86
Platen-Hallermund, Clemens Graf
  von 398–9, 401–5
Puttkamer, Karl Jesco von 390
Putlitz, Wolfgang Gans Edler Herr von and
  zu 53–4

Quistorp, Alexander von 369

Raeder, Erich 372–3
Rathenau, Walther xvii
Reichenau, Walther von 46
Reinecke, Hermann 324
Reinhardt, Max 373

Remer, Otto Ernst 371
Ribbentrop, Joachim von 87, 116, 334, 352
Richthofen, Wolfram Freiherr von 220
Ripke, Helmut 75–6, 393–4
Ripke, Ruth-Roberta (née Stahlberg) 75,
  393–4
Röhm, Ernst 43–4
Rohr, Achim von 113, 322
Rommel, Erwin 119, 155, 227, 247, 275,
  277, 303–10, 339, 359, 364, 371, 375
Roosevelt, Franklin Delano 99–100, 294,
  394
Rundstedt, Gerd von 213, 329–1, 338, 355,
  368, 377

Sack, Karl 84, 348
Schenk von Stauffenberg, Claus Graf see
  Stauffenberg
Schlabrendorff, Ernst Wilhelm Freiherr
  von 102N
Schlabrendorff, Fabian von 95, 100–5,
  199–202, 204, 301, 364
Schlabrendorff, Luitgarde von (née von
  Bismarck) 36, 100–5
Schleicher, Kurt von 8, 11–2, 17–19, 44
Schmidt-Hannover, Otto 14
Schmundt, Rudolf 223–4, 238–40, 251,
  263, 266–7, 270, 274–5, 288, 295–8, 301,
  304, 306, 326–7, 329–34, 337, 369–71
Schörner, Ferdinand 337–8, 371, 393
Schröder, Kurt Freiherr von 14
Schulz, Friedrich 210, 214, 230, 242, 246,
  256
Schulze-Büttger, Georg 257–61, 263–4,
  272, 280–3, 289–90, 300–1, 333, 335–40,
  343, 347
Schwede-Coburg, Franz 369
Schweitzer, Dr 320–1
Schweitzer, Inge 114, 319–22, 391
Schweitzer, Mareile 319–21
Schwein von Krosigk, Lutz Graf 371, 373
Seldte, Franz 15
Seydlitz-Kurzbach, Walther von 229–30,
  330, 376
Specht, "Pepo" 207–8
Speer, Albert 316–17, 395–7
Speidel, Hans 301
Stahl, Paul 40
Stahlberg, Caroline 176
Stahlberg, Hans-Conrad 36–7, 47, 61–2,
  232
Stahlberg, Spes (née von Kleist-Retzow)
  49–51, 75–6, 84–7, 148, 189–91, 377, 379
Stahlberg, Walter 344, 357–8, 378, 391
Stalin, Josef 116, 126, 154, 282–3, 294,
  349, 352, 386
Stauffenberg Claus Graf Schenk von 204,
  239–48, 285, 290, 344, 356–9, 363–4
Stieff, Helmuth 355, 357, 359, 368

Stockmar, Christian Friedrich Freiherr von 103
Strasser, Gregor 12
Stresemann, Gustav 37, 81

Thälmann, Ernst 4
Toydemir, Colonel General 301
Tresckow, Erika von (née von Falkenhayn) 10, 31–2, 348
Tresckow, Gerd von 9
Tresckow, Henning von 9–11, 32–3, 51, 70–2, 156–7, 159–61, 183, 198–204, 210, 239–40, 256–7, 279–83, 285–6, 290, 299–301, 334, 337, 347–51, 353, 364–5, 375
Tresckow, Katharina von 85
Tresckow, Rüdiger von 31
Tschirschky and Boegendorff, Fritz-Günther von 23, 38–9, 41–2, 45–6, 89

Udet, Ernst 320–1

Vansittart, Robert Gilbert 95
Vermehren, Erich 101
Vernezobre de Laurieux, Mathieu 82–3
Vilmar, Wilhelm xv–xvi

Wedemeyer, Franz-Just von 10, 391
Wedemeyer, Hans von 8, 12–3, 16–7, 22–3, 107, 216
Wedemeyer, Maria von 84, 108
Wedemeyer, Ruth von (née von Kleist-Retzow) 107–8
Weichs, Maximilian Freiherr von 214–16

Weizsäcker, Adelheid Freiin von 76
Weizsäcker, Carl-Friedrich Freiherr von 76
Weizsäcker, Ernst Freiherr von 76, 86
Weizsäcker, Heinrich Freiherr von 76, 119, 148
Weizsäcker, Marianne Freifrau von (née von Graevenitz) 76, 86
Weizsäcker, Richard Freiherr von 119
Wenck, Walther 223, 396
Werder, Colonel 287–8
Wilhelm, Linus 86
William II 17
William, Crown Prince 213
William, Prince 9–10
Witzleben, Erwin von 90, 368
Wöhler, Otto 211
Wolf 62–3
Wolf, Martin 4

Yorck von Wartenburg, Heinrich Graf 90–3, 107, 118–9, 122–8, 131, 136, 140–1, 144, 147–8, 153–4, 157, 284
Yorck von Wartenburg, Johann David Ludwig 246N
Yorck von Wartenburg, Peter Graf 154

Zedlitz und Trützschler, Robert Graf von 204
Zedlitz und Trützschler, Stephan Graf von 380
Zeitzler, Kurt 225, 229, 231, 235, 239–41, 247, 251–2, 254, 256, 259, 270, 278, 308–9, 323, 328–9, 364